THE BEATLES: THE BBC ARCHIVES 1962–1970

THE BEATLES
THE BBC ARCHIVES
1962–1970

Kevin Howlett

HARPER
DESIGN
An Imprint of HarperCollinsPublishers

CONTENTS

INTRODUCTION

'The past is a foreign country: they do things differently there.'
(L.P. Hartley, *The Go-Between*)

The Beatles arrived at the BBC for a radio audition in February 1962. At this time, the BBC was at the core of daily life in the UK. In the harrowing days of the Second World War it had provided news, laughter and comfort. During the post-war years of food rationing and austerity, the time of day was measured by the theme tunes of *Two-Way Family Favourites*, *The Archers*, *Housewives' Choice* and *Music While You Work*. In the daytime, there was nothing else to listen to but the BBC, and during the limited hours that TV was broadcast its only competitor was the young commercial upstart, Independent Television. Today's multi-channel broadcasting world rarely unites the country the way radio and TV did during the 1960s. In that era, BBC TV and radio programmes attracted weekly audiences of twenty million or more.

The invitation for the four lads from Liverpool – none older than 21 – to attend an audition at the BBC's Manchester outpost was a significant step forward in their career in show business. There is a sketch on The Beatles' Fan Club Christmas record for 1967 – *Christmas Time (Is Here Again)* – that conveys how daunting it could be to cross the threshold of the British Broadcasting Corporation:

Narrator: The boys arrive at BBC House.
THREE LOUD KNOCKS ON A DOOR
Man from the BBC: [Sternly] What do you want?

The Beatles: We have been granted permission, Oh Wise One.
Man from the BBC: Ah! Pass in peace.

Pretty soon though, The Beatles were acting like they owned the place. BBC Television was fairly late to recognize the group's potential, but they regularly appeared on the radio to perform music and chat amiably to announcers. Except for comedians, regional accents were not heard much on the wireless in those days. Part of the fun of the early broadcasts is hearing The Beatles' natural voices bumping up against the well-modulated tones of trained actors, who presented many of the shows. The appeal of the group never came just from their music. Playful in the early days, thoughtful and confessional towards the end – the BBC interviews reveal the personal charm of four men who entranced the world. As The Beatles' story unfolds through many radio and TV appearances, their emotions are palpable – ranging from bewilderment on the first exciting day in New York City in 1964 to anxious preoccupation with business affairs in 1969.

In 1982, I produced a BBC Radio 1 special called *The Beatles at the Beeb*. The BBC had been meticulous about keeping paperwork relating to its broadcasts, so it was fairly straightforward to discover on which programmes The Beatles appeared and the songs they played. In the BBC Contracts Department there was a room full of filing cabinets containing card indexes. The section for The Beatles included handwritten entries with all the recording and transmission dates of their bookings. The BBC also had a store of microfilm spools that preserved running orders with music details. Armed with a list of programme names and dates, The Beatles' BBC session history was soon revealed as I cranked the microfilm through the viewer.

Counting a highlights programme for the 1963 *Royal Variety Performance*, the group played music on 53 radio shows between March 1962 and June 1965. No fewer than 275 unique musical performances by The Beatles were broadcast by the BBC in the UK. The group played 88 different songs on radio – some recorded many times; others performed just once. Remarkably, 36 of those songs were never issued on record while the group was in existence. With the exception of the Lennon-McCartney original 'I'll Be On My Way', these unreleased tracks comprised cover versions of familiar rock 'n' roll numbers, current rhythm and blues songs and a few oddball choices.

These facts were tantalizing in 1982. Now, where were the tapes? The BBC Sound Archive in Broadcasting House had catalogued one vinyl disc with BBC-recorded songs by The Beatles. On one side of this Archive LP, there was an edited version of the Easter Monday holiday special *From Us To You*, broadcast on 30 March 1964. Made for the BBC Transcription Service to distribute to international radio stations, it did not have all the songs from the domestic programme. That was it. There had been 53 programmes with Beatles music; just one was in the Archive. Fortunately, following the international success of The Beatles and other British artists, BBC Transcription discs had soon begun to carry pop music sessions. The weekly show *Top of the Pops* was launched in 1964 (completely unrelated to the TV programme with the same name) and songs from four of the last five Beatles sessions were included in the show heard around the world. The *Top of the Pops* LPs were filed in the Transcription Service Library. There were now more songs to consider for *The Beatles at the Beeb* than just the five in *From Us To You*.

But 39 of The Beatles' sessions were broadcast in 1963 and the scripts showed that *Pop Go The Beatles* had been a treasure trove of unreleased songs. Through luck rather than managerial foresight, fifteen songs from that series had survived. In 1965, the BBC General Overseas Service aired fifteen-minute shows called *Pop Go The Beatles* featuring songs from those programmes and other sessions from 1964. At some point, a studio manager made a highlights tape for his colleagues to listen to during downtime on night shifts at Bush House – the home of the General Overseas Service. The 'Bush Tape' had fifteen songs The Beatles had never released on record. What a thrill it was to listen to that reel for the first time.

The forthcoming broadcast of so many rare tracks made *The Beatles at the Beeb* a big news story around the world. Following its first Radio 1 broadcast, the show was heard on US radio and in other countries. I returned to the material again in 1988 to produce fourteen half-hour shows called *The Beeb's Lost Beatles Tapes*. In the six years between the projects, many off-air recordings of The Beatles' programmes had surfaced on bootleg albums. Producer

Bernie Andrews had kept copies of two of his programmes with The Beatles and generously allowed them to be broadcast in 1988.

In November 1994, 56 of the BBC session songs were commercially released on *Live At The BBC*. By this time, an additional source of high-quality material had been found and used for some of the tracks on the album. No one at EMI was quite sure about the market for *Live At The BBC*. However, its release became headline news and, following this publicity, the record company was caught out. EMI's Head of Communications David Hughes admitted, 'Demand is continuing to outstrip supply. We're trying to keep everybody partly supplied and are making copies as fast as we can.' In fact, five million copies were sold around the world within six weeks. To follow up this commercial and critical success, a companion album *On Air – Live At The BBC Volume Two* was rush-released... nineteen years later.

When The Beatles' BBC radio sessions were recorded, there was very little understanding that they might have some historic or commercial value in the future. Several programmes were kept at the BBC by chance, while others were preserved by producers, engineers and home tapers. The Beatles' early BBC television appearances were also subject to similar odds of survival. Two key programmes from 1963 – *The Mersey Sound* and *It's The Beatles* – still exist; although the latter is not complete. *Juke Box Jury* with The Beatles comprising the panel was a landmark TV event, but not kept. In this era, a domestic reel-to-reel tape recorder had become an affordable item so there was a chance that somebody somewhere may have taped a radio programme or the sound of a TV show. Indeed, that famous edition of *Juke Box Jury* does exist in audio form. But videotape machines did not arrive in homes until the 1970s. Until then, if a television programme was not archived by the BBC, it was gone for ever.

If only BBC managers had had a more enlightened policy regarding the preservation of popular music programmes in this era. They were certainly meticulous about filing the paperwork. Contracts, memos and Audience Research Reports were all carefully squirreled away. It was fascinating to unearth them. Many of these enlightening documents have been reproduced in this book for the first time and they open a window into the era in which The Beatles made their historic broadcasts. They remind us that not everyone working at the BBC or in its audience liked what The Beatles were up to. Today, we are used to pop music being a few mouse clicks away; just a part of the digital babble of our 21st-century world. In the past, when The Beatles were seen and heard on the BBC, things were done differently. In 1963, George was asked if he thought it would be possible to 'settle down to a life in show business'. 'Not necessarily a life in show business,' he replied, 'but at least a couple more years ... if we do as well as Cliff and The Shadows have done up till now ... we won't be moaning.'

Kevin Howlett, August 2013

1962

Here
We Go

THE BEATLES. Those two words now signify so much to so many all over the world. In March 1962, readers might have noticed this odd name with its quirky spelling printed for the first time in an edition of *Radio Times*. The magazine listing the BBC's schedules for sound and TV revealed on the page for 8 March 1962 that The Beatles would appear in the radio show *Teenagers Turn – Here We Go*. The group had experienced rejection, failed auditions, but still believed in their potential to progress in show business. *Here We Go* gave them national exposure; put them on the crest of a wave.

Nineteen-sixty-two was the year when everything started to click into place... and not just for The Beatles. On 11 March 1962, 20-year-old Bob Dylan performed songs and spun yarns with Cynthia Gooding on her New York radio show *Folksinger's Choice*. Dylan's first LP was released eight days later. On 12 July 1962, at the Marquee club in Soho, London, a rhythm and blues group appeared for the first time with the name 'The Rollin' Stones'.

Two days before Mick Jagger, Keith Richards and Brian Jones became Stones, the US communications satellite Telstar had been launched into space. The event heralded a futuristic era where television pictures could be bounced around the globe. A pop instrumental by The Tornados called 'Telstar' celebrated this scientific marvel. The atmospheric single, reverberating with electronic rumbles and squeaks, was a number one not only in the UK, but also in the United States. This was a remarkable achievement for a British 'beat group'.

The idea of living in the 'space age' was an exciting new prospect in 1962. The year before, President John F. Kennedy had announced at a joint session of Congress that an American would reach the Moon before the end of the decade. A 'space race' against the USSR, who had made the initial running, was initiated. In February 1962, John Glenn was the first American to orbit the Earth. New York City celebrated the astronaut's achievement with a ticker-tape parade. The youthful optimism represented by America's youngest ever president was in sharp contrast to the UK's prime minister. Harold Macmillan was 68, when that age was perceived as really ancient. He had commented in

1957, the year he became PM, that 'people have never had it so good'. After many years of post-war austerity this was true. But people wanted it even better. British political satire flourished with the arrival of *Private Eye* magazine and the BBC TV show *That Was The Week That Was*. Deference to the ruling class was diminishing.

Britons viewed America as a land of prosperity – a technicolor world that was impossibly glamorous compared to the drabness of home. But the US had its troubles and deep divisions. The Civil Rights movement was gathering momentum under the inspirational leadership of Dr Martin Luther King, Jr. There were riots as James Meredith became the first African-American student to be enrolled at the University of Mississippi in October 1962. US involvement in the conflict between North and South Vietnam was increasing. The Cold War between the capitalist West and communist East was at its chilliest.

'Love Me Do' was The Beatles' first hit in their home country – entering the charts in October 1962. That month, the relationship between the USA and the USSR reached its most perilous point when the Cuban Missile Crisis took the world to the brink of nuclear war. Millions watched nervously as President Kennedy and Premier Khrushchev were at loggerheads over the installation of Soviet missiles on the Caribbean island of Cuba. The world breathed a collective sigh of relief when a solution was found to the dangerous stand-off.

The same day The Beatles' first Parlophone single was released – 5 October 1962 – *Dr No* introduced Sean Connery as James Bond to filmgoers. The year's successful movies also included David Lean's *Lawrence of Arabia* and Francois Truffaut's *Jules et Jim*. On BBC Television, three long-lasting series were first broadcast: *Z Cars*, a gritty police drama set in the North, the more comforting *Dr Finlay's Casebook* and the comedy series *Steptoe and Son*. The first regular FM 'stereophonic' radio transmissions began in the UK on 28 August 1962. On American TV, Walter Cronkite became the anchorman for *CBS Evening News*. Johnny Carson became the host of *The Tonight Show*.

Here We Go.

THE STORY OF THE BEATLES and the British Broadcasting Corporation starts with the group's manager Brian Epstein completing a form headed 'Application For An Audition By Variety Department'. The date next to his signature is 10 January 1962. The word 'variety' is significant. For many years, a British night out at the theatre promised a variety of acts, including comedians, dancers, jugglers, a magician, a ventriloquist and musical combos. Popular entertainment on the BBC's airwaves had followed that model since its broadcasts began in 1922 and there was a department dedicated to booking 'variety' artists.

When rock 'n' roll infiltrated Britain during 1955, that traditional approach was challenged. Bill Haley and His Comets had led the rock vanguard with four records in the Hit Parade, including the number one 'Rock Around The Clock'. The following year, the country experienced the seismic impact created by Elvis Presley's six hit singles and a number one album. Discovering Elvis' 'Heartbreak Hotel' in May 1956 changed the lives of The Beatles and most of their contemporaries. However, the show business establishment viewed the new music as a novelty with a limited shelf-life. Perhaps the mambo would soon replace it. The BBC thought so and paid scant attention to the popularity of rock 'n' roll.

Elvis had arrived without warning – an explosion of everything young people wanted to see and hear… and parents feared. In fact, the fuse had been lit a year and a half earlier. What happened on the night of 8 July 1954 during the WHBQ show *Red, Hot And Blue* has since become the stuff of legend. Memphis disc jockey Dewey Phillips played a single that had been recorded three days before in the local Sun Studios. The reported number of times he played 'That's All Right (Mama)' by the unknown Elvis Presley has ranged from seven to thirty. It was an example of how the growth of rock 'n' roll in the States was nurtured by maverick record spinners on local radio stations across the country.

Compared to American radio, with its fast-talking DJs playing the latest hits all day, what the wireless offered in Britain was very sedate. Nothing like Dewey's wild championing of Elvis could ever

OPPOSITE The Beatles in early 1962 – George, John, Paul and Pete Best – wearing leather. 'We looked like four Gene Vincents,' joked Paul the following year. He was referring to the rock 'n' roll star, who had been encouraged to appear onstage in black leather clothes by English TV producer Jack Good in 1960.

LEFT 'Penny for the guy, mister?' Clowning at the Cavern Club: George, John, Pete and a horizontal Paul.

happen in the UK. In 1962, the BBC had three national networks: the Home Service, the Third Programme and the Light Programme. None of these was a generic service. When the Third Programme launched on 29 September 1946, the Director General of the BBC Sir William Haley explained the BBC's policy: 'The three Programmes will not be rigidly stratified, rather will they shade into each other. Music, plays and talks, for instance, will be found in each. While the Light Programme might well play the waltzes from *Der Rosenkavalier* and the Home Service do a live broadcast of an act from Covent Garden, the Third Programme would devote an evening to the whole opera. The differences will be in approach, in treatment and in emphasis. It's difficult to talk about raising public taste without sounding superior or "governess-y", but it's our purpose and we shall see that no innovation of ours will weaken it.'

Satisfying a teenage desire for rock 'n' roll was not seen by the BBC as 'raising public taste'. Instead, it ignored what it considered primitive music in the hope that it might go away. Only the Light Programme occasionally allowed rock 'n' roll into your home. Perhaps a request for The Crickets' 'That'll Be The Day' would be selected for *Two Way Family Favourites* – if you were lucky. When the Light did feature a whole programme of popular music, because of Musicians Union restrictions, records were usually sidelined by emasculated renditions of hits performed by old-fashioned dance orchestras. There was no local radio; no land-based commercial radio. The only alternative to the BBC was a crackling, phasing Radio Luxembourg transmitted from that country at night.

The Woody Allen movie *Radio Days* brilliantly evokes the character of American radio in the thirties and forties. Kids thrill to the adventures of the Masked Avenger; panic breaks out during Orson Welles' *War of the Worlds* Martian invasion; there is a radio ventriloquist; and housewives fantasize about the glamorous lives of on-air personalities. Even at the beginning of the 1960s, the character of the BBC Light Programme was very similar to that portrayed in *Radio Days*. Its mix of comedy, daily serials, sport, variety shows, dance band tunes and classical pieces had originated during the Second World War with the reorganization of the BBC into two

networks: the Home Service and the Forces Programme. The latter was launched on 7 January 1940, charged with a responsibility to raise the morale of troops and civilians. *Music While You Work*, for example, featured a band playing lively popular tunes to keep up the productivity of wartime factory workers. The show survived to the very last day of the Light Programme in 1967.

The Beatles were granted a BBC radio audition held in Manchester on 12 February 1962. Ten months before, the group's line-up had finally stabilized as the four-man unit of John Lennon (rhythm guitar), Paul McCartney (bass guitar), George Harrison (lead guitar) and Pete Best (drums). They had acquired their solicitous and rather refined manager, Liverpool record shop boss Brian Epstein, only a few weeks prior to their first visit to the BBC.

According to his autobiography *A Cellarful of Noise*, Epstein's interest in The Beatles had been kindled by an enquiry at his NEMS shop for 'My Bonnie', a record they had made (as The Beat Brothers) with Tony Sheridan. At first only available in Germany, the single was issued by Polydor in the UK on 5 January 1962. This first UK release featuring The Beatles was mentioned on the BBC application form. The same week, Liverpool's music paper *Mersey Beat* published the results of a local group popularity poll that showed The Beatles convincingly on top. So far so good in the first weeks of

RIGHT **The first Liverpool location of the record department of the North End Music Stores (NEMS) in Great Charlotte Street. It moved in 1959 to larger premises in Whitechapel.**

Epstein's tenure until Decca Records, who auditioned the group on New Year's Day, turned them down at the beginning of February. But there was still the chance of gaining valuable national exposure by performing on the BBC – if they passed their radio audition.

On weekdays, just one half-hour show on the Light Programme was aimed at younger listeners with a yearning for music with a beat. Timed for when this potential audience had returned from school, onto the air at five o'clock came *Teenagers Turn*. In early 1962, each day of the week had its own show billed under that main title: *The Monday Show*, *The Talent Spot*, *Get With It*, *Here We Go* and *The Cool Spot*. Thursday's *Here We Go* was recorded in Manchester and produced by Peter Pilbeam: 'We used to get some terrific audiences down at the Playhouse for the teenage shows. We'd have the

Northern Dance Orchestra on stage trying to look like teenagers with their chunky jumpers on and a presenter, a singer and a guest group in each programme.'

When Liverpool alone sustained 300 groups, a great deal of searching was necessary to find the best talent, as Pilbeam remembered. 'In those days, we were spending two or three evenings a week going round the North hearing groups of a similar size and there was masses of rubbish. Then out of the blue this group turned up at one of our audition sessions, called The Beatles – a weird name and everybody said, "Whoa-yuk!" – but they impressed me at the time.' For their audition, The Beatles performed two Lennon-McCartney originals – 'Hello Little Girl' and 'Like Dreamers Do' – while John took the lead on Chuck Berry's gentle rocker 'Memphis, Tennessee' and Paul sang 'Till There Was You' from the recent musical *The Music Man*. On the audition form, Peter Pilbeam commented: 'An unusual group, not as "Rocky" as most, more C & W [Country and Western], with a tendency to play music.' He recalled that was 'high praise, indeed, because a hell of a lot of noise came out of most three guitars and drums groups'. The Beatles passed the audition.

Despite Peter's notes on his report about the singers – 'John Lennon: yes; Paul McCartney: no' – both were featured on their radio debut. The Beatles were recorded in front of an audience on 7 March 1962 and for the first time they wore the suits provided by their manager. After all, this was the BBC. Their usual stage gear of jeans and leathers was left behind from then on. The next day, the whole country had the opportunity to hear The Beatles. John was heard singing 'Memphis, Tennessee' and the Marvelettes' recent US number one 'Please Mr Postman', while Paul covered Roy Orbison's current hit 'Dream Baby'. Those who missed this historic broadcast may have been watching the BBC TV kids' show *Crackerjack*, introduced by Eamonn Andrews and featuring the antics of Leslie Crowther, Peter Glaze and The Karl Heinz Chimpanzees.

The significant radio breakthrough on *Here We Go* came three months before they signed a contract with Parlophone/EMI and seven months before their first single 'Love Me Do' was released. The Beatles had done well to make it onto the air. Their Liverpool friends Gerry and The Pacemakers (runners-up in the 1961 *Mersey Beat* poll), Billy J Kramer and The Big Three had all failed their BBC auditions with Peter Pilbeam. Fellow Cavern Club regulars

OPPOSITE **The first time 'Beatles with an A' was printed in the BBC's weekly radio and TV listings magazine** *Radio Times.*

RIGHT **George, Paul and John onstage at the Cavern Club on 22 August 1962. Granada Television visited a lunchtime session that day and The Beatles were filmed for the first time.**

The Swinging Bluegenes had been on *Here We Go* a month before The Beatles, but their style was different. With a banjo player in the line-up, their music was rooted in the safer sounds of skiffle and trad jazz. They were to change course eventually when they renamed themselves The Swinging Blue Jeans in April 1963.

Impressed again by The Beatles' performance, Peter Pilbeam booked them for another programme. The recording took place on a 'bank holiday' – Whit Monday, 11 June 1962. A coach trip was organized to take Liverpool fans across to the Playhouse Theatre in Manchester to bolster the audience response to The Beatles. The week before this BBC performance, the group had returned from a two-month residency at The Star-Club in Hamburg. Six days after their return from Germany, The Beatles entered EMI's studios in Abbey Road for the first time. This test session on 6 June 1962 was to determine whether they would secure a recording contract.

'Ask Me Why' became the first Lennon-McCartney song to be broadcast on the radio when it was heard in *Here We Go* on 15 June 1962. The group also played their versions of 'Besame Mucho' and 'A Picture Of You' – a Top Ten hit at this time for Joe Brown and the Bruvvers. By the time of their next *Here We Go* appearance The Beatles had a record of their own to promote. In Manchester on 25 October 1962, they played both sides of their first Parlophone single, 'Love Me Do'/'P.S. I Love You'. Their other song in the show was 'A Taste Of Honey'. It had been learnt from the first vocal version of the tune released by Lenny Welch in September. Most significantly, there was a new Beatle behind the drum kit. Having played his final gig on 15 August, Pete Best was replaced by Ringo Starr from Rory Storm and The Hurricanes. A sign perhaps of the gathering momentum of their career, The Beatles' fee had increased. Having previously received £26 18s (£26.90) and the cost of return rail fares to Manchester, this time they were paid £37 18s (£37.90) plus expenses.

Important steps forward had been taken through BBC radio broadcasts and the release of a record, but what about television? Their interest stimulated by fans' letters, Granada Television in Manchester had filmed The Beatles playing a lunchtime gig at the Cavern Club in August. However, the footage of 'Some Other Guy' was not shown until over a year later when British Beatlemania was at its height. However, Granada did broadcast the first Beatles TV appearance when the group sang 'Love Me Do' and 'Some Other Guy' live during *People and Places* on 17 October 1962. Meanwhile, BBC television had taken notice of two letters from Beatles fan David John Smith of Preston. Mentioning the *People and Places*

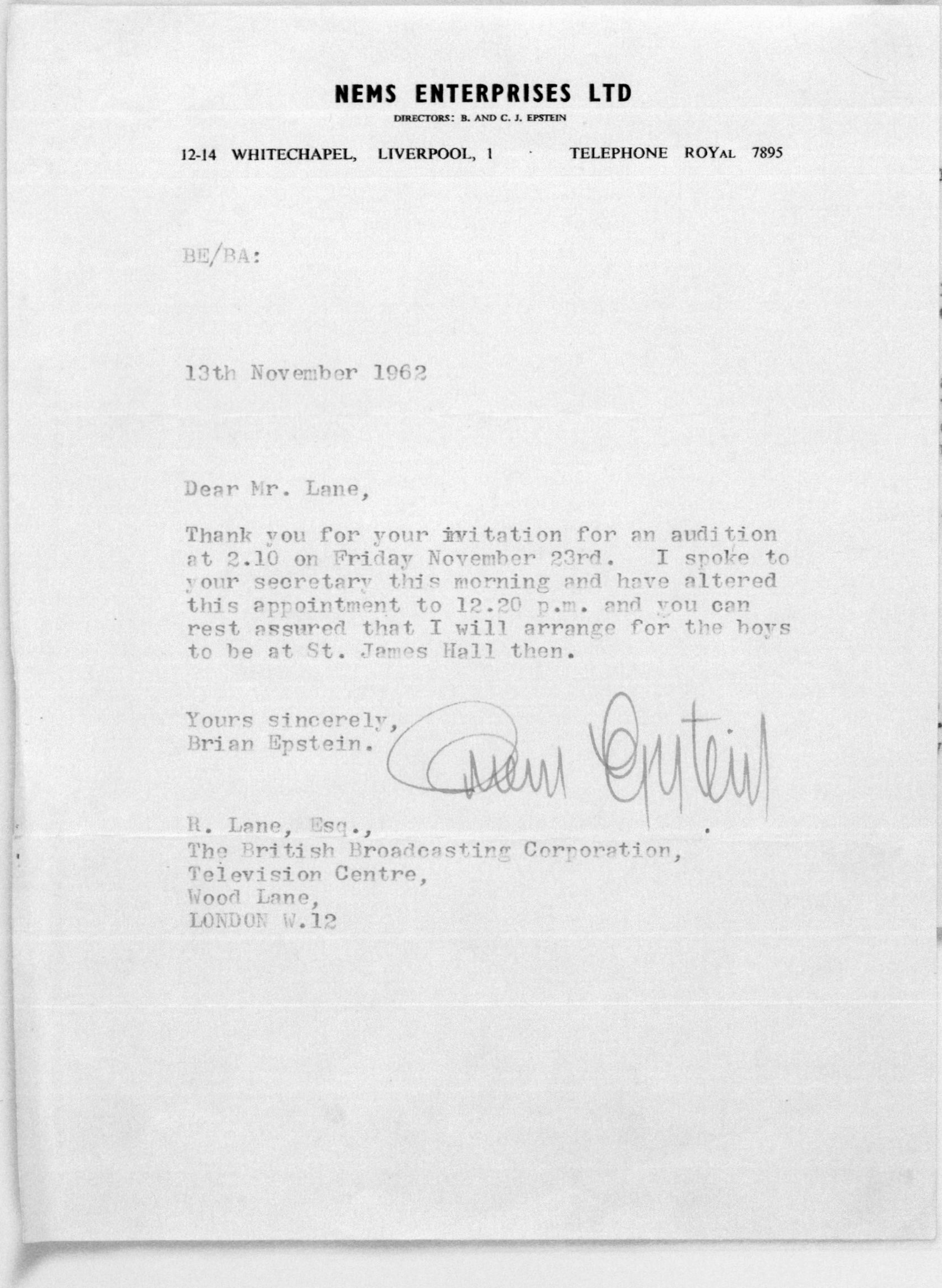

NEMS ENTERPRISES LTD

DIRECTORS: B. AND C. J. EPSTEIN

12-14 WHITECHAPEL, LIVERPOOL, 1 · TELEPHONE ROYAL 7895

BE/BA:

13th November 1962

Dear Mr. Lane,

Thank you for your invitation for an audition at 2.10 on Friday November 23rd. I spoke to your secretary this morning and have altered this appointment to 12.20 p.m. and you can rest assured that I will arrange for the boys to be at St. James Hall then.

Yours sincerely,
Brian Epstein.

R. Lane, Esq.,
The British Broadcasting Corporation,
Television Centre,
Wood Lane,
LONDON W.12

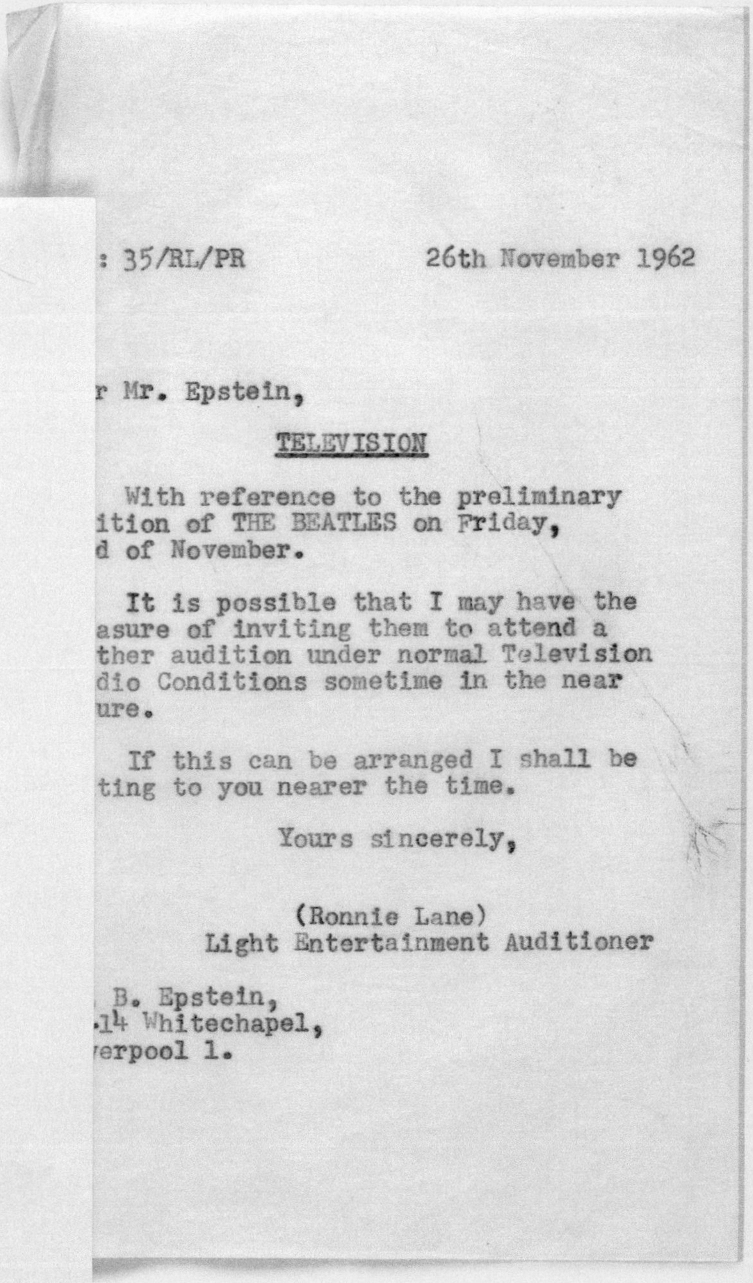

: 35/RL/PR   26th November 1962

r Mr. Epstein,

                    TELEVISION

    With reference to the preliminary
ition of THE BEATLES on Friday,
d of November.

    It is possible that I may have the
asure of inviting them to attend a
ther audition under normal Television
dio Conditions sometime in the near
ure.

    If this can be arranged I shall be
ting to you nearer the time.

                    Yours sincerely,

                    (Ronnie Lane)
                    Light Entertainment Auditioner

. B. Epstein,
.14 Whitechapel,
verpool 1.

LEFT AND ABOVE **BBC** Television was slower off the mark than BBC Radio to recognize the potential of the group. Manager Brian Epstein always referred to The Beatles as 'the boys'. When he wrote his letter in November 1962, he was aged 28 – six years older than John Lennon.

performance that was not screened outside the north west of the country, he wrote that 'with a combination of boyish, schoolboy looks and a thick rhythm and blues sound, they produce a really dynamic stage act… Believe me, if you took an interest in this very talented group of lads you would not regret it at all.'

BBC TV's Light Entertainment Auditioner, Ronnie Lane, sent a letter to Mr Smith to invite The Beatles to attend an audition at the Television Theatre, Shepherds Bush in London, W12. NEMS Enterprises then picked up the baton and a preliminary audition lasting ten minutes was arranged to take place on 23 November 1962 at St James's Hall, Gloucester Terrace, London W2. Sadly, no written information about what The Beatles played has survived, but Ronnie Lane's letter addressed to Brian Epstein stated that 'I may have the pleasure of inviting them to attend a further audition under normal Television Studio Conditions in the near future.'

With 'Love Me Do' lingering at the lower end of the charts, The Beatles' reputation was growing and they ventured further from their stomping ground in the north. In December 1962, they made appearances on local ITV shows based in Bristol and Wembley and travelled to Peterborough in the far-off Midlands for a Frank Ifield package show. On 4 December they were back on the radio in *The Talent Spot* with jazz vocalist Elkie Brooks (who would wait another fifteen years for her first hit), singer of country and western songs Frank Kelly, Mark Tracey, compere Gary Marshal and The Ted Taylor Four. The Beatles played both sides of their single and then closed the show with 'Twist And Shout'. That unbridled burst of energy must have sounded pretty cataclysmic alongside such gentle musical company.

The Talent Spot was their first radio show to be recorded in London. They had arrived in the capital the day before – 26 November 1962 – to make their fourth visit to Abbey Road. During an evening session, 'Please Please Me' and 'Ask Me Why' were completed and scheduled for single release in January. The remainder of 1962 was filled with concerts and a two-week stint at the Star-Club in Hamburg. It had been an encouraging year for The Beatles with their four BBC radio appearances oiling the wheels as they progressed through the world of British show business. As they greeted the New Year with raucous revellers in Hamburg, could they ever have imagined what it would bring?

1962 BBC RADIO APPEARANCES

TEENAGERS TURN – Here We Go
Br: 8 March 1962 – 5.00–5.29pm
– The Light Programme
Rec: 7 March 1962
Playhouse Theatre, Manchester
Producer: Peter Pilbeam
Presenter: Ray Peters
Dream Baby, Memphis, Tennessee, Please Mister Postman
Recorded in front of an audience
Pete Best – drummer

HERE WE GO
Br: 15 June 1962 – 5.00–5.29pm
– The Light Programme
Rec: 11 June 1962
Playhouse Theatre, Manchester
Producer: Peter Pilbeam
Presenter: Ray Peters
Ask Me Why, Besame Mucho, A Picture Of You
Recorded in front of an audience
Pete Best – drummer

HERE WE GO
Br: 26 October 1962 – 5.00-5.29pm
– The Light Programme
Rec: 25 October 1962
Playhouse Theatre, Manchester
Producer: Peter Pilbeam
Presenter: Ray Peters
Love Me Do, A Taste of Honey, P.S. I Love You
Recorded in front of an audience
Performed but not broadcast: *Sheila*
Ringo Starr – drummer from this session onwards

THE TALENT SPOT
Br: 4 December 1962 – 5.00–5.29pm
– The Light Programme
Rec: 27 November 1962
BBC Paris Theatre, London
Producer: Brian Willey
Presenter: Gary Marshal
Love Me Do, P.S. I Love You, Twist And Shout
First session in London

1963

Pop Go The Beatles

POP GO THE BEATLES. The group did not choose the title for their fifteen-part series broadcast during the summer of 1963 and they had reluctantly recorded the corny theme tune simply because they had to. After all, some compromise was acceptable to make their way in the show business world. Yet what made The Beatles so irresistible in their breakthrough year was how quickly they were changing the game. Aside from the energy of the music they created, their BBC broadcasts are characterized by send-ups, laughs, cheeky irreverence. This was new.

Their youthful exuberance was exactly what the UK needed as an alternative to news of a sleazy scandal engulfing the Conservative government. Revelations regarding the behaviour of MP John Profumo emerged from March onwards. Model Christine Keeler had a brief affair with the Secretary of State for War in 1961. She also had a liaison with a USSR diplomat Captain Yevgeny Ivanov who was, in fact, a Soviet spy. Profumo's impropriety, it was argued, had endangered national security. Having knowingly misled the House of Commons about his relationship with Keeler, he was forced to resign on 4 June 1963.

In America, The Beatles were largely unknown. Capitol Records, although owned by EMI Records, declined to release the group's material in the US. Licensed to independent labels, the records made no impact on the air or in the charts during 1963. The most successful pop groups in the States were The Beach Boys from the West Coast and The 4 Seasons from the East. There was also a burgeoning US folk movement with singers writing topical songs. On 28 August 1963, when 250,000 people in the 'March on Washington for Jobs and Freedom' reached the Lincoln Memorial, Bob Dylan, Joan Baez, and Peter, Paul and Mary sang for them. Martin Luther King, Jr. made his epochal 'I have a dream' speech on that day. He outlined his vision that 'my four little children will one day live in a nation where they will not be judged by the colour of their skin, but by the content of their character. I have a dream today.' The year ended in tragedy. President John F. Kennedy was assassinated on 22 November 1963. The USA entered a 30-day period of official mourning.

In 1963, The Beatles left Liverpool to live in London. The capital city was a vibrant centre for new ideas in music, fashion, theatre, art and cinema. They embraced it all. In the early years of the 1960s, provincial life had been portrayed in powerful 'kitchen sink' dramas such as *Saturday Night and Sunday Morning* and *The Loneliness of the Long Distance Runner*. Another in the sequence, *Billy Liar*, was released in 1963. In the final scene, Tom Courtenay's title character continues to live his life in a northern town; his girlfriend played by Julie Christie boards the train for London and new horizons. Black and white realism on film was making way for colourful flamboyance, as seen in the Oscar-winning *Tom Jones* and the most expensive movie ever made to this point – the epic *Cleopatra* starring Richard Burton and Elizabeth Taylor.

While the UK was still in a sombre mood following the assassination of President Kennedy, the first episode of *Doctor Who* was broadcast on 23 November. Earlier, in the summer, ITV had commissioned the pop show *Ready Steady Go!* – bringing the latest chart records, dances and stylish clothes to the screen every Friday evening, the programme assured viewers, 'The weekend starts here.' The Beatles made their first *Ready Steady Go!* appearance on 4 October 1963 to mime to 'Twist And Shout', 'I'll Get You' and their current number one 'She Loves You'. Just a few days before, the Leader of the Opposition, Harold Wilson, made a forward-looking speech at the Labour Party Conference promising that Britain under his premiership would be 'forged in the white heat of the … scientific revolution'. His message was clear: out with the old, in with the new.

AT THE BEGINNING OF 1963, Britain was experiencing its worst winter weather since 1947. The country shivered through freezing temperatures at a time when few houses had the luxury of central heating. Most of the land was covered in deep snow, making transport difficult. Undaunted, The Beatles spent many hours during those cold early months of 1963 in a van driven by their friend Neil Aspinall. They journeyed up and down the country to appear onstage at theatres and ballrooms and to perform in radio and TV studios. Before this breakthrough year, the group had worked hard at their craft – particularly at all-night sessions in the clubs of Hamburg – getting better all the time. The pressure of The Beatles' schedule never eased for a moment in 1963, but they were match-fit. Their musical expertise combined with the discipline and stamina to work incessantly proved to be an unbeatable formula. BBC radio and television embraced the group. The Beatles' voices and faces became familiar through the wireless and the telly.

'At the moment, the majority of The Beatles' fans are in their home town of Liverpool and I have a very strong suspicion it won't be long before they're all over the country.' So predicted Brian Matthew during *Saturday Club* on 26 January 1963 – the first time The Beatles were heard performing songs on the Light Programme's premier pop show. From ten o'clock to noon every Saturday, 'your old mate' Brian Matthew introduced a range of musical styles represented by artists ranging from Terry Lightfoot and his New Orleans Jazzmen (who were really from the suburban town of Potters Bar) to a genuine rock 'n' roll star like Eddie Cochran. *Saturday Club* reached an enormous audience of around ten to twelve million; a figure that doubled in size when the BBC General Overseas Service simultaneously transmitted a 30-minute section to the world.

The programme had evolved from the half-hour *Saturday Skiffle Club*, started in 1958 by producer Jimmy Grant. The appeal of groups making music with washboards and tea-chest basses soon faded, but the programme grew ever more popular after it was extended to two hours and lost the word 'skiffle' from its title. The weekly selection of pop, country and western, trad-jazz and rock 'n' roll was played from discs and tapes of specially recorded BBC

OPPOSITE Relaxing during a recording session for *Side By Side* at the BBC Paris Theatre in Lower Regent Street, London – 4 April 1963. None of The Beatles' songs recorded for the BBC featured piano playing.

'It came to us in a flaming pie and spoke these words: "From this day on you are The Beatles with an A".'

JOHN LENNON

sessions. Indeed, much of the success of *Saturday Club* was due to the assiduous search for talented newcomers to showcase. The production team's claim to have discovered leading British stars Cliff Richard and Adam Faith was a reasonable one. For anyone at all interested in popular music, *Saturday Club* was essential listening. The country's coffee bars remained free of teenagers until the show was over. It was as much a part of the ritual of a British Saturday as BBC television's *Grandstand*, *Juke Box Jury* and *Dixon of Dock Green*. Naturally, The Beatles listened regularly and, like hundreds of other ambitious musicians, hoped to be invited onto the show.

The Beatles' contract for their *Saturday Club* booking was dated 31 December 1962, revealing a swift BBC response to a preview of their new record 'Please Please Me'. A week after the single was released, the group mimed to it on independent TV's popular programme *Thank Your Lucky Stars*, also presented by Brian Matthew. The BBC's listings magazine, *Radio Times*, made their *Saturday Club* debut one of its highlights of the week with the comment: 'Any group with so uncompromising a name as The Beatles has much to overcome to win recognition from those who have little interest in Hit Parade music. Why did they choose the name? John Lennon, their leader, says (and we quote): "It came to us in a flaming pie and spoke these words: 'From this day on you are The Beatles with an A.'"'

OPPOSITE George preparing for a performance recorded at the BBC Playhouse Theatre on 3 April 1963 and broadcast in the Sunday morning show *Easy Beat*.

ABOVE The fourth edition of *Pop Go The Beatles* was recorded between 10.30am and 1.00pm on 17 June 1963 – the day before Paul's 21st birthday. Following lunch in the canteen of the BBC's Maida Vale Studios in London, he was given birthday 'bumps' in Delaware Road.

On most charts, including the BBC's own, 'Please Please Me' reached number one. When it became clear how big this hit was going to be, an EMI session was arranged for 11 February 1963. All ten extra tracks required for the *Please Please Me* album were recorded on that day. In the 1978 spoof documentary about 'The Rutles', this achievement is celebrated with the words: 'Their first album took 20 minutes; their second – even longer.' The Beatles' next visit to *Saturday Club* was broadcast on 16 March 1963, a week ahead of the LP's release.

Since their first appearance, they had travelled the country on a package tour headlined by Helen Shapiro. Although six years younger than John, she had already enjoyed five Top Ten hits including two number ones. Just as she had missed a couple of engagements because of illness, John's heavy cold prevented his participation in a few concerts on The Beatles' next nationwide tour

with American stars Tommy Roe and Chris Montez. His illness also caused the abandonment of their Monday BBC session for that week's *Saturday Club*. Recently appointed producer Bernie Andrews was supervising the music recordings for the show. He remembered that 'We started it and they couldn't get the vocals together, because John had a bad throat and couldn't sing.' The Beatles were playing in Bedford, York, Wolverhampton and Bristol over the remaining days of the week. The only option was to have The Beatles perform live during *Saturday Club*. As Bernie recalled, 'The studio in Broadcasting House was actually a Talks and small drama studio – not really a music studio at all. So we got a few extra mics in, started rehearsing about eight o'clock and went on the air live at ten o'clock'. This early morning start for the group followed two shows the night before in Bristol. In early 1963, before the M4 motorway was built, the city was a much lengthier drive from London.

It was not the first time The Beatles had played live straight onto the air. On 20 February, they had broadcast from the Playhouse Theatre for the lunchtime audience show *Parade of the Pops*. But the ability to take on a live *Saturday Club* impressed the programme's presenter Brian Matthew: 'I don't think there was another beat group who would have dared to attempt that particular feat. The Beatles did it and took it in their stride. This was the first time I saw them perform in one of our studios and I was completely overwhelmed. They were clearly streets ahead of their contemporaries.' The selected songs for the broadcast were 'I Saw Her Standing There', 'Misery' and 'Please Please Me' from the forthcoming album and three much-played stage numbers: 'The Hippy Hippy Shake' and two Chuck Berry rockers 'I'm Talkin' About You' and 'Too Much Monkey Business'.

Just over two weeks later, they met Brian Matthew again when they appeared on his gentler Sunday morning show *Easy Beat*. Nine million listened every week to a resident band led by Johnny Howard and an assortment of singers. In front of an audience at the Playhouse Theatre, The Beatles performed 'Please Please Me', 'Misery' and their new single 'From Me To You'. Their Liverpool mates Gerry and The Pacemakers were number one that week with 'How Do You Do It'. Gerry Marsden joined Brian Matthew on stage to introduce The Beatles' performance of 'From Me To You'. 'This is one that I really think is going to be a hit… hope so anyway. Nothing more I can say except… how do you do it?' Within a month, The Beatles' disc had replaced his record at the top of the charts.

Following the release of The Beatles' first album and third single 'From Me To You', the group finally entered a BBC television studio. By this time, the commercial TV channel had featured them eleven times. The Beatles' BBC TV debut was on *The 625 Show* broadcast on 16 April 1963. They performed both songs on their current single and closed the show with 'Please Please Me'. Two days later, The Beatles were back on the radio in a live broadcast from the Royal Albert Hall. *Swinging Sound '63* was the second of three Light Programme concerts from the prestigious venue. The *Radio Times* writer Tony Aspler had attended the first and witnessed 'the "cats" erupt in a paroxysm of whistles and screams of appreciation. I suppose a good scream does clear the head, but if, like me, you feel like a pigeon among the cats, it's *safer* to hear it all at home, on the radio.'

Swinging Sound '63 offered the usual Light Programme variety of music. There was trad-jazz from Ottilie Patterson with Chris Barber's Jazz Band and George Melly singing with the BBC Jazz Club All Stars; pop from The Vernons Girls and Kenny Lynch; folk from Robin Hall and Jimmie Macgregor; country-folk from The Springfields; and novelty numbers from Lance Percival and Rolf Harris. The two beat groups on the bill were Shane Fenton & The Fentones and The Beatles. The headline act, American singer Del Shannon, played his latest release 'Two Kinds Of Teardrops' and one of his six previous British Top Ten hits 'Swiss Maid'. Following the concert, Paul met his future fiancée Jane Asher, who had earlier posed for a *Radio Times* photograph showing her screaming with the other 'cats'. She was a well-known teen TV celebrity, who often judged new records for *Juke Box Jury* and had recently acted in an episode of *Dixon of Dock Green*.

At the start of April 1963, The Beatles recorded three programmes for a radio series called *Side By Side*, in which the Karl Denver Trio played host to another group. Karl Denver's yodelling had most famously been heard on the Trio's biggest hit from 1962 'Wimoweh (The Lion Sleeps Tonight)'. The show was presented by BBC staff announcer John Dunn, who jollied things along with links such as 'And here are those four Beatles… up to some no good monkey business', before John kicked off 'Too Much Monkey Business'. The group's sense of humour shone through the brief interviews. On the 13 May *Side By Side* broadcast, John explained the group's name with the usual zany 'flaming pie' pronouncement of 'Beatles with an A'. Paul introduced 'A Taste Of Honey' as one of his Auntie Jin's great favourites and, before launching into 'Boys', Ringo joked, 'They did give me a go on the LP and, between you and me, I think that's the track that's selling it!'

Although taped as long ago as 4 April, their third appearance on *Side By Side* was heard on 24 June 1963. The programme featured a Lennon-McCartney song that, at the time of broadcast, was only available on the B-side of 'Do You Want To Know A Secret' by Billy J. Kramer with The Dakotas. 'I'll Be On My Way' was never released by The Beatles in the 1960s, making it one of the most significant tracks on the collection *Live At The BBC*. The front cover photograph

for that 1994 album was taken outside the BBC Paris Theatre in Lower Regent Street, London on the day of the *Side By Side* session.

On 16 May 1963, The Beatles made their second BBC television appearance on *Pops and Lenny* presented by ventriloquist Terry Hall and his lion glove puppet. The BBC viewed pop music as pretty much for kids, so TV shows aimed at children offered opportunities for valuable publicity. Being asked for your autograph by Lenny the Lion was a small price to pay for being on television. Two days after the live broadcast, The Beatles embarked on their third nationwide tour; the headline act this time was Roy Orbison. They were great admirers of the Big O's passionate vocals on epic ballads like 'In Dreams' and 'Running Scared' and his relaxed style on 'Only The Lonely' and 'Dream Baby'. Nonetheless, audience clamour forced The Beatles to take his place at the top of the bill. However, unlike other American stars from this era, Roy Orbison remained popular with British record buyers. He had eight more Top Ten hits, including two number ones.

After three dates of the tour, The Beatles used a day off to record at the BBC Playhouse Theatre. In the evening of 21 May they headlined a 59-minute concert featuring Mark Wynter, Mike Berry, Maureen Evans, Alan Elsdon's Jazz band and the Red Price Combo. With the title *Steppin' Out*, it was broadcast on 3 June – a bank holiday called Whit Monday. Not a moment was wasted on 21 May. During the afternoon the group had taped six songs for their third appearance on *Saturday Club*. Brian Matthew confirmed their new status when he announced on 25 May, 'It's time now to hear the first one from our bill-toppers… The Beatles!' He also revealed that the show was receiving 'as many requests for The Beatles as for everyone else combined'. Some of these requests were read on air by the group, including cards sent by listeners in Egypt and Germany who heard the half-hour section of the programme relayed every week by the General Overseas Service.

Listeners were treated to spirited renditions of 'Money' and 'Long Tall Sally', which were not available on The Beatles' records at this time. There would be many more intriguing cover versions to come in a series that signified how rapidly they were rising to the top of the music business in the UK. Just three months after their first number one, the group were invited to host a radio show – *Pop Go The Beatles*.

Vernon Lawrence, Studio Manager, L.E.(S)   5070 B.H.

PROGRAMME SUGGESTION: "BEATLE TIME"   *Beatles Progs.*

A.H.L.E.(S)I   Copy to: M.O.L.E.(S)   30th April 1963

I wish to submit the following suggestion for a programme entitled
'Beatle Time'.

This programme would feature The Beatles, the current chart-toppers
of the British 'pop' music scene. As proved by recent broadcasts,
it could be compered by Paul McCartney and John Lennon, this would
also cut down the cost.

To provide a contrast, I would suggest a group directed by
Harry Robinson of seven or nine musicians. The object of this
group would be to back a guest male and female vocalist each week,
i.e. Mark Wynter and Susan Maughan.

As The Beatles produce such a distinctive sound, a group such as
Brian Poole and the Tremeloes or Russ Sainty and the Nu-Notes could
provide the 'rock' element.

The cost would be approximately £250.

I imagine a programme of this nature would be suitable for a fifty
or sixty-minute evening or weekend slot in the Light Programme.

(Vernon Lawrence)

LEFT AND BELOW Just 24 days after the memo from BBC sound man Vernon Lawrence, the first recording took place for the series *Pop Go The Beatles.* OPPOSITE Recording a session on 17 December 1963 for the Christmas edition of *Saturday Club.*

To: A.H.L.E.(S) I

From: M.O.,L.E.(S)

Prog Sugg

VERNON LAWRENCE'S PROGRAMME SUGGESTION

"BEATLE TIME"

My comments, as requested:

I'm not sure about the title, but I like almost everything else
about this. (Young Lawrence certainly has good judgment of
contemporary values.)

I think the optimum duration is 45 minutes, pre-recorded - and
I'd like to have an outlet of say 6 weeks for this, during which
we would exclude the Beatles from other shows?

D. H. MACLEAN
(Donald MacLean)   2.5.63

(Brian Epstein told me the other day that you were hoping to find
a Saturday p.m. series for the Beatles and he hoped this would
work out.)

BBC executives, who may not have registered the increasing popularity of The Beatles, were stirred into action by an enthusiastic studio manager. Vernon Lawrence drafted a memo on 30 April 1963 proposing a series called *Beatle Time*. He suggested an evening or weekend slot to be occupied by The Beatles with guest male and female vocalists – the wholesome Mark Wynter and Susan Maughan – and a rock element provided by Brian Poole and The Tremeloes or Russ Sainty and The Nu-Notes. The 'Music Organizer – Light Entertainment (Sound)', Donald MacLean, conceded that 'young Lawrence certainly has good judgement of contemporary values.' The idea evolved into a series of half-hour programmes, each featuring The Beatles and a guest group. For fifteen weeks during the summer of 1963 this Tuesday evening show was required listening for teenagers all over Britain. As presenter Rodney Burke put it: 'It's five o'clock, we're ready to pop. It's the *Pop Go The Beatles* spot!'

Only three weeks after Vernon's memo was written, the *New Musical Express* heralded the series with the headline 'Group Gets Radio Show'. The article stated that 'four shows have been planned although the series may be extended.' This was an admirably speedy and, in the context of the Light Programme, a courageous move on the part of the Corporation. Terry Henebery was appointed producer, with assistance from a new production trainee Ian Grant. The title of The Beatles' series was conceived by Frances Line, one of the production department's secretaries. As Terry Henebery remembered, 'One of the most difficult decisions is what to call the programme. You can't keep calling it the "Something-Something Show", it's so boring. Frances took a lot of interest in programmes like *Saturday Club* and *Easy Beat*, for which she worked actually, for Brian Matthew. She had a younger sister who was into pop music and she said, "We've been sitting round at home and we thought this wouldn't make a bad title – *Pop Go The Beatles*." I said, "You've got it, that is a super title!"' Frances Line rose through the ranks of the BBC to become the Controller of Radio 2 (the Light Programme's successor) in 1990.

> '**One of the most difficult decisions is what to call the programme. You can't keep calling it the "Something Something Show", it's so boring.** *Pop Go The Beatles* **– that is a super title!**'
>
> TERRY HENEBERY (PRODUCER)

wouldn't make a bad title – *Pop Go The Beatles*." I said, "You've got it, that is a super title!"' Frances Line rose through the ranks of the BBC to become the Controller of Radio 2 (the Light Programme's successor) in 1990.

The BBC loved signature tunes and the series title presented an opportunity to rock up the nursery rhyme 'Pop Goes The Weasel'. The Lorne Gibson Trio joined The Beatles on the first show transmitted on 4 June 1963. The other guest groups in the initial run were The Countrymen, Carter-Lewis & The Southerners and The Bachelors. They were all suitable Light Programme 'combos'. The Bachelors offered a particularly sugary contrast to The Beatles' repertoire. Terry Henebery confirmed that the choice of guests was solely that of the production team. 'Bearing in mind that The Beatles were new, one wanted to put some solid guest acts in; a mixture of the attractive units appearing on other programmes. There was no pressure from The Beatles to use mates or anything, because they weren't big enough to put "the heavies" on.' After a three-week hiatus, the series returned for a continuous run until September. The guest acts for these eleven shows were rockier and better matched to the style of the series. The Liverpool scene was represented by The Swinging Blue Jeans and The Searchers; Vernon Lawrence's original suggestions – Russ Sainty and The Nu-Notes and Brian Poole and The Tremeloes – were booked; and The Hollies made their sixth BBC recording for *Pop Go The Beatles*.

No one would have predicted it in 1963, but the songs The Beatles chose to perform for their radio series constitute the most fascinating element of their music sessions for BBC radio. Some groups may have been unnerved by a series that demanded six new recordings every week. Not The Beatles, who in addition to playing the comparatively small number of titles on their records, happily played songs by artists who had inspired them and tried out some contemporary material.

Eighteen Beatles tracks had been released on record by September 1963, yet 56 songs were performed for *Pop Go The Beatles*. All six of the cover versions from *Please Please Me* and eleven of the

OPPOSITE **Recording both sides of their fourth single 'She Loves You' / 'I'll Get You' at EMI Studios in Abbey Road, London on 1 July 1963.**

twelve Lennon-McCartney titles issued on that album and their singles were broadcast (the omitted song was the B-side 'Thank You Girl'). Although listeners heard all six cover versions on *With The Beatles* several months prior to its release in November 1963, none of the album's original compositions was previewed. A remarkable 39 of the songs heard in the series were not available on The Beatles' records by the end of the series; 26 of those remained unreleased during the group's existence.

The *New Musical Express* report about *Pop Go The Beatles* had stated that 'R-and-b material will be strongly featured.' The shows certainly lived up to that promise. The hundreds of hours spent entertaining the rowdy clientele of a Hamburg nightclub and the friendly regulars at the Cavern Club in Liverpool had necessitated a large and varied repertoire. In the 1988 radio series *The Beeb's Lost Beatles Tapes*, George explained that the selection of songs reflected 'What we used to do onstage because, whenever you're doing tons of material, you need to sing other people's songs as well. And we started out doing Hamburg where, as the old story goes, we used to play eight hours a day for tuppence a month and [mimicking the *Monty Python* 'Four Yorkshiremen' sketch and its refrain 'You were lucky!''] when we got home, Brian Epstein would slash us to death with a carving knife… if we were lucky! So we used to have to sing all kinds of tunes. Anything. We'd play "Moonglow" and "The Harry Lime Theme"… and we even played some Shadows songs. We sang all the old Shirelles and the old Tamla Motown tunes. As we were doing loads of those BBC shows, if we had a single or an album that we'd made, we'd obviously do some of our own stuff. But a lot of the material was just stuff that we'd be singing around the clubs.'

Ringo has also commented that the songs on the BBC tapes proved 'we were a working band… everyone gets to *Sgt. Pepper* and thinks that's what we were… but we were doing every club on the planet!' In John's candid interview with Jann Wenner of *Rolling Stone*, he also emphasized that 'in Liverpool, Hamburg and round the dance halls what we generated was fantastic and when we played straight rock, there was no one to touch us in Britain.'

OPPOSITE **Ringo's two featured vocals during *Pop Go The Beatles* were 'Boys' and the not-yet-released 'Matchbox'. This shot was taken at the session for *Saturday Club* on 17 December 1963.**

During the summer of 1963, The Beatles played theatres in several of the UK's seaside resorts. Shortened to twenty minutes of hits, their live set was drowned by screaming. Consequently, recording *Pop Go The Beatles* in the BBC's studios allowed the group not only a refreshing opportunity to romp through an old favourite, but also a chance to work on a new interpretation. As Ringo observed, 'It was fine when doing the repertoire we knew, but some weeks it'd be real hard. We'd rehearse two or three songs in the lunch break and then go and record them in the afternoon.' One result of that routine is George's *Pop Go The Beatles* choice of an obscure record by American girl-group The Donays. Although 'Devil In His Heart' did creep out on the Oriole label in the UK, hardly anyone has ever seen a copy of it. We are fortunate to have the unreleased songs caught in a fairly raw state, but well-recorded and without the constant jet-engine-whine generated by fans at concerts. Surveying the choice of songs made for *Pop Go The Beatles* is the nearest you can get to exploring the group's record collections. The original sources of the cover versions performed by The Beatles at the BBC are examined in Chapter Ten.

In the week of the fourth show of the series, *Radio Times* revealed on its highlights page that 'two days after the first broadcast, the producer Terry Henebery received over one hundred cards from listeners all over the country expressing their delight that this remarkable group now have their own programme.' The *Pop Go The Beatles* format included The Beatles reading some of the many letters sent to the BBC. The production team were swamped with many more requests as the weeks went by and the group read them on air with increasing confidence. For the initial four-week run, the presenter was Lee Peters (or 'Pee Litres', as The Beatles liked to call him). His was a familiar voice on the network. He voiced the character of David Owen in the daily soap opera *The Dales*, first broadcast in January 1948 as *Mrs Dale's Diary*.

In *Pop Go The Beatles*, Lee Peters played the role of posh BBC straight man, apparently struggling to keep order amongst the send-ups and antics of the cheeky Liverpudlians. When John interrupted him to explain he was not playing harmonica but a blues harp on

'I Got To Find My Baby', the announcer appeared to storm off in a huff. John finished the introduction with the comment: 'Love these *Goon Shows*.' He was referring to the radio comedy series that ran for 200 episodes in the 1950s, starring Spike Milligan, Peter Sellers, Harry Secombe and Michael Bentine. Like most of their contemporaries, The Beatles were fond of adopting the silly voices of Goons characters like Eccles, Bluebottle and Moriarty.

A BBC Audience Research report on the first show of the series disclosed that most of the Listening Panel agreed that Lee Peters had made a 'good compere'. The character of his introductions is typified by 'So the boys remove their shackles now to give us another track from their LP – "Chains".' Although he always mispronounced Ringo's name as 'Ring-oh', The Beatles responded well to his corny links. John seemed particularly taken with a rather good James Mason impression during an introduction to 'Baby It's You'. Lee Peters encouraged more acting when he led a round of 'Happy Birthday' during the show to be broadcast on Paul's 21st (18 June 1963), although recorded on 1 June. He even encouraged Paul to talk about his birthday party in a session recorded the day before it was due to happen. It actually turned out to be an eventful night, in which an altercation between John and Cavern DJ Bob Wooler was reported in the press.

The Beatles' playful improvisations between the songs were dazzlingly fresh for a BBC radio show. Every programme of records linked by a disc jockey had to have a script written weeks in advance. It was only allowed to be broadcast once it had been scrutinized by Anna Instone – the formidable Head of the Gramophone Department. She was notorious for returning scripts with numerous alterations marked with a blue pencil. Fortunately, The Beatles' series came under the aegis of the Popular Music Department, which permitted more freedom in the 'announcements'. As Ian Grant recalled, 'The Beatles took the Mickey. But that was it. It was right. You couldn't have scripted that and blue-pencilled that. They would never have done it. They'd have just laughed at everybody. *Pop Go The Beatles* had to have this atmosphere and Terry let it grow, really. That was an innovative thing – to have that kind of freedom. But it was all recorded so it could be edited. I don't think they'd have been allowed to go live!'

Terry Henebery recalled the fun in the studio was not confined to the speech content. 'They were very much younger and they'd come to the studio and horse about. You had to crack the whip and get on the loudspeaker talk-back key quite a lot and say, "Come on, chaps!" They'd be lying over the floor, giggling. And I can remember afternoons down at the BBC Paris Cinema Studio, where you were just looking at the clock, throwing your hands up in horror and thinking, "Will they ever settle down, stop horsing about?" I mean, people would go and get locked in the toilets and fool about. But you were, at the end of the day, getting some nice material out of them.' Ian Grant was reminded by his boss to 'sort this unruly lot out… sit on them a bit more!' 'They approached it as fun,' Ian remembered. 'But Paul was more the co-ordinator for getting things together. You could liken him to the fixer… he was the guy you could talk to if it was getting a bit out of hand.'

Terry Henebery was perceptive enough to realize that an atmosphere of send-ups and japes would enhance the series. However, the music of The Beatles and their guests was not where his heart lay. He produced the radio show *Jazz Club* and, a little later, his BBC TV series *Jazz 625* captured historic performances by many legendary artists, including Duke Ellington, Dizzy Gillespie and Thelonious Monk. The Beatles soon became aware of the producer's musical preference, as George explained in 1988: 'Yeah, Mr Henebery was a jazz fan and he hated The Beatles. At that time, Paul's girlfriend was Jane Asher and when she'd finish whatever her job was, she'd come round and sit in the control room. And then she'd tell us later what he used to say, 'cause he'd be behind the window and forget that she was there. And he'd be saying, "These bloody Beatles… they haven't got a clue! I hate this music," and all that kind of stuff.'

For the second run of eleven programmes, there was a new presenter who also had a name guaranteed to cause Beatle amusement. On one show, his opening statement 'I'm Rodney Burke' was met with John's jibe 'That's your fault!' It was too; the announcer was using a stage name. Like his predecessor, he was a trained actor. Having gained experience in Canada for two years, including parts in the TV series *Hawkeye and the Last of the Mohicans*, he had auditioned for the BBC in July 1957. He was ever cheerful throughout *Pop Go The Beatles*. 'That was a Little Richard number, "Ooh! My

OPPOSITE **A *Pop Go The Beatles* session recorded at BBC Maida Vale with announcer Lee Peters on 17 June 1963. Paul's girlfriend at the time was Jane Asher, who is sitting in the foreground, next to Ringo.

'Mr Henebery was a jazz fan and he hated The Beatles. He'd be saying, "These bloody Beatles... they haven't got a clue!"'

GEORGE HARRISON

Soul" and "Ooh! My arms" – we've just flown into Manchester here from London to record the show' was typical of his humour.

This is now great fun to hear alongside the vibrant music, but in 1963 appreciation of pop shows was often affected by when you were born. The line in the sand was usually drawn according to whether or not you were past your teens when rock 'n' roll first hit the country in 1955. This age division is evident in the comments of the Audience Research report. It was estimated that 5.3% (nearly 3 million) of the listening public aged over fourteen heard the series. Once members of the Listening Panel had given their responses, an Appreciation Index mark out of 100 was calculated. The first show received a rather low rating of 52, below the current average of 61 for Light Entertainment music programmes. But, after all, this was not *Workers' Playtime* from a factory canteen in Wrexham (a lunchtime show heard earlier in the day); *Pop Go The Beatles* was aimed at teenagers. That age group responded with favourable comments such as 'really with it', 'the finest group in the country' and 'on their way to the very top'. Even some 'old' listeners – in their twenties and beyond – were positive, describing 'a really distinctive sound' that was 'full of vitality'. But the report concluded that 'those who were not especially fond of this type of music... disliked this sort of "obnoxious noise", which seemed to them no better than that made by any other pop artists.'

When the *Pop Go The Beatles* series was extended, the BBC limited the group's appearances on other programmes. Three *Side By Side* recordings scheduled for July, August and September 1963 were duly cancelled. But summer bookings still took place for the two weekend shows presented by Brian Matthew – *Easy Beat* and *Saturday Club*. Listening back to the group's visits to these programmes and their own radio series during the summer provides convincing evidence of their escalating popularity. In *Easy Beat* broadcast on 23 June, over the screams of the audience, Brian Matthew pointed out that 'I've been overwhelmed by a shoal of letters all saying, "Will you please ask The Beatles to sing especially for me?" Well, now if I were to read out all the names I'd be here right into the middle of Jean Metcalfe's Bumper Bundle!' He was referring to the name applied to multiple requests for the same song in *Two-Way Family Favourites*. The extremely popular show, broadcast each Sunday lunchtime, linked families to their loved ones serving with British forces overseas.

The Beatles made two appearances on *Saturday Club* in June and August. During the first, the whereabouts of the enigmatic 'Harry and his box' were discussed. This was a regular enquiry heard during their radio broadcasts in 1963. John helpfully replied that 'the truth about Harry and his box is that verypardonoftentheparkywalkthrough! Tell me, you know what I mean?' Obviously.

For their next *Saturday Club* broadcast on 24 August 1963, they were heard performing both sides of their new single 'She Loves You'/'I'll Get You'. Their complete confidence as radio performers is clear on an amusing recording of John reading a request while guitar and piano are played behind him. The writer from Nottingham mentions their enjoyment of *Pop Go The Beatles* and asks for 'You Really Got A Hold On Me' – heard twice in the series by the time of this session on 30 July. An afternoon of recording for *Saturday Club* had been sandwiched between morning and evening studio time at Abbey Road to make tracks for the next album. The Beatles started this productive day in Studio Two at 10.00am and left there at 11.00pm. In all, they taped six songs for the BBC and five for EMI. As if all that were not enough, they were interviewed by bandleader Phil Tate for his regular *Pop Chat* feature in the programme *Non Stop Pop*.

AN AUDIENCE RESEARCH REPORT

(Week 23)   6
                                                      LR/63/997

POP GO THE BEATLES

Tuesday, 4th June, 1963.   5.00-5.30 pm, Light Programme

1. <u>Size of audience</u> (based on results of the Survey of Listening and Viewing
shown in full on the daily Audience Barometer.)

   It is estimated that the audience for this broadcast was 5.3% (including
   5% of the Sound only public).

2. <u>Reaction of audience</u> (based on questionnaires completed by a sample of
the audience. This sample, 114 in number, is the
6% of the B Division of the Listening Panel who
heard all or part of the broadcast.)

   The reactions of this sample of the audience were distributed as follows:-

A+	A	B	C	C-
%	%	%	%	%
10	24	35	24	7

   giving an APPRECIATION INDEX of 52.   Reported Light Entertainment music
   programmes averaged 61 during the first quarter of the year. (42% of
   the sample said they usually liked listening to this kind of music.
   Their reaction, calculated separately, gave an Appreciation Index of 68.
   The proportion of listeners under twenty was too small for their response
   to be assessed.)

3. It was clear that the Beatles were very popular with a good many fans.
   According to a few particularly enthusiastic under-twenties, they were
   'really with it'; 'the finest group in the country'; 'on their way to the
   very top'. Some older listeners were also addicted to their style of
   singing. 'The Beatles are a fascinating group', it was said, 'with a
   really distinctive sound'; their performance was 'full of vitality' and
   had 'the typical Beatles attack'.   The Lorne Gibson Trio was also very
   much liked, and the two groups were said to have combined well in a
   cheerful, lively programme.

4. Other pop fans were unimpressed. The Beatles, some evidently felt, had
   nothing better to offer than many other groups of this kind.   Some did
   not care for them at all, complaining that their singing was noisy,
   harsh and untuneful, and their choice of music lacking in variety.   They
   could not understand their present popularity.

5. Lee Peters made a good compere, fans usually seemed to agree, although in
   some cases he made no very marked impression.   'He kept the programme going
   well; it's quite a good programme for this time of day' was a comment in
   line with the half-hearted response of about one in three, but the rest
   evidently thought the programme most entertaining and well presented.

6. The response of those who were not especially fond of this type of music
   was, as might be expected, decidedly cool.   A small group, it is true,
   thoroughly enjoyed the programme, and others found it 'quite pleasant',
   although not their 'usual choice'.   They liked 'the sound of the Beatles'
   and their 'lively beat' and thought the programme well presented, and no
   doubt 'excellent for teenagers'.   Quite a number, however, disliked this
   sort of 'obnoxious noise', which seemed to them no better than that made
   by any other pop artists.

Copyright of the BBC   Audience Research Department
                                               2nd August, 1963.
EM/BML

PHIL: John, over to you for a minute. You do a lot of songwriting, I believe. Do you always work as a team?

JOHN: Mainly. The better songs that we have written – the ones that anybody wants to hear – both of us have written.

PHIL: And do you write the words and music together or does one of you write the words?

JOHN: Sometimes half the words are written by me and he'll finish them off or we go along a word each, practically!

PHIL: And did you write your new record release?

JOHN: 'She Loves You', you mean? Yeah, we wrote that two days before we recorded it, actually.

PAUL: Actually, we wrote it in a hotel room in Newcastle.

PHIL: Well, this brings me to a question from one of your fans – Vicky Owen of Chadwell Heath – how did this distinctive hairstyle come about?

GEORGE: Well, I don't think any of us have been bothered with having haircuts and it was always long. Paul and John went to Paris [in October 1961] and came back with it something like this and I went to the [swimming] baths and came out with it [just] like this!

PHIL: Are you keeping your homes in Liverpool or do you plan on moving to London or anything like that?

RINGO: I don't think any of us are moving… we must have a base in London, because we're there more than we are in Liverpool at the moment. But we're not moving our houses.

DURING THE LAST quarter of 1963, they were all living in London. Paul was staying with the family of his girlfriend Jane Asher in Wimpole Street; the others took flats in nearby Mayfair. While there, they were able to socialize a little with some media folk, including *Saturday Club* producer Bernie Andrews. He shared a flat in Shepherd Street with Terry Doran – a close friend of George and a business associate of Brian Epstein. There was another occupant – a vociferous mynah bird. Bernie recalled: 'Paul only came round to the flat once, actually, and just inside the front door of the flat there was this mynah bird in a cage. He came in and the mynah bird said, "Hello, Ringo!" which I was very embarrassed about as it was the first time Paul had been round. I apologized and said he normally didn't do things like that.'

The BBC producer's hospitality often extended to providing a favourite meal. 'The main thing that George used to come round for was egg and chips. He loved egg and chips. When they were at the height of their popularity, he couldn't just go round to some restaurant in Mayfair and order egg and chips. And he couldn't

go to a place where you could order egg and chips, because he'd get mobbed like mad. He didn't want to know about cooking it himself, so he used to come round to Bern's for egg and chips!' In 1976, The Beatles' former press officer Derek Taylor came across his notes for Brian Epstein's autobiography *A Cellarful of Noise*, for which he was the ghostwriter. The Beatles' manager had told Derek that Bernie was 'someone who I and the boys have a great deal of affection for, because he is probably one of the best producers in the Corporation.'

Bernie produced a session with The Beatles for inclusion in the fifth-birthday edition of *Saturday Club* broadcast on 5 October 1963. The celebratory show featured what *Radio Times* described as 'the most spectacular bill of stars ever invited to the *Club*'. It was quite a line-up. In addition to The Beatles, there were sessions from The Everly Brothers, Frank Ifield, Kenny Ball's Jazzmen, Joe Brown and The Bruvvers, Tommy Roe, Clinton Ford and Kathy Kirby. Taped messages of congratulation were heard from Roy Orbison, Del Shannon, Rick Nelson and Brenda Lee, and Cliff Richard phoned in from Tel Aviv. With an arrangement reminiscent of the current Heinz hit 'Just Like Eddie', The Beatles played 'Happy Birthday Dear Saturday Club'. Their other tracks included Chuck Berry's 'Memphis, Tennessee' and Little Richard's 'Lucille'.

OPPOSITE Paul, George… and Bernie – during a *Saturday Club* session, 17 December 1963. The Beatles used to visit the flat Bernie Andrews shared with Terry Doran in Mayfair. 'Sounds posh, but it was only eleven quid a week for four bedrooms,' the producer remembered.

'Everything was done instantly. We probably had a quick set-up of the amplifiers and the drums, plugged in, ran through the songs once while the engineer got a rough balance and then we did them.'

GEORGE HARRISON

Recorded on 7 September, the *Saturday Club* session was the thirty-fifth occasion they had performed songs for BBC radio during a span of 32 weeks in 1963. Given the BBC's monopoly of daytime broadcasts and how little airtime was allocated to commercial discs, The Beatles had realized these shows had to be crammed into their schedule. George remembered the circumstances of the BBC sessions: 'Everything was done instantly. We probably had a quick set-up of the amplifiers and the drums, plugged in, ran through the songs once while the engineer got a rough balance and then we did them. But before that, we used to drive 200 miles in an old van down the M1; come into London, try and find the BBC and then set up and do the programme. Then we'd probably drive back to Newcastle for a gig in the evening! That's how they all were, until a bit later when we started to stay in hotels in London. I think we'd got slightly famous by that time. But they were all done very quick – one take – and, as they say, warts and all.'

For many years, radio broadcasting had been viewed by the BBC as more important than a television service. The Corporation had opened the world's first TV channel in 1936, but it was soon closed down at the start of the Second World War. Television broadcasts resumed seven years later in June 1946, but only for a small number of hours a day and with a limited coverage of the country. However, fuelled by the entertainment programmes on a commercial channel started in 1955, the popularity of TV in the UK grew at a prodigious rate during the 1950s. Large audiences attracted advertisers and independent television knew how to lure viewers away from the BBC. It had few concerns about accusations that it was lowering cultural standards. Everyone in the UK is obliged to pay a licence to receive broadcasts. At a time when a TV set was not a fixture in every household, it was possible to choose either a radio-only licence or a more expensive one allowing the holder to receive both radio and TV. The shift in the balance of power between radio and TV occurred in the late 1950s. In 1957, radio licences outnumbered combined licences. Just three years later, the number of combined licences had grown to double that of those issued to permit only radio broadcasts.

OPPOSITE **At the BBC Paris Theatre, London with Liverpudlian comedian Ken Dodd for a recording of his radio show on 9 October 1963 – John's 23rd birthday.**

The appointment, in 1960, of dynamic Director General Hugh Carleton Greene re-energized the BBC and, in particular, its television service. Nevertheless, at the start of the 1960s, pop music was not featured as much as on its commercial rival. In 1963, only nine of The Beatles' 36 TV appearances were on the BBC. However, by the summer, it was hard to ignore the success of The Beatles and other Merseyside artists such as Gerry and The Pacemakers and Billy J. Kramer. On 12 July, the BBC's 'Representative, North West Of England', Reginald Jordan, sent a memo to Thurston Holland ('Assistant Head of North Region Programmes') drawing attention to this pop phenomenon. 'I wonder if we are sufficiently cashing in on this? I mention this because I hear that when the Liverpool groups were recently gathered together in the ITV LUCKY STARS programme [*Thank Your Lucky Stars*], it topped the figures for the whole of that series, and was one of the most popular programmes of the week on the commercial channel.' He received the reply that 'London are aware of the popularity of these people, but I doubt that this will mean that we shall get extra programmes to exploit them. We are doing our best however.'

In fact, the BBC North Region had already commissioned a documentary on the subject. Manchester-based producer Don Haworth met The Beatles on 21 July 1963 to discuss their involvement in a programme that was eventually called *The Mersey Sound*. In a letter to Brian Epstein, he wrote that he was 'much impressed by the Beatles. I think quite apart from their excellent performance, they have the personality and good humour to get the story across to an audience much wider than the one that would watch primarily for the music.'

He secured The Beatles' commitment to perform music for his programme and to be interviewed. In a shrewd move, given the deafening screams heard in theatres wherever The Beatles now played, Don Haworth's team filmed the group without an audience on 27 August 1963. The footage of 'Twist And Shout', 'She Loves You' and 'Love Me Do' was subsequently edited together with shots of rampant fans at a Beatles concert in Southport on 30 August. While not an entirely ethical approach for a documentary, this method did allow for a clear recording of the music without the inevitable technical problems caused by an extremely noisy audience.

In addition to the concert material, The Beatles are seen in various Liverpool locations. For one scene, Ringo was filmed leaving his home and then struggling through a mass of boisterous fans to reach George waiting at the wheel of an open-top car. They speed away with girls clinging precariously to the back. As the car drives through the streets of Liverpool, the camera shows numerous bomb-damaged buildings – stark evidence of the severe battering the port endured during the Second World War. To illustrate Ringo's statement that he hoped to own a chain of hairdressing salons, he was filmed at one in Liverpool, surveying the ladies under their dryers. *The Mersey Sound* also included interviews with members of Liverpool groups The Undertakers and Group One. Interestingly, *Mersey Beat* editor Bill Harry claims in the programme that The Beatles and other groups were influenced by his advice to cut their hair and to stop smoking and swearing onstage. Most importantly, The Beatles were seen for the first time talking seriously about their fame and future prospects.

JOHN: The best thing was ['Love Me Do'] came to the charts in two days. And everybody thought it was a fiddle because our manager's stores send in these… what is it? … record things.

GEORGE: Returns.

JOHN: Returns. And everybody down south thought, 'Ah, aha! He's buying them himself or he's just fiddling the charts', you know. But he wasn't.

GEORGE: Actually, we'd been at it a long time before that. We'd been to Hamburg. I think that's where we found our style… we developed our style because of this fella there. He used to say, 'You've got to make a show for the people.' And he used to come up every night, shouting, 'Mach schau!' So we used to 'mach schau' and John used to dance around like a gorilla, and we'd all, you know, knock our heads together and things like that. Anyway, we got back to Liverpool and all the groups there were doing this sort of Shadows type of stuff. And we came back with leather jackets and jeans and funny hair, 'maching schau', which went down quite well.

JOHN: We just bought leather jackets. Not for the group. One person bought one. I can't remember… and then we all liked them so it ended up we were all on stage with them. And we'd always worn jeans, 'cause we didn't have anything else at the time, you know. And then we went back to Liverpool and got quite a few bookings. They all thought we were German. You know, we were billed as 'From Hamburg' and they all said, 'You speak good English.' So we went back to Germany and we had a bit more money the second time, so we wore leather pants and we looked like four Gene Vincents, only a bit younger, I think. And that was it, you know. We just kept the leather gear till Brian came along.

PAUL: It was a bit, sort of, old hat anyway – all wearing leather gear – and we decided we didn't want to look ridiculous just going on, because, more often than not, too many people would laugh. It was just stupid. We didn't want to appear as a gang of idiots. And Brian suggested that we just, sort of, wore ordinary suits. So we just got what we thought were quite good suits, and just got rid of the leather gear. That was all.

GEORGE: And you had yours pinched anyway.

PAUL: Oh yeah, I had my pants pinched.

JOHN: They didn't laugh at the leather in Liverpool.

BY 1963, there had been no precedent for artists prolonging their careers by continuing to play pop music. Britain's first rock 'n' roll stars, Tommy Steele and Cliff Richard, had both taken the all-round family entertainer route into theatre and films. BBC TV producer Jim Casey made the point in *The Mersey Sound* that, compared to a solo act, it would be more difficult for a group to sustain success in that way. After commenting on how their fanatical following had affected their lives, not for the last time, The Beatles discussed what they would do when all the excitement fizzled out.

GEORGE: We do like the fans and enjoy reading the publicity about us, but from time to time you don't realize that it's actually about

ABOVE **Frames from the television programme** *The Mersey Sound.* This scene was filmed on 28 August 1963 at a BBC studio in Dickenson Road, Manchester. PAGES 52 AND 53 **Scenes from** *The Mersey Sound* filmed between 27 and 29 August 1963.

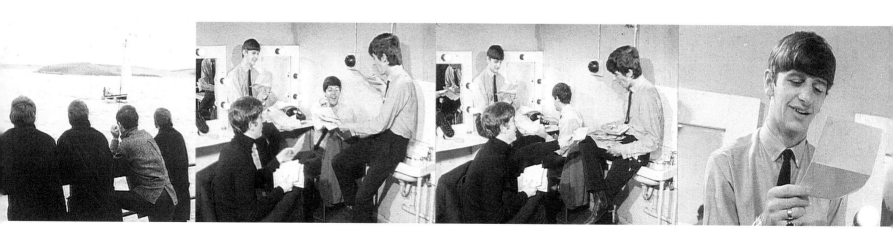

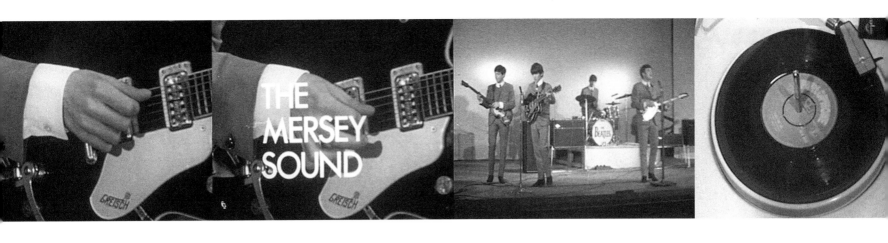

THE MERSEY SOUND

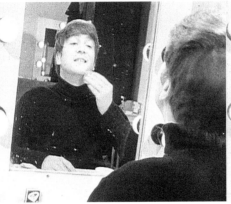

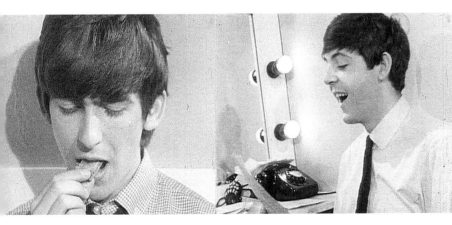

yourself. You see your pictures and read articles about George Harrison, Ringo Starr, Paul, John… but you don't actually think, 'Oh, that's me. There I am in the paper.' It's funny. It's just as though it's a different person.

RINGO: When we go home, we go in early in the morning when we've finished the job and the kids don't know you're at home. But if they find out… where I live, they get the drums out and beat it out! [laughs] 'Cause it's a 'play street' and, you know, there's no traffic or nothing bothering them. Once when the boys came for me… they popped in to see me mum and me dad, you know… we had to go out the back 'cause there's twenty or thirty outside. And they wouldn't believe me mother, you know, knocking and saying, 'Can we have their autographs?' So it built up, you know, so much. There was about two hundred kids all around the door and they were peeping through the window and knocking. [laughs] In the end, me mother was ill, you know. She was terrified out of her life – just all these kids and boys and girls and that, you know.

JOHN: It all sounds complaining, but we're not. We're just putting the point that it affects your home more than it does yourself, because you know what to expect, but your parents and family – they don't know what's happening.

GEORGE: They send us a lot of Jelly Babies and chocolates and things like that… just because somebody wrote in one of the papers about presents and things that we'd had given to us. And John said he'd got some Jelly Babies and I ate them. But ever since that we've been inundated. We had about two ton a night! But the main trouble is they tend to throw them at us when we're onstage. [laughs] And, er, once I got one in my eye which wasn't very nice. [putting his finger to an eye] In fact I haven't been the same since!

JOHN: 'How long are you gonna last?' Well, you can't say, you know. You can be big-headed and say, 'Yeah, we're gonna last ten years.' But as soon as you've said that, you think, 'We're lucky if we last three months', you know.

PAUL: Well, obviously we can't keep playing the same sort of music until we're about forty… sort of old men playing 'From Me To You'. Nobody is going to want to know at all about that sort of thing. You know, we've thought about it and probably the thing that John and I will do, er, will be write songs… as we have been doing as a sort of sideline now. We'll probably develop that a bit more, we hope. Who knows? At forty, we may not know how to write songs any more.

GEORGE: I hope to have enough money to go into a business of my own by the time we, um, do flop. [laughs] I mean, we don't know. It may be next week, it may be two or three years. But I think we'll be in the business, either up there or down there, for at least another four years.

RINGO: I've always fancied having a ladies hairdressing salon. [laughter] You know, a string of them, in fact. Strut round in me stripes and tails. You know: 'Like a cup of tea, Madam?'

ON 9 OCTOBER 1963, *The Mersey Sound* was broadcast in the north west and the London area. Despite producer Don Haworth's argument in a memo that it was 'reasonable to think that the phenomenon may be of interest for one reason or another to practically every section of our audience', other BBC regional services transmitted different programmes. The first national broadcast of the film was on 13 November, when it was watched by 20.6 per cent of the UK (around ten million viewers). Its critical reception was very positive. A written comment made by broadcaster Kenneth Allsop to Don Haworth captured the critical consensus. 'What a superb piece of work it is – beautifully done, dead accurate and, it seems to me, a classic bit of sociology.'

The Beatles had taken a well-deserved two-week holiday at the end of September. Upon their return the next month, they experienced the country completely in the grip of 'Beatlemania'. Undoubtedly, the exposure on the Light Programme's pop shows had helped the nation fall in love with The Beatles' music and personalities. But the BBC would now find it much harder to tempt them into their studios – and, soon, never for an audience show. *Easy Beat* was recorded in front of a mainly female audience on a Wednesday evening at the BBC Playhouse Theatre. Produced by Ron Belchier, it was recorded by his regular studio managers in 1963 – balancer Bev Phillips and his assistant John Andrews. Wednesday was a very busy day for the SMs, as John recalled: 'We did *Parade of the Pops* live at lunchtime with an audience, 12.30–1.30, and then we'd clear down the stage completely and set up again for *Easy Beat*. There was a rehearsal throughout the afternoon then the audience came in about seven and we did another complete one-hour show "as live".'

One of John Andrews' jobs was to indicate from the auditorium to his colleague in the sound booth whether to turn the PA system up or down once the recording had started. The system of hand signals usually worked fine, but not when The Beatles were recorded on 16 October 1963. 'The noise was totally unbelievable… even now I can remember thinking, "God, this hurts!" As soon as the lads came on, it was just solid screams – you could hear a little guitar. Bev was looking anxiously at me and I just turned around, shrugged my shoulders and put my hands in the air! There was just nothing you could do with our 75 watts of PA.' In this small theatre, the stage was about six feet from the front row of the very

OPPOSITE AND ABOVE **Performing at the BBC Playhouse Theatre for *Easy Beat* on 16 October 1963 – the day after news of the group's participation in the Royal Variety Performance was announced.**

excited audience. The authority of Brian Matthew and a few burly BBC commissionaires kept the situation under control, but Brian Epstein had already become anxious about The Beatles' safety in such situations. For example, an *Easy Beat* recording scheduled for 4 December was contracted on 10 September, then cancelled three days later. After October, there would be no more audience shows with The Beatles in BBC radio theatres.

During their last *Easy Beat*, Brian Matthew reminded listeners that it was 'now almost a year since The Beatles first hit the show business jackpot'. The recent announcement of their inclusion in the *Royal Variety Performance*, playing for the Queen Mother and Princess Margaret, now gave their success a regal seal of approval. The media were all fascinated by this news. At their rehearsal for *Easy Beat*, Peter Woods (later a TV newsreader) did two interviews with The Beatles for radio and television.

PETER WOODS: Well, lads almost unknown in January and now going into the *Royal Command Performance* in November. This is quite a rise – even for your business – isn't it, Paul?

PAUL: Yes, it's been very quick and we have been very lucky.

WOODS: How much of this is due, do you think, to pure musical talent?

PAUL: Er, dunno. No idea. You just can't tell, y'know. Maybe a lot of it, maybe none of it.

WOODS: How much would you say?

JOHN: I agree with Paul… it varies…

WOODS: How much of this is getting popularity by acting the fool a bit and playing around?

JOHN: Well, I mean, that's just natural. We don't do it for effect… we do it anyway, whether we're on stage or…

WOODS: But your funny haircuts aren't natural.

JOHN: Well, we don't think they're funny, you see, cobber!

WOODS: As far as playing your type of music is concerned, is this a new thing, do you think, Ringo?

RINGO: No, not really.

WOODS: The word in the music world is that 'We've heard this type of thing before.'

RINGO: We just play how we can and the sound we make is just us and it seems to be selling at the moment so…

JOHN: It's rock! Rock 'n' roll.

RINGO: It is rock, yeah, as John said, butting in.

WOODS: George, can I turn to you now? How long do you think you're going to be successful? You've had this monumental rise, obviously this sort of thing can't go on, but do you think you can settle down to a life in show business?

GEORGE: Well, we're hoping to. Not necessarily a life in show business, but at least a couple more years… I mean if we do as well as Cliff and The Shadows have done up till now… well, we won't be moaning… I mean, naturally, it can't go on as it has been going the last few months – it'd just be ridiculous.

WOODS: How do you find all this business of having screaming girls following you all over the place?

GEORGE: Well, we feel flattered.

JOHN, PAUL & RINGO: Flattened!

GEORGE: Yeah, and flattened. But if the screaming fans weren't there, then we wouldn't be here would we?

JOHN, PAUL & RINGO: [with exaggerated northern accents] Aye, by gum, that's right!

WOODS: Paul, coming quickly back to you again… Mr Edward Heath, the Lord Privy Seal, has said that the other night he found it difficult to distinguish what you were saying as Queen's English. Now, are you going to try to lose some of your Liverpool dialect for the royal show?

PAUL: No, you're kidding.

GEORGE: We just won't vote for him!

PAUL: No, we wouldn't bother doing that. [adopting strong northern accent] We don't all speak like them BBC posh fellas, y'know.

JOHN AND PAUL: [Northern accents] Nay, we don't. By gum, no, we don't. Right up north.

WOODS: [Assuming a northern accent] Aye, well with that I'd better wish you good luck in the show… what song will you be singing most there, do you think?

PAUL: [In a perfect upper-class drawl] Well, I don't know, but I should imagine we'll do 'She Loves You'.

JOHN, GEORGE AND RINGO: [in similar voices to Paul's] Haw, haw, haw! Jolly good, jolly good!

OPPOSITE AND RIGHT Peter Woods conducted interviews for both radio and TV concerning The Beatles' 'monumental rise' at the BBC Playhouse Theatre on 16 October 1963. 'Obviously this sort of thing can't go on, but do you think you can settle down to a life in show business?' asked the news reporter.

THE IRONY OF this final exchange was that very soon middle-class youngsters would be endeavouring to give their voices a regional twist. For example, DJ John Peel invented a new voice for himself that became gruffer and more northern as his career progressed. Soon the BBC, in general, began to reflect on air the variety of accents heard around the country.

Adding to the attention paid to Liverpool by BBC TV's *The Mersey Sound* and ITV's *Beat City*, the BBC Light Programme ran a feature on the city's importance during The Beatles' formative years. The profile was broadcast in an edition of the fortnightly entertainment magazine programme *The Public Ear* on 3 November – the eve of the *Royal Variety Performance*. There were interviews with Bill Harry, Stuart Sutcliffe's mother, Beat poet Royston Ellis, some anonymous Cavern fans and former drummer Pete Best – 'I was called into the office by Brian Epstein and for no rhyme or reason I was told that I was gonna be replaced.' The enthusiasm of narrator Tony Hall could not have been further from the cynicism of Peter Woods: 'For everyone under twenty, The Beatles still represent everything worth shouting about… and if you're older and you can't understand the teenagers, then you should *study* this music'. George set the record straight about their financial situation: 'People say we make £7,000 a week … I mean, we probably do make quite a bit, but we don't actually see it because record royalties, things like that, take months before they come in. But we've also got an accountant and a company called Beatles Limited … they see the money! … Don't forget we played for about three or four years, or maybe longer, just earning hardly anything. If we were doing it for the money, we wouldn't have lasted out all those years. We like it sufficiently to do it not for the money too… but the money does help, let's face it.' In a discussion about their abilities as musicians, Paul singled out George as being most dedicated to his instrument – 'the other three of us are more interested in the sound of the group.' George concluded that 'individually, I suppose we're all crummy musicians really!'

In a remarkable night for BBC television, The Beatles dominated the Saturday evening schedule of 7 December 1963. First, The Beatles were seen by 23 million viewers in *Juke Box Jury*. The show had been an integral part of Saturday night viewing since 1959. Based on an American format, four 'jurors' reviewed a record and then ruled whether it would be a hit or a miss. Presenter David Jacobs rang a bell if the panel's verdict was 'Hit'. A 'Miss' was rejected by the sound of a klaxon. John had appeared on an edition in June 1963, alongside frequent panellist Katie Boyle and the obligatory teenagers: actors Bruce Prochnik (playing the title role in the current West End production of *Oliver!*) and Caroline Maudling. John voted every one of the records played a 'Miss' – even 'Devil In Disguise' by his first rock 'n' roll hero Elvis Presley. 'Well, I used to go mad on Elvis, like all the groups, but not now. I don't like this and I hate songs with "walk" and "talk" in it… you know, those lyrics: "She walks, she talks". And I don't like the double beat – dum-cha, dum-cha – that bit. It's awful. Poor old Elvis. I've got all his early records and I keep playing them. He mustn't make another like this. But somebody said today he sounds like Bing Crosby now… and he does.' Katie Boyle asked John whether sounding like Bing Crosby was necessarily a bad thing. 'Well, for Elvis… yes', John replied. Within a month of the broadcast, 'Devil In Disguise' was number one in the UK.

HIT

HIT

RINGO
STARR

GEORGE
HARRISON

Juke Box Jury was usually filmed in London, but the special Beatles edition was recorded in front of members of the group's Northern Area Fan Club in the Empire Theatre, Liverpool. Once again, an Elvis record was selected on the jukebox – 'Kiss Me Quick'.

PAUL: The only thing I don't like about Elvis now is the songs. You know, I love his voice. I used to love all the records like 'Blue Suede Shoes' and 'Heartbreak Hotel'… lovely. But I don't like the songs now. And 'Kiss Me Quick'? It sounds like Blackpool on a sunny day.

[laughter and applause]

RINGO: I didn't like it at all, no.

GEORGE: I must admit I didn't like it very much. Not at all. It's an old track. And I think, seeing as they're releasing old stuff, if they'd release something like 'My Baby Left Me' it'd be number one, because Elvis is definitely still popular. It's just the song's a load of rubbish. I mean, Elvis is great. He's fine. But it's not for me.

JOHN: Well, I think it'll be a hit because it's Elvis, like people said. But I don't think it'll be very great. I like those hats, though, with 'Kiss Me Quick' on it!

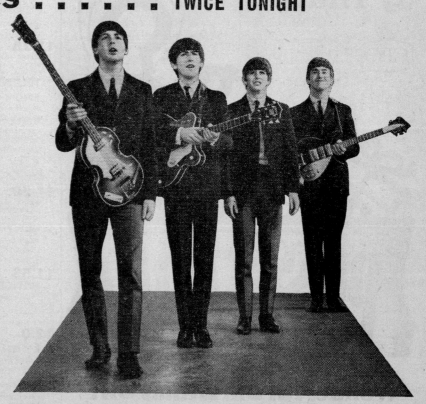

RADIO TIMES *December 5, 1963*   7

Your Weekend Saturday

The Beatles . . . . . . TWICE TONIGHT

6.5 8.10 PARENTS with teenagers in the family are advised to sit well back from the TV set: they may get trampled in the rush. And teenagers with parents in the family have a golden opportunity to show them what Beatlemania is all about—even, perhaps, to convert them. For this evening the Beatles have sixty minutes of BBC-tv time to themselves.

First, at five past six, they take over as the jury of *Juke Box Jury.* Rhythm guitarist and spokesman Beatle, **John Lennon,** was a jury member some months ago, when the first thin screams of Beatle fans were beginning to be heard in the land; now he returns with **Paul, George,** and **Ringo** under the chairmanship of **David Jacobs.**

Secondly, at ten past eight: *It's the Beatles,* in which the group will be playing many of their own favourite numbers and some new ones, and showing their individual talents as well. Among the numbers: the current Beatle hit, *I Want to Hold Your Hand.*

Both programmes will be staged at the Empire Theatre in Liverpool—*It's the Beatles* being recorded in the afternoon—before a capacity house of some 2,500 gathered for the Northern Area Convention of the Beatles National Fan Club. Mobile television cameras will roam the theatre, because as producer **Neville Wortman** says: 'The group's contact with their audience is remarkable to see. The programmes will be virtually a study in Beatlemania.'

Note for Beatle fans: *The Beatles will top the bill in a two-hour radio show on Boxing Day in the Light Programme. Also, there are still some copies of the Radio Times Portrait Gallery photograph of The Beatles available—price 2s., post free, from: BBC Publications (B.T.), Box 123, Queen's House, Kingsway, London, W.C.2.*

Radio Times (Incorporating World-Radio) December 5, 1963. Vol. 161: No. 2091.

DECEMBER 7—13

Radio Times

BBC tv Sound

SIXPENCE

HIT HIT HIT HIT

The Beatles on Saturday

BBC TV

IN JUKE BOX JURY & THEIR OWN SHOW

OPPOSITE AND RIGHT The BBC's radio and TV listings magazine *Radio Times* celebrates the double helping of The Beatles on Saturday 7 December 1963. Producer Neville Wortman told *Radio Times* that 'the programmes will be virtually a study in Beatlemania'. In reality, he was not proved wrong.

British Broadcasting Corporation   Confidential

AN AUDIENCE RESEARCH REPORT

(Week 50)   VR/63/697
                                                              IE

JUKE BOX JURY

Presented by Neville Wortman

Saturday, 7th December, 1963.   6.05-6.35pm, Television Service.

1. <u>Size of audience</u> (based on results of the Survey of Listening and Viewing.)

   It is estimated that the audience was 43%.   Thank Your Lucky Stars,
   on ITV at the time, was seen by 10%.

2. <u>Reaction of audience</u> (based on questionnaires completed by a sample of
                             the audience.   This sample, 426 in number, is the
                             37% of the Viewing Panel who saw the broadcast.)

   The reactions of this sample of the audience were distributed as follows:-

A+	A	B	C	C-
%	%	%	%	%
25	30	24	14	7

   This gives a REACTION INDEX of 63, above the average (56) for the series.

3. The overall reaction to this edition of Juke Box Jury, which had
   The Beatles as members of its panel was considerably more favourable
   than usual, mainly owing to the enthusiasm of the younger faction among
   the sample audience.   Indeed perhaps the most striking feature of the
   response to this particular edition was the wide disparity of opinion
   between the under- and over-thirties.   Considered as a group, the over-
   thirties, at the outset less interested in 'pop' music for itself, were
   all the same obviously curious to make the acquaintance of a group whose
   reputation had reached even their ears, but it seems that in the event
   they thought The Beatles added precisely nothing to the programme as such.
   Many of these viewers remarked that, with the possible exception of
   John Lennon, all four seemed incredibly inarticulate and quite incapable
   of offering reasoned comment on the records played (in themselves an
   indifferent selection) let alone constructive criticism, while in addition
   none was considered to be over-endowed with personality.   There was also
   much adverse comment on the screaming audience, many complaining that it
   had been impossible at times to hear what was being said owing to the
   'ear-splitting racket'.   Altogether, in the opinion of this group, this
   edition of Juke Box Jury, although certainly interesting in that it had
   been intriguing to meet the famous Beatles 'in the flesh', as it were,
   was in itself no more than reasonably enjoyable, and moderately entertaining.
   The Reaction Index based on the markings of this (the over-thirties) group
   (just over half the sample) was 51.

continued/

JUKE BOX JURY   (Week 50) (continued)

4. On the other hand, the under-thirties were generally enthusiastic to
   a degree.   Certainly one or two admitted that, not being Beatle fans
   and having no particular liking for 'pop' music, they had found little
   to interest them in this programme, while in addition it seems that
   some found The Beatles' 'performance' sadly disillusioning - 'They are
   "fab" on records but no good at this sort of thing.   They didn't seem
   to have any minds of their own.   I did enjoy the show but I really was
   disappointed too' (Student).   As far as most were concerned, however,
   the entire programme was 'fab - just real fab'.   All four members of
   The Beatles group had been 'just great' and who better to judge this
   type of music, many asked, than the acknowledged 'kings' of the 'pop'
   music market?   Thanks to The Beatles this edition of Juke Box Jury
   had been 'really super' and they very much hoped they would again be
   invited to act as jury in the not-too-distant future.   The Reaction
   Index based on the markings of this group was 78.

   Copyright   Audience Research Department
   of the BBC   17th January, 1964.

   EIM/DR

ABOVE The BBC Audience Research report on the special Beatles edition of the Saturday
evening favourite *Juke Box Jury* broadcast on 7 December 1963. PAGES 64 AND 65 Stills
from the surviving footage shot during *It's The Beatles* at the Empire Theatre, Liverpool.

IN A REVIEW of The Swinging Blue Jeans' version of 'The Hippy Shake', they pointed out the original was by Chan Romero and that they performed it too. Their unanimous judgement that it would be a hit proved to be true. The record that seemed to interest them most was 'The Nitty Gritty' by Shirley Ellis.

JOHN: Er, yeah. I like it. I thought it was somebody else. I've never heard of Shirley Ellis. I like all those kind of things. I'll buy it. But I believe it won't be a hit.

DAVID JACOBS: Who did you think it was?

JOHN: At first I thought it was Mary Wells. I liked that.

PAUL: The same as he said. In fact, I will say exactly the same, 'cause I agree with him. I love these kind of records, but I don't think this one will be a hit, 'cause I dunno… It doesn't say anything.

RINGO: You know, we all like this sort of thing. I'd buy it, but I don't think it'll be a hit.

GEORGE: Well, it definitely won't be a hit, in England anyway. It probably will be, or probably is already in the States. But I don't think it'll be a hit. The public haven't got round to that sort of stuff yet. When they do, I mean, that would be…

JACOBS: So, you think that our teenagers are behind the Americans in their tastes?

GEORGE: Yeah. I mean, just lately they've been going for some more way-out stuff, and rhythm and blues, and this sort of thing we've always liked. We've liked it for years. And it still hasn't caught on in England.

PAUL: Well, it's just that people who buy the records, their taste doesn't match the teenagers generally. Lots of teenagers love this kind of music but don't buy it, because they don't buy records.

A BBC AUDIENCE Research report confirmed again that appreciation of a programme featuring The Beatles depended on the age of the viewer. The 'over-thirties' were 'obviously curious to make the acquaintance of a group whose reputation had reached even their ears, but it seems that in the event they thought The Beatles added precisely nothing to the programme as such… all four seemed incredibly inarticulate… and none was considered to be over-endowed with personality.' Even some of the 'under-thirties' were disappointed – 'They are "fab" on records but no good at this sort of thing.' However, most of the younger viewers were delighted – 'just real fab', 'who better to judge this type of music, many asked, than the acknowledged "kings" of the "pop" market?' There were also comments about the 'screaming audience'. The 'ear-splitting racket' had made it impossible to hear what was said. There was more of that to come later in the evening when The Beatles were featured in a show of their own.

Following the recording of *Juke Box Jury*, the group had performed a concert at the Empire that was transmitted at 8.10pm with the title *It's The Beatles*. It was watched by 41 per cent of the population of the UK, but received much criticism – even from younger viewers. The Audience Research report and several letters in the BBC's files express the most frequent complaints. One correspondent wrote about the small number of close-ups of John, even when he was singing – 'your cameramen seem to be suffering under the misapprehension that there are but three members of "The Beatles" (an R & B group from Liverpool).' It was also felt that the cameras spent too much time showing the audience: 'we wanted to watch the Beatles, not the stupid nits in the audience' and 'we might add that when ITV shows the Beatles, it keeps its cameras on them.' One disgruntled viewer concluded, 'you say you want five pounds per licence next year – believe me, keep this up and it won't be worth five shillings.'

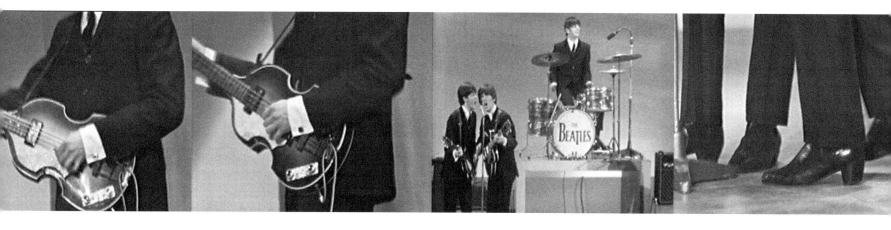

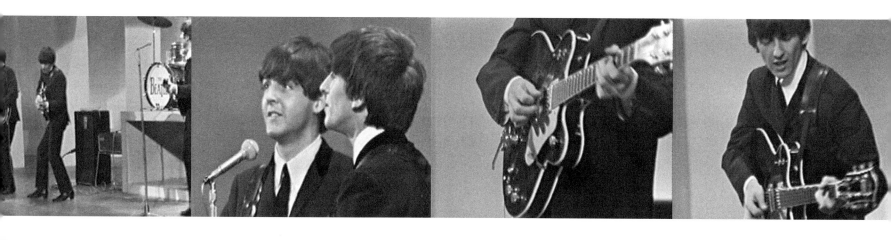

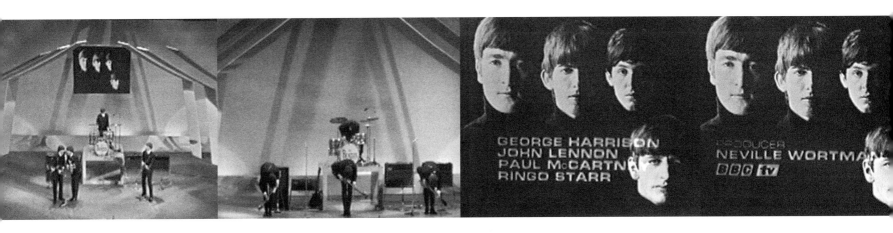

GEORGE HARRISON
JOHN LENNON
PAUL McCARTNEY
RINGO STARR

PRODUCER
NEVILLE WORTMAN
BBC tv

FOR DELIVERY VIA INTERNAL MAIL

CONFIRMATION OF MESSAGE DICTATED TO
PHONOGRAMS, BROADCASTING HOUSE, LONDON

DELIVER TO:

DONALD MACLEAN, ROOM 225 AEOLIAN, EXT 100

PRECEDENCE   ORD=

| DATE 4.12.63 |
| SERVICE SOUND CHARGEABLE |
| STAFF NO. (PERSONAL TELEGRAMS) |

TO	COPY TO
BRIAN EPSTEIN GROSVENOR HOUSE PARK LANE W1=	

PLEASE PHONE ME AS SOON AS YOU HAVE 45 SECONDS BEST WISHES= DONALD

                                        MACLEAN BBC
                                        MAYFAIR 3411+

TIME RECEIVED   1638   NO. A39 / TDG   INITIALS OF OPERATOR

A/502

ABOVE At the beginning of December 1963, BBC executive Donald MacLean sent two telegrams to The Beatles' manager – this is the second with its desperate plea. Swamped with requests, Brian Epstein's NEMS offices could not respond swiftly enough to the BBC's enquiries. Nerves soon started to fray within the Corporation.

Barney Colehan, who directed *It's The Beatles*, explained the reasons for the technical problems in a memo to Tom Sloan – the Head Of Light Entertainment, Television. 'The most important point was the totally inadequate rehearsal time available.' He was only allowed fifteen minutes for *Juke Box Jury* and twenty minutes for *It's The Beatles*. 'The camera crew could not hear my instructions due to the ear-splitting noise and the prearranged shots were useless. I had to resort to bellowing down my microphone in order to convey any instructions whatsoever.' His boss reassured him: 'I do not believe any of us had any idea of the disorganized frenzy that could take place during such a performance. I still think that in its way this was an instant documentary showing a slice of life which, whether we like it or not, exists.' Some footage of the concert has survived and reveals that the sound is much better than the protests indicated. Whatever the problems, *It's The Beatles* was certainly an example of what one of the members of the BBC's Viewing Panel summarized as 'At last, the BBC… letting themselves go. This was absolutely wonderful.'

Even after starring in *Juke Box Jury* and a televised concert, The Beatles had more work to do on 7 December. They performed in front of two 'houses' at the Odeon Cinema in Liverpool. *The Beatles' Autumn Tour* had started in Cheltenham on 1 November and continued until the final date of 13 December in Southampton. As the BBC had experienced, The Beatles' audiences screamed incessantly throughout the concerts. The fans were also an exuberant presence wherever The Beatles happened to go. The claustrophobic life soon to be portrayed in *A Hard Day's Night* was a reality. Indeed, the film's screenwriter Alun Owen observed the siege conditions of this tour for three days. Michael Braun, the writer of the excellent *Love Me Do! The Beatles' Progress*, was also in the entourage for the last two weeks of concerts. A BBC radio interview recorded on 10 December in the dressing room of the Gaumont Cinema, Doncaster gives a powerful depiction of life with The Beatles at this crazy time. Australian Dibbs Mather talked to each of them in turn for a feature distributed by the BBC's Transcription Service. The interviews were not heard in the UK at the time. Throughout the recording, the sound of girls screaming and chanting 'We want Paul! We want Paul!' is heard in the background. John munches an apple very loudly. Once more, some questions were based on an assumption that The Beatles' incandescent popularity would soon fade.

'I do not believe any of us had any idea of the disorganized frenzy that could take place during such a performance.'

TOM SLOAN (HEAD OF LIGHT ENTERTAINMENT, TELEVISION)

DIBBS: George Harrison… you're one of the reputed deep thinkers in this group, how do you see it as a peak in your life? What happens to you after this is over?

GEORGE: Well, I suppose we'll stay doing this sort of stuff for a couple of years. Naturally, we won't be able to stay at this level, but we should have another two years at least, I think.

DIBBS: And what happens to George Harrison then?

GEORGE: I dunno. I'll know by the time that comes along. Probably have a little business or something like that.

DIBBS: You don't want to go on in the profession?

GEORGE: Probably, yeah. I'd like to make records with other artists. I don't mean perform, I mean as a producer.

WHEN DIBBS MATHER talked to Ringo, he received an honest account of his younger years in Liverpool.

DIBBS: Ringo Starr, it's been suggested that boys coming from the particular area that you came from, if you hadn't found an interest in music, might have found it much more difficult to get out and make a go of life. Would you comment on this?

RINGO: I think it's true. I mean, when I was sixteen and that, I used to walk on the road with the rest of the lads and we'd have all our drape coats on. We never got to the stage of beating up old women though. Just we'd have a few 'narks' and that with other rival gangs, sort of thing. And then I got the drums and the bloke next door played a guitar and I got a job…

PAUL: [Shouts] Teddy Boy!

RINGO: [Laughs]… and we started playing together and another bloke in work made a bass out of an old tea-chest… y'know, them days – this was about '58, mind you – and we played together and then we started playing on dances and things and we took an interest in it and we stopped going out, hanging round street corners every night.

THE USUAL QUESTION of what Ringo would do when it was all over was met with his now standard reply.

RINGO: You mean when it's finished altogether? I'd like to open a business. I've been saying, this last year anyway, ladies hairdressing, but you never know what'll happen. I may open something else, but I wanna try and be successful.

DIBBS HAD DONE his homework and noticed that Paul had graduated to the sixth form at grammar school.

DIBBS: Paul McCartney… you alone of the four Beatles seemed to have had a greater incentive to go on and do other things because, on the educational side of it, you've gone further than the other lads have.

PAUL: No… Yeah, not really though. It just so 'appens, I happened to get a few GCEs. I don't think that makes me cleverer than the others… I know John's not soft at all, maybe he was a bit lazy at school, but I was as well. But I don't think that's made me feel I ought to go on and do better things.

DIBBS: What do you think you might have done if this particular thing hadn't come up?

PAUL: Well, at the time I was thinking of going to a teachers training college. I don't know whether I'd have been any good at all, but it just seemed sort of a natural thing to do at the time.

THEIR CHAT CONCLUDED with a discussion about the character of The Beatles' songs.

PAUL: Lyrics, as far as we're concerned, are just things that we might say. The main point is that they've got to be feasible. We don't like saying, 'Yeah, she's a movie queen, baby' or things like that, because they don't happen to come into our lives. But we will say things like, 'Don't go away, because I might miss you', because I'm sure that you know that everybody's felt that at some time or another. The things that *can* happen, we'll write about, but things that happen in other people's great glamorous lives – Cadillacs and movie queens and Hollywood – I'm sure we'll never write into our lyrics, because we couldn't believe it. We've got to believe our lyrics.

SO FAR, SO good for Dibbs. In a respectful and informed way, he had asked questions that were pitched higher than the more usual level of 'How did you get that funny haircut?' But his patience was tested when he faced John, who was in a mischievous mood.

DIBBS: What's been the greatest influence in your life… up to this date, up to this experience with The Beatles?

JOHN: Nell… Neil, that's our road manager.

OPPOSITE **Dibbs Mather interviewed The Beatles for the BBC Transcription programmes** *Dateline London* **and** *Calling Australia*, **distributed to overseas stations on disc.**

DIBBS: What kind of influence did he have on you?

JOHN: Er, none really.

DIBBS: [a little desperately] Is no influence better than some influence?

JOHN: Well, apart from that… [a loud munch] an apple a day, keeps the docker away!

DIBBS: It's said, John Lennon, that you have the most *Goon*-type humour of the four Beatles…

JOHN: [Quickly] Who said that?

DIBBS: I think I read it in one of the papers… [door slam]… This is all going wrong, I wanted to get a nice personality bit.

JOHN: I haven't got a nice personality.

DIBBS: What kind of personality would you say you have?

JOHN: [Cheerfully] Very nice. [Laughs]

DIBBS: Um… you were interested in poetry, at school…

JOHN: Who said?

DIBBS: [his patience finally ebbing away] It's printed in a book compiled by The Beatles and entitled *The Beatles*.

JOHN: I haven't read that book… we don't normally write those things. You can tell they're all written by the same person anyway.

DIBBS: [Despairingly] Ohh! Well, it's said that you write comic poetry, if the mood takes you about something that takes your fancy.

JOHN: Oh yeah, I do that.

JOHN THEN READ a part of 'Neville Club', which was published three months later in a collection of his verse, prose and drawings called *In His Own Write*.

A WEEK AFTER talking to Dibbs Mather, The Beatles were back at the BBC recording two shows for Christmas week. The first session was for their sixth appearance on *Saturday Club* broadcast on 21 December 1963. Following a spin of Kathy Kirby's Top Five hit 'Secret Love', the first song by The Beatles was 'All My Loving'. The verbal combat that then followed was typical of the way the group and Brian Matthew conducted their interviews. The DJ remembered that, 'They were quite sparky and always very different from any of the other artists and groups who appeared on the show. I think their main object in life seemed to be how to put me down in as good-natured a way as possible. But it was great fun always to talk to The Beatles.'

BRIAN: 'All My Loving', indeed. I never saw a more belligerent bunch in my life! What's the matter with you lot, then?

JOHN: What happened to our request, Brian Bathtubes?

PAUL: Yeah, we sent it in about two weeks ago and you haven't played it, have you, eh?

JOHN: No, he hasn't played it, has he? Oh no, not him!

PAUL: Oh no.

GEORGE: He won't play our request.

BRIAN: Have you done? Well, all right, then. Now read someone else's request.

JOHN: 'Dear John, would you please play "This Boy" by the…'

BRIAN: Get on with it!

JOHN: '… fabulous Beatles. Thank you.'

AFTER AN EXCELLENT BBC performance of 'This Boy', the programme continued with Frank Sinatra's record 'Come Fly With Me'. Their next spot in the show followed Susan Maughan singing a version of the current hit by Dora Bryan – 'All I Want For Christmas Is A Beatle'. The group responded with a quick parody – 'All I Want For Christmas Is A Bottle'. Their last BBC music session of 1963 was recorded for a two-hour 'Boxing Day' programme called *The Beatles Say From Us To You*. Naturally, 'From Me To You' was reworked as the signature tune. The show was introduced by Rolf Harris, the compere of *The Beatles' Christmas Show* at the Finsbury Park Astoria in London. Their Boxing Day guests, selected by BBC producer Bryant Marriott, included Joe Brown and The Bruvvers, Jeanie Lambe, the ubiquitous Susan Maughan and Kenny Lynch. One of the most remarkable recordings of The Beatles' radio career was broadcast during *From Us To You*. They were invited by presenter Rolf Harris to accompany him while he sang a customized 'Tie Me Kangaroo Down, Sport'.

The BBC's audience research department estimated the audience at 22.1 per cent for the first hour and 20 per cent for the second. Around eleven million had heard the broadcast, but the 'Appreciation Index' figure was a lowly 49 out of 100. Significantly, the show scored a very respectable 75 when calculated from questionnaires compiled by 31 per cent of the sample who 'usually liked listening to this kind of music'. There were not many teenagers in this portion, but even some of the 'older' listeners (those in their twenties) had enjoyed the show. Some in the older age group conceded The Beatles 'had something' and 'were full of go', but even so some felt 'they were vastly over-rated and could not really sing'. The report concluded with a positive response to *From Us To You*: 'This was definitely family listening. Teenagers, right, left, and centre and across the road had the set on. I found it quite happy and melodious, with plenty of zip. I am quite a fan of The Beatles. To me they are the new "Today", clean and wholesome and gay.'

1963 RADIO AND TV APPEARANCES

📻 Radio programme titles
📺 TV titles

★ – indicates a song not released on record by
The Beatles from 1962 to 1970.

📻 POP INN
Br: 22 January 1963 – 1.00–1.45pm
– The Light Programme, Live
An interview with Keith Fordyce before the record
of 'Please Please Me' was played

📻 HERE WE GO
Br: 25 January 1963 – 5.00–5.29pm
– The Light Programme
Rec: 16 January 1963
Playhouse Theatre, Manchester
Producer: Peter Pilbeam
Presenter: Ray Peters
Chains, Please Please Me, Ask Me Why
Recorded in front of an audience
Performed but not broadcast: *Three Cool Cats* ★

📻 SATURDAY CLUB
Br: 26 January 1963 – 10.00am–noon
–The Light Programme
Rec: 22 January 1963
Playhouse Theatre, London
Producer: Bernie Andrews and Jimmy Grant
Presenter: Brian Matthew
Some Other Guy ★, *Love Me Do, Please Please
Me, Keep Your Hands Off My Baby* ★, *Beautiful
Dreamer* ★

📻 THE TALENT SPOT
Br: 29 January 1963 – 5.00–5.29pm
– The Light Programme
Rec: 22 January 1963
BBC Paris Theatre, London
Producer: Brian Willey
Presenter: Gary Marshal
Please Please Me, Ask Me Why, Some Other Guy ★

📻 PARADE OF THE POPS
Br: 20 February 1963 – 12.31–1.30pm
– The Light Programme
Live in front of an audience
Playhouse Theatre, London

Producer: John Kingdon
Presenter: Denny Piercy
Love Me Do, Please Please Me

📻 HERE WE GO
Br: 12 March 1963 – 5.00–5.29pm
– The Light Programme
Rec: 6 March 1963
Playhouse Theatre, Manchester
Producer: Peter Pilbeam
Presenter: Ray Peters
*Misery, Do You Want To Know A Secret, Please
Please Me*
Recorded in front of an audience
Performed but not broadcast: *I Saw Her
Standing There*

📻 SATURDAY CLUB
Br: 16 March 1963 – 10.00am–noon
– The Light Programme, Live
Studio 3A, Broadcasting House, London
Producers: Jimmy Grant and Bernie Andrews
Presenter: Brian Matthew
*I Saw Her Standing There, Misery,
Too Much Monkey Business* ★,
I'm Talking About You ★, *Please Please Me,
The Hippy Hippy Shake* ★

📻 ON THE SCENE
Br: 28 March 1963 – 5.00–5.29pm
– The Light Programme
Rec: 21 March 1963
Number 1 Studio, BBC Piccadilly Theatre,
London
Producer: Brian Willey
Presenter: Craig Douglas
*Misery, Do You Want To Know A Secret, Please
Please Me*

📻 EASY BEAT
Br: 7 April 1963 – 10.31–11.30am
– The Light Programme
Rec: 3 April 1963
Playhouse Theatre, London
Producer: Ron Belchier
Presenter: Brian Matthew
Please Please Me, Misery, From Me To You
Recorded in front of an audience

📻 POP INN
Br: 9 April 1963 – 1.00–1.45pm
– The Light Programme, Live
An interview with Keith Fordyce before the record
of 'From Me To You' was played.

📺 THE 625 SHOW
Br: 16 April 1963 – 6.25–6.50pm
BBC TV
Rec: 13 Apr 1963
Lime Grove Studios, London
From Me To You, Thank You Girl, Please Please Me

📻 SWINGING SOUND '63
Br: 18 April 1963 – 9.10–10.15pm
– The Light Programme, Live
The Royal Albert Hall, London
Producers: Terry Henebery and Ron Belchier
Presenter: George Melly
Twist And Shout, From Me To You
Performed in front of an audience

📻 SIDE BY SIDE
Br: 22 April 1963 – 5.00–5.29pm
– The Light Programme
Rec: 1 April 1963
Number 1 Studio, BBC Piccadilly Theatre, London
Producer: Bryant Marriott
Presenter: John Dunn
Side By Side (with The Karl Denver Trio) ★ ,
*I Saw Her Standing There, Do You Want To Know
A Secret, Baby It's You, Please Please Me, From Me
To You, Misery*

📻 SIDE BY SIDE
Br: 13 May 1963 – 5.00–5.29pm –
The Light Programme
Rec: 1 April 1963
Number 1 Studio, BBC Piccadilly Theatre, London
Producer: Bryant Marriott
Presenter: John Dunn
Side By Side (with The Karl Denver Trio) ★ ,
*From Me To You, Long Tall Sally, A Taste Of
Honey, Chains, Thank You Girl, Boys*

📺 POPS AND LENNY
Br: 16 May 1963 – 5.00–5.30pm – BBC TV, Live
Television Theatre, London

From Me To You, Please Please Me (shortened to 1'05")
The Beatles joined the cast for the final number, 'After You've Gone' (Creamer/Layton)

📻 SATURDAY CLUB

Br: 25 May 1963 – 10.00am–noon
– The Light Programme
Rec: 21 May 1963
Playhouse Theatre, London
Producers: Jimmy Grant and Bernie Andrews
Presenter: Brian Matthew
I Saw Her Standing There, Do You Want To Know A Secret, Boys, Long Tall Sally, From Me To You, Money (That's What I Want)

📻 STEPPIN' OUT

Br: 3 June 1963 (Whit Monday) – 10.31–11.30am
– The Light Programme
Rec: 21 May 1963
Playhouse Theatre, London
Producer: Terry Henebery
Presenter: Diz Disley
Please Please Me, I Saw Her Standing There, Roll Over Beethoven, Thank You Girl, From Me To You
Recorded in front of an audience
Performed but not broadcast: *Twist And Shout*

📻 POP GO THE BEATLES (1)

Br: 4 June 1963 – 5.00–5.29pm
– The Light Programme
Rec: 24 May 1963
Number 2 Studio, Aeolian Hall
Producer: Terry Henebery
Presenter: Lee Peters
Pop Go The Beatles ★, From Me To You, Everybody's Trying To Be My Baby, Do You Want To Know A Secret, You Really Got A Hold On Me, Misery, The Hippy Hippy Shake ★, Pop Go The Beatles ★
Guest group: The Lorne Gibson Trio

📻 POP GO THE BEATLES (2)

Br: 11 June 1963 – 5.00–5.29pm
– The Light Programme
Rec: 1 June 1963
BBC Paris Theatre, London
Producer: Terry Henebery
Presenter: Lee Peters

Pop Go The Beatles ★, Too Much Monkey Business ★, I Got To Find My Baby ★, Youngblood ★, Baby It's You, Till There Was You, Love Me Do, Pop Go The Beatles ★
Guest group: The Countrymen

📻 POP GO THE BEATLES (3)

Br: 18 June 1963 – 5.00–5.29pm
– The Light Programme
Rec: 1 June 1963
BBC Paris Theatre, London
Producer: Terry Henebery
Presenter: Lee Peters
Pop Go The Beatles ★, A Shot Of Rhythm And Blues ★, Memphis, Tennesee ★, A Taste Of Honey, Sure To Fall (In Love With You) ★, Money (That's What I Want), From Me to You, Pop Go The Beatles ★
Guest group: Carter-Lewis & the Southerners.
A rowdy version of 'Happy Birthday To You' was also featured before 'A Taste Of Honey' to celebrate Paul's 21st birthday.

📻 EASY BEAT

Br: 23 June 1963 – 10.31–11.30am
– The Light Programme
Rec: 19 June 1963
Playhouse Theatre, London
Producer: Ron Belchier
Presenter: Brian Matthew
Some Other Guy ★, A Taste Of Honey, Thank You Girl, From Me to You
Recorded in front of an audience

📻 SIDE BY SIDE

Br: 24 June 1963 – 5.00–5.29pm
– The Light Programme
Rec: 4 April 1963
BBC Paris Theatre, London
Producer: Bryant Marriott.
Presenter: John Dunn
Side By Side (with The Karl Denver Trio) ★, *Too Much Monkey Business ★, Love Me Do, Boys, I'll Be On My Way ★, From Me to You*

📻 POP GO THE BEATLES (4)

Br: 25 June 1963 – 5.00–5.29pm
– The Light Programme

Rec: 17 June 1963
Studio Number 5, BBC Maida Vale, London
Producer: Terry Henebery
Presenter: Lee Peters
Pop Go The Beatles ★, I Saw Her Standing There, Anna (Go To Him), Boys, Chains, P.S. I Love You, Twist And Shout, Pop Go The Beatles ★
Recorded but not broadcast: *A Taste Of Honey*
Guest group: The Bachelors

📻 SATURDAY CLUB

Br: 29 June 1963 – 10.00am–noon
– The Light Programme
Rec: 24 June 1963
Playhouse Theatre, London
Producer: Jimmy Grant and Bernie Andrews
Presenter: Brian Matthew
I Got To Find My Baby ★, Memphis, Tennessee ★, Money (That's What I Want), Till There Was You, From Me To You, Roll Over Beethoven

---

📺 JUKE BOX JURY

Br: 29 June 1963 – 6.35–7.00pm – BBC TV
Rec: 22 June 1963
Television Theatre, London
John was one of the four panel members

📻 THE BEAT SHOW

Br: 4 July 1963 – 1.00–1.30pm
– The Light Programme
Rec: 3 July 1963
Playhouse Theatre, Manchester
Producer: Geoff Lawrence
Presenter: Gay Byrne
From Me To You, A Taste Of Honey, Twist And Shout

📻 POP GO THE BEATLES (5)

Br: 16 July 1963 – 5.00–5.29pm
– The Light Programme
Rec: 2 July 1963
Number 5 Studio, BBC Maida Vale, London
Producer: Terry Henebery
Presenter: Rodney Burke
Pop Go The Beatles ★, That's All Right (Mama) ★, There's A Place, Carol ★, Soldier Of Love ★, Lend Me Your Comb ★, Clarabella ★, Pop Go The Beatles ★
Guest group: Duffy Power & The Graham Bond

Quartet. Recorded but not broadcast: *Three Cool Cats* ★, *Sweet Little Sixteen* ★, *Ask Me Why*

📺 EASY BEAT

Br: 21 July 1963 -10.31–11.30am
– The Light Programme
Rec: 17 July 1963
Playhouse Theatre, London
Producer: Ron Belchier
Presenter: Brian Matthew
I Saw Her Standing There, *A Shot Of Rhythm And Blues* ★, *There's A Place*, *Twist And Shout*
Recorded in front of an audience

📺 POP GO THE BEATLES (6)

Br: 23 July 1963 – 5.00–5.29pm
– The Light Programme
Rec: 10 July 1963
Number 2 Studio, Aeolian Hall
Producer: Terry Henebery.
Presenter: Rodney Burke
Pop Go The Beatles ★, *Sweet Little Sixteen* ★, *A Taste Of Honey*, *Nothin' Shakin* ★, *Love Me Do*, *Lonesome Tears In My Eyes* ★, *So How Come (No One Loves Me)* ★, *Pop Go The Beatles* ★
Guest group: Carter-Lewis & The Southerners

📺 POP GO THE BEATLES (7)

Br: 30 July 1963 – 5.00–5.29pm
– The Light Programme
Rec: 10 July 1963
Number 2 Studio, Aeolian Hall
Producer: Terry Henebery
Presenter: Rodney Burke
Pop Go The Beatles ★, *Memphis, Tennessee* ★, *Do You Want To Know A Secret*, *Till There Was You*, *Matchbox*, *Please Mister Postman*, *The Hippy Hippy Shake* ★, *Pop Go The Beatles* ★
Guest group: The Searchers

📺 POP GO THE BEATLES (8)

Br: 6 August 1963 – 5.00–5.29pm
– The Light Programme
Rec: 16 July 1963
BBC Paris Theatre
Producer: Terry Henebery
Presenter: Rodney Burke
Pop Go The Beatles ★, *I'm Gonna Sit Right Down And Cry (Over You)* ★, *Crying, Waiting, Hoping* ★, *Kansas City/Hey-Hey-Hey-Hey!*, *To Know Her Is To Love Her* ★, *The Honeymoon Song* ★, *Twist And Shout*, *Pop Go The Beatles* ★
Guest group: The Swinging Blue Jeans [Producer: Ian Grant]

📺 POP GO THE BEATLES (9)

Br: 13 August 1963 – 5.00–5.29pm
– The Light Programme
Rec: 16 July 1963
BBC Paris Theatre
Producer: Terry Henebery [except for songs marked with ♦ produced by Ian Grant]
Presenter: Rodney Burke
Pop Go The Beatles ★, *Long Tall Sally*, *Please Please Me* ♦, *She Loves You*, *You Really Got A Hold On Me* ♦, *I'll Get You* ♦, *I Got A Woman* ★, *Pop Go The Beatles* ★
Guest group: The Hollies

📺 POP GO THE BEATLES (10)

Br: 20 August 1963 – 5.00–5.29pm
– The Light Programme
Rec: 16 July 1963
BBC Paris Theatre
Producer: Terry Henebery
Presenter: Rodney Burke
Pop Go The Beatles ★, *She Loves You*, *Words Of Love*, *Glad All Over* ★, *I Just Don't Understand* ★, *Devil In Her Heart*, *Slow Down*, *Pop Go The Beatles* ★
Guest group: Russ Sainty & The Nu-Notes

📺 SATURDAY CLUB

Br: 24 August 1963 – 10.00am–noon
– The Light Programme
Rec: 30 July 1963
Playhouse Theatre, London
Producer: Jimmy Grant and Bernie Andrews
Presenter: Brian Matthew
Long Tall Sally, *She Loves You*, *Glad All Over* ★, *Twist And Shout*, *You Really Got A Hold On Me*, *I'll Get You*

📺 POP GO THE BEATLES (11)

Br: 27 August 1963 – 5.00–5.29pm
– The Light Programme

Rec: 1 August 1963
Playhouse Theatre, Manchester
Producer: Terry Henebery – Ian Grant produced the Beatles session
Presenter: Rodney Burke
Pop Go The Beatles ★, *Ooh! My Soul* ★, *Don't Ever Change* ★, *Twist And Shout*, *She Loves You*, *Anna (Go To Him)*, *A Shot Of Rhythm And Blues* ★, *Pop Go The Beatles* ★
Guest group: Cyril Davies' Rhythm & Blues All Stars and Long John Baldry

📺 NON STOP POP

Br: 30 August 1963 – 5.00–5.29pm
– The Light Programme
Rec: 30 July 1963
Playhouse Theatre, London
Bandleader Phil Tate talked to the group for the 'Pop Chat' section of the show. The interview was recorded at the beginning of a *Saturday Club* session.

📺 POP GO THE BEATLES (12)

Br: 3 September 1963 – 5.00–5.29pm
– The Light Programme
Rec: 1 August 1963
Playhouse Theatre, Manchester
Producer: Ian Grant
Presenter: Rodney Burke
Pop Go The Beatles ★, *From Me To You*, *I'll Get You*, *Money (That's What I Want)*, *There's A Place*, *Honey Don't* (★ with John on lead vocal), *Roll Over Beethoven*, *Pop Go The Beatles* ★
Recorded but not broadcast: *Lucille* ★, *Baby It's You*, *She Loves You*
Guest group: Brian Poole and The Tremeloes [Producer: Terry Henebery]

📺 POP GO THE BEATLES (13)

Br: 10 September 1963 – 5.00–5.29pm
– The Light Programme
Rec: 3 September 1963
Number 2 Studio, Aeolian Hall
Producer: Terry Henebery
The Beatles' session producer: Ian Grant
Presenter: Rodney Burke
Pop Go The Beatles ★, *Too Much Monkey Business* ★, *Till There Was You*, *Love Me Do*, *She Loves You*,

I'll Get You, A Taste Of Honey, The Hippy Hippy Shake ★, Pop Go The Beatles ★
Guest group: Johnny Kidd & the Pirates

📻 POP GO THE BEATLES (14)
Br: 17 September 1963 – 5.00–5.29pm
– The Light Programme
Rec: 3 September 1963
Number 2 Studio, Aeolian Hall
Producer: Ian Grant
Presenter: Rodney Burke
Pop Go The Beatles ★, Chains, You Really Got A Hold On Me, Misery, Lucille ★, From Me To You, Boys, Pop Go The Beatles ★
Guest group: The Marauders

📻 POP GO THE BEATLES (15)
Br: 24 September 1963 – 5.00–5.29pm
– The Light Programme
Rec: 3 September 1963
Number 2 Studio, Aeolian Hall
Producer: Ian Grant
Presenter: Rodney Burke
Pop Go The Beatles ★, She Loves You, Ask Me Why, Devil In Her Heart, I Saw Her Standing There, Sure To Fall (In Love With You) ★, Twist And Shout, Pop Go The Beatles ★
There was also a short chant of 'Goodbye George, Goodbye John, Ringo, Paul, Ringo, Paul, Rodney Burke!'
Guest group: Tony Rivers & The Castaways

📻 SATURDAY CLUB
Br: 5 October 1963 – 10.00am–noon
– The Light Programme
Rec: 7 September 1963
Playhouse Theatre, London
Producer: Jimmy Grant and Bernie Andrews
Presenter: Brian Matthew
I Saw Her Standing There, Memphis, Tennessee ★, Happy Birthday Dear Saturday Club ★, I'll Get You, She Loves You, Lucille ★

📺 THE MERSEY SOUND
Br: 9 Oct 1963 – 10.10–10.40pm
(London and the north)
National broadcast: 13 November 1963
7.10–7.40pm

'This is a story about a special kind of noise – a noise worth a small fortune – a noise that has made a provincial city, for a time at least, the metropolis of pop music. This is the story of The Mersey Sound.'
Rec: 27–30 Aug 1963
27 August:
Twist And Shout, She Loves You, Love Me Do (disc used as the soundtrack to performance footage) Speech extracts were broadcast on radio programmes *Pick of the Week* and *The Week in the North*.

📻 EASY BEAT
Br: 20 October 1963 – 10.31–11.30am
– The Light Programme
Rec: 16 October 1963
Playhouse Theatre, London
Producer: Ron Belchier
Presenter: Brian Matthew
I Saw Her Standing There, Love Me Do, Please Please Me, From Me To You, She Loves You
Recorded in front of an audience

📻 THE PUBLIC EAR
Br: 3 November 1963 – 3.00–4.00pm
– The Light Programme
Rec: 3 October 1963
The magazine programme included a twelve-minute feature presented by Tony Hall about The Beatles and the Liverpool scene, in which the group and other Mersey figures were interviewed.

📻 THE KEN DODD SHOW
Br: 3 November 1963 – 2.30–3.00pm
– The Light Programme
Rec: 9 October 1963
BBC Paris Theatre, London
Producer: Bill Worsley
She Loves You

📺 SIX TEN
Br: 8 Nov 1963 – 6.10–6.31pm
– BBC TV Northern Ireland
Rec: 8 Nov 1963 – 3.00pm
An interview recorded at BBC Belfast.

📻 THE ROYAL VARIETY PERFORMANCE
Br: 10 November 1963 – 7.35–8.30pm
– The Light Programme
Rec: 4 November 1963
Prince of Wales Theatre
Producer: Arthur Phillips
Compere: Dickie Henderson
Linked by Brian Johnston
From Me To You, Till There Was You, Twist And Shout
The cast included Marlene Dietrich, Buddy Greco, Max Bygraves, Tommy Steele, Flanders and Swann, Wilfred Brambell and Harry H Corbett (playing Steptoe and Son) and Jan and Vlasta Dalibor (Pinky and Perky).

📺 SOUTH TODAY
Br: 12 Nov 1963 – 6.10–6.30pm
– BBC Local TV
Rec: 12 Nov 1963
An interview recorded with reporter John Johnston at the Royal Beach hotel, Southsea

---

📻 VOICE OF THE NORTH
Br: 20 November 1963 – 6.10–6.30pm
– North Home Service
Rec: 20 November 1963
Michael Barton recorded a two-minute interview backstage at the ABC Cinema, Ardwick, Manchester.

📻 A WORLD OF SOUND
Br: 21 November 1963 – 4.30–5.30pm
– BBC North Home Service
Rec: 7 September 1963
An edition of the programme subtitled *Liverpool: A Swinging City* featured an interview with Paul given to the programme's producer Rosemary Hart.

📺 EAST AT SIX TEN
Br: 26 Nov 1963 – 6.38–7.01pm
– BBC Local TV, Live
Reporter Jean Goodman interviewed The Beatles in their dressing room at the Regal Cinema, Cambridge.

ABOVE 'It's so long since we played a proper date like this, honest', says George. 'Shurrup', says John. 'You're on the radio now.'

📺 WACKER, MACH SCHAU

Br: 27 November 1963 – 8.00–8.30pm
– North Home Service
Rec: 20 November 1963
Michael Barton talked to George for a programme discussing the Liverpool and Hamburg music scenes.

📺 JUKE BOX JURY

Br: 7 Dec 1963 – 6.05–6.35pm – BBC TV
Rec: 2.30–3.15pm
Empire Theatre, Liverpool

John, Paul, George and Ringo reviewed records and decided whether each would be a hit or a miss.

📺 IT'S THE BEATLES

Br: 7 Dec 1963 – 8.10–8.40pm – BBC TV
Rec: 7 Dec 1963 – 3.45–4.30pm
A concert filmed in front of an audience comprising The Beatles Northern Area Fan Club at the Empire Theatre, Liverpool.
From Me To You (shortened), *I Saw Her Standing There, All My Loving, Roll Over Beethoven, Boys, Till There Was You, She Loves You, This Boy,*

I Want To Hold Your Hand, Money (That's What I Want), Twist And Shout, From Me To You (instrumental incorporating *The Third Man* theme)

📻 SATURDAY CLUB

Br: 21 December 1963 – 10am–noon
– The Light Programme
Rec: 17 December 1963
Playhouse Theatre, Manchester
Producer: Jimmy Grant and Bernie Andrews
Presenter: Brian Matthew
All My Loving, This Boy, I Want To Hold Your Hand, Till There Was You, Roll Over Beethoven, She Loves You, Beatles Chrimble Muddley ★
During their final set they sang some appropriate Christmas words to the Freddie and The Dreamers hit 'You Belong To Me'. It was in the Top Three that week below 'I Want To Hold Your Hand' and 'She Loves You'. The last session track was a 'Chrimble Muddley' based on Duane Eddy's 'Shazam!', in which John sang the titles or snippets of lyrics from the five Beatles singles to date… and 'Rudolph The Red-Nosed Reindeer'!

📻 TOP POPS OF 1963

Br: 25 December 1963 – 6.00–7.30pm
– The Light Programme
Rec: 7 December 1963
A two-minute interview was included in Alan Freeman's Christmas Day 'survey of the year's pop scene'.

📻 The Beatles Say FROM US TO YOU

Br: 26 December 1963 (Boxing Day) –
10am–noon – The Light Programme
Rec: 18 December 1963
BBC Paris Theatre, London
Producer: Bryant Marriott
Presenter: Rolf Harris
From Us To You ★, *She Loves You, All My Loving, Roll Over Beethoven, Till There Was You, Boys, Money (That's What I Want), I Saw Her Standing There, Tie Me Kangaroo Down, Sport (With Rolf Harris)* ★, *I Want To Hold Your Hand, From Us To You* ★

1964

Top Gear

TIME TO MOVE UP A GEAR. The Beatles had experienced phenomenal success by the end of 1963. The next step was to expand their reach to the place where the music they loved originated – America. The wheels had already been set in motion. By the time The Beatles arrived in the States to appear on *The Ed Sullivan Show*, 'I Want To Hold Your Hand' had replaced 'There! I've Said It Again' by Bobby Vinton at the top of the US charts. The switch symbolized a transition of power: the fresh sound from the UK swatting away one of the anodyne 'Bobbys' of current American pop, who was singing a song from 1945.

Following the death of John F. Kennedy, Lyndon B. Johnson became President. He told Congress that 'no memorial or eulogy could more eloquently honor President Kennedy's memory than the earliest possible passage of the civil rights bill for which he fought.' In July 1964, LBJ signed the Civil Rights Act, which legally ended segregation and discrimination. At the time of its Congressional passage, the country was gripped by news of the ominous disappearance in Mississippi of three young civil rights workers – Andrew Goodman, Michael Schwerner and James Chaney. Murdered by the Ku Klux Klan on the night of 21 June 1964, the bodies of the three men were not found for 44 days.

The charismatic leader of the civil rights movement, Dr Martin Luther King, Jr, became the youngest ever recipient of the Nobel Peace Prize. But Dr King's peaceful demonstrations and initiatives during the struggle for racial equality were frequently attacked. In addition to violence on its streets at home, there was trouble brewing for America in Asia. By year's end, there were 23,000 'military advisers' in South Vietnam. In the US election in November, Lyndon Johnson was elected by a landslide. In the biggest victory to date, he defeated Republican Barry Goldwater by sixteen million votes.

In the UK, a closely fought general election in October brought the Labour Party to power with Harold Wilson as Prime Minister. Thirteen years of government by the Conservative Party came to an end. In a shrewd move in March, Wilson had presented The Beatles with their Variety Club Awards – and been photographed amidst them. At the beginning of 1964, he made a speech promising his victory at the polls would be 'a chance for change. A chance to change the face and future of Britain'. Who better to symbolize this change than the successful Beatles and their foreign earning potential. 'I didn't get the bit where they said, "Earning all these dollars for Britain",' George commented at a press conference when the group returned from their first trip to America. '"Are we sharing it out or something?"'

The Beatles' first movie *A Hard Day's Night* was released in July. Witty, stylish and great fun, it consolidated The Beatles' domination of pop culture in America. Their success paved the way for a British invasion of the US charts by The Animals, Dave Clark Five, Gerry and The Pacemakers, The Kinks, The Rolling Stones and The Searchers. The third James Bond movie, *Goldfinger*, was another box-office hit and brought attention to British style. Fashion leaders such as Mary Quant and Jean Muir were making an impact with their designs, including the mini-skirt. With its fashionable boutiques, Carnaby Street became a symbol of 'Swinging London'.

The more popular TV programmes of the year included *The Avengers, Bewitched, The Man from U.N.C.L.E.* and *Bonanza*. The UK received a third television channel in 1964 when BBC 2 was launched on 20 April. However, a massive power failure in West London disrupted the network's planned programmes for its opening night. At the end of March, Radio Caroline began broadcasting from a ship outside UK territorial waters to provide an alternative to the BBC's services. Other 'off-shore' pirates set sail, including the American-funded Radio London in December 1964. 'Big L' introduced the 'Top Forty' format to British listeners and would soon describe itself as 'Your Beatle Station'.

From: Chief Assistant, Production, Popular Music (Sound)

Subject: THE BEATLES   28th January 1964

To: H.P.M.(S)   Copy to: L.E.B.M.

My comments as requested on the little heap which I return herewith. (A.H.L.E.(S)
to L.E.B.M. 20th December; L.E.B.M. to A.H.L.E.(S) 23rd December; L.E.B.M. to
A.H.L.E.(S) 1st January; Prog.Ex.N.R. to L.E.B.M. 2nd January, 2 pages;
L.E.B.M. to Prog.Ex.N.R. 21st January.)

On his return from Sweden, some time before Christmas, Brian Epstein, Jimmy Grant
and I met for about one hour.

I told him of the problems caused by the inability of our programme contracts
organisation to obtain any sort of answer to producers' enquiries about the
availability of The Beatles. He apologised profusely, said this was due to his
organisation being completely overwhelmed by the increase in the group's popularity,
and that he was taking certain steps to remedy this as soon as possible.

I asked him what sort of bookings he was likely to accept from the BBC during the
next few months. He said that the boys were enthusiastic about Saturday Club
and would like to do a reasonable amount of appearances during the year; secondly,
they would like to do studio sessions for programmes such as the Boxing Day
10.00 a.m.-12.00 noon programme (providing they had little talking to do);
that he would accept no bookings for audience shows of any sort due to the
problems of crowd control; and he would be loathe to accept any television
bookings which might have as bad a sound balance as the previous Saturday's O.B.
from the North.

I told him that I hope to persuade Light Programme to give us some major slots
on Bank Holidays in 1964 in which we could produce special programmes like the
Boxing Day one - I asked him whether our booking department would get a favourable
response when it came to the point - he promised that they would.

I stressed (as I always do) that I was not negotiating any sort of deal (in fact
he had no more desire to do so than I had) - but I did tell him explicitly that
I hoped our booking people would get quicker answers in the future and that if
he was not prepared to accept some kind of contract under any circumstances he
might tell them. He said he wasn't sure enough of this at the time and I made
it quite clear that I was going to take no action to control in any way the free
flow of requests/offers which producers might ask their bookers to make.

In summary: I am well aware of the problems caused to Programme Contracts staff
when producers or executives usurp any part of their functions - and I am disappointed to discover that L.E.B.M. should allow this pathetic little correspondence
to go on without confronting me directly with the matter.

                                                    continued....

Light Entertainment Booking Manager.   305 H.H.   P&BX 2684

LIVERPOOL POP GROUPS   23rd April 1964

Prog.Ex., North Region.   Copy to: H.N.R.P.; C.A.P.P.M.(S).;
                                         A.H.L.E.(S).;
                                         Asst. to H.P.C. (Miss Willett).

Back in December of last year I had a memo from A.H.L.E.(S). (subject
matter "The Beatles"). This moved into the orbit of a memo you sent me
in January 1964 (subject matter as above). Various other people
became involved and we got to a point when, at the end of January, I had
thought the next (and last) move would be a memo from H.P.M.(S). This
has not been forthcoming and I am writing this note so that if anybody
else has, like me, the correspondence outstanding he can now file it
away.

This was probably a case when with nobody actually wanting it nuclear
war was jolly nearly breaking out. However, there is a slight change
in the situation if only because Nems Enterprises has now moved to
London which lets you (you lucky fellow) out of it. I, too, have now
had the excitement (sic) of meeting Master Epstein face to face, though
I doubt whether he was any more impressed with me than I was with his
"shouting for his assistant" act. Anyhow, they have now taken Bernard
Lee into their office who seems to be endeavouring to get their
administration more on the rails than it has been till now.

So let's all start afresh.

                        PATRICK NEWMAN

                        (Patrick Newman)

VM

AT THE START of 1964, *The Beatles' Christmas Show* was continuing its run at the Astoria, Finsbury Park in London. This was the group that kept on giving – thirty performances were scheduled over sixteen nights. During the show's run, The Beatles' career took two leaps forward in the United States. First, their latest single 'I Want To Hold Your Hand' was rush-released on 26 December 1963. Capitol Records – EMI's company in America – had shown no interest in distributing The Beatles' previous records. When they were licensed to independent labels, Capitol's decision seemed to be vindicated as the discs made no progress whatsoever. Yet now 'I Want To Hold Your Hand' was flying off the shelves and being played on American Top 40 radio. Second, The Beatles were seen performing for the first time on US television. *The Jack Paar Show* on NBC had licensed a clip of 'She Loves You' from *The Mersey Sound*. When Brian Epstein learnt this would be shown, he was furious with the BBC. He claimed it would endanger an exclusive contract signed in November with the CBS programme *The Ed Sullivan Show*. Despite his threat to refuse further Beatles BBC TV bookings if the American broadcast went ahead, 'She Loves You' was seen on 3 January 1964. However, Paar himself was unimpressed. He responded to the performance with the smirking comment, 'It's nice to know that England has finally risen to our cultural level.'

Only three British acts had ever reached the top of the charts in the United States. Vera Lynn was the first in 1952 with 'Auf Wiederseh'n Sweetheart'. Ten years later, 'Stranger On The Shore' by Mr Acker Bilk and The Tornadoes' 'Telstar' reached number one within a few months of each other. To many, it seemed inconceivable that a British group playing R&B could compete in the birthplace of the music. Of course, The Beatles loved American music. They listened almost exclusively to rock 'n' roll and rhythm and blues. They studied it, hoping to capture its qualities in their own records. In an edition of the BBC radio show *The Public Ear*, a letter read by George revealed how evangelical they were about their favourite music.

Dear *Public Ear*,

We heard your programme on December the 29th when Tony Hall said it'd be nice if the people who liked our kind of music, would also appreciate the kind of records and music that we play at home – like Mary Wells, Miracles and not to mention Marvin Gaye.

We believe the fans would like these singers if they had the chance to hear them, y'see. Because we don't seem to hear enough of them these days on the radio.

So you'd make us very happy, Tony, and you'd [Ringo joins in] absolutely break us up, if you'd play us some.

Yours sincerely,

George Harrison and Ringo Starr.

The two Beatles were then heard discussing how Ringo's 'gag' had been missed out. Amid much laughter, Ringo explained, 'You know… Marvin Gaye… and I say "Marvin Gaye" and you say, "I told you not to mention him!"' When Tony Hall thanked George and Ringo for their audio letter, he picked up on its theme. 'Well, here's one by The Miracles that I know you're always playing at home, and the title? "I've Been Good To You".' Released in early 1962, it was the B-side of The Miracles' second Top 40 US hit on Tamla 'What's So Good About Goodbye'. 'I've Been Good To You' was, indeed, a Beatles favourite and sounds like it may have inspired John's 'Sexy Sadie'.

Tony Hall remembered, 'I'd never really heard Marvin Gaye, The Miracles and all that until George played me the records up in their flat and they absolutely blew me away. I then went on a sort of a crusade for Motown!'. George and Ringo had been recorded in Tony's home, opposite their flat in Green Street. But when they wished to visit, it could be a difficult journey. Tony recalled that on one occasion George had to take a twenty-minute detour by taxi to evade the girls keeping a constant vigil outside: 'It cost him two pounds to cross the road!' Tony and his wife often threw parties for their friends in the music business. At one get-together, Ringo and Cilla Black led the dancing to the Top Ten American single by Shirley Ellis – 'The Nitty Gritty'. It was The Beatles' favourite disc from their *Juke Box Jury* appearance in December 1963. There was

another memorable time when John, George and Ringo met Phil Spector and his girl-group The Ronettes. After an uncomfortable start, the evening soon livened up. It ended around breakfast time with Spector talking about and playing his hits. Tony observed that 'George, who was *the* record man, particularly dug it!'

The Ronettes were featured in a *Saturday Club* session broadcast on 11 January 1964. A few days before, The Beatles made a recording for the show that was kept in the can for a month. Before its transmission, The Beatles' career shifted up another gear… much to the surprise of many British cynics. Rather ludicrously, when The Dave Clark Five's 'Glad All Over' replaced 'I Want To Hold Your Hand' at number one in the UK, the 'Tottenham Sound' was predicted to hasten The Beatles' demise.

An Emwood cartoon in the *Daily Mail* pictured a group of girls waiting for autographs outside a Dave Clark Five concert. Glowering at a girl walking by, one of them comments, 'She *must* be old, she can remember when the Beatles were top-of-the-pops!' A copy of this cartoon is preserved in a BBC Beatles file attached to a note from the Chief of the Light Programme, Denis Morris, that simply read 'Greater love hath no man than not to take money off his friends

when he is on a certainty.' The recipients were Donald MacLean – by January 1964, the Chief Assistant, Production, Popular Music (Sound) and the Head of Popular Music (Sound), Ken Baynes. But even if Morris was prepared to bet that The Beatles were finished, his colleagues did not think it was all over quite yet. MacLean wrote to Baynes, 'Do you share my suspicion that somebody's jumping the gun by six months, p'r'aps maybe? (And that somebody hasn't yet seen "Billboard" 18 January issue lead story and pages 3, 8, 16, 38 and 61.)' 'Indeed I do!' was the response two days later.

The American music business trade paper *Billboard* published a 'Hot 100'. In the issue of 18 January 1964, The Beatles appeared in its chart for the first time at number 45 with 'I Want To Hold Your Hand'. There were just two other UK acts in the 100: The Caravelles with 'You Don't Have To Be A Baby To Cry' and Cliff Richard with 'It's All In The Game'. In November 1963, Brian Epstein had arranged three TV appearances for The Beatles on the top-rated *Ed Sullivan Show*. By the time they touched down in New York on 7 February, 'I Want To Hold Your Hand' was in its second week at number one. Suddenly, young America had fallen under the spell of The Beatles.

From: Chief of Light Programme   9th January, 1964

Subject: GENEROSITY

To: 1. H.P.M.(S) *Popular*
        2. Ch. Asst. Light Music

"Greater love hath no man than not to take money off his friends
when he is on a certainty."

Denis Morris.

JD

AS/20/P   **Please turn over**

From: Chief Assistant, Production, Popular Music (Sound)

Subject: BEATLES   15th January 1964

To: H.P.M.(S)   Copy to: Ch.L.P.

Do you share my suspicion that somebody's jumping the gun by six months,
praps maybe?   (And that somebody hasn't yet seen "Billboard" 18th January
issue lead story and pages 3, 8, 16, 38 and 61.)

                                        (Donald MacLean)

JPM

Donald.
Indeed I do!
            KK 17/1

AS/20/P   **Please turn over**

ABOVE AND RIGHT **This exchange of memos is a telling reminder of a prevalent attitude to pop music in the era. The show business establishment represented by these executives thought the length of time an artist would remain popular was reliant solely on the fickle taste of young fans.**

Their exultant visit to the US for *The Ed Sullivan Show* was closely monitored by the media at home. The day after their New York arrival, *Saturday Club* broadcast two items on their progress. In the first, just before 11.00am, listeners heard The Beatles talking over the phone to presenter Brian Matthew. The interview was recorded the day before at 6.00pm New York time – barely four hours since their feverish reception by hundreds of teenagers.

PAUL: It was fantastic… we just didn't believe it… when we arrived they were all just hanging all over the airport, and thousands of pressmen, and thousands of New York cops. It was just ridiculous… screaming, belting all over the place. It was marvellous, in fact… And we were just driving along, listening to the DJ show on the radio and as we were going along, it was reporting it… And just as we were getting out of the car, he says, 'Well, we hear they've arrived now!'

Paul said he was hoping to meet The Ronettes, who the others had partied with in London, and that a DJ (Murray The K) was hoping to fly in The Miracles to meet them. Then Brian talked to John.

BRIAN: Have you seen any TV yet, John?

JOHN: Yeah, we've just been watching it for the last hour or two… 'cause they've got so many programmes, so we're on all the news. Yeah, it's ridiculous.

BRIAN: What are your first impressions of arrival in America?

JOHN: They're wild!

BRIAN: Wilder than they are here in England?

JOHN: Well, it seems like it. Maybe it's just the first impression. They just seem all out of their minds!

BRIAN: John, is there anything you want to say to the fans back here at home, first?

JOHN: Yeah, well, tell 'em not to forget. We're only away for ten days and we'll be back and we're thinking of them. We're coming back to do the film for seven weeks anyway.

OPPOSITE **The Beatles' first appearance on *The Ed Sullivan Show* was broadcast live on Sunday 9 February 1964. Audience anticipation was so great the ratings registered 73 million viewers, making the programme the most-watched television show ever to that point.**

BRIAN: Oh yes, that film. And why haven't I got a part in it, pray?

JOHN: Well, we'll try and get you one pushing a barrow or something!

BRIAN: Thank you very much. Now let's have a word with Ringo, could we?

RINGO: Hello, Bri.

BRIAN: Hello. How are you?

RINGO: Fine.

BRIAN: What was the first thing you did when you got to your hotel, Ringo?

RINGO: Well, we had this big mass press interview with about 100 people there. And then we got out of that and then we had a Cadillac each! Marvellous cars.

BRIAN: Now, what sort of things did they want to know at the press reception?

RINGO: Oh, all things. Are we bald? What do we do with our money? All the usual things.

BRIAN: You proved that you don't wear wigs, I hope.

RINGO: Yeah.

BRIAN: What did you do?

RINGO: We took 'em off! … Here's George now.

BRIAN: How many of your records are in the American Hit Parade at the moment?

GEORGE: We've got six in the 100… 'I Want To Hold Your Hand', 'She Loves You', 'Please Please Me', 'From Me To You', 'My Bonnie'… which is a laugh! … and 'I Saw Her Standing There'. You know in New York, three records – 'Please Please Me', 'She Loves You' and 'I Want To Hold Your Hand' – are all number one.

BRIAN: Well, that's marvellous and we're all very proud of you.

GEORGE: All our best… see you in two weeks' time… and give our regards to Bernie Andrews.

BRIAN: I'll do that.

GEORGE: Tell him to get his hair cut!

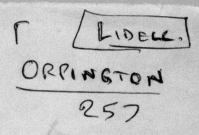

ORPINGTON
257

037ACR G23.08

EW YORK FEBRUARY 6 1964

LT BROADCASTS LONDON W 1

DONALD MACLEAN COPY JIMMY GRANT AEOLIAN HALL HAVE SPOKEN SUMMERVILLE

STOP AS BEATLES UNABLE COME TO STUDIO ONLY POSSIBLE ARRANGEMENT IS

TRANSATLANTIC TELEPHONE CONVERSATION STOP CAN MATTHEW TELEPHONE

BEATLES AT PLAZA HOTEL 2300 GMT FRIDAY FEBRUARY SEVENTH PLAZA 9-3000

STOP EYE WILL BE THERE AND ARRANGE WITH HOTEL SWITCHBOARD TO ROUTE

CALL TO ROOM ASSIGNED BEATLES PARA MALCOLM DAVIS REGULAR TODAY

CONTRIBUTOR PROVIDING APPROXIMATELY TEN MINUTES BEATLEMANIA FROM AIRPORT

TO HOTEL INCLUDING TEEN INTERVIEWS AND LOCAL DEEJAY BEATLES PROMOTION

GRATEFUL YOU BOOK TRANSATLANTIC CABLE 2400 GMT SEVENTH FOR

FEEDING STOP COULD ALSO RECORD BEATLES SIDE TRANSATLANTIC CONVERSATION

PROFEEDING SAME CIRCUIT ENABLING YOU MARRY WITH MATTHEWS LOCALLY

RECORDED

          LANG

CORRECTION SEVENTH LINE BEATLEMANIA

ABOVE A message giving details of a link-up with The Beatles in New York for a conversation with Brian Matthew to be broadcast on *Saturday Club* on 8 February 1964. In the top right corner is written 'Lidell' – this is a reference to the distinguished BBC announcer and newsreader Alvar Lidell. OPPOSITE Brian Epstein relaxing with The Beatles at the Plaza Hotel, New York on 7 February 1964.

EXTRACTS FROM THIS interview were also included in a report compiled by BBC New York correspondent Malcolm Davis. He began with the words: 'Well, they have arrived and such a reception has never been given a Head of State – at least, one that would compare with the welcome The Beatles received when they flew into New York. Friday morning I went out to Kennedy International Airport for an experience that I'm sure will never be duplicated.' Broadcast in the last ten minutes of *Saturday Club*, the feature also included fans screaming at the airport and chanting outside the Plaza Hotel. In an interview with Murray the K, the WINS DJ said he was confident that The Beatles had already made an 'initial impact' bigger than Elvis Presley.

The next week, listeners to *Saturday Club* heard The Beatles' music session recorded in January. There were two unreleased songs. John sang Chuck Berry's 'Johnny B. Goode' and Paul introduced 'The Hippy Hippy Shake' as 'one that we used to do a long time ago at the Cavern and I think it's one that most people know by now.' At the time of the broadcast it was a top three hit by fellow Cavern dwellers The Swinging Blue Jeans. The *Saturday Club* take of 'I Wanna Be Your Man' was given an excellent Bo Diddley feel that distinguished it from the version on *With The Beatles*. The group knew that when their session was broadcast on 15 February, they would be in Miami Beach, Florida to rehearse for a second live appearance the next day on *The Ed Sullivan Show*. 'It's amazing that you can hear us, seeing as we're in America now,' said John. They discussed their forthcoming film.

PAUL: We won't be acting 'cause we'll just be ourselves… we hope… None of us can act, that's the thing.

RINGO: John can act the goat!

ALL: [Laughter]

JOHN: Ringo! If I wasn't in America I'd punch you.

LEFT The Beatles played two shows at Carnegie Hall in New York City on 12 February 1964.

OPPOSITE BBC TV filmed the group's return from the US on 22 February 1964. The Beatles had taken the opportunity, of course, to buy American records. Paul holds an LP by Major Lance and Ringo has under his arm *Golden Goodies Of 1963 – Vol. 18: The Original Hit Million Sellers* issued by Roulette Records.

THE NEXT EDITION of *Saturday Club* – 22 February 1964 – was broadcast on the day The Beatles returned from America. The programme featured a telephone interview with the group, while they were at London Airport. Paul described the reception from their British fans as the 'best ever'. John agreed: 'It's the biggest thing I've ever seen in my life, it's marvellous… I'm deaf with all the noise!' Brian Matthew joked that Bernie Andrews had wanted him to go to the airport, which prompted John to ask after the producer. He was told that Bernie had, as instructed, had a haircut. 'Oh dear, well, he's out of the club, then,' John joked.

LEFT The conquering heroes talked to the press at London Airport on 22 February 1964. Another American purchase is visible next to Ringo: the LP *Recorded Live On Stage* by Marvin Gaye, released on Tamla.

OPPOSITE Stills from the coverage broadcast on *Grandstand* of The Beatles' arrival in the UK.

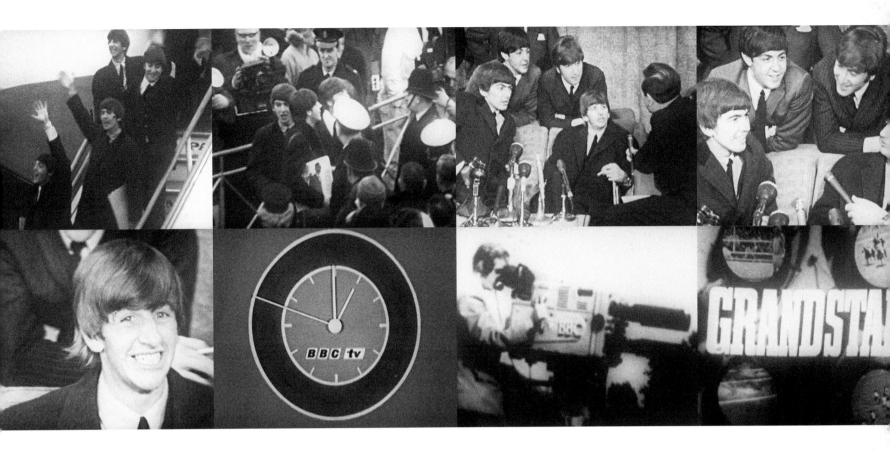

Ringo and George described their meeting in Miami with Cassius Clay (later known as Muhammad Ali), who was challenging Sonny Liston for the World Heavyweight Boxing Title on 25 February. 'You didn't fancy sparring a couple of rounds with him then?' Brian asked. 'Well, I didn't want to hurt him!' Ringo replied. The day of the fight was George's 21st birthday. To help celebrate his imminent coming of age, his mother sent a record request to *Saturday Club*. No surprise that it was a disc by his beloved Miracles that was chosen – the very appropriate 'Shop Around', which opens with Smokey Robinson singing 'When I became of age, my mother called me to her side…'

The Beatles' return from the USA was also covered on BBC TV. Each Saturday, *Grandstand* promised 'Today's sport as it happens'. On 22 February, the BBC's top sports commentator, David Coleman, was seen at the start of the show in a location with no sporting connection. 'Well, although your clock at home may show a few seconds after one o'clock, *Grandstand*, in fact, begins some six hours earlier, because as I talk to you now, the time is just after seven o'clock and I'm speaking from the observation platform at London Airport, perhaps the most sought-after grandstand in Britain today.' Reporter Polly Elwes interviewed fans who had been waiting through the early hours in temperatures below freezing. She spotted a solitary young boy amongst the girls and asked him why he had come to the airport. 'I'm just trying to get on television' was his admirably honest reply. He did offer the insight that 'most of the other groups copy their sound.' The Beatles were filmed making their way down the steps from a Pan-Am airliner. Tucked under their arms are bundles of the precious LPs they had purchased in

America. Paul is holding a copy of *Um Um Um Um Um Um/The Best Of Major Lance*. The title track was in the American Top Ten during their visit to the States. Once inside the terminal building, they were interviewed by David Coleman.

DAVID: Welcome back, boys. How does this reception here compare with America?

RINGO: Oh, it was great! It was every bit as good.

JOHN: It was better.

PAUL: Better.

RINGO: OK, it was better.

DAVID: I must say even you boys looked surprised as you came down the aircraft steps.

PAUL: Yeah.

JOHN: Well, wouldn't you be?

GEORGE: It's so early in the morning.

JOHN: Yeah, we only just got up.

RINGO: We haven't got up, we haven't been to bed yet. Don't forget, it's four o'clock in the States now.

DAVID: What do you think about America? Is it very different from your point of view?

RINGO: It's bigger.

DAVID: Did you get lost then, George?

RINGO: I'll pass you on to George now.

GEORGE: No, I didn't get lost, George.

PAUL: Nobody let him out, you know. He was in the hotel the whole time.

GEORGE: Yeah, as soon as we got there they strapped me up in bed. Injections, the lot, yeah. [laughter]

PAUL: But it's a marvellous place. We loved it.

LEFT The Beatles' first concert in America took place at the Washington Coliseum on 11 February 1964. George described the location as 'a big stadium with the audience all around and the acoustics were terrible'.

DAVID: Is it very different for performance over there than performing here?

GEORGE: Yeah.

DAVID: In what way?

GEORGE: You don't play theatres over there, you know. The places we played – Carnegie Hall and this place in Washington.

RINGO: A big stadium.

GEORGE: Yeah, a big stadium with the audience all around and the acoustics were terrible.

JOHN: So we sparred up, you know, before we left…

RINGO: Yeah, it was good.

GEORGE: But it was good for, you know… It was quite a novelty, wasn't it, John?

JOHN: Yeah it was that. Pass you on to Paul. [laughter]

PAUL: It was, too. Yes.

DAVID: Now, Ringo, I hear you were manhandled at the Embassy Ball. Is this right?

RINGO: Not really. Someone just cut a bit of my hair, you see.

DAVID: Let's have a look. You seem to have got plenty left.

RINGO: [turning his head] Can you see the difference? It's longer, this side.

DAVID: What happened exactly?

RINGO: I don't know. I was just talking, having an interview… just like I am now!

[John and Paul lift locks of his hair, pretending to cut it]

RINGO: I was talking away and then [mimes scissors snipping] there it goes. I looked round, and there was about 400 people just smiling. So, you know, what can you say? We had that in the other programme.

JOHN: What can you say?

RINGO: Tomorrow never knows.

JOHN: [laughs]

DAVID: George, how do you like being described as the Prime Minister's secret weapon?

GEORGE: It's great, yeah. The thing is, I didn't get the bit where they said, 'Earning all these dollars for Britain', like, are we sharing it out or something? [laughter]

DAVID: But we're told that you've come back from America millionaires.

PAUL: Nah, you're kidding.

RINGO: I'll buy you a drink.

JOHN: Next time.

DAVID: Now what about Miami? I mean, you were in the millionaires' playground.

RINGO: Oh, that was marvellous – Miami.

DAVID: You lived well, did you?

RINGO: Well, we lived.

PAUL: Yeah. Well, we borrowed these houses, you see. These people rang up and said, 'Do you want our house, lad?' So we said, [in a Northern accent] 'By gum, we do!' [laughter] And we went across there, and we all water-skied, and fishing.

[Paul indicated with his hands that he had caught a large fish. John countered this claim by signing a tiny fish]

RINGO: He caught a monster. All horns on its back and big teeth.

DAVID: How did it compare with New Brighton?

PAUL: [laughs] With New Brighton? It wasn't as sunny, of course, as New Brighton.

RINGO: Of course, we missed the docks.

JOHN: And the people didn't have as much money.

GEORGE: And there was more oil on the sand in Miami.

DAVID: Of course, Paul's got a grandfather since he's been away, hasn't he? Steptoe.

RINGO: Pardon, what's this?

JOHN: Oh, is it out?

PAUL: We didn't know the news was out.

RINGO: What's this?

JOHN: The film.

GEORGE: Great, the film.

JOHN: [to Ringo] We'll tell you about it tomorrow.

RINGO: You never tell me anything.

JOHN: [to Ringo] OK, Harpo?

DAVID: Now, of course, you're going out on a sporting programme this afternoon in *Grandstand*. We'd like to hear what you thought about Mister Clay.

JOHN: Very tall.

RINGO: Oh, he's a big lad.

PAUL: He's a great laugh, more than anything. He's a big lad.

GEORGE: He's gonna get Sonny Liston in three [rounds].

JOHN: He said.

RINGO: So he said.

PAUL: That's what he said. I don't think he will, though.

DAVID: I hear you were creeping up to Harry Carpenter in the training camp, Paul, and whispering things to him.

PAUL: Yeah. Well you see, the only thing was – he asked me who was going to win and I would have told him out that I thought Liston was gonna win.

JOHN: But you're a coward.

PAUL: [laughs] I'm a coward. And it was in Clay's camp, you see, and there was all these big fellas sitting around. 'Liston' – I had to whisper, you know.

JOHN: [singing; Paul joins in] 'Liston, do you want to know a secret?' [laughter]

RINGO: Plugging, you know. We're still trying to sell!

DAVID: How did Clay compare with you?

RINGO: He's bigger than all of us put together.

DAVID: We're told that he was acting though in a way that even The Beatles couldn't match.

PAUL: Yeah. He was, actually.

RINGO: He was good.

JOHN: He was saying, 'I's beautiful, and you's beautiful, too!' [laughter]

PAUL: He was lifting Ringo up.

RINGO: We thought it was funny, actually.

PAUL: Yeah, he's a showman.

RINGO: Oh, definitely.

DAVID: And what price Liverpool for the Cup?

JOHN: Oh, they've definitely got it. They'll be in the Semis.

RINGO: What?

JOHN: Didn't you hear?

RINGO: I've been away, you see. I've been in America.

DAVID: They really don't tell you anything.

RINGO: They don't. They keep me in the dark.

GEORGE: I haven't heard about that. What are they doing?

PAUL: They're winning.

GEORGE: Hooray!

RINGO: Good old Liverpool.

DAVID: Four boys can't be brought up on Merseyside without being either…

RINGO: I've been to one match in my life.

DAVID: Are you Liverpool supporters?

OPPOSITE **The Beatles are knocked out by Cassius Clay (later known as Muhammad Ali) at the 5th Street Gym in Miami, Florida. 'He's a great laugh, more than anything,' Paul told David Coleman.**

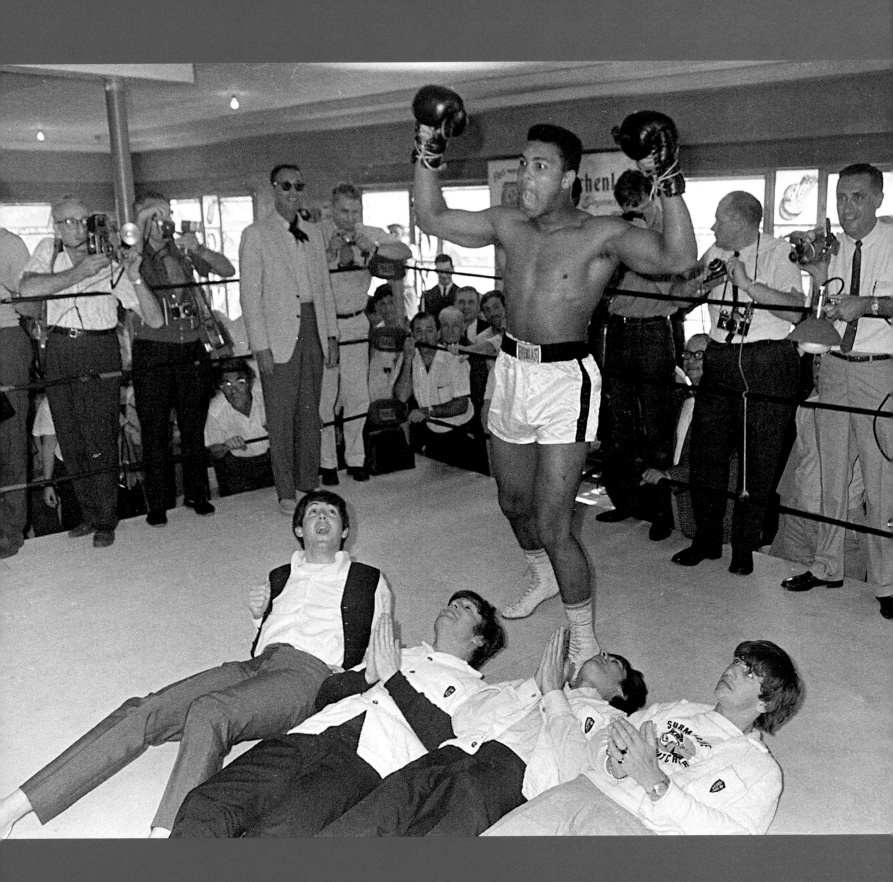

PAUL: We support whoever's winning at the time.

RINGO: Good old Arsenal!

PAUL: That's him finished.

DAVID: Well, now that you're back, you're out of the Top Ten for the first time for a long time.

JOHN: [making an exaggerated comical choking sound]

DAVID: What about it?

PAUL: Er, I don't know.

JOHN: What do you suggest?

DAVID: Have you got anything on the way?

JOHN: We could go straight, couldn't we?

PAUL: [pointing to John] He's going into Old Vic.

JOHN: Acting.

GEORGE: I'm going to try tap-dancing.

PAUL: And Ringo's doing comedy on the high-wire.

DAVID: But have you got anything on the way, apart from the film?

PAUL: We're doing recording next week.

JOHN: [to Paul] Shhh!

RINGO: Don't tell 'em.

PAUL: We're not! It's a lie. Sorry. [whispering] We're recording next week.

DAVID: We daren't ask you where.

PAUL: No.

RINGO: We couldn't tell you.

JOHN: Oh, no. Decca! [laughter]

DAVID: What about your impression of American adults? I mean, we hear your impression of teenagers and so on. I saw you, Ringo, quoted as saying something about this.

OPPOSITE **Shaking hands with the host of** *The Ed Sullivan Show* **on 9 February 1964, CBS Television Studio 50, Broadway, New York City.**

RINGO: What did I say?

DAVID: You tell me.

RINGO: I don't know. You know, I'm quoted so much it's ridiculous. [laughter] What did I say?

DAVID: You tell him what he said, Paul.

PAUL: I can't even remember. About adults?

RINGO: They're older than I am!

PAUL: No really, he's always quipping. [laughter]

DAVID: You said the adults were a bigger problem than the teenagers.

RINGO: Oh, yeah. Well, you know, they've sort of gone potty.

PAUL: Yeah, they were.

RINGO: I mean, the teenagers will ask for the autograph, and take it, and leave it at that. But the adults want to know where you've been, and what you're doing and everything.

PAUL: Yeah. Cut your hair, too.

RINGO: Yeah. Well, I don't know if it was an adult, but somebody did.

DAVID: Did you manage to get much time away from all this, and really get away by yourselves?

JOHN: We got three days at the end, after the *Ed Sullivan* in Miami, you know, we stayed on. Was it three days?

PAUL: Yeah.

RINGO: It was something like that.

JOHN: Three days, you know… nearly three.

DAVID: Anyway, nice to see you back, boys. Thanks very much for sparing the time to talk to us.

PAUL: Thank you.

RINGO: Good to see you. Keep kicking.

JOHN: [to Ringo] 'Keep kicking'?

ALL: Goodbye. Goodbye.

THE REFERENCE MADE to George not being allowed out of the hotel was because he was unwell at the beginning of their stay in New York. In fact, to ensure his recovery, he had to miss a rehearsal for *The Ed Sullivan Show* on the morning of the first live broadcast. The 'place in Washington' was the Coliseum. The Beatles were surrounded on all sides by an audience of 8,000. Every so often the drum set was swivelled round so the group could face another section of the arena in Washington, DC. Ringo's loss of some locks of hair at a British Embassy function in the city was a much talked about story. New Brighton is a seaside town near to Liverpool. It had once been an elegant resort, but by the early 1960s it had seen better times. The Beatles played several concerts at the Tower Ballroom in New Brighton, including a memorable one in 1962 when Little Richard topped the bill. Actor Wilfrid Brambell played the part of Paul's grandfather in *A Hard Day's Night*. He was famous in the UK for his role as the cantankerous rag-and-bone man Albert Steptoe in the BBC TV comedy *Steptoe and Son*. Naturally, David Coleman was interested in the group's impressions of Cassius Clay, whose fight with Sonny Liston was eagerly awaited. The BBC's boxing commentator, Humphrey Carpenter, met The Beatles when they visited Clay. Against the odds, Clay won the Heavyweight Title in six rounds. Liverpool football club did not win the FA Cup in 1964. The team was eliminated by Swansea in the quarter-finals. When Ringo is teased, John calls him Harpo – the name of one of the Marx Brothers. The quick-witted responses of The Beatles in their interviews had drawn comparisons between the group and the wisecracking film comedians. Ringo responds to John's rhetorical question 'What can you say?' with the phrase 'Tomorrow never knows'. It was used two years later as a song title.

The day after their return to Britain, The Beatles took part in the commercial TV show *Big Night Out*. During the following week they worked in recording studios – EMI's in Abbey Road and, on Friday 28 February, the BBC's Piccadilly Studios.

The BBC session was for a second 'bank holiday' *From Us To You* special made for Easter Monday – 30 March 1964. The Australian DJ Alan 'Fluff' Freeman presented the show, taking over from another broadcaster from 'down under' Rolf Harris. Fluff had planned a short visit to the UK in 1957. Having quickly become one of the country's best-loved DJs, he stayed for ever. From 1962, he

had been presenting the BBC's Sunday chart show *Pick of the Pops*. His catchphrases 'Greetings, pop pickers' and 'All right? Right. Stay bright!' were impeccably delivered over the signature tune 'At The Sign Of The Swingin' Cymbal'. In this era, it was the most exciting record show on the air in the UK.

Alan Freeman linked together performances from The Beatles and their guests – Mr Acker Bilk, The Swinging Blue Jeans and singers Marion Williams and Vince Hill backed by The Kenny Salmon Seven. Fluff had first worked with The Beatles in September 1963 in the *Great Pop Prom* held at the Royal Albert Hall. For the radio show, he brought each of them to the microphone for a chat. 'There wasn't anything terribly intellectual about it. I used to say the most inane things and they were terribly intelligent, so when I uttered inanities, they would match me with them.' These verbal vignettes are quite different in character from the banter that went on with Brian Matthew.

ALAN: George, is it true that you're a connoisseur of the classics?

GEORGE: No, it's just a rumour.

ALAN: It's just a rumour. Do you enjoy singing Beethoven?

GEORGE: No. Been singing it for 28 years now.

ALAN: For how long?

GEORGE: Twenty-eight years.

ALAN: That's incredible. Could you manage one more performance?

GEORGE: Um, possibly.

ALAN: Oh, go on, say yes.

GEORGE: Yes. [Clap] Thank you!

'ROLL OVER BEETHOVEN' followed, of course. Before singing 'Till There Was You', Paul mentioned some of his musical influences. John was heard in the background, anxious to promote his book published in March – *In His Own Write*.

ALAN: Do you have any particular idol that you've copied your singing style from?

JOHN: What about my book, then?

ALAN: John, go away.

PAUL: Used to be sort of influenced by Elvis in the old days, I think.

ALAN: Really?

PAUL: Yeah, used to love him.

JOHN: [Shouting in the distance] What about my book, then?

PAUL: Chuck Berry, Carl Perkins and Marvin Gaye and things. Can't really sing like 'em, but I like 'em, though. Love 'em.

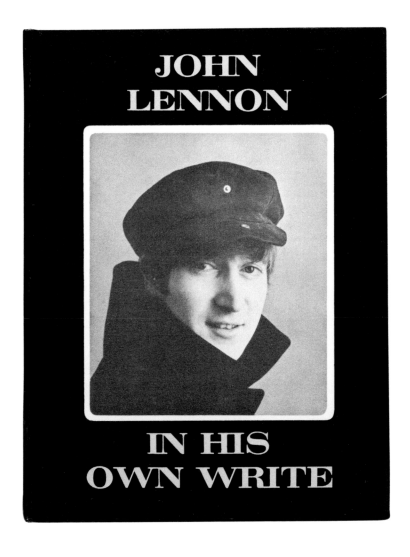

THAT WAS THE most revealing information the listener gained in *From Us To You*. However, the tongue-in-cheek exchanges with Alan Freeman amusingly portrayed the group's different personalities. For example, Ringo was cast as the isolated drummer, adrift from the main action, in this introduction to 'I Wanna Be Your Man':

ALAN: Ringo.

RINGO: Yep.

ALAN: Do you ever feel lonely at the back there playing the drums?

RINGO: Yep.

ALAN: Do you ever feel that you'd like to sing?

RINGO: Yep.

ALAN: Do you ever say anything else but 'Yep'?

RINGO: Nope.

ALAN: Would you like to be someone's loving man?

RINGO: Yep.

ALAN: Now?

RINGO: Yep.

ALAN: I thought you'd say that.

RINGO: Yep.

THERE WAS A brief discussion about their film and, of course, John's book was mentioned.

ALAN: Alongside all your singing commitments, I'm told that you're budding into a real blooming Somerset Maugham. Is that right?

JOHN: No.

ALAN: Why not?

JOHN: Hah! Well, I'm not blooming.

LEFT John's original unused title for his first book was 'In His Own Write And Draw'.

AT THIS POINT Paul broke in with a retaliatory 'What about my song, then?' George and Ringo asked 'What about us?' which prompted John to sing the title of The Coasters' record of that name. In just two and a half hours, the group recorded the opening and closing 'From Us To You' themes and eight songs that were all available on their records. Studio manager John Andrews remembered George had brought back from the States a metal cigarette packet holder. After learning the BBC's 4038 microphones were magnetic, he attempted to throw it at some audience mics hanging from the ceiling. 'I was torn between thinking, "I must let him do what he wants, this is George Harrison and I'm a lowly gofer" and "My God, if he gets that stuck on there, how the hell are we going to get it down?" Luckily, his aim wasn't very good.' Although details of the session had been kept secret, The Beatles' presence in Piccadilly was discovered. Consequently, a mob of girls chased The Beatles' car when it left the BBC studio. Alan Freeman recalled that when it screeched into a side street, 'the door flung open, hit a lamp post and came off its hinges. I thought to myself, "How do they live like this all the time?"'

A BBC Audience Research report on *From Us To You* estimated listening figures of 24.1 per cent of the population for the first hour and 22.1 per cent for the second. The 'Appreciation Index' score was 49; when calculated from the responses of 'fans', the AI was 71. However, two-thirds of the sampled audience did not describe themselves as 'pop music fans'. They had the wireless on 'mainly for the children', preferring the contributions of Acker Bilk and Vince Hill – 'an under-rated artist, who should be heard more often'. A security guard found The Beatles 'vastly over-rated; their performance was decidedly amateur, and their entertainment value nil'. There was no pleasing some people. But a solicitor, who described himself as 'definitely over-twenty', wondered, 'How can anyone fail to like them? Their music is so gay and uninhibited, and they themselves are full of *joie-de-vivre*.' Alan Freeman – and Brian Matthew – were also 'definitely over-twenty' when they worked with The Beatles. They were in their mid-thirties in 1964. 'Their music and persona freed me from middle age,' Fluff remembered. 'Because the things that were coming from The Beatles made me feel like a 10-year-old! They made us all feel tremendously happy.'

The week before *From Us To You* was broadcast on Easter

'Their music and persona freed me from middle age. They made us all feel tremendously happy.'

ALAN FREEMAN (DJ)

Monday, The Beatles were featured in the last programme of the series *The Public Ear*. John's book and movie-making were again the main talking points. Their friendship with one of the programme's contributors, Tony Hall, had allowed the show to gain enviable access to the group. Ringo described how they were coping with the demands of making a film. 'We all enjoy it. The only drag is getting up in the morning. That's the part we hate. We get up between half-six and seven, which is very early, because usually our lives are back-to-front to the ordinary person's. 'Cause we get up about four and go to six in the morning. After we've played, that's the only time we can go out. But at the moment, we're always in bed by twelve… it's like being back at school!'

Assuming the role of a BBC interviewer, George sought Ringo's opinion of *In His Own Write* and then persuaded John to read 'Alec Speaking' from his book. 'Some of you might have found it a bit difficult to understand,' said George. 'Because it's in a sort of funny lingo. Well, we get it, you see… I don't really know how you'd describe it, but it's sort of rubbish!' George also interviewed Paul during a car journey on 19 March 1964. They were travelling to the Dorchester Hotel in Park Lane, where they were to receive a Variety Club Award for 'Show Business Personalities Of 1963'. George was curious about the challenges faced when making a film.

OPPOSITE **The Beatles at the Dorchester Hotel, London to accept their awards for 'Show Business Personalities of 1963' on 19 March 1964. The clapperboard indicates the time of the TV broadcast of the Variety Club Awards ceremony.**

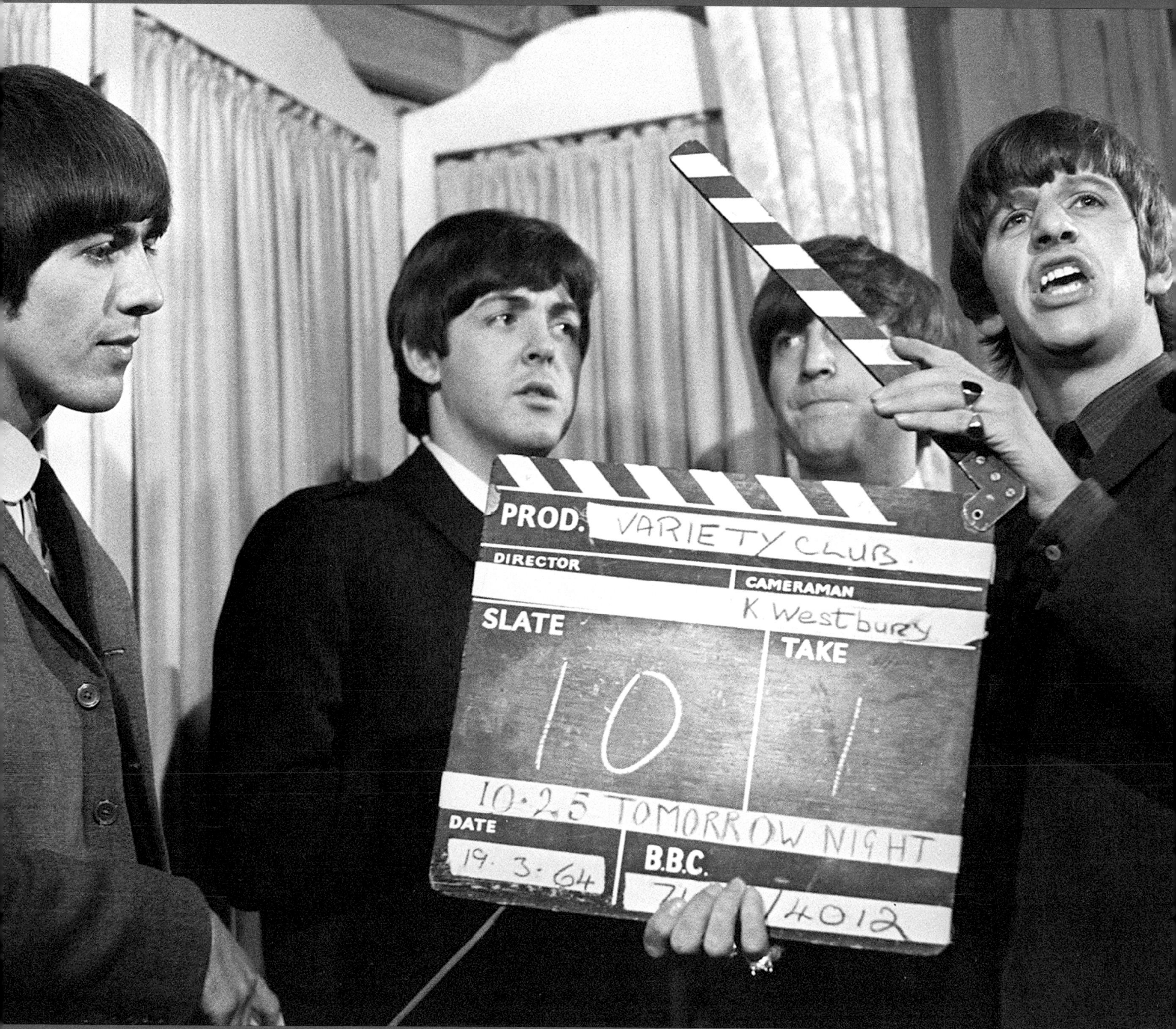
PROD.
VARIETY CLUB.
DIRECTOR
CAMERAMAN
K Westbury
SLATE
TAKE
10
1
10-2-5 TOMORROW NIGHT
DATE
19. 3. 64
B.B.C.

'Well, thank you Paul and you'll receive your three shilling fee at a later date!'

GEORGE HARRISON

GEORGE: Are you having any difficulty learning your lines or anything like that?

PAUL: Well, George, I'm a bit lazy about that. I normally learn them about ten minutes before we do the scene, actually. I feel it gives an air of 'impromptutuity'!

GEORGE: I see. How's the director of the film?

PAUL: Well, yes, Dick Lester's directing the film… what's your name? George?

GEORGE: Er, George, yeah… BBC… I'm from the BBC, *Public Ear*.

PAUL: Oh yes, it is a bit.

GEORGE: You can see it's sticking out.

PAUL: Anyway, his name's Dick Lester… and he's one of the nicest fellas I've ever met. He's a great director and I think he's gonna save the film in the cutting rooms.

GEORGE: What exactly do you mean by that, Paul?

PAUL: Well, you see George, the acting may not be very good, but if he can cut it up and slice it around and slot bits in here and slot bits in there, he may make it into a good film, y'see.

GEORGE: I see. Well, thank you Paul and you'll receive your three shilling fee at a later date!

LEFT Filming a scene from *A Hard Day's Night* with actors Edward Malin and John Junkin at Twickenham Film Studios, 12 March 1964.

From: Head of Light Entertainment Group, Television   17th March, 1964.

Subject: THE BEATLES

To: A.H.L.E.G.Tel.   Copy to: Mr.J.Stewart, Mr.L.Michell

Confirming the arrangements I entered into today.

On Thursday, in the Television Theatre - in front of a plain cyc and no
audiance - we will tape the Beatles miming to each side of their new
record. We pay £500 which means we use each side once for £250. We also
have the right to repeat each recording once for a further payment of £250.

For your information, Epstein tells me that he is being paid £1000 for
them to mime to one side of their record in "Ready Steady Go".

I think it is important that this recording is kept very quiet and that
we exercise the utmost discipline in the Theatre on this occasion.   I
do not want any possible repetition of the Liverpool business and I think
the BBC is very much on trial here.

I am sure you will want to be present on this occasion and since I asked
Epstein when we were likely to do another concert with the Beatles and
he replied rather enigmatically "I hope in the not too distant future" I
think it would be an idea for you to have a chat with him.

Would Johny Stewart please note that Epstein is also anxious to tape the
latest Jerry & the Pacemakers record for "Top of the Pops" before they
leave for Australia on March 31st.

                              Dictated by Mr. Sloan and
                              despatched in his absence by:

ABOVE A memo from Tom Sloan, Head of Light Entertainment Group, Television, regarding a filmed performance of 'Can't Buy Me Love' and 'You Can't Do That' for *Top of the Pops*. The problems encountered when filming *It's The Beatles* in December 1963 are referred to as 'the Liverpool business'. Brian Epstein was keen to have the BBC film a performance of 'Don't Let The Sun Catch You Crying' by one of his other artists Gerry and The Pacemakers.

OPPOSITE Recording a session on 14 July 1964 for the first edition of *Top Gear* in Studio S2 in the sub-basement of Broadcasting House, London.

GEORGE'S JOKE about the parsimonious BBC did ring true. ITV had begun a weekly pop show called *Ready Steady Go!* in August 1963. When BBC TV launched its competitor, *Top of the Pops*, on 1 January 1964, artists received less than the fees paid by commercial television companies. Brian Epstein pointed out to the BBC that

The Beatles received £1,000 for a performance on *Ready Steady Go!* This was double the amount received for their first appearance on *Top of the Pops* in March 1964. Although the BBC programme was based in Manchester, the group's schedule was too tightly packed for them to leave London. The Beatles were filmed miming to 'Can't

Buy Me Love' and 'You Can't Do That' on the same day George interviewed Paul on their way to lunch at the Dorchester Hotel.

The Beatles' schedule was unrelenting. Following a day spent filming a concert for their movie at the Scala Theatre, the group recorded seven songs in an evening session broadcast on 4 April 1964 in *Saturday Club*. As usual, The Beatles clowned around with Brian Matthew, read out listeners' requests and described the forthcoming film. In the 11 April edition of *Melody Maker*, Ray Coleman described the relaxed atmosphere of the BBC session:

'Only about ten people are in the big theatre, with compere Brian Matthew and producer Bernie Andrews giving the world's most popular artists plenty of freedom. And the Beatles accept it. They cavort about the stage, and take their time. They mutter, smoke, eat, drink and smoke. Producer Bernie Andrews comes down from the control box to confer with the Beatles about their programme. "Don't forget, next time we're down I'm going to do some of that Bob Dylan stuff," says Lennon. "You know, 'Blowing In The Wind' and that." Andrews nods. John plays the introduction to "Needles And Pins", although it is not in their radio schedule. "Ere, it's the gear, that, eh?" he remarks to Paul. "Great song. We ought to do it." "It's so long since we played a proper date, like this, honest," says George. "Shurrup," says John. "You're on the radio now." The red light appears. Another couple of songs are recorded.'

'Needles And Pins' by The Searchers, after three weeks at number one, was still in the Top 30 when John picked out the distinctive guitar riff in the Playhouse Theatre. George's comment confirms

how a BBC session was, at this point, still a refreshing experience for the group. Another bank holiday was coming soon, so on 1 May The Beatles shoehorned another BBC session into their tight schedule. Just the day before, they had played two shows at the Glasgow Odeon and taken part in two Scottish television programmes. During an evening session at the BBC Paris Theatre in central London, they recorded eight tracks, chatted to Alan Freeman and celebrated the holiday with their 'Happy Birthday' adaptation – 'Whit Monday To You'. The other recorded artists were Manfred Mann, Joe Brown and His Bruvvers, and singers Mark Wynter and Lulu with accompaniment from vocal group The Breakaways and The Kenny Salmon Seven.

Only Fluff could make a song title seem so naughty when he announced, 'That's right, it's The Beatles with the caution… Honey? … Don't!' When he encouraged Paul to give the writer of a request 'a nice juicy kiss', he was told, 'I think you're disgusting… You are, you know!' In a skit with George, in which Fluff feigned confusion over the title 'I Forgot To Remember To Forget', their exchange ended on what seemed like a sour note.

GEORGE: 'I Forgot To Remember To Forget'.

ALAN: You forgot what?

GEORGE: No, 'I Forgot To Remember To Forget'.

ALAN: But what do you have to remember?

GEORGE: No, 'I Forgot To Remember To Forget', you see.

ALAN: What did you forget though that you…

GEORGE: No, you see that's the song, that's what it's called.

ALAN: What's the song?

GEORGE: The song what I'm just gonna sing, any minute now, just watch me.

ALAN: What's it called?

GEORGE: 'I Forgot To Remember To Forget'.

ALAN: This could go on all morning.

GEORGE: It could… if you weren't so thick!

THEY LIKED each other really. George and John both gave long, friendly interviews to Alan Freeman in the mid-1970s. In 1987, Paul recorded a special version of 'Sgt. Pepper's Lonely Hearts Club Band' for Fluff's on-air 60th birthday celebrations: 'It was 60 years ago today…' The Whit Monday *From Us To You* received a higher than usual Appreciation Index figure of 63; the audience was estimated as slightly lower than the previous edition – 16.3 per cent and 14.5 per cent for the two hours. Highlights from the Easter Monday *From Us To You* were pressed on a Sound Archive disc; unfortunately, the other editions were not preserved by the BBC. Only the efforts of home tapers have allowed us to hear The Beatles' performances in these programmes. It was often merely by chance that taped items with The Beatles survived in the BBC's Archive. For example, there is a mysterious undated reel with the group requesting records they would like to be played.

Their selections give intriguing clues to the music inspiring The Beatles around May 1964. George chose two records from the Tamla and Motown labels: The Miracles' 'I've Been Good To You' and the first UK hit for the company, 'My Guy' by Mary Wells. He also introduced The Impressions' big US hit 'It's All Right' and 'a very old' Elvis Presley track, 'My Baby Left Me'. Ringo asked for Cilla Black's 'You're My World', which climbed to number one that month, and 'Pen and Paper' by Jerry Lee Lewis ('we all think Jerry Lee is fab. I like his country and western numbers') and 'I Forgot More Than You'll Ever Know' by Kitty Wells ('don't get her mixed up with Mary Wells'). John requested the Tommy Tucker hit 'Hi-heel Sneakers' and anything by Little Richard: 'He was my favourite when I was about 16, after Elvis. I didn't know which one I liked best… but I like Little Richard best now.' His other selection was 'I'm Gonna Send You Back To Georgia' by Timmy Shaw. 'I like it because the beat's marvellous, the voice is marvellous and it's a good song. And it's great, so play it!' Paul picked 'Hitchhike' and 'Pride and Joy', both featured on the 1963 Marvin Gaye album *That Stubborn Kinda Fellow*.

OPPOSITE AND RIGHT *Top Gear* session, 14 July 1964 – Studio S2, Broadcasting House, London.

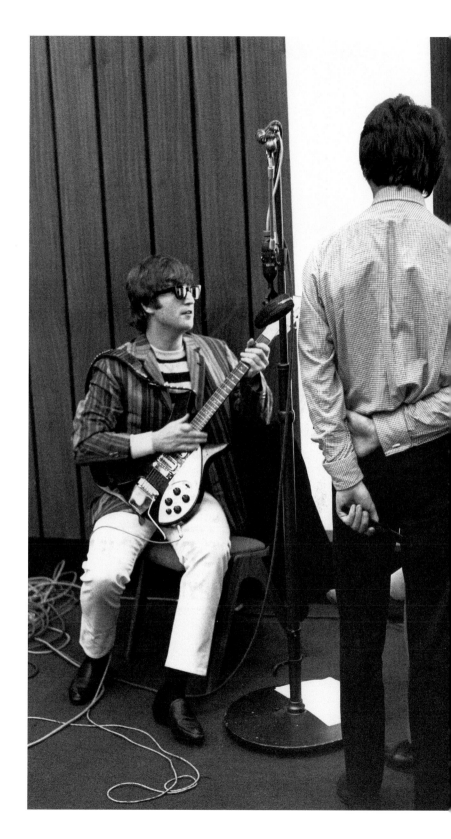

On 18 May, Paul was seen in the BBC TV programme *A Degree of Frost*. A graduate of Cambridge University, David Frost had made his name on television as the presenter of the BBC satirical programme *That Was The Week That Was* – broadcast during 1962 and 1963. Recorded in front of an audience, his new show featured Paul's first solo TV appearance. He had been filming scenes for *A Hard Day's Night* on the day of the recording, 15 April 1964.

DAVID: Paul, it's great to have you here, and one thing, as we've been rehearsing today, that I've been wondering is that whether in fact you ever expected things to be as good for you as, in fact, they've been. When you started as a group, did you expect things to go like this? Did you…?

PAUL: No. We used to sort of think of things in stages… still do, I think. When we first started off, playing in the Cavern and things, I thought first of all, 'Let's get a record contract.' We all did. We got a record contract and we said, 'Let's get a number one hit.' Got one of them…

DAVID: [laughs] So I hear… yeah.

PAUL: … and went on. You know, we do it in stages. So we never thought of it being this big.

DAVID: After you got a number one hit, you hoped for another number one hit, did you? Then what?

PAUL: Um, something like *The Royal Variety Performance*. Some sort of big thing. Then, er, what came after that? America, I think.

DAVID: Yeah, which was marvellous And after America?

PAUL: A film.

DAVID: Now, it's fairly close to the film being as big a success as everything else, I should think. Now if it is, in sort of a bit later this year, a big success, what will be the next ambition then?

PAUL: I don't know. Er, another film, probably.

DAVID: And that's a big success and what about after that?

PAUL: Oh, don't ask me, you know, I'm only doing it! [laughter]

LEFT *Top Gear* session, 14 July 1964 – Studio S2, Broadcasting House, London.

'We can turn round to Brian and say, "Could we do such-and-such a thing... like a film?"'

PAUL McCARTNEY

DAVID: Have you got any ambitions, in fact, in other spheres completely? I mean, do you want to be Prime Minister one day, does that sort of thing...?

PAUL: [shaking his head and laughing] No. I don't want to be... No, nothing like that. God! Retire. You know, that's quite... [laughter]

DAVID: Retire? And when do you think you'll achieve that ambition, in fact?

PAUL: The way things are going, about a couple of years or so. [laughter]

DAVID: When people usually ask you, 'What's the best thing about being one of The Beatles at this stage?' you usually reply 'The money' as the first quip. But what after that is one of the good things?

PAUL: Being able to do things that you enjoy doing. Rather than if... you know, you get a bit of power when you sort of reach a certain stage and then you can suggest things to people that you want to do. I mean, we can turn round to Brian [Epstein] and say, 'Could we do such-and-such a thing... like a film?' And he can say, 'Well, I'll try and fix it, boy.' He does. He's good like that, you know. [laughter]

DAVID: Useful man to have about, actually.

PAUL: Oh, he's great.

DAVID: So the power it gives you basically is the power to do what you want, is it?

PAUL: Yes. So, rather than us sort of being struggling unknowns and trying to do things that we'd never be able to do, we can now do more things that we'd like to. I think that's a sort of a good part of it.

DAVID: And when you write music, which you do a great deal with John Lennon, you write it very much, and marvellously, in the current idiom. Do you feel that later on, when you move into another period, say in five years' time, you'll be writing in the same idiom or different? Will you change with the times?

OPPOSITE Brian Epstein and Paul at EMI Studios, Abbey Road, London – 11 August 1964.

PAUL: Well, I think the point is that the tunes that we write aren't in any iddum, idiom [looking at the audience] Idiot! [laughter] I think it's just the arrangements. Like the arrangements are of today. For instance, 'From Me To You'. It could be done as an old ragtime tune – especially the middle-eight – and so, we're not writing the tunes in any particular idiom. So, in fact, in five years' time, we may arrange the tunes differently, but we'll probably write the same old rubbish! [laughter]

DAVID: How do you judge a good song when you've written it? By what?

PAUL: By us liking it. You know, John and I, if we like it and we think it's a 'good un'. It's a combination of liking it and what is commercial – what we think other people'll like as well.

DAVID: Can it be a good song if you like it and nobody was to buy it? That hasn't happened yet.

PAUL: Well, it always is for us. If we like it. In fact, we don't like bad songs. That's all there is to it, sort of thing.

DAVID: Of course, everybody, I imagine, says to you that the pop world is very short-lived and everything like that and 'What will you do when the phase passes?' Do you think the phase will pass? Does it worry you?

PAUL: No. I couldn't care less, really – I don't think – if we flop tomorrow. It'd be sad, you know. But, I mean, it wouldn't really worry me.

DAVID: Could you go back to doing something else?

PAUL: Oh, I dunno. I'd miss doing this. But I think I'd think of something else to do. Something that I'd like to do.

DAVID: What would you do?

PAUL: Um, write songs for other people.

DAVID: Yeah. Anything completely different?

PAUL: Completely different? Er, retire, you know. [laughter] That will be completely different. Not really, you know.

DAVID: Thank you very much. It will be a great pleasure to watch Paul McCartney in retirement, but it'll probably be in the year about 2010, I should think.

A PHOTOGRAPH OF David Frost and Paul was featured on the front cover of the BBC's listing magazine *Radio Times* alongside a picture of John, George and Ringo to promote *A Degree of Frost* and *The Beatles Say From Us To You*. Both shows were broadcast on 'bank holiday' Monday 18 May 1964. Inside the magazine, a page of pop star photos was headlined 'Pop For A Holiday In The Light Programme'. 'Last week we introduced *Saturday Swings*, a new two-and-three-quarter hour programme of non-stop pop in the afternoon to add to the two hours of *Saturday Club* in the morning. On the swings were up-beat, folk-beat, rhythm and blues, ballads, the whole pop lot.' The proud boast followed that with the 'bank holiday' specials – *From Us To You* and *Pop Luck* (with The Searchers) – and 'regular' shows, 'the whole lot adds up to more than twelve hours in which to sort out the Top Ten, Twenty, Fifty – and to spot a few up-and-comers of your own'. The BBC was trying to respond to the British beat boom and, no doubt, keeping an anxious ear on some new competition that had arrived a few weeks before.

On Easter weekend, March 1964, Radio Caroline began broadcasting from a ship in the North Sea – the first of a flotilla of boats that were soon anchored around the coast of Britain. Transmitting from outside territorial waters, the offshore radio stations operated beyond the reach of the law. They grabbed frequencies without licence, broadcast advertisements and paid no heed to Musicians Union regulations in force on the mainland. Without restrictions on 'needletime' – the amount of time the BBC was allowed to allocate to broadcasting records – the 'pirate' DJs could play as many discs as they liked. In stark contrast to the BBC Light Programme, the offshore stations would soon provide a mix of contemporary records presented by DJ personalities more akin to the informal and irreverent personalities on US radio. The pirates also brought brash jingles to Britain. Listeners heard American vocal groups extolling the virtues of Caroline ('The Sound of the Nation') and Radio London ('Wonderful Big L'). In its early months, Radio Caroline offered almost as much Ray Conniff, Mantovani and stage musical standards as did the Light Programme. Nevertheless, faced with some new competition, BBC executives were now prepared to run with an idea developed by Bernie Andrews for a new late-night pop show called *Top Gear*.

ABOVE **All smiles for the front cover of the 1964 Whitsun edition of** *Radio Times*, **promoting The Beatles' bank holiday radio show,** *From Us To You*, **and Paul's television interview with David Frost.**

The presenter was Brian Matthew, who recalled: 'It was supposed to be a sharper programme, all round, than *Saturday Club* had been. In other words, it didn't mix skiffle, trad-jazz, early rock – it was pretty hard rock right from the word go.' Broadcast on 16 July 1964, the first *Top Gear* included an amazing thirteen records and taped items from sessions with Dusty Springfield, Carl Perkins, Mark Wynter… and The Beatles. Bernie Andrews remembered, 'I wanted to get the pre-recorded sessions at a higher standard … somewhere near matching the record quality. When I started *Top Gear*, I tried very hard to do that.' Certainly by 1964, sessions for *Saturday Club* and other shows had been enhanced by using a primitive method of overdubbing. 'We'd record one complete track including the whole band with one vocal and then we'd play the tape again and, as we were recording onto another mono tape machine, we'd add another vocal.'

With four-track tape machines becoming more commonplace in commercial recording studios, artists came to expect the convenience of separate tape-tracks for instruments and vocals. In a session where there was always a pressure to beat the clock, the BBC's basic method of overdubbing was time-consuming. Bernie explained: 'For purely practical reasons, the mere fact that we had another group coming in at seven o'clock that evening meant we had to get the previous group out by 6.30. The balance engineer would then have to get round to the old *Ship and Shovel*, the pub round the corner, and have a bacon and mushroom sandwich and a quick pint and then get back for the evening session.'

The amount of hours Bernie spent in the studio to record artists began to increase. His BBC bosses found it difficult to understand why. 'The time I spent on that work did give me an awful lot of problems. At the time, I got more support from people like The Beatles and Brian Epstein than I did from those more immediately around me. I was very pleased when they went along with me and helped launch this programme.' At Bernie's flat, spoken 'trailers' for the new show were recorded with Paul, George and Ringo. They reminded listeners of the time and day *Top Gear* was broadcast and which artists were appearing with them on the first edition. During the show, The Beatles were invited to open *Top Gear* for business. Before that, Brian Matthew attempted to discuss Lennon-McCartney's songwriting.

BRIAN: Now all these songs in the film you had to write to a deadline. Did you find this a bit more difficult than the way you usually do them on the back of bus tickets?

JOHN, PAUL & GEORGE: Yeah, yeah.

JOHN: [Surprised] George? George!

PAUL: It was hard because we normally do them as hobbies, sort of things.

BRIAN: Hello, Ringo's just joined us!

RINGO: I thought I'd just come round.

JOHN: Did you have a hard time writing them, Ringo?

RINGO: Well, the first one was about the worst, because I had a lot of trouble with these glasses.

BRIAN: The ones he's wearing, he means, folks.

PAUL: Yes, it was 'arder.

JOHN: We did most of them in Paris and some in New York, didn't you, Ringo?

BRIAN: Right, the serious bit having got over, let's get round to the funny chat and we would like you chaps to launch the good ship *Top Gear*.

RINGO: The good ship what? *Top Gear*?

BRIAN: Bernie's new vessel.

JOHN: Ah, is it? When was the accident?

PAUL: I hereby name this ship *Top Gear*.

BRIAN: Thank you, Duchess. Right, now then, another song from the film…

GEORGE: Pity we had to sink it the first week!

BRIAN: It is a shame.

JOHN: We had a hard time writing them, Brian, anyway.

RINGO: Yeah, Brian.

BRIAN: You did – all of you. Ringo, what about your songwriting? How's that coming on?

ABOVE 'You like this programme, do you?' enquired Brian Matthew. 'Yes, *Top Gear* is our fave-rave-fab programme, as they say in all the comics,' replied John.

RINGO: Oh, yes. I've written a good one, but no one seems to want to record it.

PAUL: Now…

RINGO: Oh, Paul may record it.

PAUL: No.

RINGO: Yes, Paul. You promised.

PAUL: The thing is, I was doing the tune for you to sing it.

RINGO: I don't want to sing it, you sing it.

PAUL: [Sings] Don't pass me by…

RINGO: Rhythm and blues, soul.

PAUL: Don't pass me by, don't make me cry, don't make me blue, baby, 'cause you know why…

RINGO: I got the ice cream for you.

BRIAN: He wrote all those words?

PAUL: Yeah, blues and all that.

BRIAN: He's the Dylan Thomas of Liverpool, isn't he?

IN THEIR INTERVIEWS with Brian Matthew, Ringo was usually cast as 'the one who doesn't talk' or the one who gets picked on in the playground.

BRIAN: Now, look in my young days, when I was a lad, they used to have actors in films.

JOHN: Hey, listen.

PAUL: It's all changed now. No actors.

BRIAN: In those days, the actors used to say their best bits were left on the cutting room floor. Did you find that?

JOHN: No. Oh, no. Those were the good bits in the film. You should have seen the rest.

BRIAN: Yes?

JOHN: Rubbish.

BRIAN: Was it really?

JOHN: Even worse.

BRIAN: Who was worst?

JOHN: Oh, Paul.

PAUL: I think John was about the worst.

JOHN: No, it was you.

PAUL: Oh, Ringo was very good; he's a good lad.

JOHN: He was miming.

BRIAN: They're saying he's a new Charlie Chaplin. Do you think that's right?

JOHN: Oh yes… he's an old one! [Shouts] OK, Ring?

RINGO: [In the distance] All right, John. Can you hear me?

JOHN: Can you hear him?

BRIAN: Not really. I hope not.

JOHN: [Whispering] We've brought you the flowers.

RINGO: Oh, good.

JOHN: And the grapes.

RINGO: Oh, I like grapes!

PAUL: He likes grapes, you know.

JOHN: Brian's nose is peeling, listeners.

BRIAN: Been in the sun.

GEORGE: Been to Portugal.

BRIAN: Guess who's top of the pops in Portugal, then?

ALL: Who?

BRIAN: Os Beatles.

JOHN: Os Beatles? Great, great laugh.

BRIAN: I don't suppose you know the title of your film in Portuguese?

JOHN: Crinsk Dee Night?

BRIAN: Could be. Let's hear the number, shall we?

JOHN: [Obligingly] Right.

LEFT Recording their second and last session for *Top Gear* at the BBC Playhouse Theatre in London on 17 November 1964.

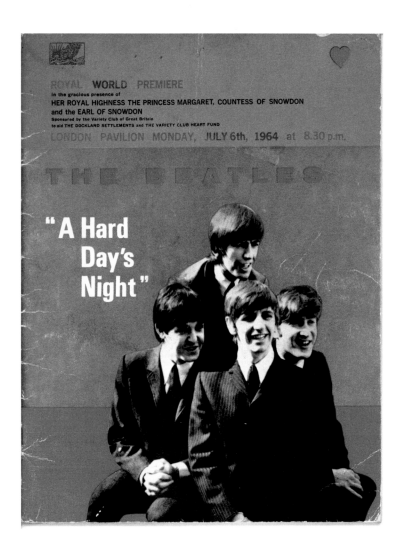

CLIFF RICHARD WAS also interviewed and gave his opinion of *Top Gear*: 'I like it very much indeed, fabulous!' Asked to choose a favourite new release, he picked 'How Glad I Am' by Nancy Wilson. Paul's choice was 'Mockingbird' by Inez and Charlie Foxx – the first release on the UK version of the Sue label. He revealed that the duo had recently shared a couple of drinks with The Beatles in a club. Bernie Andrews had promised in *Radio Times* that *Top Gear* was 'meant to be the sort of thing to make you want to get up and dance'. Paul's selection of this rhythm and blues single was perfect for that. Brian also made a tantalizing reference to having 'a smashing little bit of tape, that the lads don't know anything about, that we recorded at rehearsal with Paul and the other three giving a fabulous impression of The Animals and "The House Of The Rising Sun", but… we daren't play it!' Whatever happened to that recording?

Top Gear followed a half-hour magazine programme called *The Teen Scene*. The edition broadcast the previous week – 9 July 1964 – featured *New Musical Express* writer Chris Hutchins interviewing John about acting in the new movie. 'We're satisfied, but we're not self-satisfied. There's a lot which is embarrassing for us, you know. For instance the first bit, which is a drag as far as we're concerned, because that was the first sort of acting we had done and it looks it. It stands out more than the rest of the film… We know that we're dead conscious in every move we make… we watch each other. I know Paul's embarrassed when I'm watching him speak and he knows I am.'

The two biggest pop music stories of 1964 were The Beatles' unprecedented commercial success in the USA and the release of *A Hard Day's Night*. BBC 1 broadcast a half-hour special about the film on 3 August 1964. Called *Follow The Beatles*, it combined footage of the group during the time they were making the movie with comments on the soundtrack from the director Richard Lester, members of his crew, writer Alun Owen and actor Wilfrid Brambell. Robert Robinson introduced the film. His witty appraisal of the movie was very positive:

TOP **Paul with Richard Lester – 'He's a great director and I think he's gonna save the film in the cutting rooms.'** LEFT **The programme for the world premiere of** *A Hard Day's Night*.

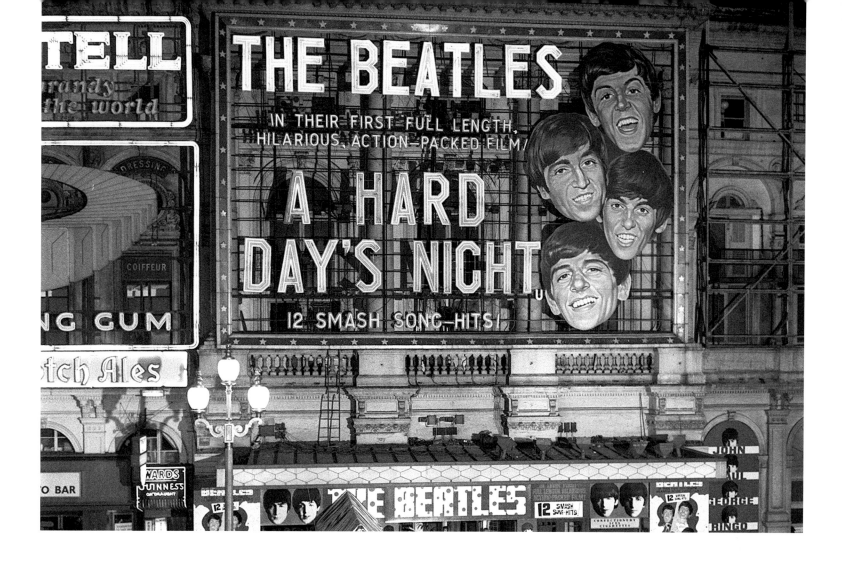

'The Beatles and the film seem to be all of one piece. The film really seems to have grown out of them. It seems to be a genuine account of the sort of people they are and the sort of music they sing. Once upon a time, you didn't expect anything from a film about a pop singer, except to clap eyes on the chap. He was simply exposed like a holy object. And you were supposed to be so jolly thankful just to see him that you didn't worry about the corny plot or illiterate dialogue. Well, the thing I felt about The Beatles' film was that they paid as much attention to the lines, and the camera work, and the acting as they would have done if The Beatles hadn't been in it. It takes place in the real world. It's a kind of documentary approach and it's a thousand miles removed from the old song-and-dance cliché into which you pop the reigning idol like a single currant in a ready-mixed pudding.'

An Audience Research report on *Follow The Beatles* reveals that not all members of the TV show's audience shared Robert Robinson's enthusiasm for *A Hard Day's Night* and The Beatles:

'A sizeable minority declared them to be talentless as musicians and repulsive as persons, and for a small proportion they can do no wrong at all, but the bulk of the sample was composed of those who took a middle line. They were not, mainly, much enamoured of Beatle music, evidently, but think the four young men themselves obviously attractive.'

ABOVE **The world premiere of *A Hard Day's Night* took place at the London Pavilion, Piccadilly Circus on 6 July 1964. Premieres of two other Beatles movies – *Help!* and *Yellow Submarine* – were also held there.**

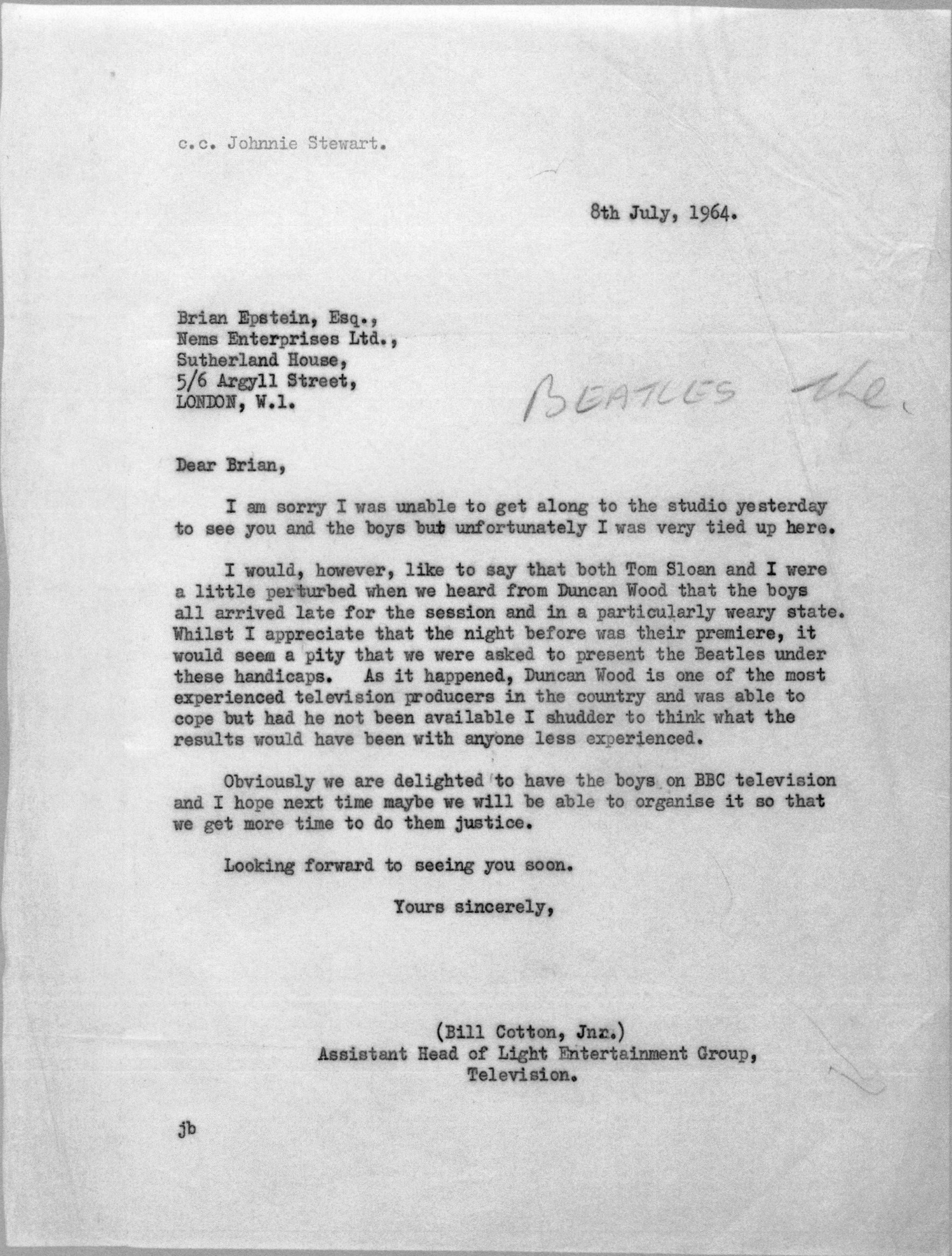

c.c. Johnnie Stewart.

8th July, 1964.

Brian Epstein, Esq.,
Nems Enterprises Ltd.,
Sutherland House,
5/6 Argyll Street,
LONDON, W.1.

BEATLES the.

Dear Brian,

I am sorry I was unable to get along to the studio yesterday
to see you and the boys but unfortunately I was very tied up here.

I would, however, like to say that both Tom Sloan and I were
a little perturbed when we heard from Duncan Wood that the boys
all arrived late for the session and in a particularly weary state.
Whilst I appreciate that the night before was their premiere, it
would seem a pity that we were asked to present the Beatles under
these handicaps. As it happened, Duncan Wood is one of the most
experienced television producers in the country and was able to
cope but had he not been available I shudder to think what the
results would have been with anyone less experienced.

Obviously we are delighted to have the boys on BBC television
and I hope next time maybe we will be able to organise it so that
we get more time to do them justice.

Looking forward to seeing you soon.

Yours sincerely,

(Bill Cotton, Jnr.)
Assistant Head of Light Entertainment Group,
Television.

jb

LEFT There had been a party at the Dorchester Hotel following the premiere of *A Hard Day's Night*. This may have led to the late arrival of 'the boys' in 'a particularly weary state' for a *Top of the Pops* recording the following afternoon. They mimed to both sides of their current single 'A Hard Day's Night' / 'Things We Said Today' and the title track of their EP *Long Tall Sally*.

The film was an enormous success. It also proved to be a strong influence on the development of pop movies and videos. However, when *A Hard Day's Night* was shown in 1964, a majority of the audience screamed as if they were at a Beatles concert. Each close-up brought yet another paroxysm of squealing from the girls, who seemed unconcerned about the realism of the acting.

The Beatles' workload during the remainder of 1964 comprised a North American tour, British concerts and the recording of sixteen tracks for a Christmas album and single. At the end of November, they loyally returned to BBC studios for two sessions produced by Bernie Andrews. On *Top Gear*, 26 November 1964, four tracks from the new album and both sides of the latest single were broadcast. In two years of working on programmes with the group, Brian Matthew had witnessed the way their fame had affected so many aspects of their personal lives. He wondered if they ever felt tired of being Beatles. He was met by a chorus of stage yawns, but then a surprisingly serious reply to his question:

PAUL: I don't think so, really. Just occasionally, you get cheesed off with certain things, but it doesn't bother you that much, you know. Just occasionally, like people writing rubbish about you, which you get often. Especially in America to roll a few points into one.

BRIAN: Do you agree with that, John?

JOHN: I agree with that. I've had 'a divorce and half a dozen kids and attacked young girls' according to…

BRIAN: Yeah, we know all that. What have they been saying in the American press?

ALL: [Laughter]

JOHN: Funny, funny. I love this Pete Murray!

BRIAN: Isn't this a big sort of drag? Don't you have to go around explaining to your wife that you're not divorced and all that?

JOHN: No, she knows I'm not divorced 'cause I keep seeing her every day, you see.

BRIAN: Yeah, there's a point. Now what about the simpler things in life like…?

PAUL: Like riding on a bus?

BRIAN: Yeah, or going to just about any restaurant…

PAUL: Oh yeah. You miss those sort of things.

JOHN: I don't. I don't miss riding on a bus, Paul.

PAUL: Don't you? I do.

JOHN: I like the red buses though.

PAUL: I like a bus… red buses, green buses.

BRIAN: What about restaurants? You've got to eat.

JOHN: We go to certain ones.

GEORGE: And we go to ones where the people there are so snobby, they're the type who pretend they don't know us. So we have a good time 'cause they're pretending they don't know us.

PAUL: Joe's caff! Social comment that, you know.

GEORGE: It is.

BRIAN: This is what we want.

PAUL: [Northern 'brass tacks' accent] We want real hard facts, son.

THE BEATLES SOUNDED a little weary in this interview. Their album for the Christmas market was given the rather cynical title *Beatles For Sale* and the faces on its cover looked jaded compared to the cheerful expressions on the sleeve of *A Hard Day's Night*.

BRIAN: I've heard it said that a lot of these would make good singles, do you think there's any likelihood at all of them being released?

PAUL: Actually, one of them nearly was.

JOHN: But the wrong one, anyway.

PAUL: But it wasn't as good as the single, we don't think, but it was nearly at one point…

JOHN: You can't release singles off an LP after the LP's been out.

BRIAN: A lot of people do.

PAUL: Well, in America they do…

JOHN: Well, they're different over there, aren't they?

PAUL: In America they do that, but it's a bit of a drag. Yes, a bit of a drag that.

BRIAN MATTHEW ASKED about *Another Beatles Christmas Show*. It was booked for a marathon run of 38 'houses' over twenty nights at the Hammersmith Odeon in London with Freddie and The Dreamers, The Yardbirds, Elkie Brooks and DJ Jimmy Savile sharing the bill. George was quizzed about any marriage plans he might have. 'He wants to stay simple!' John joked. Ringo described the black opal ring he was given in Australia.

BRIAN: Now then, what can we talk about next?

JOHN: How about records? That's what we're here for, isn't it?

BRIAN: That's what you're here for. Records. All right, talk about records. Tell me about your new one – apart from the fact that it's marvellous.

JOHN AND PAUL: Oh, Brian you shouldn't… OK, go on!

BRIAN: No, seriously. I know we always have a little laugh in our chat about your records… I think this is the best one you've made, this single.

JOHN: Oh, thanks a lot, Brian.

PAUL: Thank you, Brian.

BRIAN: I know nobody cares, but I do.

JOHN: Oh, we care. We get fed up of people saying what's that rubbish?

BRIAN: No, it's the best one you've ever made and I think the B-side's better than the A-side.

JOHN: Oh well, I don't.

PAUL: Thank you, Brian.

JOHN: Well, as long as they buy the record they get both sides anyway.

BRIAN: Well, that's for sure. It doesn't really matter. Did you both write them both?

JOHN AND PAUL: Yes.

JOHN: Community effort.

PAUL: In fact, the B-side was written the morning of the session.

JOHN: [using an upper-class voice] Actually in the studio.

BRIAN: You're joking, what the whole thing?

JOHN: [continuing in the same voice] No, no. Most of it. We had about one verse and we had to finish it off rather quickly and that's why they're such rubbishy lyrics.

PAUL: Just a bit of soul in the studio there, you see.

THEIR NEXT CHAT with Brian for *Saturday Club* was recorded on 25 November for broadcast on Boxing Day, 26 December 1964. In the section of the show simultaneously transmitted by the General Overseas Service, they were asked which of the countries visited during the year was their favourite.

JOHN: America, I think.

RINGO: Yes, I'll agree with that.

JOHN: Ringo agrees with that.

BRIAN: Why, in particular?

JOHN: 'Cause we make a lot of money. No! No, 'cause it's good. It's like Britain only with buttons.

BRIAN: I see, yes.

JOHN: That's a sort of abstract simile.

PAUL: There's more people in America, so you get big audiences and it's all wild and happy.

GEORGE: Mind you, there was quite a lot of people in Australia.

PAUL: True, true.

BRIAN: There were one or two.

PAUL: Britain's, however, still the favourite, you see Brian. Favourite place.

BRIAN: Never mind, this is the place where we chat up the people overseas!

BRIAN MATTHEW mentioned that the group's appearances on his programme were now 'few and far between'. It turned out that this tenth visit was The Beatles' final music session for *Saturday Club*. Compared to forty music performances for the BBC in the previous year, they had recorded the much lower number of eight sessions in 1964. But to the BBC's disappointment, that total was never matched again.

ABOVE A still from *A Hard Day's Night*.

📺 Radio programme titles
📺 TV titles

★ indicates a song that was not recorded by The Beatles for EMI.

📺 THE PUBLIC EAR

Br: 12 January 1964 – 3.00–4.00pm
– The Light Programme
Rec: 5 January 1964

George and Ringo were heard reading their letter for the programme's *Air Mail* slot.

📺 SATURDAY CLUB

Br: 8 February 1964 – 10.00am–noon
– The Light Programme
Rec: 7 February 1964

On the day of The Beatles' arrival in the USA they answered questions put to them over the phone by Brian Matthew. The interview was broadcast the following day together with a description by BBC correspondent Malcolm Davis of the ecstatic New York reception given to The Beatles.

📺 SATURDAY CLUB

Br: 15 February 1964 – 10.00am–noon
– The Light Programme
Rec: 7 January 1964
Playhouse Theatre, London
Producer: Jimmy Grant and Bernie Andrews
Presenter: Brian Matthew
All My Loving, Money (That's What I Want), The Hippy Hippy Shake ★*, I Want To Hold Your Hand, Roll Over Beethoven, Johnny B. Goode* ★*, I Wanna Be Your Man*

📺 SATURDAY CLUB

Br: 22 February 1964 – 10.00am-noon
– The Light Programme
Rec: 22 February 1964

The Beatles talked on a phone at London Airport to Brian Matthew, just after their return flight from America had touched down.

📺 GRANDSTAND

Br: 22 February 1964 – 1.00–5.15pm – BBC TV
Rec: 22 February 1964

David Coleman interviewed The Beatles and Polly Elwes talked to some of the thousands of fans at London Airport.

📺 TODAY

Br: 18 March 1964 – 7.15–8.40am
– The Home Service
Rec: 17 March 1964

While on location for the movie *A Hard Day's Night* at the London club Les Ambassadeurs, John was interviewed by presenter Jack de Manio about his forthcoming book *In His Own Write*.

📺 THE VARIETY CLUB OF GREAT BRITAIN AWARDS FOR 1963

Br: 20 Mar 1964 – 10.30–11.00pm – BBC TV
Rec: 19 Mar 1964

Dorchester Hotel, Park Lane, London
Leader of the Opposition Harold Wilson presented them with the award for 'Show Business Personalities of 1963'.

📺 THE PUBLIC EAR

Br: 22 March 1964 – 3.00–4.00pm
– The Light Programme
Rec: 18 and 19 March 1964

While on the set at Twickenham Film Studios for *A Hard Day's Night*, The Beatles recorded various speech items for *The Public Ear*. George interviewed Ringo about John's *In His Own Write* and also talked to John, who read 'Alec Speaking'. The next day, George interviewed Paul about the movie while in a car heading to the Variety Club Awards at the Dorchester Hotel. George and Ringo read out the programme's production credits, including themselves in the list.

📺 TONIGHT

Br: 23 March 1964 – 7.00–7.35pm
– BBC TV
Live

BBC Lime Grove Studios, London
John was interviewed about *In His Own Write*.

THE CARL ALAN AWARDS
Br: 23 March 1964 – 10.25–11.15pm – BBC TV
Rec: 23 March 1964
The Empire Ballroom, Leicester Square, London
The Duke of Edinburgh presented The Beatles with two awards for their musical achievements in 1963.

TOP OF THE POPS
Br: 25 Mar 1964 6.35–7.00pm – BBC TV
Rec: 19 Mar 1964 7.00-8.30pm
BBC Television Theatre, Shepherd's Bush, London
Miming to:
Can't Buy Me Love, You Can't Do That

FROM US TO YOU
Say The Beatles
Br: 30 March 1964 (Easter Monday) – 10am–noon
– The Light Programme
Rec: 28 February 1964
Number 1 Studio, Piccadilly Theatre, London
Producer: Bryant Marriott
Presenter: Alan Freeman
From Us To You ★, *You Can't Do That, Roll Over Beethoven, Till There Was You, I Wanna Be Your Man, Please Mister Postman, All My Loving, This Boy, Can't Buy Me Love, From Us To You* ★
This is the only Beatles session kept in the main BBC Sound Archive. Five songs were preserved on a one-sided LP disc. 'This Boy' has an ending rather than the usual fade-out.

SATURDAY CLUB
Br: 4 April 1964 – 10.00am–noon
– The Light Programme
Rec: 31 March 1964
Playhouse Theatre, London
Producer: Jimmy Grant and Bernie Andrews
Presenter: Brian Matthew
Everybody's Trying To Be My Baby, I Call Your Name, I Got A Woman ★, *You Can't Do That, Can't Buy Me Love, Sure To Fall (In Love With You)* ★, *Long Tall Sally*

MOVIE-GO-ROUND
Br: 12 April 1964 – 3.00–4.00pm
– The Light Programme
Rec: 19/20 March 1964
Twickenham Film Studios

Interviews conducted by film columnist Peter Noble at Twickenham Film Studios.

[BBC 2 opened on 20 April 1964; BBC TV was renamed BBC 1]

SCOTTISH NEWS
Br: 29 April 1964 – 6.10–6.32pm
– The Scottish Home Service
Rec: 29 April 1964
ABC Cinema, Edinburgh
The Scottish Home Service broadcast an interview recorded with Bill Aitkenhead in The Beatles' dressing room.

SIX TEN
Br: 30 April 1964 – 6.10–6.31pm – BBC 1
Rec: 30 April 1964
Evelyn Elliot interviewed them for BBC Scotland at their hotel in Callander, Perthshire.

A SLICE OF LIFE
Br: 2 May 1964 – 4.00–4.30pm
– The Home Service
Rec: 31 March 1964
In an edition focusing on 'Hobbies', John was interviewed by Brian Matthew about his pastime of writing unusual poems and prose.

FROM US TO YOU
Say The Beatles
Br: 18 May 1964 (Whit Monday) – 10.00am–noon
– The Light Programme
Rec: 1 May 1964
BBC Paris Theatre, London
Producer: Bryant Marriott
Presenter: Alan Freeman
From Us To You ★, *I Saw Her Standing There, Kansas City/Hey-Hey-Hey-Hey!, I Forgot To Remember To Forget* ★, *You Can't Do That, Sure To Fall (In Love With You)* ★, *Can't Buy Me Love, Matchbox, Honey Don't* (★ John on lead vocal), *From Us To You* ★
Plus two versions of *Whit Monday To You* – an adaptation of *Happy Birthday To You.*

A DEGREE OF FROST
Br: 18 May 1964 – 10.15–11.00pm – BBC 1

Rec: 15 April 1964
Studio 4, Television Centre, Wood Lane, London
Paul was interviewed on the first programme of the series.

ROUNDABOUT
Br: 27 June 1964 – 5.00–5.30pm
– The Light Programme
Rec: 20 June 1964
The Beatles were recorded talking on the telephone from Sydney on the third day of their concerts at the local stadium. Colin Hamilton presented this edition of a programme billed as 'an easy-going mixture of news, views and music'.

TOP OF THE POPS
Br: 8 July 1964 – 7.35–8.00pm – BBC 1
Rec: 7 July 1964 – 2.00 – 5.00pm
Lime Grove Studios
Mimed performances of: *A Hard Day's Night* (repeated 22 July and 24 December 1964), *Long Tall Sally. Things We Said Today* was recorded in this session, but not broadcast until 29 July 1964.

BELOW *Top of the Pops* producer Johnnie Stewart.

THE TEEN SCENE

Br: 9 July 1964 – 9.30–10.00pm
– The Light Programme
Rec: 7 July 1964

New Musical Express editor Chris Hutchins talked to John about the movie *A Hard Day's Night*, which had received its world premiere in London on 6 July 1964.

LOOK NORTH

Br: 10 July 1964 – 6.10–6.35pm – BBC 1
Rec: 10 July 1964

This local news magazine programme featured an exclusive interview conducted by Gerald Harrison. It was broadcast on the evening of the Liverpool opening of *A Hard Day's Night*.

TOP GEAR

Br: 16 July 1964 – 10.00–11.55pm
– The Light Programme
Rec: 14 July 1964
Studio S2, Broadcasting House, London
Producer: Bernie Andrews
Presenter: Brian Matthew

Long Tall Sally, Things We Said Today, A Hard Day's Night, And I Love Her, If I Fell, You Can't Do That

Played from a disc: *I Should Have Known Better*

JUKE BOX JURY

Br: 25 July 1964 – 5.40–6.05pm – BBC 1
Live
Studio 4, Television Centre, London

George appeared as a panelist.

JUKE BOX JURY

Br: 1 Aug 1964 – 5.40–6.05pm – BBC 1
Rec: 25 July 1964
Studio 4, Television Centre, London

Ringo appeared as a panellist.

The Beatles Say FROM US TO YOU

Br: 3 August 1964 – 10.00am–noon
– The Light Programme
Rec: 17 July 1964
BBC Paris Theatre, London
Producer: Bryant Marriott
Presenter: Don Wardell

From Us To You ★, *Long Tall Sally, If I Fell, I'm Happy Just To Dance With You, Things We Said Today, I Should Have Known Better, Boys, Kansas City/Hey-Hey-Hey-Hey!, A Hard Day's Night, From Us To You* ★

John delivered the presenter and producer credits over the closing 'From Us To You' theme and changed his voice from 'BBC-posh' to broad Scouse in the space of seven seconds.

FOLLOW THE BEATLES

Br: 3 Aug 1964 – 7.50–8.20pm – BBC 1
Rec: February–April 1964

This was a documentary centred on the filming of *A Hard Day's Night*. United Artists supplied footage of The Beatles filming and recording soundtrack songs.

THE TEEN SCENE

Br: 13 August 1964 – 9.30–10.00pm
– The Light Programme
Rec: 12 August 1964

Chris Hutchins interviewed Ringo, who talked about the North American concert tour beginning the following week.

IT'S BEAT TIME

Br: 27 Sept 1964 – 9.45–10.35pm – BBC 2, Live
Prince of Wales Theatre, London

Ringo was a member of a panel judging the final of the National Beat Group Competition.

LOOK NORTH

Br: 14 Oct 1964 – 6.35–7.00pm – BBC 1
Rec: 14 Oct 1964
ABC Cinema, Ardwick, Manchester

A group interview with David Tindall. The soundtrack of the interview was used on the BBC North Home Service programme *The Week in the North* – Saturday 17 October 1964 – 9.30–10.00am.

TOP GEAR

Br: 26 November 1964 – 10.00pm–midnight
– The Light Programme
Rec: 17 November 1964
Playhouse Theatre, London
Producer: Bernie Andrews
Presenter: Brian Matthew

I'm A Loser, Honey Don't, She's A Woman, Everybody's Trying To Be My Baby, I'll Follow The Sun, I Feel Fine

In 1988, a tape – marked Reel 2 of 2 – was uncovered in a BBC Archive. On it were false starts and several takes (complete and incomplete) of 'I Feel Fine' and 'She's A Woman'. It is the original session tape made by a BBC Transcription recording engineer. Sadly, Reel 1 remains lost.

THE TEEN SCENE

Br: 29 November 1964 – 10.45–11.31pm
– The Light Programme
Rec: 28 November 1964

Chris Hutchins interviewed John about his new house *Kenwood* in Weybridge, Surrey.

TOP OF THE POPS

Br: 3 Dec 1964 – 7.30–8.00pm – BBC 1
Rec: 16 Nov 1964 – 2.00–5.00pm
Riverside Studios, Hammersmith

Mimed performances of: *I Feel Fine* (repeated 24 December 1964 on *Top of the Pops '64*), *She's A Woman* (repeated 10 December 1964)

TOP OF THE POPS '64

Br: 24 Dec 1964 – 7.25–8.25pm – BBC 1
Rec: 22 Dec 1964
Odeon Cinema, Hammersmith

The Beatles were interviewed by Jimmy Savile. He appeared on the bill of *Another Christmas Show*, which ran for 38 performances over twenty nights.

SATURDAY CLUB

Br: 26 December 1964
– The Light Programme
Rec: 25 November 1964
Number 2 Studio, BBC Aeolian Hall
Producer: Jimmy Grant and Bernie Andrews
Presenter: Brian Matthew

Rock And Roll Music, I'm A Loser, Everybody's Trying To Be My Baby, I Feel Fine, Kansas City/Hey-Hey-Hey-Hey!, She's A Woman

'I'm A Loser', 'Everybody's Trying To Be My Baby', 'I Feel Fine' and 'She's A Woman' were repeats of the versions recorded in the November *Top Gear* session.

OPPOSITE This photograph was used to promote the BBC General Overseas Service series *Pop Go The Beatles* broadcast during 1965. The programmes included BBC session material from the 1963 Light Programme series *Pop Go The Beatles* and later recordings from 1964.

1965
The Beatles
Abroad

'GOING ABROAD' had become a regular commitment for The Beatles. They had played to fans all over the globe – even as far away as Australia – in 1964. The bigger budget of their second movie, *Help!*, allowed them to be filmed on location in the Bahamas and Austria in February and March of 1965. Their second international concert tour of the year was in North America. On 15 August, their concert at Shea Stadium in New York set a record for the largest attendance at a pop concert – 55,600 – and highest box-office revenue. 'They could almost hear us,' John commented in the BBC radio show *The Beatles Abroad*.

In that programme, The Beatles revealed that, because of the mayhem generated by their fans, they saw little of the places they visited. However, they could not fail to be aware of the tensions tearing at the fabric of American society. The struggle for civil rights was ongoing and intense. After two months of demonstrations in Selma, Alabama, President Johnson won approval from Congress to pass the Voting Rights Act. The historic legislation prohibited any form of discrimination which would 'deny or abridge the right of any citizen of the United States to vote on account of race or colour'.

American involvement in Vietnam escalated throughout 1965. In February, the first bombing of North Vietnam by US planes had occurred. An American ground force arrived in March. By the close of 1965, over 100,000 US troops were in Vietnam and a heavy aerial bombing campaign was continuing. There was widespread anti-war protest, including college campus demonstrations and the burning of draft cards in defiance of the conscription of young men to serve in Vietnam. On 4 July, Dr Martin Luther King, Jr called for an end to the war. In June, Australian troops had been deployed to support the Americans in Vietnam. While anxious to maintain his country's special relationship with the US, British Prime Minister Harold Wilson showed tactical skill in his dealings with President Johnson throughout this and following years. He pledged aid and covert support, but not a single British soldier was ever sent to Vietnam.

The political dynamics between West and East were frustrating attempts to bring peace to Vietnam. The Cold War themes of spying and subterfuge underpinned films such as *The Ipcress File*, *Thunderball* and The Beatles' own movie, *Help!*. In April, the United States launched the communications satellite *Intelstat 1*, better known as *Early Bird*. On 2 May, it was used to transmit television signals from the US to the UK for the programme *Out of this World*. Astronaut Edward White was literally out of this world on 3 June. He became the first American to walk in space.

Pop music matured during 1965 and entered a golden age. Motown was enjoying a brilliant creative and commercial streak with American number one singles by The Supremes ('Come See About Me', 'Stop! In The Name Of Love', 'Back In My Arms Again'), The Temptations ('My Girl') and Four Tops ('I Can't Help Myself'). Bob Dylan issued two astounding albums in March and August – *Bringing It All Back Home* and *Highway 61 Revisited*. The latter had been preceded by the release of the six-minute 'Like A Rolling Stone' on 20 July. It peaked at number two in the States, held off number one by 'Help!'. Anyone who heard the single should not have been surprised to see Dylan wielding an electric guitar in front of a rock band at the Newport Folk Festival on 25 July. Yet his brief performance sparked an explosive mix of booing from betrayed folk purists and some approval from the more open-minded in the audience. The Byrds had already topped the US charts in June with their electric version of Dylan's 'Mr. Tambourine Man'. They returned to number one with 'Turn! Turn! Turn!' in December. Folk-rock had become the new hit sound. 'We like folk kind of music, like Bob Dylan… man!' Paul told the BBC's Brian Matthew.

At the end of 1965, in the face of tough competition, The Beatles stunned their rivals with the LP *Rubber Soul*.

'**MAY I BE** the last to wish you a Merry Christmas.' So said comedian and jazz-pianist Dudley Moore at the start of the first episode of the fortnightly TV series *Not Only… But Also* broadcast on 9 January 1965. Following an opening credits sequence, in which Dudley and a piano rolled through a car wash, and a musical performance, the star of the show introduced his guests: Sheila Staefel, Professor Bruce Lacey, Norman Rossington, Peter Cook, Diahann Carroll and 'the book-writing Beatle Mr John Lennon'. 'What about the other three?' Dudley enquired. 'You couldn't afford them, Dudley!' was John's reply.

Clutching a copy of *In His Own Write*, Dudley with mock-seriousness intoned: 'Poetry and music – this uneasy marriage of the arts has caused a lot of controversy for a long time. Many opinions are for; many against. We leave you to judge for yourselves. What we're going to show you is a visualization and 'musicification' of a poem by a young poet – John Lennon – and the poem is called 'Deaf Ted, Danoota, (and me)'. A film followed showing John, Dudley and Norman Rossington wandering about and riding bikes on Wimbledon Common while the poem was read – with more than a hint of Laurence Olivier's style of delivery. John also joined Dudley and Norman in the studio at Television Centre for more readings from *In His Own Write*. John recited 'About The Awful' and, with Norman, 'Good Dog Nigel' and 'The Wrestling Dog'. At the end of this section, Dudley Moore advised viewers, 'Mr Lennon will be back with the answers later on in the programme.'

The new TV series had started well. The Director of Television, Kenneth Adam, congratulated producer Joe McGrath: 'I enjoyed this first effort with the whole of my family, and we are looking forward to the next. I thought Lennon fitted in quite nicely… a gay and promising start.' Joe McGrath thanked John for taking part with a note containing the 'tongue-in-cheek' remark: 'I dig what you're doing, Dad!' A BBC Audience Research report confirmed a 'warm welcome' for the series. However, some viewers were critical of John's inclusion. 'Perhaps he was out of his depth' and 'his poetry made me wonder if his presence in the programme was a touch of the cult of personality' wrote two respondents. Another, a school clerical assistant, was more enthusiastic: 'he obviously does not need the support of the other three Beatles to be very successful.'

```
                                          - 2842/3

                                   17th December 1964

Dear John,

        I dig what you're doing, Dad!

        Thanks for doing the show for
us - and a Merry Christmas.

                Yours,



                (Joe McGrath)

John Lennon, Esq.,
c/o Nems Enterprises Ltd.,
Sutherland House,
5/6 Argyll Street, W1.


JT
```

ABOVE **TV producer Joe McGrath worked with a Beatle not only on this show featuring John and Dudley Moore, but also with Paul for *A Degree of Frost* in 1964 and Ringo's movie *Candy* in 1969. He also directed promotional clips for five songs videotaped on 23 November 1965, including those for the current single 'Day Tripper' / 'We Can Work It Out'.**

OPPOSITE **On location for *Help!* at Cliveden House near Taplow in Berkshire – a short drive from West London.**

John had recorded his contributions for *Not Only… But Also* on 20 and 29 November 1964. When the programme was shown in January, The Beatles still faced a further week of performances of *Another Beatles Christmas Show* at the Hammersmith Odeon. The new year promised a rerun of the frenetic routine undertaken in 1964: record an album, make a film, tour all over the world, record another album. However, one regular commitment from 1964 all but disappeared from The Beatles' 1965 schedule: performing songs especially for BBC radio.

BBC executive Donald MacLean wrote a memo to Ken Baynes on 16 March 1965 articulating his concerns about booking The Beatles that year. The BBC was hoping for the participation of the group in 'bank holiday' programmes, but approaches 'through normal channels' had resulted in rejection. Following conversations with Brian Epstein, MacLean had secured 'firm promises' that programmes for Easter, August and Christmas would be made with the group introducing their choice of records. In the end, these did not materialize. However, The Beatles did appear in a show celebrating its one hundredth edition. *Pop Inn* featured guests talking briefly to host Keith Fordyce in order to promote their latest records. On 13 April 1965, The Beatles huddled in a BBC radio car parked at Twickenham Film Studios, where they were shooting scenes for their second movie. Keith Fordyce had just talked to American star Tony Bennett. 'We now talk to some people you met the other day, because you presented them with an award [at a *New Musical Express Poll Winners Concert* on 11 April 1965]. They're not here in the studio, but by the magic of radio we want to call up four gentlemen who have been in here twice, but today they're busy making a film… so are you there, Beatles?'

PAGES 133 AND 134 **Stills from *Not Only… But Also*, broadcast 9 January 1965 on BBC 2.**

Starred **NOT ONLY..** DUDLEY MOORE

BUT ALSO~ His guest Stars

DIAHANN CARROLL
PETER COOK
and
JOHN LENNON

Poetry by
JOHN LENNON

BBC tv ENTERPRISES

JOHN: Receiving you loud and clearly-o!

KEITH: Right. Well, I'm not going to know who's talking. I'm not gonna have a…

JOHN: It's John talking, now.

KEITH: Is it, John? Right, starting with you, what's this about you having another new book coming out?

JOHN: Oh, yeah. Oh, that's a good plug, yeah. It comes out in about two months. It's called *A Spaniard in the Works* and it's very cheap and it's lovely.

KEITH: Well, I thought we'd keep you happy first, you see.

JOHN: Yeah, thanks.

KEITH: Right, George…

JOHN: Happy Birthday to the programme, by the way.

KEITH: Thank you very much, indeed.

GEORGE: Receiving you, Keith. George speaking.

KEITH: George, good. Have you had your lunch yet?

GEORGE: We've just finished lunch. Yes.

KEITH: All feeling well fed, are you?

GEORGE:: Oh, yes. Very well fed. They're gonna feed *us* to a tiger later on this afternoon.

KEITH: You're serious?

GEORGE: Well, not really, but there is a tiger strolling around the studio. We're trying to keep well away.

KEITH: Oh, well, have a care. Ringo…

JOHN: Have an apple!

KEITH: …what have you been doing this morning? Is Ringo there?

RINGO: Yes, I'm here.

KEITH: What have you been doing this morning?

RINGO: Um, nothing very much, you know. Just messing about as usual.

KEITH: No shots for the movie?

'There is a tiger strolling around the studio. We're trying to keep well away.'

GEORGE HARRISON

RINGO: Oh, shots, yes. But that's messing about, you see.

KEITH: Oh, I see. Is it true that you're the big star of this one?

RINGO: Yes, that's true. [laughter]

KEITH: I wouldn't wish to cause dissension in the ranks. I think we might get an interesting reply. Paul?

PAUL: Yes, yes. [screams from the studio audience] Hello, Uncle Keith.

KEITH: Incidentally, you're listening to this on a radio set, aren't you? Off the Light Programme.

PAUL: Yes. We're just sitting in this car with little earphones on.

KEITH: Oh, excellent.

PAUL: Having a great time.

OPPOSITE **A scene from** *Help!* **in which Ringo lifts his beer glass and is dropped through a trap door into the pub's cellar where a terrifying tiger awaits. The exterior of the pub seen in the movie is the City Barge, Strand-on-the-Green, Chiswick in London, but the interior shots were filmed on 28 April 1965 on a set constructed at Twickenham Film Studios.**

From: Chief Assistant, Production, Popular Music (Sound)   CONFIDENTIAL

Subject: THE BEATLES   16th March 1965

To: H.P.M.(S)   Copy to: Ch.L.P.; Mr. J. Grant; L.E.B.M.;
                                   Mr. B. Willey; Mr. B. Marriott;
                                   Mr. B. Andrews; Miss A. Barr.

As you know, approach "through the normal channels" produced a turn-down
of our request for a session with the Beatles for the Easter and Whit Bank
Holiday programmes.

Since his return from the Bahamas last week I have had several conversations
with Brian Epstein.   He has agreed to the following:

1. SATURDAY CLUB, 20th March: A telephone conversation, Brian Matthew
    in London, the Beatles in Salzburg, recorded 1900 GMT Friday, 19th March.
    Walter Shenson, producer of the film, has promised to facilitate this –
    I have given Brian Willey details of phone number, etc. (THE show
    business talking point at the moment is the title of this film – it has
    been decided, Brian Epstein has approved and it is at this moment with
    the film company in America for their blessing – there is a fair chance
    that we might be able to break it in this interview.)

2. EASTER MONDAY.   We are promised facilities to record "a special interview
    with the Beatles (probably at Twickenham Film Studios) during the week
    prior to Easter and the Beatles will choose and introduce records for the
    programme.   I promised that in my absence Jimmy Grant would be in touch
    with Brian Epstein on or about 8th April to arrange details.
    (Producer: Bryant Marriott)

3. WHIT MONDAY.   I have a firm promise that we may do a proper Beatles
    programme, with their performing as well as talking.   The Beatles would
    like to do this coincident with one of their recording sessions at
    E.M.I. studios. (George Martin has agreed this in principle – we may
    have to offer a studio hire fee.) The Beatles would like a change of
    title instead of "From Us To You" and will try to think of one.
    (Producer: Bryant Marriott)

4. AUGUST BANK HOLIDAY (30th August)
5. BOXING DAY (? 27th December)
    Epstein has given me a firm promise that they will do special programmes
    for these dates.   (I took Bryant Marriott to a meeting with him last
    Friday and Epstein seemed interested in his proposal of a Beatles-planned-
    and-introduced programme, possibly with each Beatle having 30 minutes to
    himself – which will give fans an interesting insight into their personal
    tastes – and will reduce the risk of inane dialogue!)

These are, of course, agreements in principle – to be implemented through
normal channels.

                    D. H. MACLEAN

                    (Donald MacLean)

Light Entertainment   5

THE BRITISH BROADCASTING CORPORATION
Broadcasting House, London, W.1
TELEGRAMS AND CABLES: BROADCASTS, LONDON, TELEX ✳ INTERNATIONAL TELEX: 2-2182 TELEPHONE: LANGHAM 4468

Our Reference 01/PC/DD   21st May 1965   (Date)

DEAR SIR/MADAM,
    We offer you an engagement to perform for broadcasting or for recording for the purpose of subsequent broadcast reproduction
as follows :

SERVICE   Light Programme (Popular Music Department)   REHEARSALS
DATE(S) OF RECORDING 26th May 1965

TIME(S) OF RECORDING 2.30. – 6.00.pm. (Discontinuous pre-recording)

STUDIO   Piccadilly 1
(or such other place as the Corporation may direct)

DATE(S) OF BROADCAST 7th June 1965

TIME(S) OF BROADCAST 10.00.am. – 12.00.noon

PROGRAMME   "From Us To You" (Ticket To Ride)

PRODUCER   Mr. Keith Bateson

FEE 1. Broadcast performance(s) or Recording Session(s) for the purpose of Clause
     19 (c) overleaf.
     One hundred pounds (£100.0.0.)

FEE 2. Mechanical Reproduction for the United Kingdom (including simultaneous   Personnel:
     broadcast overseas) :
        (Payable in respect of each such reproduction not covered by Fee 1—   George Harrison
         see Clause 19 (d) overleaf.)   Paul McCartney
     Fifty pounds (£50.0.0.)   John Lennon
                                                                                  Ringo Starr
FEE 3. Mechanical Reproduction overseas only :
     (a) First five reproductions
     Twenty pounds (£20.0.0.)
        (Payable in respect of each such reproduction not covered by Fee 1—
         see Clause 19 (d) overleaf.)
     (b) Subsequent reproductions
     Ten pounds (£10.0.0.)
        (Payable in respect of each such reproduction.)
     (c) BBC Transcription Service
        (See Clause 19 (e) overleaf.)
     British Commonwealth and South Africa (excluding the United
     Kingdom)
     Fifty pounds (£50.0.0.)
     U.S.A. and its territorial possessions :
     Twenty five pounds (£25.0.0.)
     Rest of the World (excluding the United Kingdom) :
     Twenty five pounds (£25.0.0.)

N.B.—Fees under 2 and 3 above are payable only if a broadcast reproduction is given.

The above offer is contingent on your compliance with the conditions below and overleaf:

1. That your signed acceptance, together with all necessary particulars, is returned to us without delay.

2. That you shall attend rehearsals if and when required.

3. That you shall complete, return and submit for approval the Programme Form which is attached hereto (together
with a published copy or typescript of all songs words and material you propose to use) to :
Light Entertainment Booking Section, The British Broadcasting Corporation, Broadcasting House, London, W.1.
not later than 48 hours before the date of the performance.

4. That if it is decided /agreed that your own act is to be accompanied by an orchestra provided by the Corporation
you will provide such band parts as the Corporation may consider necessary in accordance with the size and instrumenta-
tion of the orchestra, failing which you hereby authorise the Corporation (if it so desires) to make up any shortage of
parts at your expense and to recover the cost of such parts by deduction from the amount of any fee which may be payable,
to you by the Corporation in respect of this or any subsequent engagement(s).

NEMS Enterprises Ltd. for the services of: Yours faithfully,
The Beatles, (A.201892),   THE BRITISH BROADCASTING CORPORATION
c/o NEMS Enterprises Ltd.,
Name Sutherland House,
      5/6 Argyll Street,   PATRICK NEWMAN
Address London, W.1.   Light Entertainment Booking Manager
P/352 12-64 A.E.B.
eb

ABOVE As an approach 'through normal channels' – that is the
Light Entertainment Booking Department – had resulted
in a 'turn-down', Donald MacLean had a meeting with Brian
Epstein to discuss future Beatles appearances on the BBC
Light Programme. RIGHT The contract for The Beatles' final
music session for the BBC reveals the usual title for a bank
holiday special – *From Us To You* – had not yet been changed.

KEITH: How many songs are there in this movie and who wrote them?

PAUL: There's about six or seven and they were written by Leonard Bernstein, who else? No, John and I wrote 'em.

KEITH: And what's this about The Beatles all together maybe writing a musical?

PAUL: Well, I don't know really. That's one of those things when we've got time, you know. But, as yet, there's no plans. Anyway, Happy Birthday, Keith.

KEITH: Thanks, Paul. Thank you all very much. And John, Paul, George and Ringo – let's congratulate you on the Poll Winning Awards you collected on Sunday.

ALL: Thank you.

KEITH: Have you got a special warehouse for them all yet?

PAUL: Special warehouse?

KEITH: Well, you must have got so many now. Where do you put 'em all. Be polite!

RINGO: We sell 'em!

PAUL: Flogged 'em all now, yes.

GEORGE: I melted the *NME* one down into a couple of gold teeth. [studio laughter]

JOHN: We can hear you laughing!

KEITH: Before this gets completely out of hand, I'm gonna say thanks, boys, very much indeed for being there and do try and work a bit harder this afternoon and mind that tiger, won't you?

ALL: [singing] Hold that tiger, hold that tiger!

PAUL: See you and a Happy Birthday, once again. Ta-ra to everyone.

KEITH: Right, ta-ra!

THE GROUP SINGING 'Hold That Tiger' (the vocal version of 'Tiger Rag') shows how steeped they were in pre-rock 'n' roll popular music. Ringo is, indeed, threatened by a tiger in a scene from the movie *Help!* The BBC did manage to secure a more substantial appearance by The Beatles a few weeks later. They would perform music in a 'bank holiday' radio show for Whit Monday. Donald MacLean had reported that, 'The Beatles would like to do this coincident with one of their recording sessions at EMI studios. (George Martin has agreed this in principle – we may have to offer a studio hire fee.) The Beatles would like a change of title instead of 'From Us To You' and will try to think of one.'

The reference to using a studio at EMI indicates that the group, used to more advanced recording techniques at Abbey Road, felt unwilling to tolerate the single-track recording equipment and limited session time at the BBC. Even so, on 26 May 1965 at the Piccadilly Studios, The Beatles made their 53rd and final musical performance broadcast by BBC radio. Heard on Whit Monday 7 June 1965, *The Beatles Invite You to Take a Ticket To Ride* was presented by Denny Piercy – the drummer with BBC regulars Bob Miller and His Miller Men. He admitted his script was 'all Monday and no wit'! Three of the guest groups had previously been featured in *Pop Go The Beatles*: The Lorne Gibson Trio, The Hollies and The Ivy League (formerly known as Carter and Lewis). Bank holiday regulars The Kenny Salmon Seven accompanied vocalists Danny Street and Julie Grant, and the line-up was completed by The Atlantics. Of the 49 musical items played in two-and-a-quarter hours, only seven were played from commercial discs. The Beatles chatted briefly, but amiably enough to Denny Piercy.

'I think I'm more quiet than the others, because I got fed up before the others of all these questions like, "What colour teeth have you got?"'

GEORGE HARRISON

OPPOSITE Recording sessions for *Rubber Soul* took place at EMI Studios in Abbey Road, London during October and November 1965.

LEFT The Beatles were very early users of cassette recorders, which in 1965 were not widely available. They are seen here making recordings to listen to at home of songs they have just worked on for inclusion on *Help!*.

OPPOSITE Producer George Martin's classical training proved invaluable when The Beatles began to introduce orchestral instruments into their ambitious arrangements.

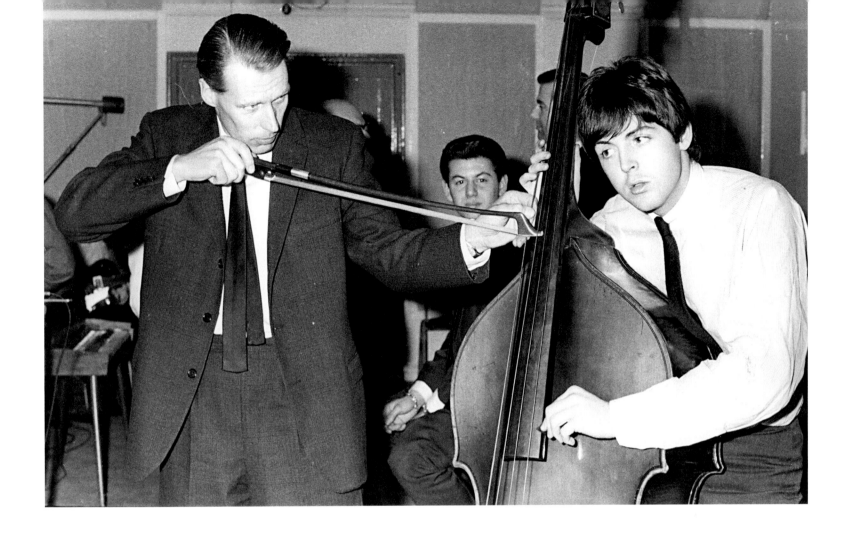

DENNY: One big question right now… the film.

PAUL: Yes?

JOHN: Yeah, that's not a question!

DENNY: Is it not a question? It's July 29th isn't it, the premiere?

ALL: Yes.

JOHN: Unless something goes wrong.

DENNY: The title is *Help!* Is that settled on now?

JOHN: Oh yes.

DENNY: What's the story behind the title?

PAUL: Well, it's just they're trying to get Ringo's ring – the baddies, you see – and we're the goodies.

DENNY: Are you a sort of Double-oh-seven, Ringo?

RINGO: No, no. I'm a sort of double entendre!

NOTHING OF GREAT significance was revealed, but The Beatles seemed genuinely amused by one introduction.

JOHN: Why do you have to do this 'imperative'?

DENNY: Because the producer asked for it. It's for his wife called Liz. Any suggestions?

JOHN: Well, Liz, how about 'Dizzy Miss Lizzy'… Liz?

DENNY: What a brilliant idea.

PAUL: 'Dizzy Miss Lizzy' – what a great idea!

JOHN: I just saw it on that piece of paper you've got there.

DENNY: Let's hear it then… 'Ticket To Ride'!

'Ringo and I are painting Buckingham Palace – green with black shutters!'

GEORGE HARRISON

THE PRODUCER WAS Keith Bateson, who had been the sound balancer for many editions of *Pop Go The Beatles* and *From Us To You*. Although this session had its moments of fun, Keith detected the group's reluctance to keep up their dutiful visits to the BBC's music studios. 'I had a sort of feeling that it may well be the last. I don't think they did. But things were getting out of hand in those days and it did appear to me that… they weren't so much getting fed up… but they'd got lots of other things to do as well. And I know that I had a certain amount of sadness. When I finished it I thought, "Well I'm not sure whether we're going to get one at Christmas."'

An Audience Research report was compiled for *Ticket To Ride*, which gave a Reaction Index figure of 47 (68 from 'the fans'). An estimated 10.6 per cent of the population tuned in at the beginning of the show, falling to 9.4 per cent by its end (roughly five million listeners). There was disappointment that The Beatles were not more present during the show, but they were praised as 'brilliant professional performers', who when chatting to Denny Piercy were 'great fun'. The 'non-fans' were for the first time in the minority (just over a quarter of the sample). They described pop music as 'ghastly', 'insane' and 'jungle music'. The Beatles' tracks were dismissed as 'monotonous bangings' – 'Oh, the deadly monotony of this kind of music!'

Tracks from The Beatles' last three sessions had been reused in a weekly show pressed on LP disc for distribution to radio stations abroad by the BBC's Transcription Service. This division of the Corporation had been established to disseminate British culture to the far-flung corners of the Empire. Recognizing that British pop music was now a very successful export, *Top of the Pops* was introduced to international broadcasters in October 1964. No commercial discs were featured; the music was exclusively drawn from BBC-recorded sessions. The presenter was the ubiquitous Brian Matthew and, around the date of the *Ticket To Ride* recording, he interviewed The Beatles for his Transcription programme. John's second book *A Spaniard in the Works* was due to be published in June 1965.

JOHN: You get more for your money this time – there's more pages and drawings.

PAUL: Same kind of rubbish.

JOHN: Yeah, same kind of rubbish. That's right, Paul.

PAUL: Pardon? I liked the first one – hate this one!

BRIAN: Heard lots of rumours and reports that you two are thinking of writing a musical. Is there anything in this?

PAUL: Thinking of it.

JOHN: Paul's thinking of it, I'm doing it.

PAUL: John's actually doing it, I just do all the brain work behind this operation.

GEORGE: Ringo and I are painting Buckingham Palace!

BRIAN: I was coming to you next.

GEORGE: That's a point of interest.

BRIAN: Marvellous. What colour?

RINGO: Green.

GEORGE: Green with black shutters.

BRIAN: I see. Do you know when you're going back to America, by the way?

GEORGE AND RINGO: August.

RINGO: For two-and-a-half weeks.

BRIAN: Thank you, George and Ringo. And this'll be a tour?

RINGO: Yes.

JOHN: Well, it won't be a one-nighter!

BRIAN: I wondered if it was just for television.

JOHN: Oh.

PAUL: I certainly hope not.

BRIAN: If I might ask you one thing on the music side. When you started hitting it big you were very much…

PAUL: Smaller than we are now.

BRIAN: … suggesting a trend which has since happened all over the world. Do you yourselves foresee any new trend at this stage? What are you listening to right now?

PAUL: We like folk kind of music, like Bob Dylan… man! No, we do, y'know. Country and Western music, 'cause we've always liked that anyway. I think all the kinds of things we like now, we always liked, but we like a few particularly.

BRIAN: You mentioned Bob Dylan, he says you write folk. What do you think about that?

PAUL: We don't.

JOHN: We don't, y'know.

PAUL: We get influenced like everybody else does.

JOHN: [In mock working-class voice] I mean as much as it's the music of the people of the day.

PAUL: [Similar voice] Yeah, the music of the working-class masses.

BRIAN: Thank you Spotty Muldoon. [A character created by comedian Peter Cook.] Well, we'll take you into some of your folk, Country and Western-influenced, Bob Dylan-inspired music now, I think. What shall it be? 'Ticket To Ride'?

GEORGE: No.

JOHN AND PAUL: Yeah, that's very folk!

SEVERAL OF THE topics in that conversation would be talking points throughout the summer of 1965 – John's second book, the American tour with its record-breaking concert at Shea Stadium and even Buckingham Palace. On 12 June 1965, news broke that The Beatles would become 'Members of the Most Excellent Order of the British Empire' – an honour more usually bestowed on retired colonels and civil servants. The group's rather bemused reaction to receiving MBEs was recorded in a BBC interview with Hugh Moran. Their flippant remarks would not have pacified those who protested the gravity of the award had been violated by The Beatles being recipients.

HUGH: Did the form come in with the rest of your fan mail or did it come separately in a very sort of impressive envelope?

RINGO: Yes, we all thought it was call-up papers! … But when we opened them it was, 'If you'd like to have an MBE, sign here.' So we did.

PAUL: Send two bottle tops and we got it!

HUGH: Paul, do you think you really deserve an award like the MBE?

PAUL: I don't know, y'know. What does it matter? We got it.

HUGH: What about when you go to the Palace for the investiture… what about the gear, how will you dress?

PAUL: Oh, some fella was just saying you have to have top hats… I hope you don't have to have top hats.

HUGH: Will you all wear top hats?

RINGO: If we have to.

PAUL: Have white rabbits coming out of them.

HUGH: And what about the hair?

PAUL: What about it?

RINGO: We'll put that in the top hat as well.

HUGH: John, having the MBE, what does it mean to you?

JOHN: I don't know until I get it. I'll read about it and see what it is really, 'cause I'm not sure what it is. I only know what I read in the papers. So I'll just check and see what I've really got. I'll find out, then I'll tell you.

HUGH: What did your wife say when she knew you had it?

JOHN: She said, 'Oh.' [Laughter]

HUGH: Just like that?

JOHN: She didn't have a clue really what it was, but she's pleased, you know. I tried to get her one, but I couldn't! [Laughter]

HUGH: George, now the MBE, what does it mean to you?

GEORGE: I don't know. I thought it was the Northern Dance Orchestra at first, but that's NDO! Um, it's great, y'know, but I don't know what we'll have to do when we've got it. I doubt if we'll have to walk up and down Buckingham Palace, will we? Showing people what it's like. I don't know. It'll just be the same only we've got a medal.

ON 16 JUNE 1965, John was interviewed about his writing for the BBC Home Service programme *World of Books* broadcast on 3 July. He talked to Wilfred De'Ath, a producer who also worked on the Light Programme show *The Teen Scene*. He was an advocate of popular culture being taken more seriously. Only three years older than John and knowledgeable about pop music, De'Ath tried his best not to patronize his guest.

WILFRED: Let me ask you first of all, how do you write? Do you write in a disciplined way or do you write when it comes into your head?

JOHN: It's more disciplined… the second book was more disciplined, because it was starting from scratch. They sort of say, you've got so many months to write a book. In the first book, a lot of it I'd written at odd times during my life.

WILFRED: Do you set aside certain hours in the day to write or do you…

JOHN: No, none of that. I haven't written enough. It's not a job, you see.

WILFRED: Would you like to discipline yourself? Do you feel a need to discipline yourself as a writer?

JOHN: No, I'm not very keen on being disciplined. It seems odd being a Beatle, because we're disciplined but we don't feel as though we're disciplined. I don't mind being disciplined and not realizing it.

WILFRED: You know, these little pieces in the book… they give an appearance of great finish, perfection… do you revise them?

JOHN: Do they?

WILFRED: Yes, they don't look all that spontaneous, they look as though they've been worked over. Do you work them over?

JOHN: They're not at all. Nobody's ever said that to me… wonderful! They are spontaneous and I hardly ever alter anything, because I'm selfish about what I write or big-headed about it. Once I've written it, I like it and the publisher sometimes says, you know, 'Should we leave this out or change that?' and I fight like mad. 'Cause once I've done it, I like to keep it. But I always write it straight off. I might add things when I go over it before it's published, but I'd seldom take anything out. So it is spontaneous.

WILFRED: Now the puns and all the other technical things – the puns, the onomatopoeia…

JOHN: The what… what?

WILFRED: That's a long word.

JOHN: That's three words I've learnt today!

WILFRED: I'll tell you. Onomatopoeia is when I say a word like 'buzz' – 'buzz' is an onomatopoeia, because in the word is captured the noise of the bee… and you, probably without realizing it… your book is full of them.

JOHN: Is it? Well, I'm glad to know that. Lot of onomatopoeias.

WILFRED: Well, you've rather answered my question, because I was going to ask you whether these were contrived…

JOHN: No, I just haven't got a clue what you're talking about, really. Automatic Pier, sounds like to me. That's probably why I change words, 'cause I haven't a clue what words mean half the time.

TWO DAYS AFTER this interview, John appeared live on BBC TV's *Tonight* to talk to Kenneth Allsop – one of a team of respected broadcasters that had appeared on the show since 1957. Other presenters seen on the evening programme included Cliff Michelmore, Alan Whicker and Fyfe Robertson. The edition of *Tonight* broadcast on 18 June 1965 was the last ever.

KENNETH: Mr Lennon, your first book is a bestseller and I shouldn't think there's any doubt that this one's going to be, too. Do you think that you'd be published were you not a Beatle?

JOHN: I could probably get published but, you know, I wouldn't sell as many. I mean, they publish a lot of rubbish anyway. But, I wouldn't sell.

KENNETH: Do you think you've got a built-in advantage in being a Beatle? I mean, are you glad about this or would you rather have earned a reputation as a writer in your own right?

JOHN: No, I never thought of it. If I hadn't been a Beatle, I just wouldn't have thought of having the stuff published 'cause I would've been crawling around, broke, and just writing it and throwing it away. I might've been a Beat poet!

RIGHT John recording at Abbey Road, during a session for *Rubber Soul*.

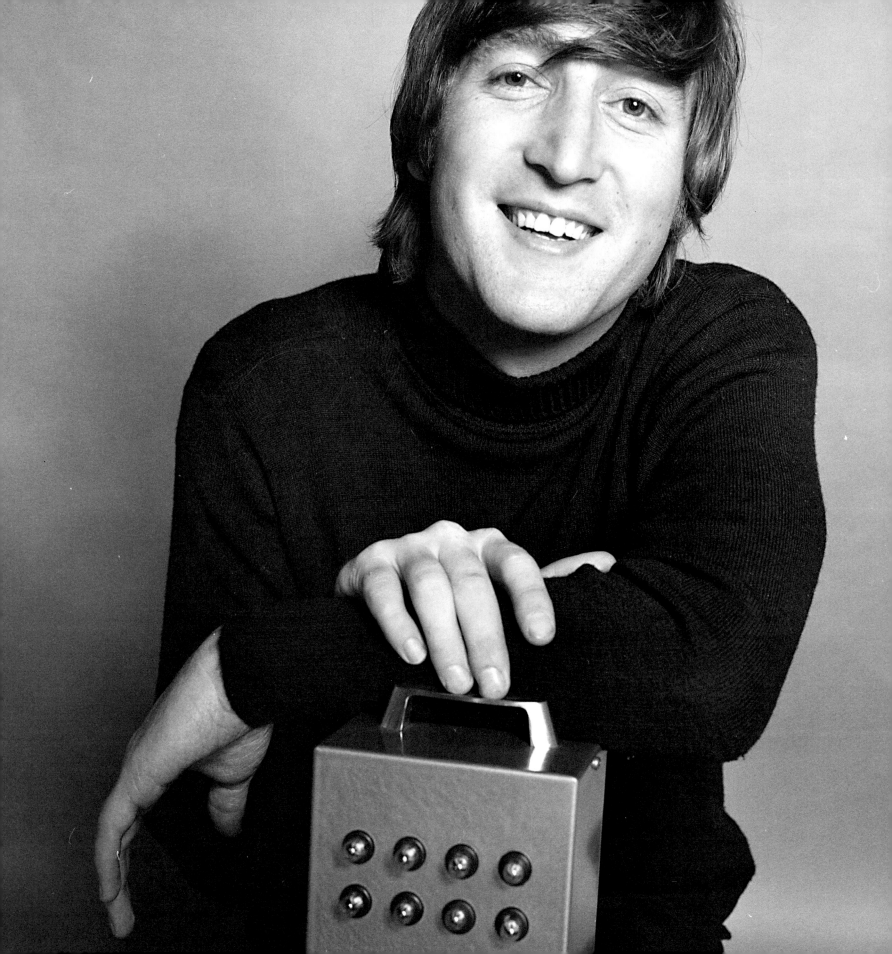

KENNETH: How did it come about that you weren't a Beat poet and that your first book was published?

JOHN: Well, some American who shall remain nameless, who's called Michael Braun [author of *Love Me Do: The Beatles' Progress*]… I showed him the stuff and he took it to the publisher, and they published it. That was it.

KENNETH: Did you ever think of publishing it under a pseudonym, not as John Lennon?

JOHN: I'd thought of that, but what's the use, you know. Because he took it to the publisher first without telling 'em who it was just to see if they would've published it. So that answers your first question as well.

KENNETH: It does indeed, yep. Living in the, you know, butterfly world of pop as a Beatle, do you find that this undermines people's serious acceptance of you as a writer?

JOHN: Er, it does. But I didn't really expect them to take me seriously, so, you know… there's nothing to say about that. They do take it more seriously than I thought, so that's good enough for me.

KENNETH: Indeed. I remember the first book was reviewed in the posh 'Sundays', and on the other side of the fence your music's recorded by people like Ella Fitzgerald. Now this is serious recognition in both areas. Which do you find more satisfying?

JOHN: Well, the book, really. Because it means more to other people that Ella Fitzgerald recorded one of our tunes than it does to us, because the tune is still something that Paul and I have written… so we still have the same faith in it. It just gives other people more faith in the tune.

KENNETH: This book's very similar to the first in being bits and pieces of poems, and bits of prose. Do you think you'd ever want to write anything longer? A novel, for example.

JOHN: Well, I tried writing… The longest thing I've written is in this book. It's one about Sherlock Holmes, and it seemed like a novel to me, but it turned out to be six pages. But I don't think I could… I couldn't do it, you know. I get fed up. I didn't know who was… I brought so many characters in, I forgot who they were.

ABOVE RIGHT *A Spaniard in the Works* was published in June 1965. 'You get more for your money this time – there's more pages and drawings,' John told Brian Matthew.

'I started all this writing long before I was a pop artist or even a Beatle, or before I had a guitar.'

JOHN LENNON

KENNETH: This happens to other writers too.

JOHN: Oh. Other writers? Good.

KENNETH: The pop business is a young man's world. It seems to have an ever increasingly young audience. Do you think that perhaps writing a book like this, and writing at all, perhaps might be an unconscious attempt to win recognition in the adult world?

JOHN: No, because I started all this writing long before I was a pop artist or even a Beatle, or before I had a guitar. So it's nothing to do with that. The guitars came second.

KENNETH: And which comes first?

JOHN: Well, now the guitars come first 'cause this is still a hobby, which it always has been.

KENNETH: Are you going on doing it, are you?

JOHN: I'll go on doing it.

KENNETH: I mean, have you written anything else? Is anything else coming after this? A third one in the series?

JOHN: Well, I don't get much time. If I had more time I'd probably write more. The publisher rang up and said, 'Have you written anything yet?' and I said, 'No, I've been writing songs,' 'cause I can't do both at once. You know, I've got to concentrate on the book or the songs. So I haven't written anything since this.

KENNETH: We'll look forward to it, nevertheless, John. Thank you very much indeed.

JOHN: Thank you.

ON 30 JULY 1965 – the day after the film premiere of *Help!* – The Beatles took time off from a private rehearsal for the TV show *Blackpool Night Out* to talk to Dibbs Mather of the BBC Transcription Service. The Australian broadcaster had first interviewed them in a dressing room at the Doncaster Gaumont in December 1963. Back then, he had wondered what they might do once their fifteen minutes of fame had expired. This time, he took a different approach.

JOHN: We enjoy English records selling in America… that's the best bit – taking over there, instead of them running everything.

DIBBS: If you had not got so rich and famous, what do you think you might be doing now?

JOHN: We'd probably be bumming round.

RINGO: Still working in clubs in England.

DIBBS: And Paul would have been teaching?

PAUL: I might have been teaching but I would have hated it, I think. I think all of us might have been – if we hadn't have stuck with the group – might have just ended up, you know, like George being an electrician, Ringo being a fitter and John being a bum. Just doing things we didn't enjoy much.

GEORGE: I think we would have been probably playing modern jazz now in some crummy club.

JOHN: Do you?

GEORGE: Yeah.

JOHN: Do we like modern jazz?

GEORGE: 'Cause no, 'cause we would have been so fed up playing the same things, that we would have progressed. But now we don't progress 'cause we play the same things every time we play somewhere.

DIBBS: But isn't this… it's a kind of a progression, though, in that the style has altered slightly.

GEORGE: Yeah, slightly. But the thing is we used to improve at a much faster rate before we ever made records. Well, I think so, because we used to get so fed up playing the same things so we'd always learn new songs all the time.

JOHN: You'd have to improvise every time. Or even with the old songs you do them different almost any time, but when you make records you've got to reproduce, as near as you can, the record. So you don't really get a chance to improvise or improve your style.

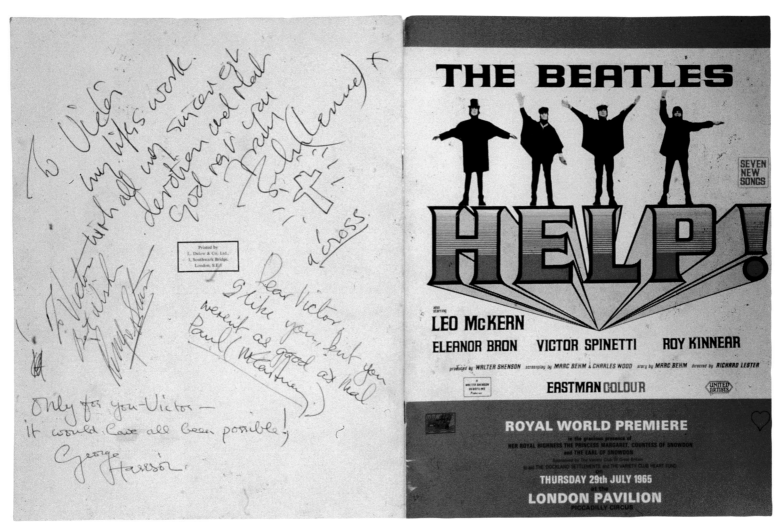

To Victor
my life's work.
with all my sincere
devotion and that
God may bless you
(John Lennon) x

Printed by
L. Delow & Co. Ltd.,
1, Southwark Bridge,
London, S.E.1

a 'cross

To Victor
for which
I like your, but you
weren't as good as Mal
Paul (McCartney)

Dear Victor
I like your, but you

Only for you-Victor —
it would have all been possible!
George Harrison.

ABOVE The Beatles autographed Victor Spinetti's programme for the world premiere of *Help!*. The actor also appeared in their films *A Hard Day's Night* and *Magical Mystery Tour*.

DIBBS: And as a result of this and your increasing popularity, how's it affected you? Is it possible you're going to become bored with being The Beatles for year after year at the top?

JOHN: You don't get bored, because there are so many different things [that] happen like MBEs or premieres… and they're all different so as soon as you start getting bored with something like a tour, the tour's over and something else starts. You don't get a chance to get bored. And there's always Ringo, isn't there?

ALL: [Laughter]

GEORGE AND JOHN expressing their dissatisfaction with playing just a handful of songs in concert was broadcast just as The Beatles undertook their third trip to the USA in August 1965. The tour's first concert was another Beatle event that, as John revealed, kept boredom at bay. Their appearance in front of 55,600 fans at Shea Stadium in New York broke world records for concert attendance and box-office revenue ($304,000).

BRIAN MATTHEW TOURS WITH THE BEATLES

The Beatles leave for their third tour of the United States
on Friday, August 13 - and with them, on behalf of the BBC
Transcription Service, will go Brian Matthew, who regularly
introduces the Light Programme's "Saturday Club", and "Top of the
Pops", a programme which is heard each week over 60 American radio
stations, 18 stations in New Zealand and other stations in Australia, the Caribbean, Africa, Malaysia and Europe.

A report from him after the Beatles' first concert in New York
will be heard in the Light Programme's daily "Roundabout" and, on
his return on August 21, he will be heard in an interview direct
from London Airport which will be included "live" in "Saturday
Club" on that date. A programme on the tour, with comments by
Brian Matthew, will be broadcast all over the world in "Top of
the Pops" and there will also be a special programme featuring
the Beatles' tour in the Light on August Bank Holiday (Monday,
August 30).

After Brian Matthew's return on August 21, Jay Peeples, a
well-known broadcaster in America, will represent the BBC Trans-
scription Service, and travel with the Beatles until their return
to England on August 31.

WITH THE COMPLIMENTS OF THE BBC

AB/mvg
6.8.65.

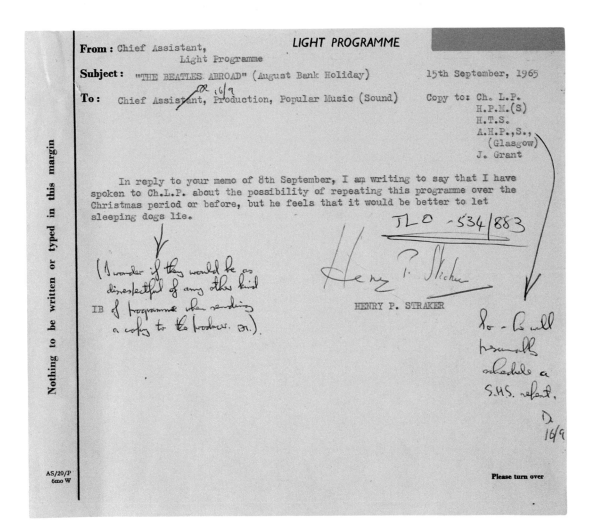

From: Chief Assistant,
Light Programme

Subject: "THE BEATLES ABROAD" (August Bank Holiday)

To: Chief Assistant, Production, Popular Music (Sound)

LIGHT PROGRAMME

15th September, 1965

Copy to: Ch. L.P.
H.P.M.(S)
H.T.S.
A.H.P.,S.,
(Glasgow)
J. Grant

In reply to your memo of 8th September, I am writing to say that I have spoken to Ch.L.P. about the possibility of repeating this programme over the Christmas period or before, but he feels that it would be better to let sleeping dogs lie.

JLO -534/883

HENRY P. STRAKER

(I wonder if they would be as disrespectful of any other kind IB of programme when sending a copy to the producer. or.)

So – he will presumably schedule a S.HS. repeat. D 16/9

AS/20/P
6mo W

Please turn over

RIGHT Some of the BBC's high-ranking executives still failed – even in September 1965 – to comprehend the magnitude of The Beatles' achievements and their popularity.

BBC advance publicity for the 'bank holiday' in August had announced a Beatles special, but the plan for a show featuring their record choices was eventually abandoned. At the beginning of the month, however, Brian Epstein agreed that Brian Matthew – who else? – should join The Beatles on tour. His on-the-spot tape recordings with the group and some fans were compiled into a show called *The Beatles Abroad* – a 45-minute documentary for the August holiday. Produced by Jimmy Grant, the programme was an innovative experiment for its time. Pop music was rarely investigated with the seriousness applied to books or other art forms. Indeed, the BBC did not produce a documentary series about a pop artist until the 1972 project *The Beatles Story*.

In Scotland, where the dates of public holidays differed from the rest of the UK, *The Beatles Abroad* was not broadcast on 30 August. Consequently, a repeat broadcast to the whole of the UK was proposed. The BBC correspondence that ensued was indicative of the hierarchy's haughty attitude to pop. Donald MacLean, a supporter of the cause of disappointed Beatles fans in Scotland, received from the Chief Assistant, Light Programme a terse reply dismissing any idea of repeating *The Beatles Abroad*. 'I have spoken to the Chief of the Light Programme [Denis Morris, who had been so eager for The Beatles' downfall in January 1964]… he feels that it would be better to let sleeping dogs lie.' A copy of this memo had also been sent to Jimmy Grant. A handwritten note on the file copy drily observed, 'I wonder if they would be as disrespectful of any other kind of programme when sending a copy to the producer.' This sort of lofty attitude towards pop music was evident in the opinions of various newspaper critics. It annoyed Brian Matthew. In his first *Top Gear* broadcast he had remarked, 'Why is it these so called intellectuals go cloth-eared when asked to review anything popular?'

'It was the
biggest live show
anybody's ever done,
they told us, and
it was fantastic.
It was just great.
They could
almost hear us
as well, even though
they were making
a lot of noise,
because the
amplification was
terrific.'

JOHN LENNON

In *The Beatles Abroad*, the group sounded relaxed with their 'old mate' Brian Matthew and gave candid replies to his questions.

PAUL: I don't really get nervous when there's that many people, because they can't hear you! So we just listen to them… The thing is even if something really terrible goes wrong…

BRIAN: Nobody's going to know?

PAUL: I don't know, maybe they will!

FROM THE MOMENT the group bounded out of a Wells Fargo armoured truck onto the baseball field of Shea Stadium, it was obvious that John was enjoying himself.

JOHN: It was marvellous… It was the biggest live show anybody's ever done, they told us, and it was fantastic. It was just great. They could almost hear us as well, even though they were making a lot of noise, because the amplification was terrific.

BRIAN: It was very good actually. I must confess I could only distinguish about three of the numbers, which I happened to know.

JOHN: Yeah, well the well-known ones you can pick up.

BRIAN: Did you do anything that you don't normally do in your concerts?

JOHN: We did 'I'm Down' so 'cause I did the organ on the record I decided to play it onstage for the first time. I didn't really know what to do, 'cause I felt naked without a guitar, so I was doing all Jerry Lee [Lewis] – I was putting my foot on it and George couldn't play for laughing! Y'know, I was doing it for a laugh.

BRIAN MATTHEW'S EXPOSURE to the mania surrounding The Beatles in America gave him an insight into what their life on the road was like. 'It was quite bewildering… you can hear about it, but until you actually experience it first hand, you've no conception of what it could possibly be like. Kids crawling up the wires and just wanting to get out and touch. Being with them when they ran onto the ball park in Chicago and a cop with a night stick grabbing me and saying, "Where are you going, buddy?" and Paul turning round saying, "It's all right, he's with us!" and dragging me in.' Observing how The Beatles were virtual prisoners within hotel rooms, cars and planes, he asked George how he coped with this lack of freedom.

GEORGE: We don't mind. When we start a tour, we know very well it's going to be wild with lots of people and that we're going to be stuck in a hotel. We don't think we're coming over here to see the sights… In fact, over the last few years we've been in hotel rooms, we find a way of keeping ourselves amused.

HAVING BROKEN THROUGH the 'shyness barrier', as Brian Matthew put it in the programme, he asked Ringo why the two Beatle wives were not present on the tour.

RINGO: It would be unfair to fetch 'em on tour 'cause we travel about so much and they'd have to keep packing their bags the same as us. And if they go out, they get bothered as well when we go abroad.

BRIAN: Would you think that it's made any difference at all to The Beatles as a group that two of you are now married? Once upon a time it did make a difference to pop stars.

RINGO: I think about 1957, '58, it was a big thing that pop stars weren't married.

BRIAN: Why do you think this has changed?

RINGO: I think all the fans realize that we're just human beings and we drink, smoke and get married like anybody else.

IN RECOGNITION OF the invaluable insights contained in *The Beatles Abroad*, the programme was selected for the BBC Sound Archive. It was copied onto an LP disc, but not in the form broadcast on the Light Programme. The archived show is a speech-only version prepared by the BBC Transcription Service, including extra interview material. It is also lacking some of the speech broadcast in the UK.

OPPOSITE **On 3 December 1965, a sixth album would be added to the four previous LPs displayed here and the unseen *With The Beatles*.**

Its preservation had been recommended by Donald MacLean. In October 1965, he opened negotiations with Brian Epstein with the hope of a Christmas special with The Beatles. Following a lunchtime meeting, he reported to Ken Baynes – the Head of Popular Music. 'I managed at last to get Emperor Epstein to talk business again… I told him frankly that we were disappointed at the now total absence of Beatles on radio except for their discs, and asked how we could do business. We had a long – very honest talk, and at the end he as good as promised them for Christmas morning 'Saturday Club' – perhaps as a self-contained 30-minute feature.'

There had been previous discussions about recording music for the radio at one of The Beatles' EMI sessions scheduled during October and November. They did turn up on Christmas Day in *Saturday Club*, but only for a few comic moments with Brian Matthew. There was no exclusive music performance for the BBC.

Following the August tour of North America and a six-week rest, The Beatles spent four busy weeks working on their new album and single to be released in December. Fourteen original songs were recorded for *Rubber Soul* and the double-A-sided single 'Day Tripper'/'We Can Work It Out'. During 1965, pop music had taken some giant steps away from frothy beat music to something more heady and mature: Dylan's two electric albums *Bringing It All Back Home* and *Highway 61 Revisited*, The Rolling Stones' 'Satisfaction', 'protest music', diverting debut hits by The Byrds, The Who and The Yardbirds. Always aware of the latest developments, The Beatles once again set the pace. *Rubber Soul* inspired Brian Wilson, for example, to reach for the heights achieved on The Beach Boys' LP *Pet Sounds* released in 1966.

After using advanced studio techniques to create *Rubber Soul*, the idea of The Beatles submitting to the limitations of a BBC music session had become fairly unlikely. On the other hand, so was the brief British tour undertaken in December. On 29 November 1965, four days before the first concert, they visited the BBC. The first item recorded was The Beatles singing a version of the instrumental

signature tune 'Saturday Jump', heard every week at the beginning of *Saturday Club*. On the broadcast, it was preceded by a quick burst of tomfoolery. 'Ad lib, man, you're famous for it!' John tells Ringo on the unedited tape that has survived. Next they were asked to comment on Brian Matthew's version of the Stanley Holloway monologue 'Brahn Boots' in 'Beatle Box Jury' – a parody of *Juke Box Jury* presented by David Jacobs. They had not heard Brian's impersonation of Stanley Holloway, but, nevertheless, reviewed it by sending up the fossilized phrases uttered regularly by the jurors on TV. 'A nice fat tapper … really get the kids swinging' (Ringo); 'The beat the kids adore these days' (Paul); 'I thought it was nice to dance to but I don't know about the Top Twenty' (John); 'I don't like all these protest songs about boots' (George). The familiar phrase 'Two say will, two say won't' brought 'Beatle Box Jury' to a Hit-or-Miss end.

Brief Christmas greetings were delivered, along with some thoughts on how they might spend the rest of the festive day – eating and watching television were the unsurprising choices. As the tape rolled between takes, it captured John enthusing to Paul about a new Chuck Berry record (probably *Fresh Berry's*) and receiving an album he had ordered by jazz bassist and composer Charles Mingus. Paul is heard asking whether the *Saturday Club* audience might wonder 'why we didn't happen to play on this one'.

The next day – 30 November 1965 – Brian Matthew met up again with John and George to record separate interviews for the BBC Transcription series *Pop Profile*. The intention of the series was to sketch in the personal background of 'top personalities from the world of popular music'. Two programmes were pressed on either side of a seven-inch disc running at 33 1/3 rpm and distributed to radio stations around the world. Each interview lasted around eight minutes and was opened and closed by a version of 'Outrage' by Booker T. & The M.G.'s. The original, the B-side of 'Boot-leg' by the M.G.'s, was on one of the discs John loaded into his portable Swiss KB Discomatic jukebox taken on tour in 1965.

BRIAN: Now John, you have from time to time been criticized – attacked is probably a better word – on the basis that you just don't care about anything or anybody. I'm sure this isn't true, but would you tell us what is the thing that you care most about?

JOHN: Well, I mean, obviously the first thing you think about is yourself and your family. So I care about them so whoever said I didn't care about anybody is wrong for that. There's plenty of things I care about. All the things I'm known for not caring about are things that a lot of people don't care about. And it's usually, you know, a certain type of person that cares about them. You know, just things in general that aren't important to me, that seem important to other people, you know. And it's not a sin or a crime.

BRIAN: No, I'm not suggesting it is…

JOHN: Yeah, I know, but there are people who think it is. Only, I can't think of them, because they're so general, it's just when I come across them I realize that I don't care about them, because I've never thought of them before.

BRIAN: OK, tell us a bit about your home, where you live now, John. How big is the house and what sort of area does it cover?

JOHN: Well, it's in what they call the stockbroker area. Everybody thinks you move… pop stars… I don't know what other pop stars move into places like that for. I moved in, 'cause it was about the third house I looked at and I had to get out of a flat quick. And I didn't care where it was as long as it was somewhere quite quiet and I really wanted to live in London, but I wouldn't risk it till it's really quietened down.

BRIAN: How big, in fact, is the house you're in?

JOHN: The house? I don't …it's quite big. It had a lot of bedrooms, but it said it had about ten when I got in there. But they call anything a bedroom, you know. It's probably got about six now. It's three floors so it's quite big.

BRIAN: Did you change it a lot internally?

JOHN: I knocked the whole inside out, practically. I didn't mean to. I meant to just get in and live for five years till the sort of fan fever settled down and then, sort of, go out looking properly, 'cause I could hardly look at houses, never mind live in it. It seemed massive when I walked in, but it gets smaller as you get used to it. I only realize how big it is when I go home again to Liverpool or visit any relations and I realize the size of their house compared with it. But it feels like a normal house now, and I can't find enough room for… I need more rooms for more instruments and things like that. I've got one room that's blue, green and… and some other colour. I don't know, I just painted it myself… and with about fourteen guitars in it, twenty pianos, organs, tape recorders, everything. The next room's for those racing cars. The next room's got a desk in where I write and draw. And the next room's got one-arm bandits and football games and all those things that you put tanners in. So I go up there and sort of play about there and the rest of the house is normal, you see. So it's almost…

BRIAN: You're nearly there!

JOHN: But it's not big enough, you see, I'd need a giant place.

BRIAN: Yeah. What about the… I don't know whether it is the latest car that you've acquired, you seem to have had a string of cars, but the big black job, John.

JOHN: Oh, that Rolls? Well, when I first got the original Rolls, I couldn't drive. Well, I hadn't passed my test – never bothered, because I wasn't very interested in it anyway – driving. But when all the others passed, I thought. 'Oh, I'd better do it or I'll just sort of get left!' So I got the first Rolls… sort of used to be embarrassing sitting in a Rolls, you know. You draw up, people think I got black windows to hide completely. Well, it's partly that and also 'cause it's good when you're coming home late at night and it's still… if it's daylight when you're coming in, it's dark inside the car. You just shut all the windows and you're still in the club, you know.

BRIAN: But you've had the whole thing black, haven't you, John?

JOHN: The whole… all of it's black. The wheels are black. The only thing still normal is the radiator which they wouldn't do black at the time, but I quite like it silver, now.

BRIAN: But is it all black inside – upholstery, woodwork?

JOHN: Inside, it's black carpet.

BRIAN: The black windows I understand, but why did you have everything else black?

JOHN: Because I like black, you know, and if I've gotta make a choice of colours, either in a hurry or one that I know I can live with, I can always… it saves me thinking about another colour scheme. And I'm always comfortable if it's black, you see. I don't mind if it's black.

BRIAN: Here's a point, when you came round to visit us in our studios the other day, John, you parked or somebody parked the Rolls, right out there in the middle of a parking meter 'No Parking' belt. And it was just left and it was fine, and you came out and went away. Do you think that this is a sort of a passport to anywhere, a Rolls? I mean, I've heard this suggested before.

JOHN: It is a bit of a passport. You see, you get some policemen that'll sort of… keep… you know sort of… shut their eyes a bit if they see a Rolls, especially a big black one, which is quite a good advantage some times. But also you get the other type of policeman that's got it in for anybody that, you know, Capitalist 'thingies' and that. So he'll pick on you just because you are in a big car even though, you know, they don't know they're biased, but their attitude is that even though they have got a Rolls, I don't care who it is.

BRIAN: [Laughing] Do you have any kind of – you just threw in this capitalist bit I know flippantly – do you have any kind of political leanings at all?

JOHN: I don't… I'm… yeah. I have, you know, but I can never place what they are. Do you know what I mean? I don't go on about it.

BRIAN: They don't fit into any party line?

JOHN: Not any party line I've heard of, yeah. I don't object to people inheriting money or having a big lot of money. I never did. But I do object to people being stoney broke and starving, you know.

BRIAN: What about sort of feelings and attitudes as a father, John? I mean, obviously you could afford to give your son any kind of education you would choose. Will you, in fact, do that do you think? Or would you like to leave a lot of it to him?

JOHN: Er, obviously you gotta choose his school up till he's 14. Well, I've worked out… I would never send him to a public [private] school, because… just of the snob value, that he'd be snobbish to people that didn't go, but the people there would also be snobbish to him because of what I am, so I'm not gonna let him go through that. If I send him to an ordinary school, just an ordinary day school or a grammar school… if he was at a grammar school, his father would be that much richer than most of the people there, that he's bound to get, you know, some sort of difficulty there and because of what I am. So the only school, I worked out, would be best for him until he's 12 is the French school, that one where they teach them in French.

BRIAN: The Lycée, yes.

JOHN: Yeah, I can never remember the name of it. So there, I reckon, if it's like I've been told, you get all nationalities, all colours. I think that's the most sort of classless school I can think of.

BRIAN: Yeah, but beyond that, would you give him complete freedom of choice or would you try to direct him at all?

JOHN: I don't know, you see. I can't imagine I'm… I'm trying not to do all the things I disliked, but not all of them – because some of the things I disliked, they *were* right at the time, even though, I was so annoyed with them…

BRIAN: Can you think of an example?

JOHN: Well, it's a joke in the family now… you know, 'The guitar's all right for a hobby.' That's the big thing, 'But it won't earn you any money.' Now I know that, I always keep thinking that I should have… you know, I was obviously musical from very early, and I just wonder why nobody ever did anything about it 'cause… maybe 'cause they couldn't afford it.

BRIAN: Lets sort of confine it to this then, John. If your son, when he got to a reasonable sort of age, I mean, early teens, felt very strongly that he wanted to do anything at all, would you encourage him?

OPPOSITE **The EMI factory in Hayes, Middlesex – 24 November 1965.**

JOHN: Yeah, whatever it is. I would, yeah. The only thing, I'd hope it was something like I like, but I know I'm gonna not do that. You know, I mean, I'm already sort of: 'Get on that piano,' and he's only two! When he gets on, I mean he does it himself and all that kind of thing. But I dunno whether all kids of two-and-a-half do. Obviously, he's gonna be a bit influenced, 'cause there's music, and my kind of music, on all the time at home. And the thing is I'm just turning out like all other parents, you see!

BRIAN: [laughing] Obviously.

JOHN: I try and think about it when he's not there. I try and be rational. I'm trying to do it all right, but I suppose he'll just turn out the same. I'm gonna try not to, you know, at least I'm thinking about it now.

BRIAN: With that much experience behind you now, would you like to have more children?

JOHN: Yeah, I'd… just as many as come, you know! 'Let 'em roll out!' I say. I like large families, the idea of it.

BRIAN: Good. Fine, John. Thank you very much.

JOHN: It's a pleasure.

JOHN, HIS WIFE Cynthia and son Julian had moved out of central London to Weybridge, Surrey in 1964. The house, called Kenwood, had been built in 1913 in a mock-Tudor style. The Lennon family lived in the servants' flat on the top floor for a year while the considerable alterations to the building took place. Julian first attended Heath House School in Weybridge until he moved from the area following his parents' divorce. He did not go to the Lycée Français Charles de Gaulle school in Kensington, London.

George's *Pop Profile* was an enlightening and honest feature.

BRIAN: Now George, I wonder if first of all you'd tell me a little bit about your own background before you ever became a Beatle.

GEORGE: Yeah, well… start say at school, because it's pointless really going back before then and I probably wouldn't remember anyway. At school I was a very bad pupil. In fact I was probably one of the worst pupils they've ever had in the school, but I realize that now, [but] at the time, I was all for having a good 'laff' and if this hadn't have worked then I don't really know what I would have been doing. 'Cause I left school, I was an electrician for about… or apprentice electrician… for about four months and I decided… I remember asking my big brother, 'Would you pack in work and have a go at this, if you were me?' And he says, 'Well, you might as well. You never know.' And he said, 'If you don't, you're not going to lose anything by just working in that job.'

BRIAN: Was there anything at school that you liked at all?

GEORGE: The only thing I liked really was art. And I realize now that it was because the teacher at art was a nice fella. He'd come round and try and… you know, he'd say, 'Well, why don't you do it this way?' The others, if you'd go up and say, 'I'm a bit doubtful about…' they'd shout at you or give you a belt in the gob, which didn't really help! Anyway, after school, and this job which only lasted a bit, I joined full time. Well, the others – Paul and John – were still… John was at art college and Paul was doing an extra year at school. So by the time I'd been at this place for four or five months, then they were just due out of school and we got the opportunity to go to Scotland and then on to Hamburg. And then after that I just forgot all about nine till five.

BRIAN: I'm sure you did. George, I don't know whether you'd accept this, but it seems to me that you've emerged with the image of, in so far as any of you are ever silent, the silent Beatle.

GEORGE: Yeah. Well, I think I'm more quiet than the others, because I got fed up before the others of all these questions like 'What colour teeth have you got?' You know, just stupid questions you have no interest in any longer. And I think everybody… well, all fans, I think, all know what colour eyes we've got and what we drink for breakfast and all that. And they don't wanna know that any more. So I just shut up until somebody asks me something worth answering.

BRIAN: Yeah. What do you care about most now, George?

GEORGE: Music is my main interest, naturally. And not just pop music – all sorts of things. I like a lot of folk – much more folk than I did say a year or two ago. I like quite a lot of them and I think Dylan, Donovan and Pete Seeger and Jack Elliot – that type – are the good ones. But as with most music, there's good and bad.

BRIAN: Yep. George, you've recently started to write rather more than you had in the past. This must have been kinda difficult for you, sitting alongside the two most popular writers in the world today.

GEORGE: Well I think, um, I don't know really whether I would've written more songs by now or better songs by now had Paul and John not been with us, because probably I mightn't have even thought of writing songs, only for those two. But it was hard trying to get in on it, because I didn't wanna write… Well, I've written so many songs that I've just thrown away as I've been writing them, because I've wanted, when I've finally recorded one of mine, I've wanted it to be worth putting on the LP alongside Paul and John's. I feel now I've got more idea about how to write songs.

BRIAN: Yeah. What about sounds in general, George, which way do you think we're heading?

GEORGE: More arrangements, definitely. Well, from the songs and the singers that we follow – you know, our favourites, each instrument's doing a definite thing and you can hear everything, if you want to. You can hear a tambourine, even if it's just in the background and there's better arrangements coming. And so just generally I think pop'll progress so that every member of the group's doing his own bit rather than… you know, I think the bad thing about some groups is the lead guitarist likes to be the star, and the drummer likes to be the star and also the singer's out there in the front, who *is* the star of the group. And that's all wrong. I think with us we try and… everybody is a bit of, you know, one whole.

BRIAN: Right, George, you've told us how you think and how you work. How do you live now? Do you have a house or are you in a flat?

GEORGE: Yeah, I've been living in a house of my own for almost two years now. Because it got, at one point, so bad… for Ringo and I had flats… we first lived in hotels in London, we'd realized we were down here so much we'd better get a flat. So Ringo and

'I don't know really whether I would've written more songs or better songs by now had Paul and John not been with us.'

GEORGE HARRISON

I shared about three or four flats and it worked out we'd have a lease for a few months and after that, even if we liked the flat, we couldn't stay there 'cause they didn't want us to stay 'cause of kids and noise and trouble and all that. So I decided the only way is to move out of town, and so I got this house, which I've been in for about two years and it's great.

BRIAN: It's virtually in the country is it, George?

GEORGE: Yeah, yeah, in Surrey.

BRIAN: Is it big?

GEORGE: No, it's a bungalow, actually. But it's built like an Australian ranch house, the man told me, who built it. And it's just like a wander-in bungalow, sort of bedrooms right down one end and you can be in bed with all the noise in the world going on in the lounge and you won't hear it.

BRIAN: Is there a lot of ground round it?

GEORGE: No, not really. It's not an acre. But the great thing is it's isolated by a big wall, which is [an] old sort of National Trust wall, which you can't knock down.

BRIAN: Oh, great. Do you have a staff looking after you?

GEORGE: No, just one woman, who comes in, cleans up and cooks… and smiles! [laughter]

BRIAN: Nice! I don't suppose you're there all that much, are you?

GEORGE: Yeah, well we're able to be at home much more now, because as everybody probably knows, we're doing less touring and we're just having more time for ourselves. We were able to spend more time on recording. Now, we've got more time to think about the things that we do. And so we hope that even if we do less things, that when we do them they're gonna be better than if it was all a big rush, and also we all enjoy being at home now. The good thing about going away is you appreciate coming home again.

BRIAN: Yeah I'll bet! Good. And what about as a sort of subject, rather than any particular aspect of it, do you want to have a family?

GEORGE: Well, I don't know about that!

BRIAN: Well, do you like kids? Let's put it that way.

GEORGE: Well, I like some kids and I dislike some others. I don't really… I can't see myself being a father yet. I couldn't stand… I'm too young for that. I don't mind admiring other people's kids and thinking, 'Oh, coochy coo, isn't he nice?' but I don't think I want 'em for myself, right now. [laughs]

BRIAN: Is there anything you really do want for yourself right now, other than what you've got?

GEORGE: Well, nothing I'm conscious of. I just wanna carry on progressing with music; you know, writing more and just learning more about it.

BRIAN: And being left to live your own life a little bit?

GEORGE: Mmm, yeah.

BRIAN: Good. Thank you very much, George.

GEORGE: Thank you.

GEORGE EXPRESSED HIS disdain for the ephemeral nature of most pop interviews. The *Pop Profile* series took a new approach to interviewing musicians; consequently he sounded very relaxed and thoughtful as he talked to Brian Matthew. Like Paul, George had attended the Liverpool Institute Grammar School, where he claimed he was 'a very bad pupil'. He mentioned his growing interest in folk music and name-checked the new generation represented by Bob Dylan and Donovan, and the older singers who had inspired them – Pete Seeger and Rambling Jack Elliott. When the interview was recorded, The Beatles' LP *Rubber Soul* was about to be released. The album does show signs of being influenced by the current vogue for folk music. George's composition 'If I Needed Someone' has the jingle-jangle sound of The Byrds. Formed in 1964, they had been inspired by The Beatles and had appropriated the chiming sound of George's Rickenbacker twelve-string guitar. George bought the bungalow in Esher, Surrey – called Kinfauns – in July 1964. He lived there until his 1970 move to Friar Park, Henley-on-Thames. Kinfauns was later demolished and a new property built on the plot.

The *Pop Profiles* featuring John and George were transferred to disc and mailed out in March 1966. Paul and Ringo recorded their interviews for the series in May of that year. Compared to 1963 and 1964, there had been only a small number of radio appearances by The Beatles on the BBC's UK networks in 1965. There were even fewer occasions when they were featured on BBC TV. The commercial television channel fared better. ITV showed several programmes with Beatles performances: *Thank Your Lucky Stars*, *The Eamonn Andrews Show*, *Poll Winners Concert*, *Blackpool Night Out* (six live songs) and *The Music of Lennon & McCartney*. For 42 weeks in 1965, Radio Luxembourg scheduled a fifteen-minute programme presented by Chris Denning called *The Beatles*. There were snippets of interviews and requests read by the group spread fairly thinly across the series. Pirate radio stations also broadcast Beatles material in 1965. The group recorded a message to welcome the launch of Radio Scotland and Christmas greetings for Radio Caroline. Paul was also featured on Caroline's Boxing Day programme *Pop's Happening*. Pop was happening, but in comparison to the offshore stations spinning non-stop hits, it was not happening much at the BBC. Pirate Radio London DJ Kenny Everett made jingles boasting 'Big L' was 'your official Beatle station'. No wonder The Beatles were less enthusiastic about adding to their heavy workload by accepting bookings for shows on the old-fashioned BBC Light Programme.

🔲 Radio programme titles
🔲 TV titles

🔲 NOT ONLY... BUT ALSO
Br: 9 Jan 1965 – 9.20–10.00pm – BBC 2
Rec: 20 Nov 1964
Wimbledon Common, London
Location filming with John, Dudley Moore and Norman Rossington to illustrate a reading of 'Deaf Ted, Danoota, (and me)'.
Rec: 29 Nov 1964 – 8.30pm
Studio One, Television Centre, London
John, Dudley Moore and Norman Rossington read prose and poems from *In His Own Write*: About The Awful (John), Good Dog Nigel and The Wrestling Dog (John and Norman Rossington), All Abord Speeching (John, Dudley Moore and Norman Rossington), Unhappy Frank (Dudley Moore and Norman Rossington).

🔲 SATURDAY CLUB
Br: 20 March 1965 – 10.00am–noon
– The Light Programme
Rec: 19 March 1965
The group were heard talking to Brian Matthew over the phone from a hotel room in Obertauern,

Austria, where they were on location for their second movie *Help!*

🔲 POP INN
Br: 13 April 1965 – 1.00-1.55pm
– The Light Programme, Live
100th Edition
Sitting in a BBC 'radio car', The Beatles' voices were beamed from Twickenham Film Studios onto the air.

🔲 TOP OF THE POPS
Br: 15 April 1965 – 7.30-8.00pm
– BBC 1
Rec: 10 April 1965
Studio Two, Riverside Studios, Hammersmith
Mimed performances of: *Ticket To Ride* (repeated 29 April and 6 May 1965), *Yes It Is* (repeated 22 April 1965).
[25 seconds survive of 'Ticket To Ride', as it was used in *Doctor Who* on 22 May 1965]

🔲 TONIGHT
Br: 18 June 1965 – 7.00–7.35pm
– BBC 1, Live
Lime Grove Studios, London
John talked about *A Spaniard in the Works* with Kenneth Allsop and read: We Must Not Forget The General Erection and The Wumberlog (Or The Magic Dog).

🔲 THE BEATLES Invite You to Take a Ticket To Ride
Br: 7 June 1965 (Whit Monday) – 10.00am– 12.15pm – The Light Programme
Rec: 26 May 1965
Number 1 Studio, Piccadilly Theatre, London
Producer: Keith Bateson
Presenter: Denny Piercy
Ticket To Ride (short version), *Everybody's Trying To Be My Baby*, *I'm A Loser*, *The Night Before*, *Honey Don't*, *Dizzy Miss Lizzy*, *She's A Woman*, *Ticket To Ride*

🔲 LATE NIGHT EXTRA
Br: 11 June 1965 – 10.35-11.30pm
– The Light Programme
Rec: 11 June 1965
Paul was interviewed over the telephone when

news broke of The Beatles receiving MBEs in the Queen's Birthday Honours List.

🔲 TODAY
Br: 21 June 1965 – 7.15–8.40am
– The Home Service
Rec: 16 June 1965
The programme included John talking to reporter Tim Matthews and reading two verses of 'The National Health Cow' from his new book *A Spaniard in the Works*.

🔲 THE WORLD OF BOOKS
Br: 3 July 1965 – 10.10–10.40pm
– The Home Service
Rec: 16 June 1965
NEMS Enterprises, Sutherland House, Argyll Street, London
John was interviewed about *A Spaniard in the Works* by BBC producer Wilfred De'Ath.

🔲 LANCE A'GOGO
Br: 31 July 1965 – 12.00–12.29pm – The Light Programme
Rec: 30 July 1965
Lance Percival interviewed The Beatles for his show, billed as 'half an hour of quiet pandemonium'.

🔲 THE BEATLES ABROAD
Br: 30 August 1965 (August Bank Holiday) 10.00–10.45am – The Light Programme
Rec: 15–20 August 1965
Brian Matthew presented a 45-minute behind-the-scenes feature about The Beatles' tour of North America with a particular focus on the Shea Stadium concert in New York. The group were heard talking – and George strumming a guitar – in hotel rooms.

🔲 SATURDAY CLUB
Br: 25 December 1965 (Christmas Day) 10.00am–11.30am – The Light Programme
Rec: 29 November 1965
Brian Matthew engaged the group in merry banter, including a *Beatle Box Jury* verdict on his performance of Stanley Holloway's monologue 'Brahn Boots'. They sang a version of the show's instrumental theme tune 'Saturday Jump'.

1966

At the
Phonograph

IN AUGUST 1966, Paul appeared on a BBC radio show called *David Frost at the Phonograph*. The title was a joke – no one called a record player a phonograph any more. On the other hand, it was a production by the BBC's Gramophone Department – who still called a record player a gramophone? Certainly not the many offshore 'pirate' radio stations beaming a constant stream of records to the UK and making the BBC seem very out of touch with the vibrant British pop scene of 1966.

Despite a busy international touring schedule planned for the summer of 1966, The Beatles' entire musical focus was on creating something revolutionary in the studio. The result of the ambitious approach taken during sessions lasting from April to June was *Revolver*. None of the songs on the album was ever played live by The Beatles. The group in concert now bore little relation to the master record-makers of *Revolver*. The Beatles' tour of North America started in Chicago with John explaining that an observation in an interview that 'we're more popular than Jesus now' had been 'taken wrong... and now it's all this'. What he meant by 'all this' was death threats from the Ku Klux Klan and bonfires fuelled by Beatles records. Asked on this tour about the Vietnam War, he spoke out for the first time. He later recalled it was 'a pretty radical thing to do, especially for the Fab Four. I burst out, because I could no longer play that game any more.'

The war in Vietnam was the major news story of 1966. It was now being waged with the full might of the US military with a force of over 385,000. Over six thousand Americans were killed in Vietnam during the year – more than three times the number for 1965. Anti-war protests were widespread. On 15 May, 8,000 encircled the Pentagon building. Boxer Muhammad Ali (formerly Cassius Clay) refused to be drafted into the war. He was given a prison sentence the following year for his act of defiance. At a time when images of warfare were broadcast nightly on network news programmes, Staff Sergeant Barry Sadler had a five-week run at number one with a patriotic tribute to his army combat unit called Special Forces. 'The Ballad Of The Green Berets' sold a million copies in its first two weeks on sale in the US.

Another element that characterized 1966 was satirized in The Kinks' single 'Dedicated Follower Of Fashion'. 'The Carnabetian Army' dressed in flamboyant clothes was marching through 'Swinging London'. Michael Caine starred in *Alfie* – a film showing the title character living a hedonistic lifestyle of 'birds and booze' in the trendy city. On 30 July, the country was elated when England beat West Germany 4-2 at the final of the football World Cup. In October, the UK was similarly united as it was shocked by the tragedy that occurred in the Welsh village of Aberfan. Slag-heap waste from the local coal mine had slid down a hillside and engulfed a junior school, causing the deaths of 116 children and 28 adults.

The space race continued. On 1 March, the Soviet craft *Venera 3* crashed on Venus – the first man-made object to reach the planet's surface. The Russians were also first to put a spacecraft, Luna 10, in orbit around the Moon. The sixth manned NASA space flight was made by *Gemini VIII* under the command of Neil Armstrong, who carried out the first docking of two spacecraft in orbit. Fascination with adventures in the universe was reflected in *Star Trek*, which launched on American TV in September 1966. The mission of the starship *Enterprise* was to 'boldly go where no man has gone before'. The same month, the TV series *The Monkees* made its debut. Its mission was to go where The Beatles had already gone before. The four actors playing members of a fictional pop group were required to follow a formula set by The Beatles' escapades in their movies *A Hard Day's Night* and *Help!*. It worked. The TV series was a hit and The Monkees' records sold millions. Their timing had been perfect. The Monkees assumed roles that the original Fab Four had just vacated when, after their last concert of 1966, they dropped out of that game.

FOLLOWING THE LAST concert of The Beatles' UK tour on 12 December 1965, the group took a break lasting several months. A long absence from BBC radio and TV schedules was interrupted by the screening of *The Beatles at Shea Stadium* on 1 March 1966. It was produced by three companies: Sullivan Productions (founded by Ed Sullivan), Brian Epstein's NEMS Enterprises and The Beatles' own Subafilms. The pandemonium generated during the concert on 15 August 1965 caused several technical problems with the sound recording. As part of post-production work on the film, some musical 'fixes' were made by the group on 5 January 1966. These repairs included re-recording 'I Feel Fine' and 'Help!' in their entirety at CTS Studios in London. The concert sound for 'Act Naturally' was completely replaced by the version of the song released on *Help!* The film footage provides compelling evidence of the fan frenzy that erupted that August night in the baseball stadium used by the New York Mets.

The BBC 1 audience for the first broadcast of the film was measured at 23.1 per cent of the population. An impressive figure, it was nevertheless eclipsed by *Amos Burke Secret Agent* in the same time slot on ITV, which reached 27 per cent of the country. There were three channels to choose from at this time, but the other alternative – BBC 2 – had a very small number of potential viewers. An Audience Research report stated that a quarter of the Viewing Panel who had watched 'derived little enjoyment of the programme – as an illustration of Beatlemania it was, perhaps, not without interest but there was certainly nothing entertaining in this exhibition of "mass hysteria"… musically the programme was a "dead loss"'. As in previous reports on The Beatles' programmes, there were some strongly worded negative comments: 'a vastly over-rated group'; 'the Beatles' "inane" comments added little to this excessively noisy and unedifying spectacle'; 'I thought this an appalling show, the girls in the audience made me despair for their sanity'.

RIGHT Kenneth Adam went straight to the top – the Director General Hugh Carleton Greene – for a decision regarding Brian Epstein's plans to advertise the BBC broadcast of *The Beatles at Shea Stadium*.

OPPOSITE The BBC's Audience Research report on *The Beatles at Shea Stadium* included the usual wide range of comments – from 'nothing entertaining' to 'the next best thing to being present at Shea Stadium'.

From: Director of Television

Subject: THE BEATLES AT SHEA STADIUM   15th February 1966

To: D.G.

I am very sorry to commit you to reading this as soon as you get back, but it is urgent and complicated.

Basically, the situation is this: The Epstein Organisation made a film of the Beatles in the U.S. and sold us the rights to televise this twice. We were not concerned in the production in any way. We have no other rights of any kind. They want to advertise our first showing in the Daily Mirror.

Advertisement by artists (including those who do appear in BBC productions - see the Al Read clipping attached) are constantly appearing in the trade press, and sometimes in local and national newspapers. Usually very unostentatiously, but the practice has been established over the years. The difference here is one of size - and circulation. The Epstein Organisation can afford a full page in the Daily Mirror. Few artists are worth this kind of money.

I enclose a clear note of the situation from Peacock. My own view is that if we were to get Epstein to feature prominently his production company credit (Peacock's paragraph 6) we should not try and stop this.

(Kenneth Adam)

AS/20/P
6mo W

lha

encs

URGENT

Please turn over

British Broadcasting Corporation   Confidential

AN AUDIENCE RESEARCH REPORT

(Week 9)   VR/66/129

THE BEATLES AT SHEA STADIUM

Tuesday, 1st March, 1966. 8.00-8.50 pm, BBC 1

1. <u>Size of audience</u> (based on results of the Survey of Listening and Viewing.)

   It is estimated that the audience for this broadcast was 23.1% of the population of the United Kingdom. Amos Burke, Secret Agent, on ITV at the time, was seen by 27%.

2. <u>Reaction of audience</u> (based on questionnaires completed by a sample of the audience. This sample, 385 in number, is the 18% of the BBC 1 Viewing Panel who saw all or most of the broadcast.)

   The reactions of this sample of the audience were distributed as follows:-

A+	A	B	C	C-
%	%	%	%	%
17	31	26	19	7

   giving a REACTION INDEX of 58. It's the Beatles - a programme relayed from the stage of the Empire, Liverpool in Week 50, 1963 - gained a figure of 59.

3. Reaction to this film of the Beatles performing before an audience of 60,000 teenagers was mainly one of astonishment at the sheer frenzy of the scene, a display that was made even more incomprehensible by the fact that the persistent and deafening screaming made it appear unlikely that any of the near-hysterical fans could even hear their idols. Over a quarter of the sample, in fact, derived little enjoyment from the programme - as an illustration of Beatlemania it was, perhaps, not without interest but there was certainly nothing entertaining in this exhibition of 'mass hysteria', they felt and musically the programme was a 'dead loss'. Some had never cared for the Beatles and saw nothing in the broadcast to make them change their minds - 'a vastly over-rated group' - but even those who admired their singing sometimes remarked that they could, on this occasion, hardly compete with the general hubbub and came over well below their best. The supporting artists - with the possible exception of Sounds Incorporated - were pretty poor, it was also observed, while the Beatles' 'inane' comments added little to this excessively noisy and unedifying spectacle. 'Interesting as a phenomenon but painful to listen to. I did not enjoy the music of any of the artists. I do not usually like the Beatles but even so I thought them well below form, while as speakers they were inarticulate and uninteresting'; 'Whilst I enjoy some of the Beatles' programmes, I thought this an appalling show. The girls in the audience made me despair for their sanity'.

Continued /

THE BEATLES AT SHEA STADIUM (Week 9) (Continued)

4. About half the sample, nevertheless, had thoroughly enjoyed the programme. Several declared themselves ardent Beatle fans and much appreciated the opportunity of seeing them on their American tour, while others, usually no more than moderately entertained by the group, were nevertheless struck by the warmth and enthusiasm they brought to their singing and the programme as a whole was evidently felt to have captured most successfully the excitement of the occasion. Some viewers, it is true, found the photography jerky, disliking the 'odd camera angles' and the abrupt switches from one subject to another but many others particularly admired the way in which the camera panned from artists to spectators and agreed that the photography throughout had been extremely good. 'Marvellous. The Beatles always generate such excitement that one gets swept along with the fantastic enthusiasm of the fans. One really got the feel of the mounting heat and frenetic hysteria of the young screaming, weeping fans and of the energy put into the performance by the Beatles themselves. This programme was the next best thing to being present at Shea Stadium'. Several, too, said they particularly enjoyed the aerial views of New York (taken from the Beatles' helicopter) and the lads' own comments on their tour.

Copyright   Audience Research Department
of the BBC   22nd March, 1966.
RG/BB

However, half of the reporting viewers did enjoy *The Beatles at Shea Stadium*. 'Marvellous. The Beatles always generate such excitement that one gets swept along with the fantastic enthusiasm of the fans. This was the next best thing to being present at Shea Stadium.' Brian Epstein regarded the televising of the film as an effective medium to demonstrate his group's phenomenal success. He booked space to advertise the BBC broadcast in the *Daily Mail*, *NME* and five other trade papers. This ruffled feathers. As a public service broadcaster, the BBC had to be seen as separate from commercial practices. The Corporation did not buy advertising to publicize its programmes. In fact, it was so wary of indirectly advertising products that even the brand names above the keyboards of pianos were blacked out. The Director of Television Kenneth Adam wrote to the Director General of the BBC, Hugh Carleton Greene with the advice that 'if we were to get Epstein to feature prominently his production company credit… we should not try and stop this'. The Controller of BBC 1 agreed with this course of action. He pointed out: 'We are concerned with the most successful group of artists in the history of show business, and their goodwill and that of the Epstein Organisation is of great importance to us.'

At this time, the Transcription Service was more successful at gaining access to The Beatles than were the BBC's domestic services. Having recorded highly personal interviews with John and George for *Pop Profile*, Brian Matthew interviewed Paul and Ringo five months later, on 2 May 1966. The Beatles had resumed recording songs at Abbey Road on 6 April – nearly five months since they had completed work on *Rubber Soul*. The sessions for the new album – eventually called *Revolver* – ran until June. The album merged a variety of elements absorbed from outside the usual sphere of pop music. Interwoven with exotic Indian instruments, dreamy drones, loops, backwards tapes, a string quartet, clavichord and French horn, the sound of the album was a dazzling leap forward from *Rubber Soul*. Paul's *Pop Profile* interview clearly revealed his willingness to absorb inspiration from a variety of new sources. Curious about anything innovative, he'd recently attended an avant-garde concert by electronic composer Luciano Berio.

BRIAN: Do you at any time, pause, cease to think of yourself as Beatle Paul McCartney?

PAUL: Yes, I try to do that quite a bit, because… really the best thing about before all of this sort of happened for us was that you could just sort of wander around and never have to think, 'Oh, look. Why is that person looking at me?' 'Cause I'm famous. Nobody ever looked at you, you know, and so it was great just to walk around like that. So those times, yes.

BRIAN: Looking ahead, how do you feel about it?

PAUL: Oh, I don't mind, you know. I don't mind about it.

BRIAN: And when you're not being a Beatle, what sort of things interest you most?

PAUL: I like lots of things. I like music, just anyway. I like writing music. I mean, that's sort of almost even apart from The Beatles. Mind you we record everything we write, but I just liked doing things like that – music. Oh, I don't know, [there are] lots of things I wanna do, but I haven't got round to them yet. But I will do.

BRIAN: You've attracted a fair amount of publicity of late by attending unusual sort of concerts and plays and things, haven't you?

PAUL: Yeah. Well, it's funny that. Because it's a drag that it does attract that funny kind of publicity, because the only reason I'm going is not the way people seem to think of it in the newspapers and things. I mean in one of the newspapers they wrote up… I went to see this fellow who is just a composer and I'd heard some of his music and a bit of it was electronic and it was quite interesting. It sounded all new and everything. And I went along and then papers sort of wrote it up: 'No wonder he was there, it was about electronic music.' And it was a drag! Because that's the trouble, you get put into a pigeonhole.

BRIAN: Now, I don't want to ask you the corny old question that you must get asked so often of 'When are The Beatles going to stop being Beatles?' or anything like that, but obviously there must come a time when the group ceases to be a group. Is there anything you want to do then? Obviously, you wouldn't have to do anything.

RIGHT Recording in Studio Three, Abbey Road during the sessions for the LP *Revolver*. Producer George Martin is visible through the control room window.

PAUL: No. Well, the thing is that I'd – like any of the others – I don't like doing nothing, particularly. I think all of us enjoy something… enjoy doing something that's enjoyable. That's all there is to it and it can be anything. All kinds of music, for instance. There's millions of kinds of music I haven't listened to yet. But I've heard a few kinds, only sort of extracts of them really, but I suddenly realized I like 'em. And I always thought I didn't. And it's funny, you know, just suddenly realizing, 'Yes, that's quite good.' But I wonder why I always turned that off when it came on the radio. You know, Indian music, for instance. Whenever you get on an Indian channel, you know, when you're fiddling through the radio, I always used to just turn it off. And George got this big sort of Indian kick and he's dead keen on it. And we've been round to his house a couple of times and he plays you and er… [it's] so boring! [laughing] No, no. It's good, you know. And you sort of hear millions of things in it that I never realized were in it. And [the same] in classical music, some classical music.

BRIAN: OK, you also do from time to time visit theatre for straight plays.

PAUL: Yeah.

BRIAN: Anything…?

PAUL: Well, that's the same thing again, because when I was in Liverpool I used to, once or twice, just go to Liverpool Playhouse, which was a repertory then. And I wasn't very keen on it. I mean I used to just go to see if I liked going to see these plays. I wasn't very keen on it. I just never went again. But I went when I came down to London and I went to something that wasn't like those plays that they did in repertory. So, I don't know, you just come down and you see some great actors acting in great plays, and you just think, 'Wow, that is good!' I was wrong to say that it's just rubbish.

BRIAN: But your interest in it is just sort of a personal experience and appreciation of watching other people do it.

PAUL: Well I mean…

BRIAN: It stops there?

PAUL: Yeah, I think so. I mean I'm not, for instance, interested in producing…

BRIAN: This is what I want…

PAUL: … for stage or anything, because I don't think I could do it for one and I don't think I'd get enough enjoyment out of it to merit me learning how to do it. But there are some things that I'd love to be able to do.

BRIAN: Such as?

PAUL: Oh, I don't know. The whole idea of making films is good. But I don't mean very big expensive films, but films that you sort of just make because you fancied making a film. But, I mean, the only thing is that already having got the kind of image that we've got, if any of us wanted to do anything like that, we would tend to get beaten down because people would say, 'Oh, look. He's not trying that old trick of making a film,' or, you know, 'He's not going classical.' And it sounds like that, but the only thing is that… and I thought exactly like that about people who did that too. I always used to think, 'Oh, there he goes, going the same old path they all go – all-round entertainers.' But, it's just that you find there are some things which are just as interesting as what you've been doing for a certain amount of time.

BRIAN: Right, let's get onto a, if we can, a kind of domestic level, Paul. The other three boys, all being married, need or choose to have large-ish houses. What about you for a pad? What's your ideal? You've recently bought a house, haven't you?

PAUL: I've bought a house. Yeah. I love it. I love houses. I always have. I always like going to visit people and seeing their houses and things, because it's always the character of houses that gets me. You go into a small house and it's that kind of character – it's still great. You go into a big house and it's completely different and they are things on their own anyway. I like that.

BRIAN: What sort of house have you bought?

PAUL: Um, a big one. 'Cause I like big houses. And it's an old one, because I like old houses.

BRIAN: And it's in town, is it? Or near?

PAUL: Well, it's near.

BRIAN: Are you, by and large, sick and tired of travelling or would you still like to do more?

OPPOSITE AND RIGHT **Paul at Abbey Road in April 1966.**

PAUL: I don't like travelling. I never have liked travelling. I never liked travelling as a kid in someone's car or something. I always got sick. But I don't get sick any more, I just don't like it. I got sick *of* it. And I don't care how many statistics they produce, I'm still a bit nervous about flying.

BRIAN: So you wouldn't want to take that up?

PAUL: It's funny you should say that, because I had a go of a plane. Some fella gave me a go of a plane and he was a trained instructor and so he just said, 'I'll give you a lesson.' And I was flying it and it was different then, because you know when you're a driver and you're in the back seat of someone else's car and they're driving – I'm terrified. I don't like it unless I'm driving. Because I'm not worried about whether we're going to crash if I'm driving. And it was like that with the plane. It was fantastic so that made me…

BRIAN: It fits the pattern, I think, so really you'd say you're a doer and not a watcher.

PAUL: Er, I think so, probably. I think I'm a watcher up to a point. I like watching until I think it would be good to do or I might be able to do that and get something out of it. I mean enjoy it. That's what it is, you know.

BRIAN: Well, I hope you go on doing things that you get pleasure out of and I'm sure we shall for a long time. Thank you, Paul.

PAUL: Thank you.

THE INTERVIEW REVEALED Paul's enthusiasm for low-budget 'films that you sort of just make because you fancied making a film'. Less than a year later, Paul formulated his plan for the do-it-yourself Beatles film *Magical Mystery Tour*, which went into production in September 1967. The Beatles' movies released in 1964 and 1965 had been directed by Richard Lester – an inspired choice made primarily because the group loved a short film he made in 1960 with comedians Spike Milligan and Peter Sellers called *The Running Jumping & Standing Still Film*. Asked whether he would direct another Beatles movie, Lester replied: 'I have a very great respect for The Beatles' talents and believe they shouldn't be limited to the conventions of the professional film-maker. They should go on and develop their talents in this field and make a movie as they make their albums.'

'The whole idea of making films is good… I don't mean very big expensive films.'

PAUL McCARTNEY

OPPOSITE Paul taking an interest in the filming of promotional clips for 'Paperback Writer' and 'Rain' in the grounds of Chiswick House, West London on 20 May 1966.

In Brian Matthew's *Pop Profile* interview with Ringo, he heard how the drummer had first been attracted to music when in hospital. In his early teens, he developed a severe case of pleurisy, which affected one of his lungs. Consequently, he spent two years in the Royal Liverpool Children's Hospital in Heswall on the Wirral peninsula.

BRIAN: Ringo, what's been the most important aspect of being a Beatle to you?

RINGO: Important?

BRIAN: Yeah.

RINGO: I… Oh, I was tapping. I was tapping, folks. Your set isn't wrong. I don't know, it's all… sort of important in good ways, and it's unimportant in other ways, you know.

BRIAN: Could you say what's pleased you most about it?

RINGO: The most?… To pinpoint it would be hard. I just like being in The Beatles. It's the best thing for me anyway. There's nothing better than that.

BRIAN: What do you find the most enjoyable aspect of life *now*? The way The Beatles are operating now, which is on a sort of limited…

RINGO: Yeah. Well it's much nicer. We used to work every night, practically. We were always tired and hungry! [laughs] But now we have plenty of time off and it's great because it doesn't get on top of you. You can just have a rest and then we do a bit of work.

BRIAN: What do you do during the time that you're off?

RINGO: Sit around most of the time. I just don't do anything. Just play records. You know, all the usual stuff anybody does when they sit round.

BRIAN: Yeah. Do you think you'd be content to do that for the rest of your life or is there anything you'd like to do outside of being a musician?

RINGO: Um… no, there's nothing I'd rather do. Really. I mean, I like playing and things like that, but I think I would turn into a blob if I was left to do nothing.

BRIAN: You would do that?

RINGO: Yes, I could easily turn into a lump of nothing – just sitting on a chair!

BRIAN: How much do material possessions matter to you? Do you need the trappings of luxury now?

RINGO: I like them, you know. That's why I have 'em. So, it's nice to have a good house and a bit of land and a couple of good, you know, couple of cars instead of one terrible old car. I enjoy all that. I mean anyone would.

BRIAN: Well, I'm sure. Do you like being a family man?

RINGO: Yes, I enjoy that too. 'Cause then that's good again for me, you see, because if I sit around, at least there's something going round. You know, there's the baby slobbering on me! Things like that. Lovely baby.

BRIAN: Would you like to have more kids?

RINGO: Yes, yes. They're good fun. They sort of crawl round and break all the ashtrays and that.

BRIAN: Have you any thoughts about what you'd like your own children to do?

RINGO: No. No, I don't know. Honestly, don't know.

BRIAN: Would you be happy to have a family of…?

RINGO: That's the worst thing, you know. As soon as the baby arrived, you've got all these sort of… 'Well, what do we do now? If we tell him to do this, is it right?' Just have to go along, but I haven't planned anything for him. I just hope he's OK, himself. He can make it.

BRIAN: Would you be happy to have a family of blobs all sitting around doing nothing?

RINGO: Well, as long as I was one too!

BRIAN: That's what I meant.

RINGO: I wouldn't mind. That would be OK. Then you'd have no worries, would you?

BRIAN: I guess. No, no.

RINGO: And that's what I like, you see, no worries. I hate worries.

BRIAN: Do your outside activities extend to wanting to travel anywhere and really see places that you've maybe been to and not seen as a Beatle?

RINGO: No, not yet. No.

BRIAN: Where do you like to go on a holiday for instance?

RINGO: Well, we always go somewhere where it's quiet. We phone up the office and say, 'Well, how is it here?' and she'll say 'Oh, it's snow.' 'Cause we don't know much geography. Well, I don't. And they'll say, 'Well, this is very nice.' So we all go there thinking, 'Yeah, great and all peaceful and quiet.' But after two weeks… Well, I get bored after two weeks of just sitting around doing nothing in the sun. I like to sit at home doing nothing, because if you do want to do something it's right there. But I always get bored laying round after two weeks.

BRIAN: That's very strange.

RINGO: Yeah, I don't know, you know. I think it's 'cause I like being home anyway. I love staying at home.

BRIAN: You say you play records and so on. Can you tell us what sort of things, or do you range over a pretty wide field?

RINGO: I play anything. Just anything.

BRIAN: Are there any artists or musicians you'd go out of your way to listen to?

RINGO: Er, not right out of me way.

BRIAN: Well, no, as far as records go.

RINGO: As long as they're on the way into town, it'll be all right. Um, records? I sort of get mad things, you know. I sort of go potty on people just after hearing one record and I buy a couple of LPs and that's it. I may play one of the LPs and then I never bother again. I'm like that with most things. I want things and then I get them and then I get tired.

BRIAN: Like what other things? Can you think of anything that you've felt that way about?

RINGO: Well, more when I was a kid. You know, 'I wanna bike, gimme a bike!' – spoiled brat! And I'd get a bike and then I'd swap it for a steering cart or something, and me mother would say, 'Well, I paid a lot of money for that bike.' And some kid made the steering cart in his back yard. And then I'd swap that for a tom-tom [drum]. Things like that. I just kept wanting things till I got them.

BRIAN: So even when you were a kid, I mean obviously your sights were lower than they are now, you were still able to get most of the things you wanted?

RINGO: Well, I mean I didn't want much, did I? You know, an eight quid bike and things like that. I never wanted anything big, so… just soft little things. And I just wanted them and I tried to get 'em. And got most of them, and then just got rid of them!

BRIAN: So would you say on the whole that you've had a fairly easy life?

RINGO: Yeah, I've had an easy life. Yeah. I've never been hungry. Never been cold. I've had a good life. I wouldn't change any of it, you know. Even the bit before. This bit's much better, mind you!

BRIAN: Well, obviously. Yeah.

RINGO: Yeah, but it still wouldn't bother me to go through all the rest again, because…

BRIAN: Are you from a big family or a small family?

RINGO: I'm the only child.

BRIAN: Ah. Well, there you go.

RINGO: Oh, 'There you go,' you see. People say, 'Oh, only child. You must have been spoiled.' But I wasn't spoiled where I could have everything, because me mother went out to work and she was the only one getting any money. So, therefore, I suppose it was one of the reasons I never asked for big things. I just asked for little things, which may have seemed big, but they weren't really.

OPPOSITE **On 4 October 1966, Ringo and his wife Maureen flew to Spain, where they visited John on location for the movie *How I Won the War*.**

'I got this bass drum and I used to bash it. Bashing it to the BBC!'

RINGO STARR

BRIAN: When did you first get interested in music?

RINGO: When I was about fourteen in hospital. They used to have a… to keep us happy, all the kids, 'cause I was fourteen, they had a sort of ward band and the teacher came along and she put a big board up with all yellow dots and red dots and when she pointed to red or yellow or green – the triangles or the drums [would play]. Silly little band, but it was great fun and I would never play unless she gave me a drum, you see. I used to fight for the drums [even] then. And I think that's when I first became interested and then I used to sort of bang on a desk, on the locker next to the bed and things. And then I came home and I put little bits of wire on top of biscuit tins and used to bash them with pieces of fire wood. And then I got a 30 bob bass drum, which used to drive them all mad. I was about fifteen-and-a-half, I think… 16. And I got this bass drum – just a one sided bass drum and I used to bang it. Bashing it to the BBC and things like that!

BRIAN: [laughing] Did you ever have any kind of tuition at all or was the whole thing…?

RINGO: I had about three lessons. Once I got interested, I thought, 'Right, I'll go and read music and learn how to play.' Only, I went to this little man in… it was just in a house, sort of thing. And he played drums and he said, 'Get a manuscript.' And he wrote it all down and I never went back after that, 'cause I couldn't be bothered. It was too routine for me – all that paradiddles, and that. And I couldn't stand it. I don't think I'd ever bother learning now.

BRIAN: No. Well, OK Ringo. I think that sort of takes it to the end. It's time I let you go and do some more ligging about, isn't it?

RINGO: Thanks a lot then, Brian. Well, all the best.

BRIAN NEVER FORGOT Ringo's comment about being content to turn into a 'blob'. Ringo was his guest in the BBC Radio 1 programme *My Top Twelve* broadcast on 7 April 1974. The long-running series invited guests to select tracks for an imaginary compilation album of their favourite music. During their conversation, he played the 'blob' section of the 1966 interview to Ringo. Brian pointed out that for someone who had expressed such a view, he was now extremely industrious – directing and acting in films, session drummer duties ('I played on twelve albums one year') and the recently released solo album *Ringo*. 'Some blob,' he joked. 'I haven't had a holiday for two-and-a-half years,' Ringo responded.

ON THE SAME day that Paul and Ringo were interviewed for *Pop Profile*, all The Beatles had talked to Brian Matthew for features to be included in the 400th edition of *Saturday Club*.

BRIAN: Now a question I must ask you. Why have you been silent as far as the British scene is concerned for so long?

JOHN: Couldn't you hear us?

PAUL: We're very quiet, really.

BRIAN: You've been very quiet.

PAUL: Quiet, rural characters. [adopting a rustic accent] On the farm, you know. Up in the morning, milking the cows. Peaceful life.

BRIAN: Don't you think it's cutting it a bit fine with the fans generally, who think they wish they had a little bit more of you?

JOHN: I don't know how we could see more of them and go anywhere else.

BRIAN: Not just see them, but you don't perform on radio, television or anything.

PAUL: Oh, of course we do. Not actually working?

OPPOSITE **Robert Whitaker's still of Ringo was taken at Chiswick House during the filming of a promotional clip for 'Paperback Writer' on 20 May 1966.**

GEORGE: We spend more time on recording now, because we prefer recording.

JOHN: We've done half an LP in the time we would take to do a whole LP and a couple of singles. So we can't do it all and we like recording.

BRIAN: Can you disclose any secrets about this LP? Have you introduced any unusual instruments this time? … You can't use a sitar, 'cause everybody's using them.

JOHN: Yes we can!

GEORGE: I play sitar on another track, but I don't care if everybody's using them. I just play 'cause I like it.

BRIAN: When's it going to be finished?

GEORGE: It should be finished in about two or three weeks' time really, because if it's not, then we won't be able to get another holiday. We'll never be able to get another holiday in before we go away again.

PAUL: If we don't get it done soon, guv, we'll lose our jobs!

THEY NEVER DID get that holiday. Just two days after completing work on *Revolver*, they embarked on an international tour. They played in West Germany, Japan and the Philippines. In the last of those countries, it was alleged they had snubbed the First Lady, Imelda Marcos, by not accepting her invitation to attend an event. Their Asian expedition came to an undignified and dangerous end amid scuffles at Manila airport. On his return to London on 8 July, George told Tom Mangold on the BBC's *Today* news programme 'We're going to have a couple of weeks to recuperate before we go and get beaten up by the Americans.'

The interviews recorded at the BBC Playhouse Theatre for *Saturday Club* and *Pop Profile* took place the day after an historic concert. On 1 May 1966, The Beatles played five songs at the *New Musical Express* Poll-Winners concert at the Empire Pool in Wembley. It was the last time they were seen onstage in the UK. The following month, they made their final performance on a television pop show.

OPPOSITE **The Beatles photographed in Studio One, Abbey Road where they were videotaped miming to 'Paperback Writer' and 'Rain' on 19 May 1966. The following day, other versions were filmed at Chiswick House and its grounds.**

ABOVE **Robert Freeman – the photographer for the sleeves of *With The Beatles*, *A Hard Day's Night*, *Beatles For Sale*, *Help!* and *Rubber Soul* – took this picture of George and John recording at the Abbey Road sessions for *Revolver*.**

Top of the Pops had been running since January 1964, but The Beatles had yet to make a live appearance on the show. For their recent singles, the programme was supplied with filmed performances, which were also shown on TV in other countries. For their first single of 1966 – 'Paperback Writer'/'Rain' – director Michael Lindsay-Hogg made various promotional clips shot in Studio One at Abbey Road and in the conservatory and garden of Chiswick House, London. *Top of the Pops* producer Johnnie Stewart wrote to Brian Epstein on Monday 13 June to express his disappointment that The Beatles had been 'regrettably barred from making any personal appearances… *Top of the Pops* is generally accepted as the Number One pop show, and yet is almost the only show of its kind in which the group has not yet appeared in person.' If there could be a reversal of policy, he promised 'every facility to make such an appearance as quick and easy as possible'. The *NME* reported Brian Epstein's news that 'I put it to the boys late on Tuesday and they said, "Yes".' Consequently, on

LIVE APPEARANCE TX. 16.6.66.

Beatles.

13th June 1966

Dear Brian,

Once again the Beatles have made a Number One record, but once again they have regrettably been barred from making any personal appearances. I think you will agree that Top of the Pops is generally accepted as the Number One pop show, and yet is almost the only show of its kind in which the group has not yet appeared in person. I am writing, therefore, to ask if you would reconsider the position and allow them to appear personally with their new No.1 record on Top of the Pops on any Thursday.

With the show in London we could arrange minimum rehearsals and accord them every facility to make such an appearance as quick and as easy as possible.

With best wishes,

Yours sincerely,

(Johnnie Stewart)

Brian Epstein, Esq.,
Nems Enterprises Ltd.,
Sutherland House,
5-6 Argyll Street,
London, W.1.

EMB

Thursday 16 June, Pete Murray introduced The Beatles miming to both sides of their new single on *Top of the Pops*.

There was an interval of a month between the tense encounters in Asia and a summer tour of the USA and Canada starting in August. While at home, Paul was a guest on the radio show *David Frost at The Phonograph*, broadcast on 6 August 1966. Later, both John and Paul consented to be interviewed for a programme scheduled for August Bank Holiday Monday – 29 August 1966. There had been a previous discussion with Brian Epstein about his radio proposal for a 'Beatles Story'. The BBC concluded that insufficient archive Beatles interview material would require a 'start from scratch' on the project. Presumably, that halted progress on the idea. However, Epstein accepted the request for the participation of John and Paul in *The Lennon and McCartney Songbook*.

The programme was devised by producer Derek Chinnery, who would eventually become the Controller of Radio 1. 'The Beatles, of course, were already tremendously popular in 1966 and for the first time we found artists outside the pop field recording their songs – people like Ella Fitzgerald and even the Band of the Irish Guards. I thought it would be interesting to get John and Paul to comment on what they felt about artists, who to a previous generation were already great big stars, recording their songs. The whole concept was just an idea I had at the time that something unique was happening here that hadn't happened before.' For the recording on 6 August, Derek and Keith Fordyce – a well-known figure from ITV's *Ready Steady Go!* and radio programmes *Pop Inn* and, from 1964, *Easy Beat* – visited Paul's house in Cavendish Avenue near Regent's Park, London. It is doubtful whether John and Paul had heard more than half of the records featured in *The Lennon and McCartney Songbook*:

> The Band Of The Irish Guards – 'She Loves You'
> Peggy Lee – 'A Hard Day's Night'
> Andy Williams – 'Michelle'
> Ella Fitzgerald – 'Can't Buy Me Love'
> Peter Sellers – 'Help!'
> Nancy Sinatra – 'Day Tripper'

OPPOSITE Johnnie Stewart's letter to Brian Epstein received a swift response – a live appearance on *Top of the Pops* just three days later, on 16 June 1966.

> Matt Monro – 'All My Loving'
> The Boston Pops Orchestra – 'I Want To Hold Your Hand'
> Lena Horne – 'And I Love Him'
> Frankie Vaughan – 'Wait'
> Keely Smith – 'If I Fell'
> The Mamas and The Papas – 'I Call Your Name'
> Brenda Lee – 'He Loves You'
> Pat Boone – 'Yesterday'
> The George Martin Orchestra – 'This Boy'

Derek Chinnery recalled: 'I think Paul was quite interested – not necessarily as amazed as I thought he might be – that these people were recording their songs. John, bless him, was far more cynical about the whole thing and said, "Why don't you just play our versions?" He didn't seem to understand that people, certainly of my generation then, thought it was wonderful and something special that their songs were being recorded by so many different artists. We were in Paul's house, sitting in the living room on the floor, if I remember. And John was wandering around the place. We kept stopping the tape to try and get him to come back and join in the conversation, because his comments, we thought, would be valuable.'

Derek's concept for the show precluded some choices that might have made the conversation a little more comfortable for Lennon and McCartney. For example, 'I Wanna Be Your Man' by The Rolling Stones, Del Shannon's early pick-up on 'From Me To You', the returned compliment from Motown of The Supremes' recording of 'You Can't Do That' and Marianne Faithfull's delicate version of 'Yesterday'. One comic moment was prompted by Keith Fordyce asking whether 'Wait' from *Rubber Soul* was written specially for the vaudeville song and dance man Frankie Vaughan. 'No! We weren't thinking of Frankie at the time,' replied an incredulous John.

Paul sounded relaxed and cooperative, while John often seemed tired and unenthusiastic. On the programme's insert tape kept by Derek Chinnery, there is an unedited discussion about closing the show with a joke based on the title of *Pop Inn* regularly presented by Keith. John mutters, 'Not a peep out of me.' Paul encourages him to participate, saying, 'No, no, come on.' However, John's sense of humour did break through when the arrival of refreshments was captured on tape.

PAUL: Come in, Mrs Higgins!

KEITH: Your milk, John.

JOHN: Oh, thank you.

KEITH: Mrs Higgins arriving with three glasses of milk.

PAUL: [taking a sip of something that presumably was not milk] That's not even Mrs Higgins, either.

KEITH: Oh, well. [laughter]

JOHN: It was Mr Higgins!

THE INTERVIEW CONTAINS some interesting details about the two Beatles' songwriting and who had influenced them.

KEITH: Have you got any thoughts on other composers – people whose work you particularly admire?

PAUL: There's lots of them actually, but they're not big as composers, mainly. I like, still I think, Goffin and King. They're the kind of writers we set out to be… what we wanted to be originally. They wrote all the big hits at the time…

JOHN: And they were all nice as well.

PAUL: … always nice, commercial, great, easy to sing.

JOHN: But not horrible.

PAUL: Never sickly.

KEITH: How far do you feel that your individual talents are dependent upon each other? I mean, are you sort of Gilbert & Sullivan or Rodgers & Hammerstein? Do you need to work together as composers?

JOHN: No, not really, but it helps a lot. You get another point of view.

KEITH: Just on the old maxim of two minds are better than one?

JOHN: Mmm. You get another point of view as well.

RIGHT Following their *Top of the Pops* live appearance on 16 June 1966, The Beatles worked long into the night at Abbey Road on 'Here, There And Everywhere'.

ABOVE AND OPPOSITE John, George and Paul study the sleeve of The Rolling Stones' album *Aftermath* released in April 1966 and their Decca single 'Paint It, Black', issued the following month. Mick Jagger and Keith Richard had been slower off the mark than Lennon and McCartney to compose songs for their group. Their fourth UK album, *Aftermath*, was the first Stones LP to consist entirely of self-composed material.

PAUL: We can do them on our own, but often one of us will just do a song and there'll be say one verse in it that's very bad or very corny. If I've written it then I'll take it along and sing it to John. And he'll say that verse is terrible and that verse is corny.

JOHN: You still get so involved with something; you finish it and if you're on your own, you haven't got the energy to go over it and see if it really makes exactly what you want. So if you sing

it over to each other, even if it's a finished song with almost the [complete] arrangement, it's still sort of: 'Yes, that's fine.'

KEITH: Do you consider that the two of you think alike or do you think differently and therefore help each other?

PAUL: We think nearly alike, but pretty differently at the same time. But we can write a song like 'Day Tripper' where we've got to write one and can write it, thinking the same about it. But if we each wrote it individually, it would be a completely different song.

KEITH: Do you both have to be in the right mood when you're working together, collaborating on a song? Does one have to wait for the other to start?

JOHN: Very seldom, you know. If we both don't feel like it, we just have another ciggie.

PAUL: The only time we've got to do that – to actually force ourselves to write it – is when we've got an LP coming up or a film. Then it's a bit of a drag for the first, say, two songs… in fact, the last LP [*Revolver*]: Wow! We took weeks just trying to get one written to get back into the swing of it. 'Cause we don't write in between LPs, normally. Maybe just write one or two and then we have a great big batch [to do].

KEITH: I would have thought it's quite impossible really to say, 'Right, we've got to write twelve songs for an LP. Let's settle down to it.'

JOHN: It is some days. This last time was very impossible. Holiday spirit.

KEITH: Would you tell me a personal reaction on 'Day Tripper' and 'We Can Work It Out'. Were these songs written under pressure or were they inspired? To me, personally, they were less inspired than all your other songs that I've heard.

JOHN: 'Day Tripper' was under complete pressure based on an old folk song I wrote about the month previous. It was very hard going, that, and it sounds it. Glad you spotted that. Two house points!

PAUL: [Clearing his throat] However…

JOHN: 'We Can Work It Out' wasn't.

PAUL: No. Bad marks for 'We Can Work It Out'. Lose three Brownie points.

KEITH: I don't know how many thousands of times you've been asked which is your own favourite composition. I'm not going to ask you that, I'm going to tell you that one of mine is certainly 'Can't Buy Me Love'. It's got a zip and gaiety about it that is perhaps way ahead of the others. Were you in that sort of mood when you wrote this song?

PAUL: Zipping away in Paris, we were, when we wrote that one.

JOHN: I thought we just recorded it there.

PAUL: I mean, you can draw your own conclusions from that, you know, Keith.

KEITH: Do you prefer writing at night? Are you night workers?

JOHN: No, no. Any time, really. When you're awake. Not too near the morning when you're half-asleep and not when you're tired, so it doesn't matter what time it is. Just the period when you feel quite healthy.

KEITH: Do you use piano, guitars? What when you're writing?

PAUL: Anything. Piano or guitar – that's about our limit.

JOHN: I'm just finding I don't know enough chords to write 'em with guitars, so I'll have to get some old fella to come in and play to me.

PAUL: Gorra be an old fella, though! Couldn't be one of these young whizz-bang kids, you know.

JOHN: They wouldn't have time.

KEITH: Well, there it is. It's been very enjoyable in your own… in the incredible quiet of your own sitting room, Paul.

PAUL: It's very quiet in here, Keith. Except for the dog howling [Paul's seven-week-old puppy, Martha] and the clock ticking. Well, it's been nice to have you, really.

KEITH: John, thank you very much too.

JOHN: It's a pleasure. It was wonderful. Nice pad he's got, isn't it? As they say in the teen rave…

PAUL: Teenage rave. Well, thanks, Keith and if you're ever round this way again – pop in!

'Wow! We took weeks just trying to get one written to get back into the swing of it.'

PAUL McCARTNEY

British Broadcasting Corporation   Confidential

AN AUDIENCE RESEARCH REPORT

(Week 35)   LR/66/1298   6

THE LENNON AND McCARTNEY SONGBOOK

Produced by Derek Chinnery

Monday, 29th August,1966. 4.30-5.30pm, Light Programme

1. <u>Size of audience</u> (based on results of the Survey of Listening and Viewing.)

   The audience for this broadcast was estimated at 3.8% of the population of the United Kingdom.

2. <u>Reaction of audience</u> (based on questionnaires completed by a sample of the audience. This sample, 115 in number, is the 7% of B Division of the Listening Panel who heard all or most of the broadcast.)

   The reactions of this sample of the audience were distributed as follows:-

A+	A	B	C	C-
%	%	%	%	%
10	23	47	15	5

   giving a REACTION INDEX of 55, which is somewhat below the current average (63) for record programmes (excluding requests) on all Services except Third Programme.

3. 'I enjoy the Beatles' own renderings but with two or three exceptions, these did not stand up in comparison with them' declared a Housewife, one or a number of listeners who apparently considered these arrangements of Lennon and McCartney numbers by artists like Ella Fitzgerald, Matt Munro and Frankie Vaughan 'not a patch' on the originals and would much have preferred a straightforward selection of Beatle records. A handful did not in any case, care for music of this kind ('the melodies are pretty tuneless and the words are either meaningless or horrible') and one or two were inclined to agree with a Student that 'if, as Keith Fordyce stated, there had been over 300 records of Beatle songs, I fail to see why such boring ones were chosen'. In many opinions, nevertheless, this was an interesting selection of records that were not only enjoyable in themselves but helped to illustrate the undoubted range and musical ability of this talented pair, whose own singing might not be to everyone's taste but who could certainly 'write a good tune'. The songs were varied, as were the artists, it was said, and this was a well chosen and arranged selection that made entertaining listening. In the words of a Housewife: 'I was greatly impressed by the quantity and quality of the compositions. Although a confirmed pop-hater, I was enthralled with the Beatles' songs. Surely the variety and the fact that any singer can sing them with success proves they are of lasting excellence'.

4. Some listeners found their pleasure in the music marred by the 'inarticulate mumbling' of John Lennon and Paul McCartney in conversation with Keith Fordyce. While Paul was, perhaps, the better of the two, the Liverpool accent of both boys was difficult to listen to, their speech was slovenly and they were unable to express themselves with any degree of fluency, it was remarked, and Keith Fordyce had his work cut out to keep the conversation going at all - 'a pity that Lennon and McCartney don't learn to speak clearly, as I'm sure they said some interesting things, if only one could have understood them'. Nevertheless, although by no means polished speakers, the two Beatles earned a good deal of praise for their lively, natural and forthright comments on the business of song writing. Despite their unprecedented rise to fame, they remained modest and likeable, it was widely agreed, and their down-to-earth and entertaining comments were always well worth hearing. Keith Fordyce's questioning was sometimes considered rather dull and unimaginative but more often he was felt to have handled the boys well and listeners liked the informal nature of the conversation.

Copyright of the BBC   Audience Research Department
RG/BB   26th September,1966.

LEFT The bank holiday special with John and Paul was scheduled to follow *The Billy Cotton Band Show* (with 'Mr Wakey Wakey' himself), *Swing into Summer* (including Gerry and The Pacemakers, Kenny Ball's Jazzmen and Vince Hill) and *Robinson Cleaver* (at the theatre organ in the Granada, Tooting).

OPPOSITE John attempted to explain his 'more popular than Jesus' remark at a press conference held on 11 August 1966 at the Astor Towers Hotel in Chicago. The Beatles' final tour opened in the city the following day.

DEREK CHINNERY RECALLED that 'the programme, as far as I remember, was quite well received probably by the older generation listening, rather than the youngsters who might have agreed with John – "Why don't you play The Beatles' records?".' As always in BBC Audience Research reports, contrary views were expressed. 'I enjoy the Beatles' own renderings but with two or three exceptions, these did not stand up in comparison with them,' thought a 'Housewife'. Others agreed that they were 'not a patch' on the originals. A 'Student' wondered 'if, as Keith Fordyce stated, there had been over 300 records of Beatle songs, I fail to see why such boring ones were chosen.' However, many were won over by the selection: 'Although a confirmed pop-hater, I was enthralled with the Beatles' songs. Surely the variety and the fact that any singer can sing them with success proves they are of lasting excellence'. There was also criticism of the interviewees' Liverpool accents and 'slovenly speech': 'A pity that Lennon and McCartney don't learn to speak clearly, as I'm sure they said some interesting things, if only one could have understood them.' The report concluded that 'although by no means polished speakers, the two Beatles earned a good deal of praise for their lively, natural and forthright comments on the business of song writing' and that they 'remained modest and likeable.' The Reaction Index score was 55 – 'below the current average (63) for record programmes'.

On the day of the recording, Brian Epstein had hurriedly flown to New York in an attempt to quell a storm of controversy. America was in uproar over an observation John had made a few months before in a London newspaper interview with Maureen Cleave: 'Christianity will go. It will vanish and shrink. I needn't argue with that; I'm right and I will be proved right. We're more popular than Jesus now'. When printed out of context in the US teen magazine *Datebook*, his pronouncement provoked the banning and even burning of The Beatles' records. These were not ideal circumstances for imminent concerts in the States. Indeed, anxiety about the tour may well have affected John's mood during the interview with Keith Fordyce.

A week later, John was repeatedly pressed for an apology at the first press conference of the tour in Chicago. 'If I'd have said television is more popular than Jesus, I might have got away with it... I'm not saying that we're better or greater or comparing us with Jesus Christ as a person, or God as a thing, or whatever it is, you know. I just said what I said and it was wrong... or was taken wrong and now it's all this.' News reports on the BBC covered the events unfolding across the Atlantic and included John's 'apology'. This was a different breed of Beatlemania. Adoration of the cute 'moptops' had flipped over to something sinister. The sight of young Americans gleefully tossing Beatles records into the flames in protest at John's remark was shocking. The frustration and peril the group experienced on tour pushed them to breaking point. The day *The Lennon and McCartney Songbook* was heard in Britain, The Beatles knew they were playing their last concert in San Francisco.

Their response to the madness was to retreat almost completely from public life, including BBC TV and radio. Both had virtually nothing to broadcast with The Beatles during the rest of 1966. One exception was a glimpse of John in a Boxing Day edition of *Not Only... But Also* broadcast on BBC 1. In a sketch featuring Peter Cook's character Hiram J. Pipesucker Jr., John played Dan – doorman of the exclusive gentlemen's club the 'Ad Lav'.

RIGHT **On 27 November 1966, John and Peter Cook were filmed outside the 'Public Convenience' for Gentlemen in Broadwick Street, London, W1.** This was used as the location for the 'Ad Lav' club shown in the Christmas edition of the BBC 2 comedy show *Not Only… But Also*.

📻 Radio programme titles
📺 TV titles

📺 THE BEATLES AT SHEA STADIUM
Br: 1 March 1966 – 8.00–8.50pm – BBC 1
(Repeated 27 August 1966 – 6.15–7.05pm
– BBC 1)
Rec: 15 August 1965
Shea Stadium, New York, USA
I'm Down (the closing number), *Twist And Shout*
(shortened version), *I Feel Fine* (new recording
made on 5 January 1966 used on the soundtrack),
Dizzy Miss Lizzy, *Ticket To Ride*, *Can't Buy Me
Love*, *Baby's In Black*, *Act Naturally* (the recording
released on *Help!* was used on the soundtrack), *A
Hard Day's Night*, *Help!* (new recording made on
5 January 1966 used on the soundtrack)

📻 SATURDAY CLUB (400th Edition)
Br: 4 June 1966 – 10.00am–noon
– The Light Programme
Rec: 2 May 1966
The BBC Playhouse Theatre
The Beatles were featured several times in con-
versation with Brian Matthew, but it was Cliff
Richard and The Shadows who topped the bill of
the artists recorded in session for this special show.

📺 TOP OF THE POPS
Br: 16 June 1966 – 7.30–8.00pm
– BBC 1 – Live
Television Centre, Wood Lane, London
Miming to: *Rain*
Paperback Writer (repeated on *Line-up Review* – 17
June 1966 – BBC 2, on *Top of the Pops* – 30 June
1966 – BBC 1 and on *Top of the Pops '66 – Part 1* –
26 December 1966 – BBC 1)
This was The Beatles' last appearance on a
TV pop show.

📻 TODAY
Br: 8 July 1966 – 7.15–8.40am
– The Home Service
Rec: 8 July 1966
London Airport
George and Ringo were interviewed by reporter
Tom Mangold upon their arrival from India. They
were returning home after concerts in Tokyo and
the Philippines.

📺 DAVID FROST AT THE PHONOGRAPH
Br: 6 August 1966 – noon–1.30pm
– The Light Programme
Rec: 1 August 1966
Paul was interviewed for this programme of
gramophone records and chat.

📻 THE LENNON AND McCARTNEY SONGBOOK
Br: 29 August 1966 (August Bank Holiday Monday) – 4.30–5.30pm – The Light Programme
Rec: 6 August 1966
Paul's home in Cavendish Avenue, London
Keith Fordyce sought the writers' comments on a
collection of cover versions. Paul was diplomatic
and tried hard; John remained subdued and did
not pay attention.

📻 THE LIVELY ARTS
Br: 11 December 1966 – 4.00–4.30pm
– The Home Service
Rec: 20 September 1966
George was interviewed in Bombay by the BBC's
correspondent Donald Milner about his burgeon-
ing interests in India in an item billed as *A Beatle
Goes East*.

📺 NOT ONLY... BUT ALSO
with Peter Cook and Dudley Moore
Br: 26 Dec 1966 – 9.00–9.50pm – BBC 1
Repeated 7 February 1967 – 9.05–9.50pm
– BBC 1
Rec: 27 Nov 1966
Broadwick Street, London
John acted the role of Dan – doorman of the
'Ad Lav' club.

1967

Where
It's At

THE PHRASE *'WHERE IT'S AT'*, like many idiomatic expressions used in the Sixties, originated in African-American culture. For example, in a rousing R&B hit from 1966, Etta James and Sugar Pie DeSanto sang about being down 'In The Basement' because 'that's where it's at'. The phrase may have lost a little credibility when, in 1967, it was adopted as the title of a Saturday afternoon show on the BBC Light Programme. To be fair though, *Where It's At* did live up to its name when it featured interviews with John, Paul and Ringo during an early preview of The Beatles' album *Sgt. Pepper's Lonely Hearts Club Band*.

The title of the LP had been inspired by the unusual names of groups emerging in America. Following the British musical invasion of 1964, the US sprang back with harmonious music by The Beach Boys, The Byrds, The Lovin' Spoonful, The Mamas and The Papas, and Simon & Garfunkel. By 1967, new FM stations were providing an alternative to the musical diet of Top Forty AM radio. There was a greater focus on albums. Bands associated with the burgeoning counterculture, such as Buffalo Springfield, Country Joe and The Fish, The Doors, The Grateful Dead and Jefferson Airplane, began to break through. Near San Francisco, where hippies hung out in Haight-Ashbury, the three-day Monterey International Pop Festival took place in June. The varied bill ranged from Ravi Shankar and soul star Otis Redding to the powerful rock of The Who and The Jimi Hendrix Experience. Founded on the principles of jazz and folk festivals, Monterey established a new way to stage pop music. The film of the event, released in December 1968, promulgated a vision of the 'Summer of Love' revolving around 'psychedelic' music, the consumption of illegal drugs and 'flower power'.

The ideals of love and peace were not much in evidence in the hard news stories of 1967. In June, the Six-Day War was waged between Israel and an Arab coalition with forces from Egypt, Jordan and Syria. Israel's victory resulted in its capture of the Gaza Strip, Sinai Peninsula, Golan Heights, West Bank and East Jerusalem from its neighbouring countries. In the war in Vietnam there was yet more death and destruction. The US military presence increased to nearly half a million personnel. The number of Americans killed during 1967 was over 11,000. There was also loss of life in US cities as the streets burned during race riots in Boston, Newark and Detroit. Some of the year's hit movies reflected the turbulent times. Race relations in America was a theme in *Guess Who's Coming to Dinner* and *In the Heat of the Night*.

In the UK, the population anxiously followed news of the shipwrecked *Torrey Canyon*. Riven in two when it struck a rock in March, the supertanker leaked 120,000 tons of crude oil into the sea. In attempts to sink it and burn off the oil slick, the vessel was bombed by air-force planes. The Cornish coastline was contaminated for seventy miles and thousands of seabirds died from the pollution. The year saw steps to accommodate more liberal attitudes to sexual behaviour and drug-taking. Homosexuality between consenting adults aged over 21 was decriminalized when the Sexual Offences Act passed into law on 27 July. A few days before, *The Times* published an advertisement with a petition signed by eminent figures, including all four Beatles, calling for the legalization of marijuana. Pop star drug busts had become headline news during the year. *The Times* ran an editorial in protest against the jail terms given to Mick Jagger and Keith Richards. Quoting Alexander Pope, the leader column asked 'Who Breaks a Butterfly on a Wheel?' The sentences were quashed a month later by an appeal court.

To show their solidarity with Mick and Keith, John and Paul sang on the Rolling Stones single 'We Love You'. It was recorded on 12 June, a couple of weeks before the Stones attended The Beatles' live TV broadcast of 'All You Need Is Love'. 'We Love You' was a tongue-in-cheek riposte from Jagger and Richards to representatives of the traditional establishment who, they believed, were victimizing them. In contrast, The Beatles' song was a sincere message to *Our World*. Even when watched in black and white, it was clear the flamboyantly dressed 'beautiful people' in Abbey Road on 25 June 1967 were at the focal point of pop culture. However, The Beatles were inviting 350 million viewers around the globe to join them.

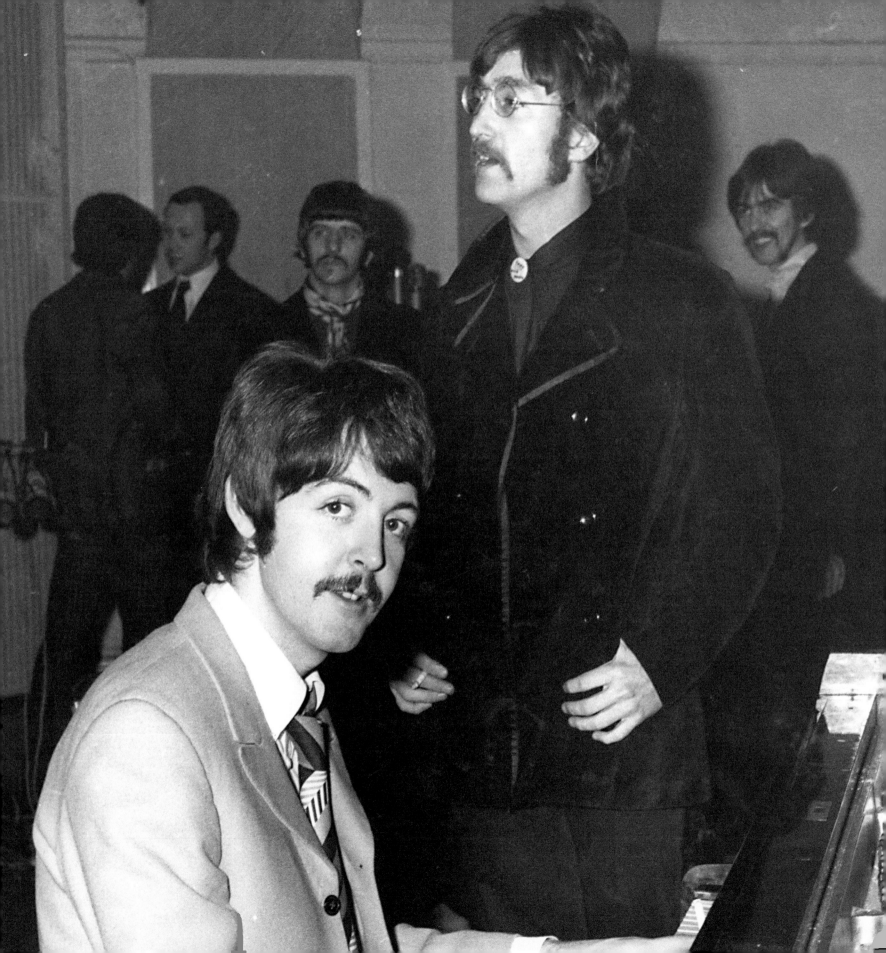

THE BEATLES GAVE their farewell concert on the stage of Candlestick Park, San Francisco on 29 August 1966. Their decision to withdraw from performing was not made public, but it soon became apparent the group had made an escape from a relentless cycle of recording, touring and media appearances. Since the release of *Revolver* in August, no single or album with new material had arrived in the shops by the end of 1966. The year proved to be their least productive – just sixteen new songs were released compared to thirty-three in 1965.

Viewed from a 21st-century perspective, the songs on *Revolver* and the single 'Paperback Writer'/'Rain' would sustain a modern-day band for several years before releasing their next project. However, as several months went by without anything new, there was much speculation about what The Beatles might be doing. Although keeping a low profile, they were, for three months, busy not being Beatles. Within a week of the last concert, John was acting in the film *How I Won The War*. He recalled during his BBC interview with Andy Peebles in December 1980 that: 'After The Beatles' last tour where the Ku Klux Klan were burning Beatle records, we decided no more touring. That's enough of that. I'm not going to put up with it. And I was dead nervous, so I said "Yes" to Dick Lester, that I would make this movie with him. I went to Almeria, Spain for six weeks… because I didn't know what to do. What the hell do you do all day?' Paul was soon immersed in composing a score for the film *The Family Way*. George flew to India to study sitar with Ravi Shankar.

The long wait for the next Beatles record ended when the double A-side 'Penny Lane'/'Strawberry Fields Forever' was released in February 1967. The promotional films for the songs supplied to *Top of the Pops* gave clear indications of the group's new interests. Both had imagery that was unexpected. For example, much of the action in the clip for 'Strawberry Fields Forever' revolves around a dismantled piano attached to a tree. The Beatles had entered uncharted territory for pop musicians – far from the kind of family-friendly films made to broaden the appeal of British singers such as Tommy Steele and Cliff Richard.

After a seven-month absence from BBC radio, John and Paul were heard on 27 March 1967 during *The Ivor Novello Awards for 1966*. The awards were named after a British singer and actor who composed the First World War favourite 'Keep The Home Fires Burning' and parlour songs such as 'We'll Gather Lilacs'. An 'Ivor' remains to this day a prestigious honour to recognize the achievements of composers. A week before the broadcast, Brian Matthew had interviewed Lennon and McCartney about their latest awards during a recording made at EMI Studios in Abbey Road. First, John and Paul responded to 'Yellow Submarine' winning in the category of 'the UK's best selling A-side of a single during 1966'.

PAUL: We are truly grateful.

JOHN: [excitedly] Great, great.

PAUL: That is really wonderful. I see it's inscribed on the side of it.

JOHN: That's an old one from Brian's piano!

PAUL: [laughs] Well, this is wonderful. And I'd like to thank everybody, on behalf of John, George, Ringo and myself.

BRIAN: Yes.

PAUL: Thank you.

BRIAN: Good. Who was principally responsible, Paul or John?

JOHN: Paul.

PAUL: John, really.

JOHN & PAUL: No. No.

BRIAN: I see.

JOHN: Ringo.

PAUL: No, it's the old patter, you know. The old vaudeville. I suppose I thought of the idea and then John and I wrote it. There's your correct answer, Brian.

BRIAN: Yeah. What were you setting out to write? I mean, did you think of a song for Ringo in the first place, or what?

PAUL: We just sort of thought, we have to have a song. That it was… sort of a bit of fantasy in it, you know. And the only way to do that would be to have it so kids could understand it, and anyone could take it on any level. Multi-level song.

BRIAN: Yeah. I heard a funny sort of story that you used to perform this to your nephews. Is that all wrong?

PAUL: That's all wrong. That was Mozart's Piano Concerto!

BRIAN: [earnestly] Oh, I see.

[laughter]

BRIAN: John, earlier before we started recording, you said it was, in effect, written as two separate songs.

JOHN: Yeah. I seem to remember, like, the submarine… the chorus bit, you coming in with it.

PAUL: Yeah.

JOHN: And wasn't the other bit something that I had already going, and we put them together?

PAUL: Well, yeah. Right. Yeah.

JOHN: And it made sense to make it into…

PAUL: Yeah, the bit… [singing the melody of the verse] 'Dut-ta-da, da-dut-ta-da'.

JOHN: With Ringo in mind, again.

BRIAN: Yes.

JOHN: Always thinking of him, you see, at times like this.

[laughter]

JOHN: And that's what happened.

BRIAN: And they, like, gelled.

PAUL & JOHN: Yeah.

BRIAN: And now on to the most performed work of the year. And this, I should explain, includes live broadcast, television performances, and performances in ballrooms throughout the country. And the winner for 1966 was 'Michelle'. Paul, do you even remember this song?

PAUL: [sings] 'Michelle, ma belle.' I know the one.

BRIAN: Good. Did you write it or did John?

PAUL: Well, you know…

JOHN: I think Paul wrote that one. I remember saying, 'Why don't you pinch that bit from so-and-so's song?' and he said 'Right.'

BRIAN: What was it pinched from?

JOHN: Er, I'm not telling.

PAUL: It was pinched from something. Most of them are, Brian.

BRIAN: [laughing] Are they?

PAUL: But you've got to own up eventually. [laughs] No, it's just a slight pinch, but you never notice, you know.

BRIAN: No.

PAUL: And, I mean, I couldn't tell you because the P.R.S. [Performing Rights Society] would probably rip me.

[laughter]

JOHN: It's a wonderful award and we'd like to say 'Bon, oui.'

BRIAN: Oh, because it's a French song.

JOHN: Yeah.

BRIAN: The last award to be presented to The Beatles… they have become runners-up to themselves. Give us the inside story on the song 'Yesterday'.

JOHN: Ah well, this is John saying I don't know anything about

OPPOSITE John, George and Paul discussing one of their recordings for *Sgt. Pepper's Lonely Hearts Club Band* at EMI Studios, Abbey Road, London. Tape operator Richard Lush looks on.

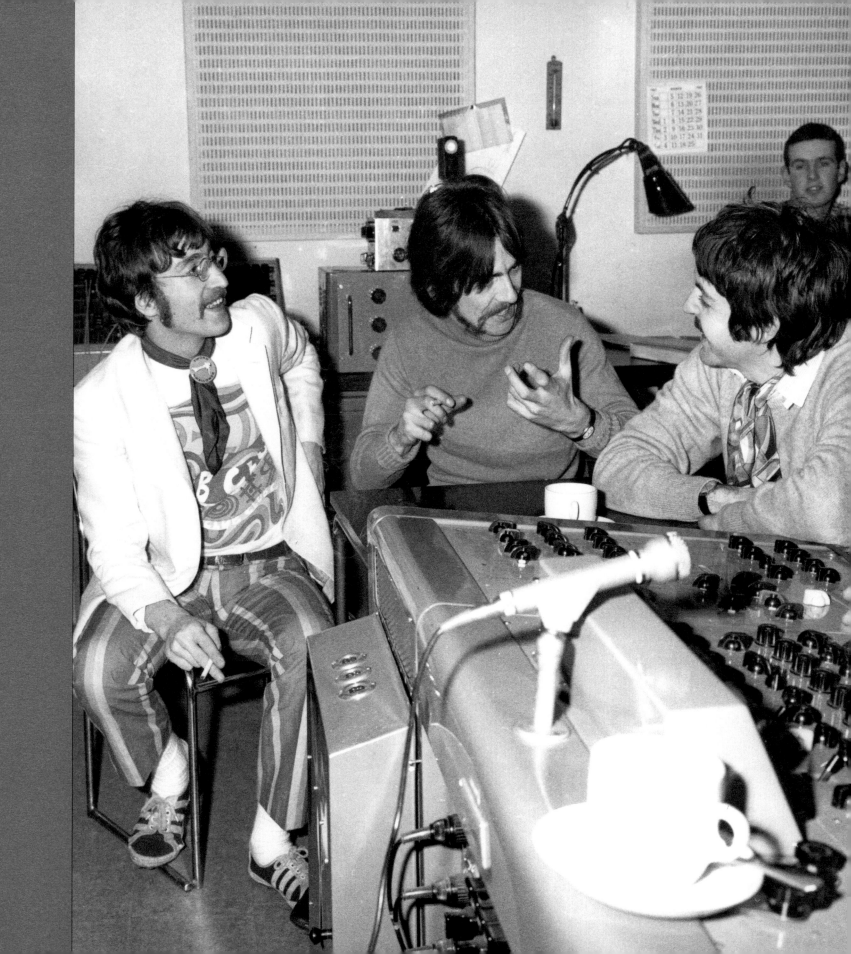

that one. I'll hand you over to Paul.

PAUL: [laughs] This is Paul, taking up the story in a holiday villa in Corsica. Strumming away on a medieval guitar, I thought [sings] 'Scrambled Egg'. But I never could finish it, and eventually I took it back in. With the ancient wisdom of the east, John came out with [sings] 'Yesterday'.

BRIAN: Apart from being the runner-up in the most performed section, I think that must have been the most recorded number last year… must've been about 400 versions of it. You must have heard some of them. Is there any one that you think is a standout performance?

JOHN: Er, one by a young fellow called Paul McCartney had a sort of plaintive approach.

PAUL: [laughs]

BRIAN: A naive charm.

PAUL: Yes, er… Andy Williams.

JOHN: The arrangement of the strings was wrong.

PAUL: Yeah.

JOHN: That was the trouble with Andy's version.

BRIAN: There was Matthew Monro.

JOHN & PAUL: Yeah.

PAUL: That was arranged by a good friend of ours – Charlie Drake!

BRIAN: Ah.

[laughter]

PAUL: And he did a very good arrangement. I would like to thank him personally.

BRIAN: Yeah, good. So would you say that probably is your favourite version of them all?

PAUL: Er, well I think Charlie Drake.

JOHN: Yeah, Charlie Drake.

PAUL: Charlie Drake and Matt did a fine, fine record on that.

RIGHT **Producer George Martin in the studio during the making of** *Sgt. Pepper.*

DESPITE THE FLIPPANT nature of the interview, their thoughts about 'Yesterday' are revealing. The Beatles' version has a string arrangement that is distinctly classical. A string quartet was used because it had what producer George Martin called a 'clinical sound'. The sugary strings in the lush arrangement of 'Yesterday' recorded by Andy Williams was just the sort of style The Beatles had not wanted. George Martin produced Matt Monro, a singer described as Britain's answer to Frank Sinatra, Indeed, Sinatra himself was an admirer of Matt Monro. George Martin had also recorded comedy records with Charlie Drake, including the Top Twenty hit 'My Boomerang Won't Come Back'. At the time of the interview, Charlie was in an ITV comedy series called *Who Is Sylvia?*

At the same session Brian Matthew had his last bout with John and Paul for BBC Transcription's *Top of the Pops*. Perhaps encouraged by the reflective interviews The Beatles had contributed to his recent BBC Transcription series *Pop Profile*, Brian attempted to elicit a serious account of their future plans. As he was visiting Abbey Road, he knew they were making a new album and was given a few clues about the content of what would soon be released as *Sgt. Pepper's Lonely Hearts Club Band*.

In the UK, 'Penny Lane'/'Strawberry Fields Forever' had reached number two – the first Beatles single not to top the UK charts since their debut hit 'Love Me Do'. It had been eclipsed by the year's best-selling record, 'Release Me' by Engelbert Humperdinck. Although the British pop scene of 1967 included dazzling experimental music by The Beatles, The Rolling Stones, The Who, The Small Faces and The Pink Floyd, there was still a big demand for safer fare. Most of the biggest singles sales of the year were earned by artists such as Engelbert, Tom Jones, Val Doonican and Vince Hill singing romantic ballads.

BRIAN: 'Penny Lane' failed to make number one... did you feel at all put out by that?

PAUL: No. The main thing is that it's fine if you're kept from being number one by a record like 'Release Me', 'cause you're not trying to do the same kind of thing as 'Release Me' is trying to do. So that's a completely different scene altogether, that kind of thing. So it doesn't really matter anyway.

BRIAN: But you have in the past said – or at least been reported as having said – that in the event of a record not going to number one, you'd seriously think about packing it all in. Do you feel like that?

PAUL: Well, John packed it in, actually. But we're trying to persuade him to stay with the group at the moment. I don't want to start any rumours over in the States or anything.

BRIAN: Pity. The thing is, I mean, you've obviously reached a stage where you don't have to write any more songs for any reason at all other than that you like doing it.

PAUL: But it's always been like that. That's the good thing.

BRIAN: Yeah.

PAUL: 'Cause it has been a hobby, and it still is, you know. Mind you, it gets – around about the time when you're doing an LP and you've got to start working – it gets like a job. But, you know, you do it in your time off anyway, so it is a hobby. So it'll go on forever, probably.

BRIAN: Good. Can you, without giving away any trade secrets, tell us anything about the numbers that you're engaged on at the moment for this new album that you're working on?

JOHN: Oh, we've done about nine or ten... and there's a couple of strange ones, a couple of happy-go-lucky Northern Songs.

PAUL: Mmm... couple of whimsical... you know, folk, folk-rock...

BRIAN: Have you this time augmented again, used any strange line-ups at all?

PAUL: Well, we've used sorts of things that aren't us quite a bit.

JOHN: We've used The Monkees on a few of the tracks!

PAUL AND BRIAN: [Laughs]

PAUL: Yeah, right. But they wouldn't go along with the TV series that we had planned for them.

BRIAN: Yeah, yeah. Has George written anything this time?

PAUL: Oh yeah. He's done a great one. [Laughs] A great one.

JOHN: A great Indian one. We came along one night and he had about 400 Indian fellas playing 'ere and it was a great swinging evening, as they say.

PAUL: So there's a few things going on.

BRIAN: Yeah. Is there going to be another Beatles film?

JOHN: Yes.

PAUL: Oh yeah.

JOHN: As soon as we finish this LP we'll be starting on this mythical film that we've been on about for the last year.

PAUL: We wanna do a TV show and a film, sort of next.

BRIAN: And is touring now completely out? Everywhere?

JOHN: I reckon so, yeah… says John.

PAUL: Well, the thing is, we're working on an act where we run on in brightly coloured suits…

BRIAN: [Not fooled] Yeah…

PAUL: … and switch on five tapes…

BRIAN: Ah! Yeah, yeah, that's a thought.

PAUL: … and then we do a juggling act at the front of the stage while these tapes play Beatle melodies.

BRIAN: Yeah. Why is it? I don't know why this microphone sends you barmy, because when I was talking to John earlier, he was quite serious and said, 'No. No more tours.'

PAUL: No, that's the only possibility. You never know.

JOHN: I said, 'No more tours, no more 'She Loves You's.' But going on with a million tape recorders and a brightly coloured suit… well, that's something else, you know.

BRIAN: No more big tours of America or around the world?

JOHN: No.

PAUL: I don't think so. Not in the same kind of pattern as we've been doing so far anyway. But you never know.

BRIAN: You never know. I see. Right. And one final bit then. There have been reports in the last week or two about you writing this musical we've been hearing about for years. True or false?

PAUL: Er, false, I think.

JOHN: False, I think.

PAUL: False.

JOHN: False.

PAUL: False.

JOHN: False rumour.

BRIAN: You're not going to do it.

PAUL: I don't think so.

JOHN: Unless it's a musical with a thousand tape recorders and brightly coloured costumes!

BRIAN: We're no nearer this projected musical.

PAUL: All of those kinds of things, you know, we might do in the next few years. But this is the idea, to give us a chance to try other things. We don't know what they're going to be yet.

BRIAN: But you are going to go on writing?

PAUL: Oh, there's going to be a lot more other things, but we want to make them sort of different, you know. [adopting a strong Liverpool accent] You know, Brian?

BRIAN: Well, thanks for giving us the facts!

JOHN: It's a pleasure. Thank you.

'I said, "No more tours, no more 'She Loves You's." But going on with a million tape recorders and a brightly coloured suit… well, that's something else.'

JOHN LENNON

LEFT Paul, John and George Martin during a session for 'A Day In The Life' in January 1967. An alarm clock is heard ringing on the recording just before Paul sings, 'Woke up, fell out of bed'.

THE GENUINE FUSS generated by the first Beatles single of 1967 failing to reach number one was unique to Britain. 'Penny Lane' topped the US Hot 100. Its flip-side was listed separately, because radio play was used in tandem with sales to compile the American chart. The 'mythical film' was a reference to the fact that The Beatles should have made a third movie in 1966, but most of the scripts they were offered followed the *Help!* formula. A TV series with manufactured group The Monkees proved there was plenty of commercial potential left in that mode of wisecracking humour and running, jumping and standing still. John's reference to The Monkees was not simply a joke. Two of the group – Michael Nesmith and Micky Dolenz – had attended *Sgt. Pepper* sessions in February. George's 'great Indian one' was 'Within You Without You', which had no other Beatle performing on it. The fantasy about tape machines playing Beatles melodies was echoed two years later at the media launch of the Plastic Ono Band single 'Give Peace A Chance'. Following a car crash in Scotland, John and Yoko were unable to attend. Instead, at the Chelsea Town Hall in London, the press were introduced to perspex 'robots' with microphones, tape machines and amplifiers.

Sgt. Pepper's Lonely Hearts Club Band was released on 1 June 1967 and could not have been more in tune with its time. In what was later described as 'the Summer of Love', elements of the 'underground' culture of hallucinogenic drugs, colourful clothes and trippy music began to filter into the mainstream. *Sgt. Pepper* provided the ubiquitous soundtrack to the period. However, the album proved to be timeless; reverberating through the decades that followed. At the time of its release, it would have been fascinating to have heard interviews about the innovations made during the 700 hours of recording. But that was not to be. Instead, three Beatles appeared very briefly on the Light Programme's preview of the LP during *Where It's At*.

Presented by former Radio Luxembourg and pirate Radio London DJ Chris Denning, *Where It's At* had started in early 1967. Producer Johnny Beerling liked the offshore pirate stations and wanted his show to sound just as 'groovy'. He even introduced jingles to the BBC. 'On the station of the nation, this is *Where It's At!*' announced Duncan Johnson. Denning, his voice treated with echo and tape-reverb, speedily introduced the music. Most significantly,

> # 'We wanted to make a "Happening" happen… and it happened.'
>
> PAUL MCCARTNEY

only records were played. Listeners did not run the risk of hearing versions of The Beach Boys' 'God Only Knows' or The Rolling Stones' 'Paint It, Black' by resident big bands such as Joe Loss and his Orchestra or the Northern Dance Orchestra – regular hazards elsewhere within the Light Programme schedule. The playlist between the two *Sgt. Pepper* sections that opened and closed *Where It's At* is a fair representation of the music scene in May 1967.

The running order included two Tamla Motown discs by Brenda Holloway ('Just Look What You've Done') and The Marvelettes ('When You're Young And In Love'); current Top 20 records by The Tremeloes ('Silence Is Golden'), The Who ('Pictures Of Lily'), The Kinks ('Waterloo Sunset'), The Beach Boys ('Then I Kissed Her'), Bee Gees ('New York Mining Disaster 1941') and Arthur Conley ('Sweet Soul Music'); and future hits by The Young Rascals ('Groovin''), PP Arnold ('The First Cut Is The Deepest'), Petula Clark ('Don't Sleep In The Subway'), Dusty Springfield ('Give Me Time'), Procol Harum ('A Whiter Shade Of Pale') and Dave Dee, Dozy, Beaky, Mick & Tich ('Okay!'). There were also a couple of early slices of British 'psychedelia' by The Purple Gang ('Granny Takes A Trip') and The Mirage ('The Wedding Of Ramona Blair') and an update of 'Portrait Of My Love' by American vocal group The Tokens.

RIGHT *Sgt. Pepper's Lonely Hearts Club Band* was launched on 19 May 1967 at Brian Epstein's home in Chapel Street, London, SW1. Photographer Linda Eastman was present at the select press party. She and Paul were married on 12 March 1969.

FROM: Assistant Head of Gramophone Programmes.   12.5.67

SUBJECT: SONGS AND LYRICS ALLEGED TO CONTAIN REFERENCES TO DRUGS.

TO: A.D.S.B.   Copy to: C.L.P., H.G.P.

I am sending you with this note a tape (at 7½ i.p.s.), which we asked the publisher to let us hear, of one of the tracks from the new Beatles L.P. to be issued at the end of May. Also attached is a Press cutting from "Disc and Music Echo", and a photostat of the lyrics.

For Light Programme production "Where It's At" will be featuring the L.P. on Saturday May 20th, and although they need not play this particular track, it is thought by the experts to be one of the best on the album, and other programmes may well want to play it later. H.G.P. and I have listened to the tape, and neither of us is sure about the content, nor about whether or not it should be broadcast. We would welcome a ruling from you at the earliest opportunity.

Whilst on the subject, wewould like to have your advice also on the use of the word "Psychedelic". In our opinion, which I believe is shared by C.L.P. this word derives exclusively from the use of the drug L.S.D., and it might be wise if we were to instruct all D.J's not to use it. On the other hand this is only our opinion, and other people claim that the word is not connected exclusively with drugs at all.

Certainly while the Pirates are still on the air our position in deciding these things is especially difficult. There have been cases in the past year when both London and Caroline have banned discs that we have played. When this occurs however, it is seldom news, except perhaps in the trade press, but if we ban anything we hit the headlines.

Would you please advise us on both points, and on our policy regarding all discs alleged to contain references to, or to be based on, drugs and drug taking?

(Mark White).

HMD

LEFT Mark White's letter requesting advice about whether 'A Day In The Life' should be broadcast on the BBC. He refers to the leading offshore pirate stations Radio London and Radio Caroline banning records that the BBC had played on air. The day Mark White wrote the letter, Radio London played *Sgt. Pepper* from start to finish, including 'A Day In The Life'.

THE SGT. PEPPER preview pieces were put together by the maverick DJ Kenny Everett. Encouraged to pursue a career on the wireless by BBC producer William De'Ath, he had made his name on pirate Radio London. His playful manipulation of sound through tape-editing, echo and phasing was startlingly inventive in 1967. His interview technique was light years away from that of Brian Matthew. Kenny giggled and mumbled casually with The Beatles, keen to show he was locked on to their wavelength. John was heard delivering three amusing and rather stoned-sounding introductions:

'We're sitting in the hushed semicircular theatre waiting for the Sgt. Pepper's Lonely Hearts Club Band to come out and here they come now playing the first number, ah! Let's go! … All right? I can't do it for them all, man, or I'll be dizzy.

'… Now we'd like to play you one. It's a sad little song… where's it gone? … Oh, this is it, yeah… 'Picture yourself on an old-fashioned elephant'. 'Lucy In The Sky' for everyone… now.

'… Phasing is great! Double-flanging, we call it… You name the one it isn't on. You spot it, you get a prize and you get a Sgt. Pepper badge. Phasing is toooo much!'

Paul's clips were a little more informative.

KENNY: How many takes did you usually do on this album before you got the perfect take?

PAUL: We did quite a few on each one, but it's just 'cause it's changed. Like in the old days of the LP *Please Please Me*, we went in and did it in a day 'cause we knew all the numbers. We'd rehearsed them and been playing them for about a year. But nowadays, we just take a song in and all we've got is the chords on a guitar and the words and the tune. So we've got to work out how to arrange it. So we do a lot of takes on each one.

KENNY: Do you like to have a lot of people in the studio when you're recording or do you like to do it completely alone?

PAUL: It doesn't matter. We had a lot of people on some of the tracks. Sometimes we use them – ask them to clap and that. Depends. If it's good people, who don't hassle anyone and don't try and mess a session up, then it's great, you know. 'Cause it's company, good company.

KENNY: I hear you had The Rolling Stones in this session.

PAUL: They came down 'cause we had a lot of people there. It was a big session and we wanted to make a 'Happening' happen… and it happened!

IT HAPPENED ON 10 February 1967 when the orchestral rush was added to 'A Day In The Life'. Serious players wore an assortment of silly red noses and joke shop paraphernalia, while various friends – including some Stones and a Monkee – joined them in the studio. Kaleidoscopic images from the event were made into a film using the song as its soundtrack. It was never televised in the 1960s – principally because, for several years, 'A Day In The Life' was banned from both BBC TV and radio.

The BBC picked up an early warning when 'A Day In The Life' was front-page news in *Disc And Music Echo* (6 May 1967). It was reported that several Los Angeles radio stations had obtained four *Sgt. Pepper* tracks and had placed a ban on the song, because of inferred drug references. An advance tape was requested from The Beatles' publishing company Northern Songs. Mark White, the Assistant Head of Gramophone Programmes, wrote a memo to the Assistant Head of Sound Broadcasting, Mr RD Marriott:

'Our Light Programme production "Where It's At" will be featuring the LP … and although they need not play this particular track, it is thought by the experts to be one of the best on the album, and other programmes may well want to play it later. Head of Gramophone Programmes [Anna Instone] and I have listened to the tape, and neither of us is sure about the content, nor about whether or not it should be broadcast. We would welcome a ruling from you at the earliest opportunity.'

There was also a worry that 'the word "Psychedelic" derives exclusively from the use of the drug LSD and it might be wise if we were to instruct all DJs not to use it.' The suspect word was heard in *Where It's At* (although further usage was officially discouraged), but 'A Day In The Life' was not played. Roland Fox – Assistant Head of Publicity – wrote to his colleagues confirming that the BBC would not broadcast the song as it could 'encourage a permissive attitude to drug-taking'.

Radio Times (Incorporating World-Radio)
June 22, 1967. Vol. 175: No. 2276.

LONDON AND SOUTH-EAST

JUNE 24—30

Radio Times

SIXPENCE

OUR WORLD

DIRECT
BY SATELLITE
ON BBC-1

FOR THE FIRST TIME TV ENCIRCLES THE EARTH

On 23 May, Frank Gillard – the Director of Sound Broadcasting – wrote an explanatory letter about the BBC decision to the Chairman of EMI, Sir Joseph Lockwood:

'I never thought the day would come when we would have to put a ban on an EMI record, but sadly, that is what has happened over this track. We have listened to it over and over again with great care, and we cannot avoid coming to the conclusion that the words 'I'd love to turn you on' followed by the mounting montage of sound, could have a rather sinister meaning.

'"Turned on" is a phrase which can be used in many different circumstances, but it is currently much in vogue in the jargon of the drug-addicts. We do not feel that we can take the responsibility of appearing to favour or encourage those unfortunate habits ...'

'A Day In The Life' was not broadcast until the early 1970s and was one of only two records from the 1960s absolutely banned by the BBC, rather than being subject to the less draconian-sounding 'restricted'. Nevertheless, amid the controversy, The Beatles appeared in an historic television event broadcast the same month *Sgt. Pepper* was released.

Our World was the first TV show to link five continents by satellite. Work on the project originally began with the title *Round the World in Eighty Minutes*. The programme eventually spanned over two hours with a range of short features from many of the countries linked together by the exciting new technology. On 28 February 1967, a letter from the BBC was sent to The Beatles' manager Brian Epstein explaining that one section would 'show man's greatest current achievements in the field of art and entertainment. Within this section we would like to offer from Britain the subject of the Beatles at work... in a recording studio making a disc.' It was agreed that there could be an outside broadcast from EMI Studios, Abbey Road while the group recorded their next single. BBC producer Derek Burrell-Davis met The Beatles on 17 May to discuss their contribution. In a telegram to the project's coordinator Aubrey Singer, he reported: 'Our World beat group in two hours meeting – aware challenge – enthusiastic actuality setting – responsive to world stage – writing new number with words such as Hello Love You Me Us Them We Together. Intend indicate Swinging London. Happening hoped for. Promise participate all rehearsals.'

28th February 1967

Dear Mr. Epstein,

I am writing to you as a result of a telephone conversation with
your assistant, Mr. Peter Brown.   I am working on a unique television
programme for which we would very much like to book the Beatles, if this
is at all possible.

The programme will be called, in English "Our World".   It is to be
the first ever world television programme in which twenty or more countries
will join together to create and present a single programme to a potential
audience of 500,000,000 viewers.   It will be a two hour programme on the
theme of man and his world; and one section will show mans' greatest current
achievements in the field of art and entertainment.   Each country
contributing will offer the finest exponents they can of the particular
subject they are to show, e.g. we hope that France will offer us Picasso at
work.

Within this section we would like to offer from Britain the subject
of the Beatles at work.   Ideally we would like, since the occasion seems
big enough to warrant this, to hear them in a recording studio actually
making a disc.   This would be live Outside Broadcast coverage, and would,
I hope, give us the first ever public airing of their next single.

All this would happen between 8.00 and 10.00 p.m. British Summer
Time, next June 25th (a Sunday).   In this country the programme will be
at least on BBC 1.

I wonder if as soon as possible I could have your initial reactions
to the idea I have outlined for the Beatles, if they are at all able to be
available at that time?

Yours sincerely,

(David Filkin)

Brian Epstein Esq.,
NEMS Enterprises,
Southerland House,
5-6 Argyll Street,
W.1.

ABOVE The letter that made the first overture
to Brian Epstein regarding The Beatles'
participation in the ambitious *Our World*
programme scheduled for four months later.
RIGHT The telegram that confirms that 'All You
Need Is Love' was written especially for the
global *Our World* broadcast on 25 June 1967.

PAGES 222 AND 223 Stills from *Our World*
showing The Beatles singing 'All You Need Is
Love' direct to the world. Studio One in Abbey
Road is festooned with flowers and balloons
for the hoped-for 'Happening'.

PLEASE RETURN
TO ROOM 4012.

BBCTELOBS LDN
LO/TVOBS 9   TC11   17 MAY   2120
COPIES TO :-
1. MR PETER DIMMOCK 4105 KH
MR RAY COLLEY 3081 KH
MR JOHN MILES 2018 TC   =

FROM DEREK BURRELL-DAVIS RM 3082 KH
=FULL = MR AUBREY SINGER LA SALLE HOTEL MONTREALCANADA =
=FULL = MR AUBREY SINGER CARE LAURIER HERBERT CBC MONTREALCANADA =
V
OUR WORLD BEAT GROUP IN TWO HOURS MEETING   AWARE CHALLENGE
ENTHUSIASTIC ACTUALITY SETTING RESPONSIVE TO WORLD STAGE
AGREE FIVE MINUTES PARTICIPATION STOP WRITING NEW NUMBER WITH BASIC
WORDS SUCH AS HELLO LOVE YOU ME US THEM WE TOGETHER STOP 8
POSSIBLE WORDS SUNG IN SEVERAL LANGUAGES WITH MULTILINGUAL

HELD GRAPHICS STOP INTEND INDICATE SWINGING LONDON STOP HAPPENING
HOPED FOR STOP PROMISE PARTICIPATE ALL REHEARSALS STOP REPORTER
STEVE RACE STOP DIMMOCK COLLEY FULLY INFORMED STOP REGARDS =
DEREK BURRELL-DAVIS+++

CCTN :- RD
   STOP POSSIBLE

+.
TOD TVOBS 2122 VR

BBCTELOBS LDN
ERASE V AT BGNG +

PAUL

JOHN

GEORGE

LONDON,
UNITED KINGDOM

ロンドン、
イギリス

RINGO

RINGO

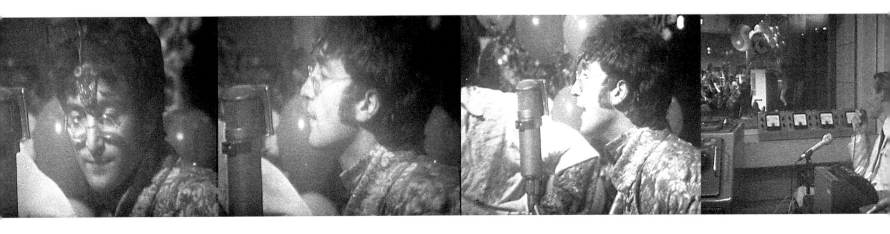

In addition to the hoped-for 'Happening', the other UK item for *Our World* was an outside broadcast from the Scottish new town of Cumbernauld with Magnus Magnusson for a section entitled 'The Crowded World'. There were hopes expressed in press information that 'the world will take a step closer to Marshall McLuhan's concept of a "global village" as an estimated 500 million persons in 30 nations witness the first globe-girdling telecast in history.' This optimism was punctured by current events. On 21 June 1967, four days before the scheduled broadcast, the Soviet Union refused to take part. It believed that the US, UK and West Germany were lending support to Israeli aggression in the Middle East, which was against the humanitarian spirit of *Our World*. Four countries from Eastern Europe – Czechoslovakia, East Germany, Hungary and Poland – followed the Soviet example and withdrew. Denmark was quickly invited to take part, resulting in the final show having fourteen contributing countries. It was broadcast to thirty nations.

For British viewers eagerly anticipating The Beatles, there was a very long wait. Cliff Michelmore cued the section from Abbey Road Studios an hour and 39 minutes after *Our World* had commenced. Their performance of 'All You Need Is Love' followed five other examples of 'Artistic Excellence': Franco Zeffirelli directing *Romeo and Juliet* in Tuscany, Italy; a rehearsal of *Lohengrin* at the theatrical home of Wagner opera in Bayreuth, Germany; artists Joan Miro and Alexander Calder at work in Fondation Maeght in France; Mexican folk song and dancing; and pianists Leonard Bernstein and Van Cliburn at the Lincoln Centre in New York.

When a worldwide audience estimated at 350 million was linked to Abbey Road, George Martin was seen in the control room talking to The Beatles over the studio talk-back system. Broadcast commentary was by Steve Race:

'The supervisor is George Martin, the musical brain behind The Beatles' records. There's the orchestra coming into the studio now and you'll notice that the musicians are not Rock & Roll youngsters. The Beatles get on best with symphony men. The boys began by making a basic instrumental track on their own. Then they added on top of that a second track of vocal backgrounds and they've just added a third track. Now comes the final stage. It brings in a solo vocal by John Lennon and, for the first time, the orchestra. Here

then is "Final Mixed Track Take 1" of a song which we offer to the whole world – "All You Need Is Love".'

The TV performance has become emblematic of Sixties idealism. Lending support in the studio are The Beatles' friends Mick Jagger, Keith Richards, Marianne Faithfull, Jane Asher, Eric Clapton, Keith Moon, Graham Nash – all wearing flamboyant clothes and carrying placards with translations into several languages of the message 'All You Need Is Love'. If *Our World* had been seen in the Soviet Union, where any glimpse of The Beatles was repressed, it would have been a monumental moment. Soviet Beatle fans had adopted extraordinary methods, at considerable personal risk from the authorities, to try to hear the forbidden records and see what the group looked like.

Despite the technical marvels of the programme, some British critics were less than enthusiastic. George Melly wrote in the *Observer*: '*Our World* dragged its interminable length across the screen last Sunday.' Maurice Wiggin of the *Sunday Times* did note 'the BBC's stunning technical achievement in linking umpteen countries live in *Our World*. When I say stunning I am picking my word with morbid precision; it stunned me very nearly to sleep.' A BBC Audience Research report contained responses from the Viewing Panel that voiced their disapproval of The Beatles representing the UK: 'Surely this isn't the image of what we are like?'; 'We did not do ourselves justice'; 'What a dreadful impression they must have given the rest of the world – I hope they do not think this is typical'; 'After all the culture etc. shown by the other countries, the Beatles were the absolute dregs (incidentally I am a Beatles fan).'

Quickly released as a single, 'All You Need Is Love' topped the UK charts during July and August 1967. *Sgt. Pepper* continued its long run at the top of the album chart. It was a glorious summer. However, for pop fans lucky enough to live in areas of the UK served by the many offshore radio stations, there were dark clouds on the horizon. Both the government and the BBC were unhappy about the popularity and proliferation of the pirates. Before 'A Day In The Life', the only song given a blanket ban was, unsurprisingly, 'We Love The Pirates' by The Roaring 60's. The single was made in 1966 as a protest against planned legislation to outlaw the stations.

ABOVE The script read by Steve Race to describe the methods used to record 'All You Need Is Love'.

OPPOSITE Brian Epstein relaxes with George, John and Paul during rehearsals for *Our World*.

> ## 'What we need isn't material, it's spiritual. We need some other form of peace and happiness.'
>
> GEORGE HARRISON

In August 1967, offshore radio was sunk by the Marine Offences Act and so, with the exception of a defiant Radio Caroline, during daytime the radio dial was returned to the monopoly of the BBC. But the popularity of the pirates had signalled a need for a network that did not schedule *Where It's At* within hours of *Those Were The Days* with Old Time sequence dancing played by Sidney Davey and his Orchestra. BBC Radio was obliged by the government to reorganize and so a fourth channel was added – Radio 1. Just a few months after the BBC's worries about ' A Day In The Life', their new pop station had jingles promising it would 'turn you on'.

On Radio 1's first day of broadcasting, 30 September 1967, an interview with George was heard in the pop magazine programme *Scene and Heard*. The Beatles had embarked on a new project – the TV show Paul had mentioned to Brian Matthew in March – *Magical Mystery Tour*. On 11 September 1967, The Beatles had set off in a bus for a week of filming on location in the west of England. Travelling with them were people of all ages, shapes and sizes. Some were actors, for example George Claydon playing 'Little George The Photographer' and Jessie Robins in the role of Ringo's aunt. Some were just along for the ride, such as the National Secretary and three Area Secretaries of The Official Beatles Fan Club.

George talked to reporter Miranda Ward at the Atlantic Hotel, Newquay, where the coach party stayed for three nights. Listeners had not heard him talk on a pop show since June 1966 and it soon became clear that his fascination with Indian culture now ran deeper than simply playing the sitar:

'I first noticed that I was interested in this, with the music first of all and along with that I'd heard stories of people in caves – Yogis as they're known – people levitating and dematerializing and doing all sorts of wondrous things. And then through the music, with meeting Ravi [Shankar], it was great, because he's a Brahmin, which is a high sect. Just all the groovy people are Brahmins – the scientists, religious people and musicians. And I learnt a lot from him and by going to India I realized there was more to all these rumours and mystic stories that you hear about in the West. They're actually there doing it and it's real and there are people like Jesus Christ, who are there all the time and they're always gonna be there.

OPPOSITE: **George and Ravi Shankar at a press conference held on 3 August 1967 – the day before the sitar virtuoso's concert at the Hollywood Bowl. While in LA, George and his wife Pattie rented a house on Blue Jay Way. The street name became the title of a song featured in** *Magical Mystery Tour.*

From: Controller, BBC-1

Subject: THE BEATLES : I AM A WALRUS

To: H.C.A.G.Tel.; H.F.G.Tel.; Ed.Tel.N.; H.M.P.Tel.;
             H.A.F.Tel.; H.P.S.; H.P.N.I.; H.P.W.; H.P.N.;
             H.P.M., H.P.S.W.

             Copy to: H.L.E.G.Tel.   27th November 1967

     I am passing on, for your information, a note from H.L.E.G.Tel.
which is self-explanatory.

     "In the Beatles film (so far uncompleted) "The Magical
     Mystery Tour", they sing a number called "I am a Walrus".
     A disc has now been issued.

     The lyrics contain a very offensive passage and after talking
     to Anna Instone, we have both agreed not to play it on radio
     or television.

     Although not officially banned, it will not be heard on "Top
     of the Pops" or "Juke Box Jury".

     I should be grateful if you would ensure that any other possible
     outlets are similarly blocked off."

                              PAUL FOX

AMF   (Paul Fox)

'One thing led to another, just snowballed, got bigger and bigger. And then in the end, I'd like to become this myself. I'd just like to have this quality that these people have, which is a spiritual thing. And I think with us having all the material wealth that we need, then… you know, the average person feels that if they had a car and a telly and a house then that's where it's at. But if you get a car and a telly and a house… and even a lot of money… your life's still empty because it's still all on this gross level. What we need isn't material, it's spiritual. We need some other form of peace and happiness.'

George gave a brief synopsis of *Magical Mystery Tour*: 'a typical coach tour, but anything can happen… because it's magic'; and his view on TV shows like *Top of the Pops*: 'It was okay for whenever it was invented, but it's still the same. The times change so fast yet those TV shows go on and on and on being the same old thing.' When asked about the long-awaited third Beatles movie, George used an apt analogy: 'Over the last two years since *Help!*, we've had thousands of ideas [sent to us]. But they've all been *Help!* and *A Hard Day's Night* revisited. It's no good… How we visualize the film, it's got to be at least the difference between the song 'Help!' and *Sgt. Pepper*. The movie's got to be that progression too.'

Where It's At had survived the demise of the Light Programme to be given a Saturday afternoon slot on Radio 1. The edition of 25 November 1967 featured John chatting to Chris Denning and Kenny Everett. They seemed most interested in capturing some off-the-wall streams of consciousness for trailers and jingles…

KENNY: 'Cause interviews are a bit old hat, as you'll have gathered, do a few Lennonisms that we can chuck in every now and then.

JOHN: It's easier said than done, Ken. I mean give us a clue as to what you want.

SUBJECTS FLITTED IN and out of the conversation. John commented on the shortcomings of the equipment at Abbey Road: 'EMI are just about to buy some eight-track machines and that's not enough'; post-production work on *Magical Mystery Tour*: 'we planned three weeks to edit it and put the sound on but it's taken eight weeks to edit and we're just getting into the sound now'; and the songs in

the TV film. The BBC had its knickers in a twist again about … well, knickers. 'I Am The Walrus', the B-side of the current Beatles single 'Hello, Goodbye', included the line 'Boy, you been a naughty girl, you let your knickers down.'

JOHN: Are you going to play 'Walrus'? Somebody heard Joyce Grenfell singing about 'Pull your knickers up!' yesterday. So listen Sir Henry Fielding, or whoever it is running the BBB!

OPPOSITE **Despite his advice to 'block off' possible outlets that would allow the British public to hear 'I Am The Walrus' over the airwaves, the Controller of BBC 1 did not demand the song be removed from the broadcast of the** *Magical Mystery Tour* **film on 26 December 1967.**

ABOVE **John on the** *Magical Mystery Tour* **coach on the day of departure for filming in the West Country, 11 September 1967.**

EVEN AS LATE as November, there had been no decision about whether *Magical Mystery Tour* would be shown on the BBC or the commercial TV channel. As the editing neared completion, an outlet for the film was finally confirmed when the Controller of BBC 1, Paul Fox, sealed a deal at a meeting in his office with Paul McCartney. *Magical Mystery Tour* was transmitted on Boxing Day (26 December) 1967 at 8.35pm in black-and-white. It was repeated ten days later in colour on BBC 2. Very few homes had the special aerial needed to receive BBC 2, and fewer still a very expensive colour TV set, so only a small audience experienced the film as it had been intended by its creators.

The screening of *Magical Mystery Tour* on British TV derailed a long-running train of triumphs for The Beatles. There had been instances of unfavourable publicity in Britain before. For example, the group receiving MBEs in the Queen's Birthday Honours list in 1965 had caused some grumpy remarks that the gravity of the award had been violated. But that was mild disgruntlement compared to the newspaper headlines following the first broadcast of *Magical Mystery Tour*. 'Magic Leaves Beatles With Almighty Flop' and 'Beatles Mystery Tour Baffles Viewers' were the verdicts of the *Daily Express* and *Daily Mirror*. Certainly, the film's visual power was weakened by its transmission in black-and-white, particularly the clouds changing hue for 'Flying' and the montage of mountain views with Paul as 'The Fool On The Hill'. But the film's generally hostile reception was more affected by its placement on Boxing Day. Light entertainment had been expected – not an experimental fantasy. After all, it was preceded by a variety show hosted by Petula Clark and normal service was resumed after *Magical Mystery Tour* with a film called *The Square Peg* starring comedian Norman Wisdom.

TOP Ringo on the bus with his fictional Aunt Jessie played by Jessie Robbins. The Beatles' road manager Mal Evans is in the background. MIDDLE The Beatles wearing animal masks for the 'I Am The Walrus' scene filmed for *Magical Mystery Tour* at West Malling Air Station, Kent – September 1967. BOTTOM Out and about in the West Country – Paul is in the foreground; George and Mal Evans are behind him. OPPOSITE John directing the film crew on the cliffs at Holywell near Newquay, Cornwall on 13 September 1967. The sequence did not appear in the final cut of *Magical Mystery Tour*.

According to a BBC Audience Research Report, 25.7 per cent of the UK population watched *Magical Mystery Tour* on Boxing Day. This was a very impressive number. However, three-quarters of those on the Audience Research Viewing Panel 'could hardly find a good word to say for the programme, considering it stupid, pretentious rubbish which was, no doubt, intended to be very clever and "way out" but which was, they thought, a complete jumble with neither shape nor meaning, and certainly no entertainment value whatsoever'. 'Positively the worst programme I can remember seeing on any TV channel,' reported one viewer. In the small minority of those who enjoyed 'the refreshing departure from the usual run of programmes' was a schoolboy who described it as as 'one of the best Christmas programmes we have had for a long time. The idea was clever as well as original. It was very funny in parts. A marvellous programme in black and white – in colour it would be indescribable.'

The six new songs from *Magical Mystery Tour* were released in the UK on a double EP (two 45rpm discs). It was runner-up in the UK singles chart to 'Hello, Goodbye'. This chart-topping success at Christmas was a fitting end to a year of large-scale achievements, including the biggest TV audience up to that point for 'All You Need Is Love' and the indomitable *Sgt. Pepper's Lonely Hearts Club Band*. True, their adventurous film had signified that The Beatles could no longer expect universal acceptance for every project. But Brian Matthew had accurately summarized the group's attitude at the end of his BBC Transcription interview in March 1967: 'As unpredictable as ever – The Beatles!'

ABOVE The last day of filming for *Magical Mystery Tour* – for the 'Blue Jay Way' sequence – took place in the garden of Ringo's home in Weybridge, Surrey on 3 November 1967. OPPOSITE John sitting in the field near Newquay where the 'magic tent' sequence was filmed on 14 September 1967.

1967 RADIO AND TV APPEARANCES

📺 Radio programme titles
📺 TV titles

📺 TOP OF THE POPS
BBC Transcription Service
Rec: 20 March 1967
Brian Matthew talked to John and Paul about their current activities and future plans for a feature distributed on disc for broadcast outside the UK.

📺 THE IVOR NOVELLO AWARDS FOR 1966
Br: 27 March 1967 (Easter Monday) – 2.00–3.00pm – The Light Programme
Rec: 20 March 1967
John and Paul won three awards for 'Yellow Submarine', 'Michelle' and 'Yesterday', but did not attend the ceremony. An interview about the songs was taped during session time for *Sgt. Pepper's Lonely Hearts Club Band* at Abbey Road.

📺 MAN ALIVE – *What Is a Happening?*
Br: 17 May 1967 – 8.05–8.35pm – BBC 2
Rec: 29 April 1967
John was filmed at the *14 Hour Technicolor Dream* event at Alexandra Palace.

📺 WHERE IT'S AT
Br: 20 May 1967 – 4.00–5.30pm – The Light Programme
Rec: May 1967
Kenny Everett assembled features with John, Paul and Ringo introducing all but one of the songs on *Sgt. Pepper*. The Light Programme's 'grooviest' show was presented by Chris Denning.

📺 OUR WORLD
Br: 25 June 1967 – 7.57–9.59pm – BBC 1 – Live
The Beatles were shown recording 'All You Need Is Love' at EMI Studio One, Abbey Road from 9.36 to 9.42pm.

📺 'All You Need Is Love' was repeated in two *Top Of The Pops* broadcasts on 6 July and 3 August 1967 and in *Top Of The Pops '67 – Part Two* – 26 December 1967

📺 WHERE IT'S AT
Br: 1 July 1967 – 4.00–5.30pm – The Light Programme
Rec: June 1967
Chris Denning's show included Paul talking to Kenny Everett about the forthcoming single 'All You Need Is Love'.

📺 BBC NEWS REPORTS
Br: 27 August 1967 – BBC 1
Rec: 27 August 1967
John and George were interviewed in Bangor, North Wales about the sudden death of their manager Brian Epstein from a drug overdose. Looking shocked, John struggled to make sense of the news: 'We don't know what to say. We just loved him and he was one of us'.

📺 SPOTLIGHT SOUTH-WEST
Br: 13 September 1967 – 5.55–6.15pm – BBC 1, local news for south-west region
Rec: 12 September 1967
John and Paul were interviewed by Hugh Scully while filming on location in Plymouth for *Magical Mystery Tour*.

📺 SCENE AND HEARD
Br: 30 September 1967 – 6.32–7.29pm – Radio 1
Rec: 13 September 1967
George was interviewed by Miranda Ward for the first edition of a pop magazine programme broadcast on the launch day of Radio 1. Recorded at the Atlantic Hotel in Newquay, he talked about the filming of *Magical Mystery Tour* and his devotion to Indian culture and spirituality.

📺 SCENE AND HEARD
Br: 7 October 1967 – 6.32–7.29pm – Radio 1
Rec: 13 September 1967
Part two of Miranda Ward's interview with George.

📺 SCENE AND HEARD
Br: 14 October 1967 – 6.32–7.29pm – Radio 1
Rec: 14 September 1967
During filming of scenes for *Magical Mystery Tour*, Miranda Ward had also talked to Ringo at the Atlantic Hotel, Newquay.

📺 WHERE IT'S AT
Br: 25 November 1967 – 2.00–3.00pm – Radio 1
Rec: November 1967
Kenny Everett and Chris Denning interviewed John. From out of their casual ramblings emerged some details about the editing of the *Magical Mystery Tour* film. Paul also recorded a musical jingle for the programme with the repeated line 'Kenny Everett and Chris Denning all together on the wireless machine'.

📺 LATE NIGHT EXTRA
Br: 5 December 1967 – 10.00pm–midnight – Radio 1 & Radio 2
Rec: 5 December 1967
John and Cilla Black talked to Brian Cullingford at the launch party of the Apple boutique in Baker Street.

📺 TOP OF THE POPS
Br: 7 December 1967 – 7.30–8.00pm – BBC 1
Rec: 21 November 1967
To provide a visual accompaniment to 'Hello, Goodbye', a film was made of The Beatles editing *Magical Mystery Tour* with Roy Benson at Norman's Film Productions, London.

📺 MAGICAL MYSTERY TOUR
Br: 26 December 1967 – 8.35–9.25pm – BBC 1; repeated on 5 January 1968 – BBC 2

1968
Release

UNLIKE TODAY, the gap separating an artist's records during the 1960s was measured in months not years. In February 1968, just a few weeks after the release of the soundtrack songs for *Magical Mystery Tour* and the Christmas chart-topper 'Hello, Goodbye', The Beatles completed recording their next single 'Lady Madonna'/'The Inner Light'. Their job done, they then travelled to Rishikesh, India to study Transcendental Meditation with Maharishi Mahesh Yogi. The Beatles' time spent in the peaceful ashram above the Ganges was far removed from events that prevailed in 1968: war, assassinations, street riots, revolution in the air.

The Tet Offensive launched by the North Vietnamese at the beginning of the year had brought the most intensive and bloody battles of the Vietnam War. The ferocity of its enemy's attacks shook the US military's belief in a successful and imminent conclusion to the conflict. American personnel involved in the war numbered over 540,000. The US death toll for the year was 16,592. Through the year there were preliminary peace talks and troop withdrawals and the cessation of North Vietnam bombing by the Americans.

On 4 April 1968, Dr Martin Luther King, Jr was assassinated while standing on the balcony of the Lorraine Motel in Memphis. The previous day he had spoken about the possibility of his early death: 'I've been to the mountain top … and I have looked over and I have seen the Promised Land. I may not get there with you, but I want you to know tonight that we, as a people, will get to the Promised Land.' Following his murder, riots erupted in over a hundred cities across the States. President Lyndon Johnson had decided not to stand for re-election as President. While in Los Angeles as part of his campaign to be the Democratic Party's candidate, Senator Robert Kennedy was shot on 5 June 1968. He died a day later. At the funeral, his brother Edward delivered the eulogy: 'He said many times, in many parts of this nation … "Some men see things as they are and say why. I dream things that never were and say why not."'

In the last week of August, the Democratic Party's National Convention was held in Chicago to nominate a presidential candidate. Thousands of anti-war protestors gathered in the city to express the need for change. In what has been described as a 'police riot', the demonstrators were subjected to brutal attacks by the forces of law and order, who greatly outnumbered them. The nominated Democratic candidate Hubert Humphrey was defeated by Republican Richard Nixon in the closely fought November presidential election.

There had been street fighting in several countries throughout 1968. In France, student protest at the universities of Nanterre and Sorbonne had developed into a general strike and civil disobedience. There were riots in West Berlin. On 20 August, 650,000 troops from the Soviet Union and other Warsaw Pact countries invaded Czechoslovakia to halt the sequence of liberal policies introduced by Alexander Dubcek, the first secretary of the Communist Party. 'The Prague Spring' was quickly brought to an end.

Although pop musicians had begun to sing about the troubled times, particularly the events of the civil rights campaign and Vietnam War, The Beatles usually did not. Paul has explained that 'Blackbird', recorded in June, was written in support of the struggle for racial equality in America, but the most direct political statement was made in 'Revolution'. On 6 June, a week after the first recording of his song, John was interviewed for the BBC TV programme *Release*. His strongly expressed opinion about what was happening in the world was an early sign of what was to come from him a year later.

The innovative animated film *Yellow Submarine* was released in July 1968. With a soundtrack of The Beatles' music and actors impersonating their voices, it told a tale of Love and Music triumphing over the Blue Meanie forces of Evil. Featuring remarkable visual effects for its time, *2001: A Space Odyssey* was a rather more enigmatic story. Significant progress was made in real-life space exploration during 1968. In September, the unmanned Russian craft *Zond 5* was the first to loop round the Moon and return to Earth. The American space programme launched *Apollo 8* in December. On Christmas Eve, it became the first manned spacecraft to circle the Moon. In a live TV broadcast from their lunar orbit, the three astronauts showed pictures they had taken of the Moon and Earth. For the millions watching, this was a calming and thought-provoking event to close out such a tempestuous and sorrowful year.

IN SEPTEMBER 1967, when actor Victor Spinetti arrived at an airfield in Kent to take part in *Magical Mystery Tour*, he was struck by an unusual item on the shooting schedule. A meditation session was timetabled to follow lunch. His day playing a loquacious drill sergeant was during the second week of filming – less than a month after the sudden death of The Beatles' manager Brian Epstein on 27 August. The group had received the shocking news in Bangor, North Wales, where they were to spend the week learning about Transcendental Meditation with Maharishi Mahesh Yogi. On the third day, their attendance at the course at the Normal College in Bangor ended abruptly with a distressing phone call from London. The media had already descended on Bangor to cover a quirky story about The Beatles meeting an Indian guru. Newsgatherers now found themselves ideally placed to record the group's initial feelings following the sad loss of their manager.

INTERVIEWER: I understand that Mr Epstein was to be initiated here tomorrow.

JOHN: Yes.

INTERVIEWER: When was he coming up?

GEORGE: Tomorrow… just Monday, that's all we knew.

INTERVIEWER: Had you told him very much about the Spiritual Regeneration Movement?

GEORGE: Well, as much as we'd learned about spiritualism and various things of that nature, then we tried to pass them on to him. And he was equally as interested as we are, as everybody should be. He wanted to know about life, as much as we do.

INTERVIEWER: I understand that this afternoon Maharishi conferred with you all. Could I ask you what advice he offered you?

JOHN: He told us… er… not to get overwhelmed by grief and whatever thoughts we have of Brian to keep them happy, because any thoughts we have of him will travel to him wherever he is.

OPPOSITE **On 25 August 1967, The Beatles arrived in Bangor, North Wales to study Transcendental Meditation with Maharishi Mahesh Yogi.**

INTERVIEWER: Had he ever met Mr Epstein?

JOHN: No, but he was looking forward to meeting him.

INTERVIEWER: Did the Maharishi give you any words of comfort?

JOHN: Meditation gives you confidence enough to withstand something like this, even the short amount we've had.

GEORGE: There's no real such thing as death anyway. I mean, it's death on a physical level, but life goes on everywhere… and you just keep going, really. The thing about the comfort is to know that he's OK.

Five days after Brian Epstein's death, The Beatles met in London to decide what to do next. At Paul's urging, *Magical Mystery Tour* – a TV project they had first discussed five months before – was given a green light. They planned to resume their study of transcendental meditation at the Maharishi's centre in Rishikesh, India once the film was completed in October. However, *Magical Mystery Tour* took longer to edit than anticipated so their trip was postponed until February 1968. Ringo and his wife Maureen spent less than two weeks in Rishikesh. Paul and his girlfriend Jane Asher were next to leave after five weeks. The day they returned to England, the audio from a filmed interview at London Heathrow Airport was broadcast on Radio 4's *The World at One* news programme.

INTERVIEWER: What exactly have you been doing? How do you meditate?

PAUL: You sit down, you relax and then you repeat a sound to yourself. And it sounds daft, but it's just a system of relaxation and that's all it is. There's nothing more to it so that we meditated for about five hours a day in all. Two hours in the morning and maybe three hours in the evening. And the rest of the time we slept, ate, sunbathed and had fun, you know.

INTERVIEWER: Ringo came back a bit early and he described this place as a holiday camp. Would you agree?

PAUL: [laughs] Yes. Well, it is a bit like that. But that's a good description not disparaging.

INTERVIEWER: One Indian MP accused this place of being an espionage centre and you, in fact, of being a spy for the West.

PAUL: [laughs] Well, don't tell anyone, it's true!

INTERVIEWER: It is?

PAUL: We're spies, yes. The four of us have been spying… Actually, I'm a reporter and I joined The Beatles for that very reason, but the story's out next week in the paper which shall be nameless.

ABOVE Stills from a BBC News interview with George and John about the death of The Beatles' manager Brian Epstein on 27 August 1967.

OPPOSITE The Beatles made their pilgrimage to the Maharishi's ashram in Rishikesh, India in February 1968. George celebrated his 25th birthday there.

FAR FROM THE distractions of life in England, the relaxed atmosphere in Rishikesh had inspired a prolific period of songwriting. The Beatles began to record their cache of newly composed songs at Abbey Road on 30 May. A week later Kenny Everett visited Abbey Road. The DJ was moving from his Sunday morning slot to a daily show on Radio 1 and encouraged John, Paul and Ringo to improvise 'Goodbye Jingles'. John strummed an unplugged electric guitar and was joined by Paul for an instantaneous song, 'Goodbye to Kenny Everett, he is our very pal'. Ringo also led a chorus of 'Goodbye Kenny, see you in the morning', which evolved into 'Goodbye Kenny, we hear you got the sack!' As for 'the interview', even Kenny was aware of how bizarre it was.

KENNY: Well, that's about thirty seconds' worth.

JOHN: Nah, there's an LP out of this, Ken… This is ad nauseam, straight from the mouth that bit me… I hope we're gonna hear this, listeners, because we have a lot of fun doing them. But never quite hear them, listeners, when you get home… So, Wonderful Radio One-ders!

KENNY: Have you got anything to say that our listeners would understand?

JOHN: How about 'Good Morning'?

JOHN TREATED KENNY to a quick blast of the Leadbelly song 'Cottonfields' with a word change: 'When I was a little bitty baby, my mama used to *smash* me in the cradle!' Asked to choose a favourite new record, John requested Nilsson's cover version of 'River Deep Mountain High' or, as he renamed it, 'River Deep Mountain Dew'. It was on the singer's debut album *Pandemonium*

LEFT AND OPPOSITE **The Beatles in EMI Studios, Abbey Road in June 1968. The ever-helpful Mal Evans is standing by Paul.**

PAGES 246 AND 247 **Stills from the BBC 2 arts show *Release*, which included an interview with Victor Spinetti and John filmed at Abbey Road.**

Shadow Show, which also included an ingenious cover of The Beatles' 'You Can't Do That' incorporating snatches of several more of their songs. Kenny Everett recorded a Nilsson composition from the same album, 'It's Been So Long'. In an unbroadcast version of the interview, all the Beatles are heard enthusing about the eccentric falsetto singer and ukulele player, Tiny Tim. His album *God Bless Tiny Tim* had recently been released in April 1968. He was most well-known for his take on 'Tip-Toe Thru' The Tulips With Me' and appearances on the American TV show *Rowan & Martin's Laugh-In*. 'Play Tiny Tim!' John suggested. 'That's what you gotta play. Tiny Tim! He's the greatest ever, man. You see if I ain't right, Kenny Everett. He's the greatest fella on earth. Play Tiny Tim, gentle-readers.'

On the same day he had clowned around with Everett, John gave an extremely lucid and serious interview for the BBC 2 television show *Release*. John and Victor Spinetti discussed *The Lennon Play: In His Own Write*, a dramatization for Sir Laurence Olivier's National Theatre Company of the two books published in 1964 and 1965. The idea to adapt John's books for the stage had come from Adrienne Kennedy. Parts of the interview with Peter Lewis have been preserved on film by the BBC. The following transcription includes material (shown in italics) that was not transmitted.

JOHN: 'My houseboat and I take great pressure in denouncing this lovely ship'!

PETER: *John Lennon, you only saw the play after it had been in rehearsal for several weeks. What did you think when you were suddenly met by it?*

JOHN: *I thought what a clever lot of people. The first thing I saw when, after Victor had cut it up was… it was just what I thought.*

PETER: *You mean it was how you felt when you wrote?*

JOHN: *Yes.* When I saw the rehearsal of it, I got quite emotional, as if I'd written it.

VICTOR: *He said to me afterwards, 'That's what I was thinking when I wrote these things.'*

PETER: *That's marvellous. Well, did you in fact think of it as being one boy's experiences and he grows up and becomes a man.*

JOHN: *No, no. To see that objectively took this to happen to it. Somebody*

A Most Unwarrantable Intrusion
John Maddison Morton

In His Own Write
Adrienne Kennedy   John Lennon
Victor Spinetti
(Based on "In His Own Write" and
"A Spaniard in the Works" by John Lennon)

JOHN
LENNON

IN HIS
OWN WRITE

.U.C. against the
s the Duck of Ed
celess Margarine
ou might well an
ve his pension.

Panorasthma (BBC)
same questium was asked thre
d worjing folk about —
ou prepare Rinkled Dinglebon

he headlines. 'MOR
d there was, but it
'JACK THE NIPPI
er, it was Sydnees a

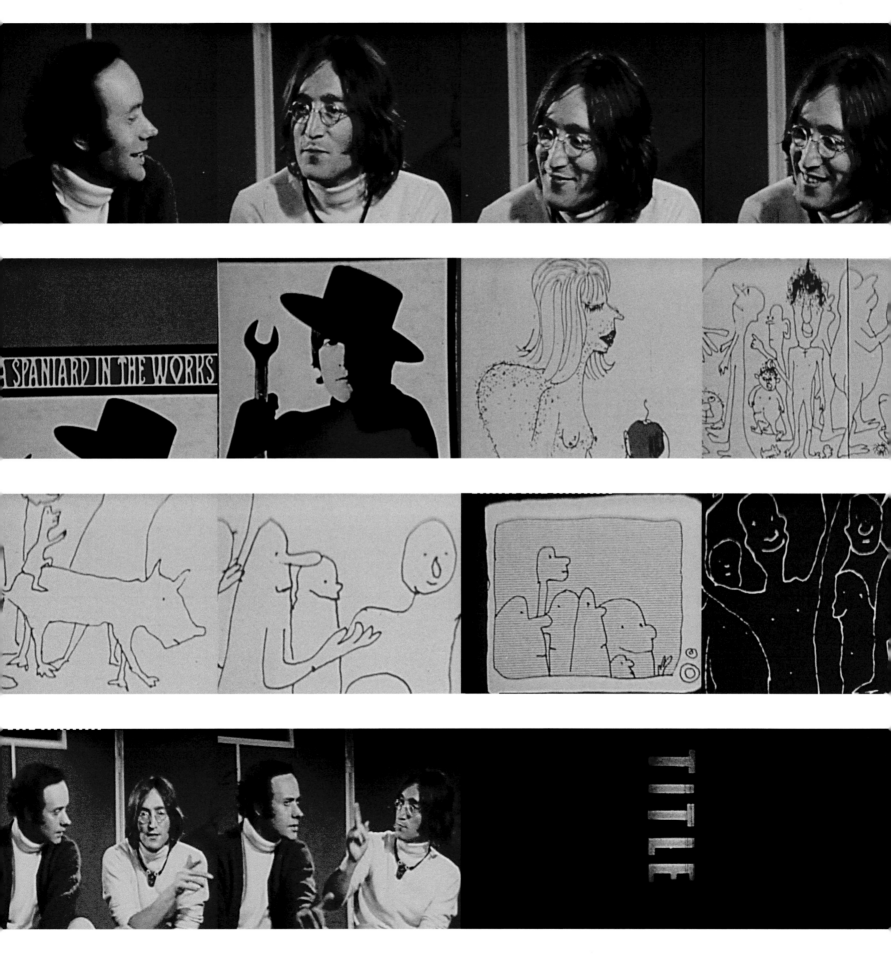

else to take it and say that they were all you. I mean, I knew in my heart of hearts who was who and what the book was saying, but not enough. I was too involved with it when it was written. And any criticism it had was either just rubbish or still only writing about what was on the paper so it took something like this to happen to make me see what I was about then, you know.

VICTOR: Are we rehearsing?

JOHN: Or are we on?

PETER: We're on.

VICTOR: We're on. What was interesting about it to me… the play was brought to me to act in, you see, and when I read it I began to feel, by reading the poems and the stories, the kind of things that happened to me as a kid and the kind of things I heard. And thank God, it corresponded with, when John came to see it, the kind of things that influenced him. The most important line in it is really 'The infleances upod us'. The things that make us what we are. Make you what you are now. Or make us what we were. The things we half-heard as kids.

PETER: Well, some of the influences, one of the big ones, is the family. The family glued round the television. How did you feel about that?

JOHN: Well, that was fine, you see. I didn't have a family glued round the television 'cause I only really lived with an auntie and we didn't really get a television until I was going out and didn't really watch it. But I mean it was going on all around me.

PETER: Well, an awful lot of the play is about radio and TV.

JOHN: Well I mean, that's all I ever heard, didn't I?

PETER: Yeah.

JOHN: I mean you go home…

VICTOR: [with humorous voice] Comic books. You got the church…

JOHN: [using the same sort of voice] You got your comic books, your classic comics, your *Beano*s.

VICTOR: Your church. Your classic comics. Your school.

JOHN: Aye, your school, your pub, and your TV and your radio.

PETER: Exactly.

JOHN: And that's it.

PETER: Funny thing you didn't put in pop music.

JOHN: No, because up till then it hadn't hit me. Pop music didn't hit me till I was sixteen and this is all before. The things that happened before sixteen.

VICTOR: But it's not really John's childhood. It's all of ours, really. Isn't it, John?

JOHN: [laughs] It is. We're all one, Victor. We're all one, aren't we?

VICTOR: It is, you know.

JOHN: I mean, what's going on?

PETER: Yeah. And the thing that you feel, all the way through, is that there's this boy trying to get out.

VICTOR: Sure.

JOHN: Well, I did, you see. [laughs] I got out. That's the joke. But that's just a sort of picture of somebody who is still in it. I mean, you get out in your mind.

PETER: Yeah. All the time he's dreaming his way out.

JOHN: But I mean, you do, until you actually physically get out of it.

PETER: Dream your way out into being Sherlock Holmes or…

JOHN: Whatever.

VICTOR: Whatever.

JOHN: Whatever.

VICTOR: *But I think that we come out of that reality into the real world of fantasy. I think the real world is fantastic.* And when the boy leaves at the end, I don't see him going into reality. His reality is his closely knit family locked up in television or locked up in those… He's going into fantasy, which I think is a real world. *Look what's happening around us now. You know, it's too fantastic, more fantastic than we could put on stage.*

PETER: *There's another thing about this boy. And that is,* he won't talk plain English. He invents his own language…

JOHN: Yeah.

PETER: … which is what you did when you started writing, when your books started coming out.

JOHN: Well, yeah. That was just a hangover from school, you know. I mean, I used to make the lads laugh with that scene, talking like that, and writing poetry. I used to write them and just give them to friends to laugh at, and that was the end of it. So when they all go down in a book, when it turns into a book and into a play, etcetera, etcetera. It's just my style of humour. *It's punning. You know it's just puns.*

PETER: *Well, you made the language up. A lot of it is extremely clever in the way you change words, distort words. I mean I wish they actually existed.* Instead of saying 'for example' as I was going to, you say 'forsample'.

VICTOR: Forsample, yes! And 'He was astoundaghast'!

JOHN: Well, some of them… 'cause I was never any good at spelling, all me life. You know, I never quite got the idea of spelling. English and writing, fine. But actually spelling the words. So… And also I typed a lot of the book, and I can only do it very slowly with a finger. So the stories would be very short because I couldn't be bothered going on.

VICTOR: [laughs]

JOHN: And also I'd spell it as you say it, like Latin really, you know. Or just try and do it the simplest way to get it over with. 'Cause all I'm trying to do is tell a story, and what the word is spelt like is irrelevant, really. But if they make you laugh because the word used to be spelt like that, that's great. But the thing is the story. And the sound of the word. *And just because we're English and we have, you know 'for example' or whatever the word is, this is a lot of crap, you know. It doesn't mean a thing.*

PETER: *You know when you say 'In the early owls of the morning…'*

JOHN: *Morecambe, actually. Yeah, that's fun. I enjoyed it.*

PETER: A lot of people wrote about your books and said, 'Oh! James Joyce, Edward Lear,' and so on. What did you think when they said that?

JOHN: Well, when they said James Joyce, I hadn't… I must have come across him at school, but we hadn't done him like I

'After you write something, a song or anything, you get the sadness and then you perform it or you put it on paper and then that's gone.'

JOHN LENNON

remember doing Shakespeare and remember doing so-and-so. I remember doing Chaucer a bit, or somebody like him doing funny words. But I don't remember Joyce, you see. So, the first thing they say, 'Oh! He's read James Joyce,' you know. So I hadn't. And so the first thing I do is buy *Finnegans Wake* and read a chapter. And it's great, you know, and I dug it and I felt as though he's an old friend. But I couldn't make it right through the book. And so I read a chapter of *Finnegans Wake* and that was the end of it. So now I know what they're talking about. But I mean, he just went… he just didn't stop, you know. Yeah.

PETER: What actually, though, had you read that you know was important to you when you were young?

JOHN: Only kids' books, you know. *Alice in Wonderland, Treasure Island, Kidnapped* and all those things.

PETER: *Yes, I see. But some of those poems…*

JOHN: The poems are all from *Jabberwocky*… started me into that kick.

PETER: Did it?

JOHN: And drawing. I started trying to draw like Ronald Searle when I was about eight. So there was *Jabberwocky* and Ronald Searle, I was turning into by the time I was thirteen. You know, I was determined to be Lewis Carroll [laughs] with a hint of Ronald Searle. *Then I sussed both of them when I was about seventeen. I moved off.*

PETER: *Well, we've got Shamrock Womlbs and Doctored Whopper.* Were you a Sherlock Holmes reader?

JOHN: No. I had a holiday, after we first made it big as Beatles in Tahiti. And there was nothing else on the boat but books. And Tahiti, we're on all those islands, great, but I still got into reading. So I was writing *Spaniard in the Works* and I knew… I never got past a story longer than a page. So I read a whole stack, sort of 'The Madman's Sherlock Holmes' where you get all the stories in one, and realized that every story was the same story. So I just wrote one 'Shamrock Womlbs' after three weeks of Sherlock Holmes in Tahiti. And that was the end of it.

OPPOSITE Victor Spinetti, John and Yoko Ono at the Old Vic for the opening night of the National Theatre production *In His Own Write* – 18 June 1968. This evening marked the first time John and Yoko were seen together at a public event.

VICTOR: *And Jock The Nipple.*

JOHN: *Yeah, but I missed out that he took cocaine, you see, readers… I missed the great point of him taking it.*

PETER: *You write it to be funny?*

JOHN: *Yes. And to be serious.*

PETER: *And to be serious. And some of it's pretty desperate in a way.*

JOHN: *We're all pretty desperate, you know, inside.*

PETER: There's a very, very sad poem at the end of the play about Kakky Hargreaves who is some sort of person whose name changes during the poem who's gone lost. Who was Kakky Hargreaves?

JOHN: Well, nobody, you know. It was Kakky, or Kathy, or Tammy. So it was all those people. But the point is that you got it: the sadness that I wrote into it. But after you write something, a song or anything, you get the sadness and then you perform it or you put it on paper and then that's gone. And the only way you get the joy back of writing it or the sadness back, is when somebody like Victor, or somebody else, comes and reads it to you, or acts it out. Like, when I first saw the rehearsal of the play, and they said these words back to me and I got the sadness from Kakky Hargreaves like I'd never heard it before.

PETER: You wrote that one when you were very young.

JOHN: Yes. That was, sort of, pre-Beatle. Eighteen, nineteen.

VICTOR: [laughs]

PETER: And have you written lately?

JOHN: Well I write, I think, all the time. So I mean, it's the same. I actually don't put it on paper so much these days, but I mean it goes into songs. A lot of the same energy that went into those poems. I don't know what I actually do with the thoughts, but they come out either on film, or on paper, or on tape. I've just got lots of tape, which I suppose if I put onto paper it would be a book. But it's just a matter of, do I want to make those tapes into paper or make the tapes into records?

PETER: Does it feel the same to you when you're writing something on paper and when you're writing a song lyric?

JOHN: It does now. In the old days I used to think that songwriting was this: you know, 'I love you and you love me,' and my writing was something else. Even if I didn't think of it quite like that. But I just realized through Dylan and other people… Bob Dylan, not Thomas… that it is the same thing. That's what I didn't realize, being so naive, that you don't write pop songs, and then you do that, and then you do that. Everything you do is the same thing, so do it the same way.

PETER: *Yeah, you get a lot of the same feeling in 'Strawberry Fields Forever'.*

JOHN: *It is the same thing really. But it's still a different feeling.* You see sometimes I'll write lyrics to a song first and then I'll get the same feeling as Kakky Hargreaves or a poem and then write the music to it after. So then it's a poem, sung. But sometimes the tune comes and then you just put suitable words to fit the tune. If the tune's [sings] 'Doodle-loodle loodle-lay,' and then you have 'Chag-a-boo choo-cha.' You know, you have sound-words then, just the sound of it as opposed to lyrics.

PETER: *Are you very aware of sound? You must be, John.*

JOHN: *Oh yeah.* 'Cause it is all sound. Everything is vibrations, I believe, you know. Everything is sound, really, or vision. And just, the difference between sound and vision I'm not quite sure about. But it's all just 'voo-woo-woo-woo-woo-woo' to me.

PETER: You live in a 'voo-woo-woo-woo'.

JOHN: Yes. Well, I'm just aware that that is going on all the time. Like that camera is purring and those people are humming over there. And you're breathing and inhaling. And he's humming. And I'm talking on a 'hmm hmm'. [with vibrato in his voice] So all the time, this is going on like this all the time. So I'm aware of that, really.

PETER: The boy [in the play] hates a lot of things and, in a way, you could say you were attacking these things… like, organized religion, the way people teach you in school.

JOHN: I feel the same now, really, about organized religion, education, and all those things that everybody's still laughing at. But I mean, I expressed it that way then. I don't know how I'd express it now, you know. It'd be slightly different, really.

'I think our society is run by insane people for insane objectives. Don't you agree?'

JOHN LENNON

VICTOR: But there's a tremendous amount of compassion in his writing, which I love. It really is saying, 'Come on, do what you want to do.'

JOHN: Because I've always sort of suspected that there was a God, even when I thought I was an atheist. You know, [whispering] just in case. But I believe it, so I mean I am full of compassion, really. You can still dislike things. I just hate things less sort of… I can't think of the word… strenuously than I did. I haven't got as big of a chip about it, because maybe I've escaped out of it a bit. *So the church particularly, readers, the maniacs that I'm against don't have so much control over me now. So I can… I'm not giving into them… but I've just got better ways of sort of attacking them.*

PETER: *Looking at life, does it still seem to you full of people trying to hem you in?*

JOHN: *Yeah. Not me, particularly. Just,* I think our society is run by insane people for insane objectives. And I think that's what I sussed when I was sixteen and twelve, way down the line. But I expressed it differently all through my life. It's the same thing I'm expressing all the time. But now I can put it into that sentence that I think we're being run by maniacs for maniacal ends, you know. If anybody can put on paper what our government, and the American government, and the Russian, Chinese… what they are actually trying to do, and what they think they're doing, I'd be very pleased to know what they think they're doing. I think they're all insane. But I am liable to be put away as insane for expressing that, you know. That's what's insane about it. I mean, don't you agree?

PETER: I do, actually.

JOHN: It's not just a bit strange. It's just insane and nobody knows. All the people in the street, half the people watching this are going to be saying, 'What's he saying? What's he saying?' You know… That you are being run by people who are insane, and you don't know. *[They'll say]* '*How does he know? Bloody pop star. How does he know what's going on?*'

VICTOR: The real world is so insane that the fantasy world becomes something much better. We are living in insane times, aren't we? You know, we really are.

PETER: *Does this make you melancholy?*

JOHN: *Well, yeah.* The universal sorrow just hits you about once a week now. Bang. And then you say, 'Oh. Oh, well.' And then you're back to: 'Well, get on with it.' You know, get on with it.

PETER: And laugh?

JOHN: Well, I mean there are laughs to compensate, 'cause if there weren't, I mean it would be very melancholy.

PETER: And at the end of the play there's this big family group and there's a great big family row.

JOHN: [to Victor] Is there?

VICTOR: Yes. 'Brummer Striving'.

JOHN: Oh, 'Brummer Striving'.

PETER: It's all about 'Brummer Striving'.

JOHN: Yeah.

PETER: Do tell us about 'Brummer Striving'.

JOHN: 'Brummer Striving' is 'Brummer Striving' – all those jobs that people have that they don't want. And there's probably about 90 per cent Brummer Strivers watching in at the moment.

VICTOR: Yeah.

JOHN: But you don't have to be a Brummer Striver, you see. It depends how involved in 'Brummer Striving' you are. But 'Brummer Striving' – Paul explained it at the beginning of the book. Er, it doesn't… [laughs] What does he say he was saying? 'What is 'Brummer Striving'? It isn't anything.

VICTOR: Well, it's grafting.

JOHN: It confused Sir Laurence too, didn't it? 'Brummer Striving'.

VICTOR: Sir Laurence said, [impersonates Olivier] 'I've no idea what "Brummer Striving" is. What is "Brummer Striving"?' I said, 'It's any kind of job you have to graft at. Like going to a steel works or to a coal mine and follow your father.'

PETER: [to Victor] You've had it now!

VICTOR: What by doing [impersonating] him?

JOHN: No, he'll love it, won't he?

VICTOR: He'll say, 'Thanks for immortalizing me.'

AS WITH THE WORLD OF BOOKS Lennon interview in 1965, this TV programme provided a fascinating insight into the origins of John's wordplay and early literary influences. He also mentions 'trying to draw like Ronald Searle when I was about eight'. Searle's cartoon books recounting the unruly adventures at St Trinian's boarding school for girls were popular with young readers. Indeed, *Hurrah for St Trinian's*, the first of the series, was published in the year John turned eight – 1948.

BBC 2 screened this edition of *Release* on 22 June 1968. This was four days after the one-act play had opened as part of a triple bill at the Old Vic in London where the National Theatre was based. The day before the broadcast, various scenes from the drama were filmed at Television Centre to illustrate the discussion. Ronald Pickup played the central character simply known as 'Me'.

Significantly, John took an opportunity to look directly at the camera and state: 'You are being run by people who are insane, and you don't know.' A week before he was filmed, John had recorded 'Revolution 1' – a song that revealed his concerns about current political events. It was a tumultuous time. In the opening months of 1968 there had been violence on the streets of Paris, London and in West Germany. In America, the intensity of US military actions in the Vietnam War led to clashes between protestors and police. Following the assassination in April of Dr Martin Luther King – a leader of non-violent protest for Civil Rights – many cities across the States were set ablaze. On the day John spoke out, it was announced that US presidential candidate Robert Kennedy had died following his shooting a day earlier in Los Angeles.

In a note to producer Colin Nears on the eve of the broadcast, John enquired 'Why have you cut the only bit of real communication out of my "Release" interview?' Adding in a handwritten postscript 'or so I've heard'. In his reply, Nears assured him that such a cut was 'absolutely untrue! All the bits to camera were kept in and were very effective.' As activities over the next few years proved, using the media for the communication of a message became a central concern for John and his new partner Yoko Ono.

By 1968, the status of pop music had been elevated by the attention of British Sunday supplement magazines and TV arts programmes. That year, the BBC's flagship arts documentary strand *Omnibus* commissioned a film from Tony Palmer that subjected the pop music scene to serious analysis. A Cambridge University graduate, Palmer was a contemporary of The Beatles and passionate about both classical music and pop. His first major documentary for the BBC had been *Benjamin Britten & His Festival*. His next was *All My Loving*, which featured exclusive interviews with Paul and Ringo and fellow musicians Ginger Baker (drummer with Cream), Eric Burdon, Donovan, Jimi Hendrix, Pete Townshend and Frank Zappa. The film began with a caption displaying a verse from 'Yellow Submarine' followed by the portentous chords of the Ninth Symphony by Ralph Vaughan Williams.

As early as December 1963, *The Times* critic William Mann had assessed the songs of Lennon and McCartney in terms usually applied to classical works. He observed that 'one gets the impression that they think simultaneously of harmony and melody, so firmly are the major tonic sevenths and ninths built into their tunes and the flat submediant key switches, so natural is the Aeolian cadence at

'The universal sorrow just hits you about once a week now.'

JOHN LENNON

ABOVE John's illustration for 'The Singularge Experience of Miss Anne Duffield' – his 'long' piece in *A Spaniard in the Works*.

RIGHT 'I started to draw like Ronald Searle when I was about 8.'

'Prudence is new to St. Trinian's,
I want you to take care of her, girls.'

the end of "Not A Second Time" (the chord progression that ends Mahler's *Song Of The Earth*).' Speaking to Tony Palmer in May 1968, Paul agreed with one of the ideas offered in the film that ambitious pop music should have equal status with 'serious' music:

'I was always frightened of classical music. And I never wanted to listen to it because it was Beethoven and Tchaikovsky, and sort of big words like that... and Schoenberg. I mean, like... a taxi driver the other day had some sheet music of a Mozart thing and I said, "What's that?" And he said, "Oh, that's the high-class stuff. You won't like that. No, no, you won't like that." And I said, "Well, what is it?" [laughs] He said, "No, you won't like it. It's high-class, that. It's very high-brow." And er, that kind of way, I always used to think of it. I used to think, "Well, you know, that's very clever, all that stuff." And it isn't. It's just exactly what's going on in pop at the moment. Pop music is the classical music of now... I have no idea if there's any Aeolian cadences and... miasmic climaxes and all of that!'

Paul was also asked about how pop music could reflect the time in which it was created: 'Because like everyone else, we read the papers... we go through all the things that most people go through. So when everyone wants to say a thing at a certain time, it's handy being a songwriter. You know, you can put your finger on it.'

Sitting in front of a studio mixing desk at Abbey Road, Ringo explained the vogue for experimentation when making pop records. 'There's more fun in the record if there's a few sounds that you don't really know what they are. We have a special man who sits here and goes like this... and the guitar turns into a piano or something. And then you may say, "Why don't you use a piano?" Because the piano sounds like a guitar!'

All My Loving was broadcast on 3 November 1968. Two weeks later, director Tony Palmer wrote about *The Beatles* – soon known as 'The White Album' – for the *Observer* newspaper. His appraisal echoed one of the themes of his recent documentary: 'If there is still any doubt that Lennon and McCartney are the greatest song writers since Schubert, then next Friday – with the publication of the new Beatles double LP – should surely see the last vestiges of cultural snobbery and bourgeois prejudice swept away in a deluge of joyful music making, which only the ignorant will not hear and only the deaf will not acknowledge'. The review was reprinted on the UK sleeve of The Beatles' *Yellow Submarine* soundtrack LP released the following January.

'The White Album' was brimming with 30 new tracks of extraordinary variety. Yet none of the Beatles talked in detail about it on BBC radio or TV. Only an interview with George for *Scene and Heard*, broadcast two months before 'The White Album' was released, had revealed any details. He told *NME* writer Alan Smith, 'This next album is much simpler than "Pepper" because it's more down to guitars, bass and drums, and maybe piano.' Although George maintained his spiritual beliefs were as strong as ever, his future songs would not be as mystical: 'It's all still "Within You Without You", but I don't want to go into that any more 'cause now I'm being a rock 'n' roll star! I now want to write songs that don't have any meaning, because I'm a bit fed up with people coming up and saying, "Hey, what's it all about? What does it mean?"'

BBC TV had not featured a Beatles live performance since they sang 'All You Need Is Love' to the world in 1967. When Apple announced on 7 November 1968 that The Beatles would 'give three live concerts in London next month... a one-hour TV spectacular may be built around the shows', Bill Cotton Jr., the Head of Variety and Light Entertainment, was quick to respond. Writing directly to Paul McCartney, he wondered 'whether there was any possibility of the BBC and yourself getting together in the production of this programme'. Neil Aspinall replied on 12 November that 'our plans are complete, it will be produced by Apple Films Limited in American colour video. I feel sure that you will be fascinated by the end product, and we look forward to talking to you about it then.' However, the promised concerts 'at London's Chalk Farm Roundhouse for three successive nights starting December 15 or 16' did not take place. During 1969, The Beatles were seen and heard only separately on BBC TV and radio. As the public witnessed a variety of Beatles solo endeavours and media appearances, the major interview topic throughout the year was whether the group would, in fact, stay together.

OPPOSITE In November 1967, Paul had personally agreed a deal for the broadcast of *Magical Mystery Tour* with the Controller of BBC 1, Paul Fox. This may explain why, a year later, this exploratory letter from Bill Cotton was addressed to Paul rather than the Managing Director of The Beatles' company Apple.

BEATLES

8th November, 1968

Dear Paul,

Having read my papers today and seen that the Beatles are intending to mount a television Special based on three live concerts in December, I wondered whether there was any possibility that the BBC and yourselves could get together in the production of this programme.

If you think that this is a feasible proposition, I would be only too pleased to meet you and discuss it whenever its convenient for you.

Yours sincerely,

(Bill Cotton Jnr.)
Head of Variety
Light Entertainment, Television

Paul McCartney Esq.
Apple
3 Savile Row
London W.1.

APPLE CORPS LIMITED
3 SAVILE ROW LONDON W1
TELEPHONE 01-734 8232
CABLES APCORE LONDON W1

BEATLES

12th November, 1968.

BEATLES SPLIT UP
10-4-70

Bill Cotton Jnr.
B.B.C.
Television Centre,
Wood Lane,
London W.12.

Dear Bill Cotton,

With reference to your letter dated 8th November addressed
to Paul McCartney, thank you for your offer to help with
our TV special.   However, our plans are now complete, it
will be produced by Apple Films Limited in American colour
video.   I feel sure that you will be facinated by the
end product, and we look forward to talking to you about it
then.

Yours sincerely,

Neil Aspinall
Managing Director

DIRECTORS N ASPINALL D O'DELL H PINSKER

LEFT Despite Neil Aspinall's reply
to Bill Cotton's letter stating
that 'plans were complete',
the concerts promised for
December 1968 did not happen.

📻 Radio programme titles
📺 TV titles

📻 THE KENNY EVERETT SHOW
Br: 4 February 1968 – 10.00am–noon – Radio 1
Rec: 27 January 1968
John was interviewed at his house in Weybridge, Surrey for Kenny Everett's Sunday morning show.

📺 CILLA
Br: 6 Feb 1968 – 8.00–8.50pm
– BBC 1, Live
BBC Television Theatre, London
The show featured Ringo and Cilla Black singing 'Do You Like Me?'.

📺 BBC NEWS REPORTS
Br: 26 March 1968
– BBC 1 and Radio 4
Rec: 26 March 1968
Paul and Jane Asher were interviewed briefly at London Heathrow Airport on their return from Rishikesh, India.

📻 THE KENNY EVERETT SHOW
Br: 9 June 1968 – 10.00am–noon

– Radio 1
Rec: 6 June 1968
Kenny's interview was primarily with John, who toyed with an unplugged electric guitar and burst into song occasionally. Paul and Ringo joined them for some 'goodbye jingles' to mark Kenny's transfer from his Sunday slot to a weekday evening show called *Foreverett*. The interview was recorded at Abbey Road during the first phase of recording of *The Beatles* ('The White Album').

📺 RELEASE
Br: 22 June 1968 – 10.05–10.45pm – BBC 2
Rec: 6 June 1968 – 5.00pm
EMI Studios, Abbey Road, London
Following his madcap radio chat with Kenny Everett, John joined actor Victor Spinetti and journalist Peter Lewis for a filmed discussion about the National Theatre production *In His Own Write*. John's eloquence was in marked contrast to his earlier mood when talking to Kenny.

📺 LOOK NORTH
Br: 1 July 1968 5.55–6.15pm – BBC 1, Yorkshire edition of local news magazine programme
Rec: 30 June 1968
Exhibition Road, Saltaire, Yorkshire
Paul was in Yorkshire to produce a session at Victoria Hall, Saltaire with the Black Dyke Mills Band. They recorded 'Thingumybob' (a McCartney-composed theme for a London Weekend Television situation-comedy series) and 'Yellow Submarine'. Reporter Tony Cliff's interview with Paul was seen the following day.

📻 LATE NIGHT EXTRA
Br: 6 August 1968 – 10.00pm–midnight
– Radio 1 & Radio 2
Rec: 6 August 1968
BBC reporter Matthew Robinson interviewed John – and Pattie Harrison and fashion editor Suzy Menkes – at a fashion show in the Revolution discotheque in Mayfair, London.

📻 SCENE AND HEARD
Br: 28 September 1968 – 6.32–7.00pm
– Radio 1
Rec: 18 September 1968
George was interviewed by *NME* writer Alan

Smith for the weekly magazine programme presented by Johnny Moran.

📺 OMNIBUS: ALL MY LOVING
Br: 3 Nov 1968 – 10.40–11.35pm – BBC 1
Repeated: 18 May 1969 – 9.30–10.25pm – BBC 2 in colour
Rec: 23 May 1968
EMI Studios, Abbey Road, London
Paul and Ringo were interviewed for Tony Palmer's pop documentary film.

📻 NIGHT RIDE
Br: 11 December 1968 – 12.05–1.00am – Radio 1 & Radio 2. Live
John and Yoko took part in the filming of *The Rolling Stones' Rock and Roll Circus* in Wembley and then visited John Peel during his eclectic hour of the Wednesday *Night Ride* programme. They discussed *Unfinished Music No. 1: Two Virgins*, which was released the previous week. Peel remembered that one reverend gentleman complained to the BBC about the programme – describing the silences as obscene.

1969

Scene and Heard

THE BBC RADIO 1 programme *Scene and Heard* provided a weekly round-up of pop news, records and interviews. Ten of its editions in 1969 featured a Beatle in conversation with David Wigg. Their interviews with him are relaxed and remarkably candid. When the question about whether the group will break apart is asked repeatedly throughout the year, there is often a feeling that each Beatle is saying something he hopes the others might hear. 'Spiritually, you can't split because, if you're listening, I'm the walrus too!' George jokes at the end of an interview broadcast in October 1969.

Away from the pop scene, the recurring theme of the year was the Vietnam War and the protests against it. Following his inauguration as President in January, Richard Nixon predicted he would bring an end to hostilities by 1970. In February, he authorized the covert bombing of Cambodia to attack North Vietnamese bases in that neighbouring country. The US death toll in Vietnam during 1969 was 11, 616. On 12 November 1969, news broke of the killing of over a hundred villagers by US troops in an incident in March 1968. For many, all the horror of a senseless war was encapsulated in the massacre that took place in My Lai; others called for leniency during the sentencing of William Calley, the officer in charge when the killing spree occurred. One of several mass demonstrations, the 'Moratorium to End the War in Vietnam', took place on 15 October. A month later, 500,000 demonstrators took part in the 'Moratorium March on Washington'. Pete Seeger led the singing of John's song 'Give Peace A Chance', which had been released by The Plastic Ono Band in July.

There was an unexpectedly large gathering at Max Yasgur's dairy farm, 43 miles from the town of Woodstock. Billed as 'An Aquarian Exposition' of '3 Days of Peace & Music', the festival was attended by at least 400,000 – causing traffic chaos and food shortages. A film of the event released in 1970 enhanced the significance of the Woodstock festival and furthered the careers of many of the artists who had performed. Facing unfavourable conditions caused by heavy rain and mud, the huge crowd remained peaceful and cooperative. Two weeks later in England, the second Isle of Wight Festival took place with headliners Bob Dylan and The Who. In December, a free festival starring

The Rolling Stones was staged at the Altamont Speedway in northern California. It was hoped that Altamont would represent the West Coast equivalent of the spirit of Woodstock. Instead, it was marred by chaos, three accidental deaths and the murder of a spectator by a Hells Angel. For some, Altamont symbolized the sad end to the idealism engendered by the younger generation during the Sixties. The potent footage seen in the documentary film *Gimme Shelter* only amplified that view.

Two planes making their maiden flights during 1969 offered opposite approaches to the future of air travel. Concorde was a sleek supersonic airliner founded on the concept that the speed of a journey, rather than passenger capacity, was paramount. The wide-body Boeing 747 'jumbo jet' was designed to transport a large number of people. It was the jumbo that embodied the successful aircraft of the future, while Concorde was mainly patronized by the super-rich jet set.

The most historic event of the year was the fulfilment of President Kennedy's challenge to put a man on the Moon by the end of the decade. On 20 July 1969, Neil Armstrong radioed back to Earth: 'Houston, Tranquility Base here. The Eagle has landed.' Nearly seven hours later, Armstrong was the first man to set foot on the surface of the Moon. Stepping down from the lunar module's ladder, he spoke to half a billion people watching on TV: 'That's one small step for man, one giant leap for mankind.' Viewers in the UK watched Neil Armstrong and Edwin 'Buzz' Aldrin walking on the Moon in the early hours of Monday 21 July. Later that day, The Beatles performed 'Come Together' during a session for the last album they recorded – *Abbey Road*.

In October, a comedy sketch show was shown for the first time on BBC Television. *Monty Python's Flying Circus* became a must-see programme for young Britons. Its revolutionary approach to comedy writing and acting exerted an influence that has echoed through the decades. One of the show's famous lines, used to connect disparate sketches, may have captured a feeling within The Beatles at the end of 1969: 'And now for something completely different...'

ALTHOUGH THE PROMISE of three Roundhouse concerts in December 1968 had not been fulfilled, the project evolved into a much more ambitious plan. Derek Taylor, the head of Apple's press office, had indicated in November that songs from the current double album would be played. The brave new year concept was to show The Beatles rehearsing a set list of brand new songs – even though they had delivered a fresh batch of 30 just a few weeks earlier. Viewers would be able to observe the development of each song from an initial run-through to the final version performed in a televised live concert. To continue what George had described as the 'simpler' approach of 'The White Album', the group's intention was to return to their origins as a live rock band.

Time at Twickenham Film Studios was booked to start on 2 January 1969. The location for their televised return to live performance was yet to be decided, but would probably be an exotic one. Rehearsing in the chilly draughts of a vast sound stage at Twickenham was in marked contrast to the familiarity of sessions at Abbey Road studios. George observed at Twickenham, 'It reminds me of being at Lime Street Station' [Liverpool's railway station]. As the cameras rolled, they captured some tense moments and the occasional argument. On 10 January 1969, George quit the group. His succinct diary entry for that day was 'rehearsed until lunchtime, left the Beatles, went home'. He agreed to rejoin five days later, but with two conditions. The plan for a televised live performance must be abandoned and work on their songs would switch from Twickenham to the basement studio of Apple headquarters in Savile Row, London.

On 21 January, the day before The Beatles' musical reunion at Apple, Ringo was recorded for the Radio 1 programme *Scene and Heard*. During a car journey to London, *Daily Express* writer David Wigg enquired about tensions tearing at the group's bonds. It was not known at the time that Ringo had walked away from the sessions for 'The White Album' on 22 August 1968 and, so he thought, out of the group for ever. Twelve days later, following a holiday in Sardinia, he returned to work at Abbey Road. On 4 September, his second day back in the fold, Ringo took part in the promotional films for the group's first record issued with an Apple label – 'Hey Jude'/'Revolution'. As far as the world knew, the unity of The Beatles had never been in danger. But in January 1969, there were worrying signs.

DAVID: Last week was quite a controversial week for The Beatles. How close are you? We've had reports that you're not as close as you used to be and The Beatles aren't as rich as everyone thought they were and they might have to close down Apple. How true is this?

RINGO: Well, shall we take 'em, one at a time?

DAVID: [laughing] Yes.

RINGO: [laughing] All right, what was the first one?

DAVID: Are you as close?

RINGO: Yes. There's that famous old saying 'You always hurt the one you love', and we all love each other and we all know that. But we still sort of hurt each other occasionally, where we just misunderstand each other and we go off and it builds up to something bigger than it ever was. And then we have to come down to it and get it over with and sort it out. And so we're still really very close people. What was the second one?

DAVID: Do you see The Beatles going on like they are at the moment, for a long time in the future, or do you see a split very soon?

RINGO: It depends what you mean as a split, I mean, we split…

DAVID: Go your separate ways.

OPPOSITE **On 27 June 1969, Ringo and his wife Maureen flew to the South of France for a holiday. It was also a vacation month for Paul and Linda, who arrived from Corfu on 17 June, and George and Pattie, who returned from Sardinia six days later.**

RINGO: Completely, no. We'll never go… oh, I can't say never… but we won't go our separate ways after this album. And we'll always be tied up with each other in some way, because we signed a lot of papers that say we stay together for twenty years or something! And Apple closing, you know, is… is silly. We have spent a lot of money, because we don't earn as much as people think, 'cause if we earn a million then the government gets 90 per cent. And we didn't sort of realize how much we were spending, you know. Like, someone pointed out, to spend ten thousand you have to make 120 [thousand]. But we just spent it as 120 [thousand]. So what we're doing now is tightening up on our own personal money and on the company's money, you know. We're not just giving as much away and handouts and things like that, you know, and as many projects. We're gonna cut down a bit till we've sorted ourselves out again and do it properly as a business.

DAVID: Do you feel you have been a bit careless with money?

RINGO: Yes, I think we have. But it's not that we're broke. On paper we're very wealthy people. Just when it gets down to pound notes, we're only half-wealthy. [laughing]

DAVID: Are you concerned about public opinion? Because there is a suggestion that your popularity isn't as strong as it used to be.

RINGO: No, it isn't. It's because when we first started we were the nice clean 'moptops' and every mother's son and everyone loved us. And then suddenly there's a few things that they don't understand and they don't get; they don't like… and so it turns them off us a bit. But I still think we're very popular. It's just that we're men now, you know. We're a bit older than those lads that started out. And we've got a lot of things to do, you know. And you've got to do a few of them. It doesn't matter what people say, you can't live all your life by what *they* want. You know, we can't go on for ever as four clean little moptops, playing 'She Loves You'.

THAT LAST TOPIC was also discussed by Paul and David Wigg in a *Scene and Heard* interview recorded in September 1969. 'You see, you grow up. Everyone grows up. And it's always a great pity to see a baby turn into an adult, 'cause it's always nicer when they're a baby and they go 'Goo! Goo!' and they do everything you want. It's lovely. In a certain period of our career, we were particularly nice. We had a very all-round appeal. It wasn't put on, we were more like that. But as we've grown up, you become more individual… we're more true to ourselves these days.'

> # 'It's just that we're men now. We're a bit older than those lads that started out, but I still think we're very popular.'
>
> RINGO STARR

Each Beatle gave several lengthy interviews to David Wigg for *Scene and Heard*, in which their individual concerns and the future of The Beatles as a unit were frequently explored. In March 1969, George had spoken about his frustration with Britain's negative attitude to the group, especially as it was expressed in the press. On 8 May 1969, John was asked whether he had noticed a change.

DAVID: George said that he thought the British were against The Beatles. Do you agree with this, John? Do you feel an anti-attitude towards you at the moment, which you haven't experienced before in your career?

JOHN: Oh, we've experienced it before. We've always been treated the same; The Beatles are treated like Britain's children. And it's okay for the family to insult us, but see what happens if abroad starts insulting us. The British will stick up for us and it's just like a family. And it's all right for them to slap our face, but if the neighbour does it, you watch out! And it's always been like that. And George was very depressed, and it is depressing when the whole family's picking on you. We do get hurt, because Britain appreciates us least.

WHEN JOHN AND YOKO Ono married on 20 March 1969, their honeymoon in Amsterdam was turned into a seven-day 'Bed-in' to publicize their campaign for peace. The Vietnam War was continuing to alarm the world with large numbers of casualties on both sides. Earlier that month, Chinese and Russian soldiers had clashed on the border between their countries. There was continuing unrest in Czechoslovakia following an invasion by a Soviet-led army the previous August, which had crushed a move towards a more liberal regime in the Iron Curtain country. As John told Andy Peebles in 1980, 'The point of the Bed-in, in a nutshell, was a commercial for peace as opposed to a commercial for war, which was on the news every day and in the newspapers.' Proving the adage 'if you build it, they will come', for a week the world's media trooped through Room 902 at the Amsterdam Hilton Hotel and relayed what the couple had to say. BBC news recorded John's message on 30 March: 'We're here to talk to the press, because the press and the TV are the communicating channels. You can protest against violence in many ways and this is one.'

RIGHT **The Amsterdam Hilton, March 1969. John told the BBC: 'In London, they'd say, "Oh, it's the freaks again." So we have more effect on Britain if we're abroad.'**

John and Yoko seemed content to generate publicity for peace, whatever derision might be heaped upon them. A month after their Amsterdam Bed-in, David Wigg's sympathetic questions brought calm responses that always revolved around a central theme – Peace.

DAVID WIGG: John, what do you and Yoko hope to achieve together? Because you seem to be concentrating an awful lot of effort these days on LPs together and on your own things together.

JOHN: Yeah. We hope to achieve peace, really. You know, that's what we're aiming at. And it's a big achievement and we're just doing our best for it, you know.

DAVID: Do you feel your week in Amsterdam, lying in bed, has achieved anything? Have you had any encouraging results?

JOHN: Yeah, there was a lot. We made people laugh and that's good. You know, I mean, John and Yoko are like the wind. You can't see it, but when it passes the trees bend. You know, and that's what we do.

DAVID: A lot of people also feel that if everyone goes to bed and stays in bed for a week or a few days for peace, as a protest for peace, the whole country will come to a standstill.

JOHN: Well, wouldn't it be better than producing arms and bombs? Imagine if the American army stayed in bed for a week and the Vietnamese army. Or Nixon… and Kosygin, Chairman Mao. Imagine it, if the whole world stayed in bed. There'd be peace for a week and they might get to feel what it was like. The tension would be released.

DAVID: What do you want out of life most of all now, John?

JOHN: Peace, you know. Really that's all I want.

DAVID: If anything happened to you, how would you like people to remember you?

JOHN: As the great peaceniks.

DAVID: That before your music?

JOHN: Oh sure, yeah.

DAVID: John, you seem a lot more relaxed in yourself now. What has happened? What do you put this down to? Because before, you were always a little bit frightening.

'We are Laurel and Hardy, that's John and Yoko. We're willing to be the world's clowns.'

JOHN LENNON

JOHN: Yes, yes. I put it down to Yoko. She's brought out the real me. I get nervous and tense like anybody else, but I'm more relaxed than I ever was… since I was a child anyway.

DAVID: But the only thing that disturbs me a little is that a lot of people are jeering, aren't they? And making fun, not taking you seriously.

JOHN: But that is good. That's part of our policy – not to be taken seriously, because I think our opposition, whoever they may be in all their manifest forms, don't know how to handle humour. And we are humourists. We are Laurel and Hardy, that's John and Yoko. And we stand a better chance under that guise, because all the serious people like Martin Luther King and Kennedy and Gandhi got shot.

DAVID: Yes, that's a very interesting point. So you don't mind being the court jesters, John?

JOHN: No, no. We're willing to be the world's clowns.

A WEEK LATER, Paul gave an interview to Roy Corlett, a fellow ex-pupil from the Liverpool Institute grammar school. The recording was made in Paul's father's house, called 'Rembrandt', in the town of Heswall, Cheshire. The ambience created by the familiar setting and a friendly face from school days seemed to help Paul relax in front of Roy's microphone. As Paul pointed out, the last few months had been very busy for The Beatles and he was looking forward to a holiday. The destination was Corfu, not France as Paul stated in the interview. This was a ploy to mislead any journalists pursuing him, his wife and stepdaughter. On the day of the interview, The Beatles' Midas touch was evident in the charts. In the UK, 'Get Back' was number one. Mary Hopkin, signed to the group's label Apple, was also in the top five with Paul's song 'Goodbye'.

Paul is first heard spinning a pun on the show's title. A 'local' is a colloquial term for the nearest pub for a drink. 'Set 'em up, Mary!' he jokes at the end of the interview.

PAUL: The time is now 12.31 and this is Paul McCartney with *A Light at the Local*.

ROY: Er, I think you got the title wrong, Paul.

PAUL: Oh, *Light and Local*.

ROY: [laughs] That's a bit better.

PAUL: Right.

ROY: Yes, it is 12.31. It is *Light and Local* and that was Paul McCartney. We'll be hearing more from him later in the programme.

PAUL'S RECENT MARRIAGE to Linda Eastman was the first topic. They had married on 12 March 1969 at Marylebone Register Office, London. An enquiry about whether he and Linda would like to have children was answered enthusiastically. However, he did not say that his wife was already pregnant. Their daughter Mary was born three months later on 28 August. The baby is pictured nestled under Paul's jacket on the back cover of his first solo album, *McCartney*, released in April 1970.

ROY: Well, Paul, you've been married, what, a couple of months now?

PAUL: Couple of months, yeah.

ROY: What's it like, being the last of the bachelor Beatles, now you're married?

PAUL: It's terrible, you know [laughs]. It's OK, you know. It's the same as being married for everyone, you know. It's married.

ROY: You're liking it, anyway.

PAUL: Yes, it's fine.

ROY: It's meant to you, of course, that you've got an instant family as well. You've got a daughter.

PAUL: Yes, aged six. Young Heather, who's star struck and would love to be on the programme, but I've put her back in the box!

ROY: [laughs] How do you get on with her, in fact?

PAUL: Oh, great. She's a great kid, you know. She's lovely.

ROY: Do you see much of her, in fact?

PAUL: Oh yeah, sure. Well, you know, 'cause I don't sort of go out to work, so the only time I don't see her is when she's at school. Oh, I see her and read goodnight stories and all that stuff, you know.

ROY: Do you take her out much?

PAUL: Yeah, sure. Well, we're going on holiday today. Got her off school for a bit, so we're off. I see a lot of her, you know.

ROY: Where are you going for your holidays?

PAUL: Going to France. Trying to get a bit of sunshine.

ROY: How long will you be away?

PAUL: I hope, in all, to be away for about a month. 'Cause we've got nothing on for the next month and we've had a lot on for the past couple of months, as you might have heard from a couple of newspapers here and there. So I'm just trying to get a break now.

ROY: Yeah, well tell us about what you have got on, Paul.

OPPOSITE **Paul pictured with Linda Eastman on their wedding day – 12 March 1969. Linda's 6-year old daughter Heather is in the foreground. She was born in Tucson, Arizona (the home town of 'Jo Jo' in The Beatles' first single of 1969 'Get Back').**

PAUL: Well, we've been doing a lot of stuff. We've had a lot of stuff happening down at Apple, you know, and we've been making records ourselves. We've been working, like, till four in the morning making records and the Northern Songs bid has been on so it's been high finance down there for the last couple of months. But it seems to be going OK now, so I'm just taking a break, [to] get away from it all.

ROY: You talked about high finance. The Beatles to me, now, seem to be more businessmen than performers.

PAUL: Yeah, well the thing is… when we started off as Beatles, we knew nothing about the business side of it. And one thing that does happen in the business is that if you're the artist or if you're the singer or something, you do get agents and people, you know, who are on the business end of it and sometimes you can get a bit carved up, you know. So that we've had a lot of… we've been involved in a lot of contracts and a lot of things, you know. It's all very boring, but we've had a lot of contracts and stuff that we had to try and straighten out now, so that we've become a bit more business-minded. But I still can't stand business. I'd much rather… you know, the four of us are really just a rock band, you know, but we've got to actually sort of think now when we sign a contract, 'What's it mean?' It's all… it's growing up. You've got to do it one time in your life.

ROY: Well, talking about growing up, one night I remember very well was the night you made this tremendous homecoming to Liverpool and the reception at the Town Hall. Do you long for those days, when every time you appeared anywhere you were mobbed?

PAUL: Oh, no. I don't think so. Those things – they're fantastic at the time. It's great at the time – all that. But, I tell you, we were playing… round about that time we were in New York and we'd played to 56,000 people at Shea Stadium and just after that, you just sort of think to yourself what more can you do? The only thing you can do more is to play to 57,000 or 58,000 next time; so you start to realize that you've either got to keep trying to play to more and more people and try and be involved in bigger and bigger events, or else just sort of cool it down a bit. So that's what we're doing now: cooling it down and living a bit more normal lives than we would have done; trying to sort out the business bit. But I mean, I sometimes think, 'Well, we're not working very hard.' Like you say, 'cause we don't make that many appearances.

But, in fact – I was just thinking about it the other day – we work harder than we've ever done now. We're slogging away. As I was saying, recording till about four in the morning. Then you get up the next day and you've got a meeting, a couple of business meetings, then recording later in the evening. And between all of that, you've got to write all the songs for it. So we work quite hard.

ROY: I've often heard it said by Beatle fans in Liverpool that they've always been sad that The Beatles have never come back to the city since they really became big time.

PAUL: Yeah, yeah. Well, that's one of the things, you know. I mean we've come back when we've been doing tours and stuff. We've always played the Empire, and always come back and done that. But it's not just a question of not coming back to Liverpool. We haven't come back to anywhere. So the people in Runcorn say 'You haven't been back to Runcorn.' The people in New York say you haven't been back to there. The people in Japan say, 'You haven't been back.' But the idea is generally that we don't want to do as many performances, 'cause I was saying you get to this point where you say what else can you do? What can you do that was bigger than the last one? So that instead of trying to keep getting bigger and bigger and bigger we decided to concentrate mainly on records. So after that we did *Sgt. Pepper*, you know, and then we did *Magical Mystery Tour*, which was a new thing we tried then.

ROY: So, from your point of view, were they a success? Certainly the *Magical Mystery Tour* came in for some criticism.

PAUL: Yeah, oh it did, yeah. The thing is… see, at the time, I'll tell you what was… there's a couple of main things that were really hashed up about that… One was that we made it in colour. It was a sort of colour thing and it was put out first of all in black and white. So there are whole big sequences that you couldn't understand, 'cause they looked… I saw it on the telly and they just looked mad, in black and white, 'cause there were sequences where the colours changed. So that was a bit daft. The thing itself was… we just did it off our own bat, you know. And I think it was put on at the wrong time on telly when everyone's expecting sort of Christmas extravaganzas and we put on this mad film. But I've since seen it. A lot of people have since seen it. For instance, it's been around America since and it's being very successful at the moment. 'Cause now people are sort of catching up with what it's about now. So it's now beginning to be very successful. It wasn't on the day it was out. The first day it was out in Britain there was a

'It's growing up.
You've got to do it
one time in your life.'

PAUL MCCARTNEY

lot of comment about it. But, as I say, it's been shown in America. It's been shown in a lot of places since and now it's getting very successful. I think it's going to be, in about ten years' time, one of those films where you say, 'Let's have a look at that again,' and it'll be like an old, you know, sort of like *Rock Around the Clock* and them. Now they look better than they did then. You know what I mean? 'Cause they get nostalgia and stuff. At the time, it was just a bit sudden and it was a bit sort of too quick. But I still like it as a thing. I still think it's great.

ROY: You've had a very varied career, Paul, what…

PAUL: Not 'alf!

ROY: [laughs] What sticks out? Is there anything that sticks out most in your mind? Anything that's happened or anything you've done that really gives you a great deal of satisfaction?

PAUL: Well, it's, I think, mainly the things that give me the satisfaction are the things like the receptions you get. Like you said, the Liverpool reception, you know. That was fantastic at the time. It was incredible. Those are the highlights for me. There was another one just like that in Adelaide in Australia and we had the same kind of reception. It was like being the Queen or something! We came in from the airport – it was the same in the Liverpool one – and we came in from the airport and there were all the crowds lining the route. And we're giving the thumbs up and we went to the Town Hall, with the Lord Mayor of Adelaide there. And we're giving the thumbs up. But in Liverpool, it's OK, 'cause everyone understands the thumbs up. But in Australia it's a dirty sign! [laughter] So they all wondered what we were doing.

BELOW **Paul driving away from the Apple building at 3 Savile Row in London,** April 1969.

'They're my three best friends. They're good lads, I tell you.'

PAUL MCCARTNEY

ROY: Paul, let me, if I may, turn for a minute to your personal lives. The Beatles have come in for a lot [of] criticism about things that have happened in their personal lives. Do you think it's all been justified? How've you felt about it when you've had these criticisms?

PAUL: The criticism's OK, you know, 'cause, people are allowed to criticize. See, the thing is, our whole thing on the surface of it, 'cause, you know, you read about us in the newspapers, hear about us on interviews and stuff. All of that on the surface of it, I understand why it comes in for criticism, because I'll tell you one thing about us, we've never been dishonest. So that, for instance, if John… because you're talking about John and Yoko mainly; most people do. So if John marries Yoko and divorces Cyn, a lot of people think, 'Well he's just mad, you know, 'cause he's gone off with this mad Japanese girl instead of Cynthia, who's a great girl.' But the truth about it all is that he loves Yoko, so that whether you like it or not… I tell you, he said one thing to me which made me understand what they were up to just as two people, not as anything else. Just as two people. He just said, 'I tell you, it's like holding hands on the back row of the pictures.' And I suddenly realized: they're not freaks. You know, they may look like freaks. 'Cause, I mean he says that, John… he says, 'It's too bad if I look… if we look, like people think we're funny. It's too bad. This is how we are and we're very straight.' 'Cause they are, really. They're two great people, you know, and they're very much in love. So you can't say anything more than that.

ROY: What about the other side of it, the attitude of The Beatles towards drugs?

PAUL: Well, again, you see, that's another thing. It's like someone comes up and asks you. They say, 'Now, what do you think about drugs?' OK, so if you've been involved in it and if you've tried drugs and stuff, then what can you say? You can only lie, if you want your public image to be great. The only way out is to lie like so many people do. That's the Hollywood star thing. 'It's wonderful in your country. It's so wonderful, everything's rosy, it's beautiful.' 'Do you take drugs, Mr Hollywood?' He'll say, 'No, no. It's terrible.' But the thing is we're honest. So that, if people are awkward enough to go and ask us that question, they're going to get an honest reply. And it may be something that they may not like. They may like it, they may not. But I'll tell you, one thing is that it's honest. At least, it's an honest reply. At least, we didn't mess around saying, 'Oh, no, no, no. We've never touched them,' and 'Oh, it's terrible,' and all that. At least, we're honest about it and I think you can't really go far wrong. You can get people… I mean we get a lot of the older generation really moaning at us and saying it's terrible. I met a fella coming up on the train and he said – he asked for my autograph for his daughter – and he said, 'It's good to see you looking so healthy. From what we hear about The Beatles, we expect them to be a real depraved lot. We expect them to be washed out and really looking terrible and everything.' We were having a laugh about it and I was saying, 'I understand,' 'cause from what you hear about us, you'd think we've gone potty! But I tell you, just as four people we're all right. There's nothing seriously wrong.

ROY: You've remained friends on the surface, anyway, for a great length of time. Is there really this great bond of friendship between you, would you say?

PAUL: Yes, sure there is. Yeah, 'cause we're each other's mates and we've come through all of this together. [sings] 'We've been together now for 40 years.' So, I mean, you can't help but be friends anyway. They're my three best friends. They're good lads, I tell you.

ROY: Is there anything which The Beatles, as a whole, or you personally, would like to do? You've done a lot already. Is there anything, you feel, that is left that you can achieve, that you really want to achieve?

PAUL: Well, the main things in that are just in music. We've still got a lot to do in music, as far as we're concerned. We've just finished an album now and we're onto the next one already before this one's been released. So we're working hard on the music thing. But as far as performances and stuff, as I say when you play to 56,000 in a big stadium, you can't really do much more than that, unless it's like get on Telstar and have an hour playing to everyone in the world. You can't really top 56,000. So we don't have too many performance ambitions left. But the ambitions are all in the music as far as I'm concerned.

ROY: Anything particular?

PAUL: Just to do better music. It's always been there. It's like we started off with 'Love Me Do' and the second record we wanted to be better. So we did 'Please Please Me' and we wanted the next one to be better. That's where the ambition is: to make music that satisfies us and other people.

ROY: Why do you feel The Beatles have been so successful in their songwriting?

PAUL: Well, see, the trouble with asking a question like that is you get an answer which could sound big-headed, because I think it's 'cause we write good songs. I don't think it's anything other than that.

ROY: Is there a reason why you write good songs?

PAUL: I don't know. No, I don't know.

ROY: Have you a formula?

PAUL: John and I is a good combination. 'Cause I'm very… you know… if I'm left on my own to write songs, I'll write songs that are a bit sloppy, which I like. I'm a bit more sentimental on the surface. Now, John will write harder songs so that if we come together, then you get a bit of each. You get a bit of [tea cup rattles] that's a cup of tea, folks! … you get a bit of the sloppy stuff and the hard stuff. So then you get a nice combination.

ROY: How about personal ambitions? You've just got married now. Would you like a family of your own?

PAUL: Of course.

ROY: You've got an instant family, as you say. How many children would you like yourself?

PAUL: As many as I can put up with! I love kids. When I say I love kids now, I haven't got that many. I've got one at the moment and I love her, so I really don't know what I'm going to be like with a large family, but I fancy a large family.

ROY: How do you imagine yourself, say, in twenty years' time, Paul?

PAUL: Old! [laughs]

ROY: Do you think you'll still be in the same business or will you have retired long before then?

PAUL: Oh, no. I tell you, I think we'll be in music. See, this is why if you say performance, OK, you can perform. See, the only thing the four of us don't particularly want to do, speaking from now, is end up at about 60 with grey hair, you know, rocking around. You don't want to have to do it then. So this is why we're sort of trying to lay the thing now saying, 'Look, we're going to do what we want to do.' If we build up a following, then we suddenly say, 'We're not going to play any more,' you've got to bear with us 'cause that's what we're gonna do. We're gonna do it as we want to do it. And it's too bad if people want us to perform when we're 60 and we say, 'Well, we're not going to'. You know what I mean? So that side of it, we're not too concerned about. If we want to do shows and stuff, we'll still do them. But we don't want to be tied down to shows. But in the music, you can continue singing and playing till the day before you die. So we intend to do that. The music will always be there. Well, that's all, folks, from *Light and Local* and Paul McCartney, here with a light down at the local. Set 'em up Mary! Goodbye.

ROY: And we'll all be back, except Paul McCartney, the same time, 12.31, on Monday.

OPPOSITE **Paul and Ringo rehearsing at Twickenham Film Studios in January 1969 – footage from this time eventually appeared in the movie *Let It Be*, released in May 1970.**

ONLY A FEW days before, there had been acrimony when Paul refused to add his name to papers appointing Allen Klein as Apple's business manager. But with Roy Corlett he was supportive both of the group – 'they're my three best friends' and John and Yoko – 'they're two great people and they're very much in love.' The use of the word 'freaks' did not have a pejorative meaning in 1969. In the counterculture it was a benign alternative for the word 'hippie'. In their discussion of The Beatles' use of illegal drugs, he told Roy Corlett, 'If people are awkward enough to go and ask us that question, they're going to get an honest reply.' It was a reprise of an argument he had made when interviewed for ITN TV News on 19 June 1967. Asked on camera whether he should have admitted

publicly to taking LSD, he stated, 'I was asked a question by a newspaper [reporter] and the decision was whether to tell a lie or tell him the truth. I decided to tell him the truth. It's his responsibility for spreading it, not mine.'

BBC local station Radio Merseyside was heard in the city of Liverpool and the surrounding area on either side of the River Mersey. The many pirate radio stations broadcasting from around the coast of Britain from 1964 to 1967 had demonstrated not only a demand for a dedicated pop music channel, but also a positive audience response to a service aimed at a specific geographical

ABOVE **Ringo and George – 8 July 1969.**

area. An initial eight BBC local stations were opened as a two-year experiment, beginning with Radio Leicester in November 1967. Roy Corlett's interview with Paul betrays no sense of awe or anxiety about asking probing questions. The 26-year-old Paul McCartney sounds very comfortable talking to his old school friend. Decades later, the interview provides a revealing insight into his life at that hectic time.

In harmonious sessions compared to those for the now shelved project begun at Twickenham, The Beatles worked on *Abbey Road* during the summer of 1969. To promote the album's release in September, three of The Beatles were featured on several editions of *Scene and Heard*. David Wigg was again in attendance, ready to talk about the new record and the continuing rumours about the survival of the group. He talked to Paul on 19 September 1969. Six days earlier, John had returned to the stage playing with a hastily convened Plastic Ono Band in Toronto.

Asked for his personal favourites on the soon-to-be-released *Abbey Road*, Paul selected 'Come Together', 'Something', the 'long one' (the medley that concludes the album) and 'Because'. He proudly described his new baby Mary – 'the best-looking baby you've ever seen' – and faced up to the inevitable question.

DAVID: Paul, what about the future of The Beatles? I happen to know that the organizers of the Isle of Wight Pop Festival are going to ask you and the rest of The Beatles if you will top the bill next year at the Isle of Wight. What's your reaction to a thing like that? Are you likely to go back on stage and perhaps do a show like that?

PAUL: I don't know. I've never known. I didn't know when we were playing the Cavern that we'd be on the Royal Variety Performance. And after that all the papers said, 'Well, what's left for them?' So then we went to America. Then they said, 'What's left for them?' And then we got into making better albums and stuff. I mean, I just don't know what's going to happen. It'll be all right though… I don't see how we can retire. It's like Brigitte Bardot and Greta Garbo. Although they tried to retire, you can't, 'cause you're always there.

WHEN IT WAS George's turn to sit down with David Wigg in October 1969, he seemed equally sure of the group's continuation.

GEORGE: All I'm doing is acting out the part of Beatle George and we're all acting out our own parts. You know, the world is a stage and the people are the players. Shakespeare said that… and he's right.

DAVID: Do you expect another part later?

GEORGE: Oh, many parts. [laughs]

DAVID: Do you enjoy it now?

GEORGE: It's the same as any job. It's up and down. Life is up and down all the time. Maybe for us it goes up higher, but it comes down lower. Relativity. So if we have a bad time it's really bad. And if we have a good time, maybe it's really good. The same law operates for everybody.

DAVID: Two of the most beautiful songs on *Abbey Road* are from yourself when we've been so used to Lennon/McCartney compositions and, of course, people have been commenting this week about 'Something' and 'Here Comes The Sun', which are your own compositions. How did this all happen? It's so unusual for you to contribute so much to an LP.

GEORGE: Well, not really. I mean, the last album we did had four songs of mine on it. I thought they were all right. So I thought these, 'Something' and 'Here Comes The Sun', were OK… maybe a bit more commercial. but as songs not much better than the songs on the last album. But I've been writing for a couple of years now. And there's been lots of songs I've written which I haven't got round to recording. So, you know, in my own mind I don't see what the fuss is, because I've heard these songs before and I wrote them quite a while back. And it's really nice that people like the songs, but…

DAVID: You don't look upon yourself as a late developer as regards songwriting then? Because it's kind of hit everyone in that way, you know.

GEORGE: Late, early… you know, what's late and what's early?

DAVID: [laughs] But you hadn't really got the reputation as yet as a songwriter, had you?

GEORGE: No, no. I wasn't Lennon or I wasn't McCartney. I was me. And the only reason I started to write songs was because I thought, 'Well if they can write them, I can write them,' you know. 'Cause really, everybody can write songs if they want to. If they have a desire to and if they have sort of some musical knowledge and background. And then it's by writing them, the same as writing books or writing articles or painting – the more you do it, the better or the more you can understand how to do it. And I used to just write songs. I still do. I just write a song and it just comes out however it wants to. And some of them are catchy songs like 'Here Comes The Sun' and some of them aren't, you know. But to me they are just songs and I just write them and some will be considered as good by maybe the masses and some won't. But to me they're just songs, things that are there that have to be got out.

DAVID: What inspired 'Something', for example?

GEORGE: Maybe Pattie, probably.

DAVID: Really?

GEORGE: I wrote it at the time when we were making the last double album. And it's just the first line, 'Something in the way she moves', which has been in millions of songs. It's not a special thing. But it just seemed quite apt. I usually get the first few lines of lyrics and melody both at once. And then I finish the melody usually first and then I have to write the words. Like, there's another song I wrote when we were in India about two years, eighteen months ago, and I wrote it straight away. And the first verse I wrote just said everything I wanted to say, like that. And now I need to write a couple of more verses and I find it much more difficult. But John gave me a handy tip once, which is, once you start to write the song, try and finish it straight away while you're in the mood. And I've learned from experience, because you go back to it and then you're in a whole different state of mind and it's more difficult. Sometimes it's easier, but on the whole it's more difficult to come back to something. So I do it now, try and finish them straight away.

DAVID: Is it the first time that one of your songs has been released as a Beatles single?

GEORGE: As an A-side, yeah.

DAVID: As an A-side.

GEORGE: They blessed me with a couple of B-sides in the past. But this is the first time I've had an A-side. Big deal, eh?

DAVID: Yes, and 'Here Comes The Sun'. That sounds a more obvious one. You must have been inspired by the sun, but where were you?

GEORGE: The story behind that was, like Paul sung 'You Never Give Me Your Money'. I think, because whatever you're involved with rubs off and influences you, 'You Never Give Me Your Money' is, I think, during all these business things that we had to go through to sort out the past, so it came out in Paul's song.

DAVID: Was that written as a sort of dig, or was it written as a sort of…?

GEORGE: No, I don't think so. I think it's just written as that's what it is, you know. That's what we are experiencing, you know. Paul, in particular. But 'Here Comes The Sun' was the same period. We had meetings and meetings and with all this, you know, banks, bankers and lawyers and all sorts of things. And contracts and shares. And it was really awful, 'cause it's not the sort of thing we enjoy. And one day I didn't come in to the office. I just sort of… it was like sagging off school.

DAVID: [laughs]

GEORGE: And I went to a friend's house in the country. And it was just sunny and it was all just the release of that tension that had been building up on me. And it was just really nice sunny day. And I picked up the guitar, which was the first time I'd played the guitar for a couple of weeks because I'd been so busy. And the first thing that came out was that song. It just came. And I finished it later when I was on holiday in Sardinia.

DAVID: What was your own personal response to the *Abbey Road* album? How do you feel comparing it with previous albums?

GEORGE: I thought it was quite nice on the whole. I think it's a pretty good album.

DAVID: What are your own personal favourites? Which ones that you really do like?

ABOVE **George** with his wife Pattie Boyd in 1969. They married on 21 March 1966 at Esher Register Office, Surrey.

The British Broadcasting Corporation

To:
LIGHT ENTERTAINMENT BOOKING MANAGER,
THE BRITISH BROADCASTING CORPORATION,
HAREWOOD HOUSE,
HANOVER SQUARE,
LONDON, W.I.

TALKS REQUISITION/CONTRACT

Copy No. 1   (Registry)

...ee specified in the appropriate form of
...rleaf relating to all types of contributions
contributions.

A.201892
Beatles & Co., for the services of:-
George Harrison, Esq.,
c/o Beatles & Co.,
3 Savile Row,
London, W.1.

PLEASE SIGN AND RETURN

Programme Numbers	PA1972Q
Service:	Radio 1
Title:	SCENE AND HEARD
Rehearsal/recording date and time:	4th March 1969 as arranged
Transmission date and time:	12th April 1969 1.00 – 2.00 p.m.
Location/Studio:	Outside studio
Duration/nature of contribution: (Note: Final manuscripts of scripted talks contributions must be received by the BBC not later than ten days before the broadcast or recording date(s), unless otherwise agreed).	4'30" interview with David Wigg
Producer's name (and signature if appropriate)	Mr. Ted Beston PABX 3105 Date: 24th April 1969

For   Accounts   use   only

If you wish to accept please sign the form of acceptance contained in Part B or C below, as appropriate.
This offer may be cancelled if your signed acceptance is not received within five days of this offer. If the fee
proposed below is paid before we receive your signed acceptance of this contract then we shall be at liberty
to treat your acceptance of the payment as confirmation that you accept the contract.

If you receive notice of any claim for defamation in respect of your contribution(s), you are asked to notify the
BBC before taking any steps to deal with the claim.

Signed on behalf of the BBC by _David Dove_   Date 24th April 1969
Assistant to Light Entertainment Booking Manager
NOTE: Part C is only intended for use where a contributor accepts the offer at the time of performance. In any other circumstances
(when Part C may be detached by the BBC) the contributor wishing to accept should sign Part B.

B For signature by the contributor when he accepts the offer at some time other than the time of
performance

The contributor should retain copy No. 2 of this Agreement marked for him and sign and return copy No. 1 to:
Talks Booking Section, The British Broadcasting Corporation, Broadcasting House, London, W.1.

Fee: Six Pounds (£6.0.0.)

I accept the offer in consideration of the fee mentioned above and on the terms and conditions stated.

Contributor's signature _George Harrison_   Date.

ABOVE The standard BBC 'Talks'
contract for the interview George
gave to David Wigg on 4 March 1969.
Their conversation was broadcast in
the weekly pop magazine programme
Scene and Heard.

GEORGE: I like… My favourite one is, I think, 'Because'.

DAVID: Oh, yeah.

GEORGE: Just because I like three-part harmony. We've never done something like that for years, I think, since a B-side. [sings] 'If you wear red tonight' and 'This is what I said tonight' ['Yes It Is' – B-side of 'Ticket To Ride']. So I like that. I like lots of them. I like 'You Never Give Me Your Money' and 'Golden Slumbers' and things.

DAVID: That's beautiful.

GEORGE: You know, Paul always writes nice melodies. In fact, I don't know where he finds them half the time.

DAVID: [laughs]

GEORGE: He's amazing for doing that. I like Ringo's song.

DAVID: Yes. It's great fun.

GEORGE: Because, I mean, most people say, 'Oh well, it's Ringo', or you know, 'Ha, ha' or something. But it's great that Ringo *should* do it. You know, why shouldn't he do it. And it's just like a country and western tune anyway. And it's a happy tune and it's all that. And I like what he's saying about '… rest our head on the sea bed'. And all that. 'We could be warm beneath the storm'.

DAVID: The little kids are gonna love that.

GEORGE: Well, yeah. Maybe some big kids like it. I've heard a few people already who are big kids saying that it's their favourite track on the album. So, you know, you can't… What one person may dislike certain things, somebody else likes it, which makes it difficult doing albums, because we're all influenced by different things. And The Beatles has always been a lot of different music. It's never been one sort of 'bag'. [laughs] But the thing is that you can set a high standard and it doesn't necessarily have to be a hit. You know, this is one thing. The market for hits is… you know, I just can't figure it out. I know when The Beatles put out a single it's a hit. But I don't know if… sometimes I feel that if somebody else had put out the same thing, but done in their way it mightn't be a hit. I don't know. It's very difficult. I've really decided I haven't got a clue what's commercial and what isn't. And that's

the problem, you know, trying to decide what is and what isn't a single. I think the American idea is really good where they just put out an album and the stations over there, you know, they have a lot of independent stations, unlike Britain. You see that's a problem with Britain. You've got your good old BBC – full stop. You know, maybe Radio Luxembourg if the weather's fine.

DAVID: Would you like to see The Beatles performing on stage live again?

GEORGE: Er, I don't know. I wouldn't mind playing, you know. I like playing the guitar with people and singing a few songs and stuff. But I don't know as to going on clubs and things like that.

DAVID: Yes. You can't split, can you?

GEORGE: No, well, I think it's a mental concept. But to physically or spiritually split is impossible. Well, maybe not physically. Spiritually, you can't split.

DAVID: No. So that doesn't bother you.

GEORGE: Because, if you're listening, I'm the walrus too!

EIGHT WEEKS AFTER the interview, George slipped into Delaney and Bonnie's band during their tour of Britain. Over three years had elapsed since he had last played on a British stage with The Beatles at the Empire Pool, Wembley. When John and Yoko talked to David Wigg in October 1969, the likelihood of a Beatles concert was again on the agenda.

JOHN: Performing as a Beatle is a harder problem than performing as John Lennon and Yoko, or The Plastic Ono Band, 'cause you don't have that big aura around you. You saw what happened to Dylan in the Isle of Wight. There was nothing wrong with his performance and the audience appreciated him, but they were expecting Buddha or Jesus to appear! And if you imagine the four Beatles are going to come on the Isle of Wight, whatever happens we're gonna get knocked. Whatever happens, we have such a thing to live up to. It's not out of the question. It's just a big responsibility. There's such a mystique about The Beatles that they'd be expecting God to perform and we're not.

JOHN HAD ALREADY asked for 'a divorce' from the group in September. When asked what he wanted for The Beatles in the future, John referred to the group in the third person: 'For them to be happy. To do whatever they want to do. 'Cause whatever happens to The Beatles, so-called, we'll always be friends. So all I want for The Beatles is their individual happiness and whether that's in a collective form or not remains to be seen.'

As if The Beatles did not have enough to deal with, in October 1969 a preposterous story swept through America. According to Russ Gibbs – a DJ on Detroit station W-KNR – cryptic clues hidden on Beatles records and album covers revealed the dark secret that Paul had died in 1966 and been replaced with a lookalike. In the wake of this nonsense, Radio 4 newsman Chris Drake was granted an interview with Paul, who had retreated with his family to the Mull of Kintyre in Scotland. He didn't actually persuade Paul to say 'I'm alive!' but Paul's wife Linda expressed the couple's annoyance – 'it ruins our life, that kind of thing.' Drake reported that Paul 'lives contentedly in isolation, walking in the day and watching television at night. He does have a telephone but it's nearly always left off the hook. He's in no hurry to return to civilization, there's no need to.' Paul explained: 'I've done all my work for this year, because The Beatles have… We've made a film and another album, besides *Abbey Road*, which are unreleased yet. So I've finished my work till about March of next year, so I'm laughing! I may not be back in London at all this year.'

While Paul remained out of the spotlight, Ringo recorded tracks for his solo album *Sentimental Journey*. During 1969 he had acted in *The Magic Christian*, whose other cast members included Peter Sellers, Richard Attenborough, John Cleese, Christopher Lee and Raquel Welch. The Paul McCartney song 'Come And Get It' by Apple recording artists Badfinger is heard as the credits roll at the beginning of the film. When *The Magic Christian* was released in December, Ringo agreed to be interviewed for BBC TV's *Late Night Line-Up* to promote it. Although there is only a brief reference to the film in the conversation, he does point to a badge on his hat displaying the words 'Magic Christian' and grins: 'That's why I'm here, folks!'

Ringo's first BBC interview of 1969 had been in a car driving to London from his house in Elstead, Surrey. His last BBC interview of the year was also recorded on the road with one of the regular *Line-Up* presenters. As he climbed into the back seat, Ringo asked Tony Bilbow about one of his colleagues: 'And how is the lovely Joan Bakewell?' Another part of the interview was conducted on the River Thames with Ringo and, occasionally Tony Bilbow, at the oars of a rowing boat. One of their topical discussions was about the impact of lowering the minimum age requirement for voting in UK elections from 21 to 18.

RINGO: Members of Parliament are getting younger and so I think it will work itself out. With the young vote and the younger members of Parliament then we can get somewhere. You don't have to be like 45 or 50 before you actually get into the House.

And I think, maybe in the next generation, the Prime Minister will not only be black, but he'll be beautiful and 26. [laughs]

TONY: You had a lot of illness when you were a child. So much so that you lost out on a lot of your education.

RINGO: Yes.

TONY: Does this now bother you?

RINGO: Occasionally. When I talk to people as intellectual as you talk.

TONY: Ah! But only with people like me.

RINGO: Only with people like you. No, sometimes it does… where people put words that I really have never heard in my life, and I have to sort of stop and say, 'Excuse me what does that mean?' It's just a bit of a hang-up like that. But it doesn't bother me too much any more.

TONY: But I mean, you've got time now if you wanted to, to have a little course of self-education if you like.

RINGO: No.

TONY: Do you read a lot, for instance?

RINGO: Yes, I read all the time. See, I always say, 'I'm intelligent, but uneducated.' [laughs] 'Cause I'm quite intelligent. You know, that's how I put it. But I don't know the actual spelling of the words. I can read any word you want to give me and I know what a lot of them mean, but I can't spell most of them.

As the boat meandered over the water, talk turned to Ringo's burgeoning acting career.

RINGO: It started when we finished touring, everyone sort of found something to do… like Paul and George produced [records for] people. John then got with Yoko and produced himself and Yoko. And I was sort of at a loose end for a while; and I always enjoyed filming.

TONY: More than the others do you think?

RINGO: Yes. And when Brian [Epstein] was alive I said, 'Well, let's make a film with something', you know, and he had a few scripts then. We decided that *Candy* was the best one. And *Candy* was good for me as a trial, because it was only two weeks' work and I had a small part, so I didn't have to sort of hold anything up, you know; it [the success of the movie] wasn't on my head. And after *Candy* I thought it was so easy that *Magic Christian* came in. It was also by the same writer, Terry Southern, who I think is a fantastic writer. 'Cause I think the lines in a film are important… more important than the camera. You know, what you have to say. And so I decided to do *The Magic Christian*. [joking about the progress of the rowing boat] This is the slowest trip we've ever been on! [laughs]

TONY: You said you want to be a film star. I don't really believe that; you don't really want to be a film *star*, do you?

ABOVE **Stills from Ringo's nautical interview with Tony Bilbow filmed on 1 December 1969.**

RINGO: No, no. I want to be a film *actor*. I don't want to be like Cary Grant or one of them who, like, really do the same performance in everything, and the story is the only thing that changes.

TONY: Would you be prepared, for the sake of argument, to go to drama school or something?

RINGO: No, no. I'm not interested in that part of it, because I think it's much better if you can just, you know… I keep reading about how I've got natural ability. [laughs]

TONY: 'Cause your co-star is Peter Sellers…

RINGO: Yeah.

TONY: … and he's somebody who really came to film acting from a very different sort of background.

RINGO: Not really, because he was a drummer as well, in a band. How did he come different? The only difference… he had to work at it. He started with, like, walk-on parts and then he got a bit bigger part, and then he got his own films. The only difference is I, because of the name Ringo as a Beatle, I was allowed to walk right into a good slot. I didn't have to stand-in, or do any of the small jobs. I'm getting sick personally of message films. I think it's about time we got back to Doris Day… films like that where you can get involved. I can't get involved in films any more. I want it to be like when I was a kid, where whatever was on… if it was a Western, I'd come out the theatre and I'd be shootin' and ridin' and whatever you do. And if it was a buccaneer film I'd sword-fence everyone in the street. And I'd like to get films back to that, you know, because that's what the function was… was to take you out of the real world. James Bond films, you know. Guys come out after seeing James Bond films… [laughs] Some wives have a great time, you know, when the guys come out there…

TONY: [laughs]

RINGO: … they strut up to her and say, 'Howdy, honey. I'll have me Horlicks shook not stirred!'

FOLLOWING RINGO'S DAY with a BBC film crew, John and Yoko were followed by cameras from 2 to 6 December 1969. *The World of John & Yoko* was screened on 15 December in the BBC 1 programme strand *24 Hours*. Constantly together, John and Yoko are seen chatting in bed, travelling in their Rolls-Royce, recording at Abbey Road studios and being interviewed in their office at Apple. One of the most remarkable scenes was their highly charged encounter with the London *New York Times* correspondent Gloria Emerson. She was deeply concerned about the Vietnam War and the following year began her award-winning reports from the country. Her writing focused on the suffering caused by the war to soldiers and civilians caught up in the conflict. But she had no sympathy with what John and Yoko were doing to promote peace. The week before John had returned his MBE medal to Buckingham Palace and had written a letter to Prime Minister Harold Wilson explaining his action. It was, he wrote, 'in protest against Britain's involvement in the Nigeria-Biafra thing, against our support of America in Vietnam and against "Cold Turkey" [the current Plastic Ono Band single] slipping down the charts'. His mixture of the serious and the flippant did not impress Gloria Emerson.

JOHN: If I'm gonna get on the front page, I might as well get on the front page with the word 'peace'.

GLORIA: But you've made yourself ridiculous.

JOHN: To some people. I don't care if…

GLORIA: Some people? You're too good for what you're doing.

JOHN: If it saves lives…

GLORIA: You don't think you… Oh! my dear boy, you're living in a nether-nether land.

JOHN: Well, you talk to her…

GLORIA: You don't think you've saved a single life.

JOHN: Well, maybe we'll save some in the future.

GLORIA: You've probably helped 'Cold Turkey' move up the charts.

JOHN: It didn't do a bit of use… it's still gone down so it didn't do anything.

GLORIA: I mean you don't equate the civil war that's going on in Nigeria…

JOHN: Look, listen…

GLORIA: … with that… and then talk about, 'Well, this is my form of protest, because…

'We did an advertising campaign for peace. Can you understand that?'

JOHN LENNON

JOHN: Well, look…

GLORIA: '… people in anti-war campaigns are too *serious*…

JOHN: Yes.

GLORIA: … and they get battered.' What do you know about a protest movement, anyway?

JOHN: I know a lot about it. I've…

GLORIA: It means a lot more than sending your chauffeur in your car back to Buckingham Palace.

JOHN: You're just a snob about it. The only way to make…

GLORIA: You're a fake! … Can't you give up something else that would mean a little bit more?

JOHN: It's not the sacrifice… you can't get that into your head, can you? You've stated a half a dozen times the MBE is irrelevant. I agree. It was no sacrifice to get rid of the MBE, because it was an embarrassment.

GLORIA: Then what kind of a protest did you make?

JOHN: We did an advertising campaign for peace. Can you understand that?

GLORIA: No I can't!

JOHN: A very big advertising campaign for peace.

GLORIA: I think it shows you're vulgar and self-aggrandizing. Are you advertising John Lennon or peace?

JOHN: Oh, you want nice middle-class gestures for peace and intellectual manifestos…

GLORIA: Maybe.

JOHN: … written by a lot of half-witted intellectuals and nobody reads 'em? That's the trouble with the peace movement.

GLORIA: Well, it just seems a nether-nether land. I mean I can't think of anyone who seems more remote from the ugliness of what's happening than you. I do see you getting up on a Tuesday morning and thinking, 'Let's see what shall we do today? What war is going on?'

PAGES 290 AND 291 **Stills from** *24 Hours – The World of John & Yoko*, broadcast on 15 December 1969. Shots from the confrontational interview between Gloria Emerson and John are towards the end of the sequence.

JOHN **AND** YOKO

DIRECTED BY
PAUL MORRISON
A **BBC tv** PRODUCTION

YOKO: Well, that's your imagination, you know, really.

JOHN: You know, you carry on. Why don't you make a film while you're at it.

GLORIA: I'm someone who admired you very much.

JOHN: Well I'm sorry you liked the old moptops, dear, and you thought I was very satirical…

GLORIA: Well, I mean, talking about cashing in on The Beatles…

JOHN: … and witty and you liked *Hard Day's Night*, love. But I've grown up, but you obviously haven't.

GLORIA: Have you?

JOHN: Yes, folks.

GLORIA: What have you grown up to?

JOHN: Twenty-nine.

IN THE NEXT edition of *24 Hours*, presenter David Dimbleby commented on the audience reaction to *The World of John & Yoko*.

'Most of the people I talked to liked it and thought it amusing, but there was a ferocious response afterwards from people telephoning the BBC. There were over a hundred of them. They said it was "drivel", "absolutely disgusting", "the most disgusting programme *ever*", "abominable", "pernicious rubbish", "tripe", "disgraceful", "filthy". The hostility was directed entirely at John Lennon and his Japanese wife. It's interesting when you think that only a few years ago, he was one of the four lovable mop-heads from Liverpool.'

The best-selling album of the year, *Abbey Road*, was number one in the UK every week, bar one, from October to the end of December. For nine weeks from the end of April to the middle of June (with a one-week interruption), The Beatles had topped the singles chart with 'Get Back' and 'The Ballad Of John And Yoko'. Clearly, the group remained a powerful artistic and commercial force in 1969. But seeing and hearing The Beatles on BBC TV and radio offered evidence that each member had, indeed, grown up and asserted his individuality. The last track listed on side two of *Abbey Road* was called 'The End'. No one listening at the time had realized that it was.

'Only a few years ago, he was one of the four lovable mop-heads from Liverpool.'

DAVID DIMBLEBY

SEQUENCE 6/LENNON PAY OFF AND GOODNIGHT (DD/af)   19.12.69

VISION	SCRIPT AND DETAILS
34'50	On Monday you may have seen our film profile of John Lennon and his wife Yoko. It was about a week in the life of that happy couple, driving around in their white Rolls Royce, and organising their publicity campaign for 'Peace', while being interviewed by an endless procession of questioners. Most of the people I talked to liked it and thought it quite amusing but there was a ferocious response afterwards from people telephoning the BBC. There were over a hundred of them. They said it was Drivel, Absolutely disgusting, the most disgusting programme ever, abominable, pernicious rubbish, tripe, disgraceful, filthy. There was one lady who said that the Lennons couldn't even speak English and had used "yunno" 58 times: Imagine sitting right through a film you hate and solemly counting up the times they said "yunno". The film itself didn't have any of the kind of sequences that have Mrs. Whitehouse and the rest reaching for their telephones. The hostility was directed entirely at John Lennon and his Japanese wife. It's interesting when you think that only a few years ago he was one of the 4 lovable mopheads from Liverpool. But now Lennon no longer seems to want the adulation of the crowd - as came out very clearly in the film - and his old admirers are apparently replying in kind. A swift passage from Love to hate on both sides.

RIGHT David Dimbleby's 'Pay off and goodnight' script from the edition of 24 Hours broadcast four days after the previous programme devoted to the activities of John and Yoko.

Radio programme titles
TV titles

SCENE AND HEARD
Br: 25 January 1969 – 1.00–2.00pm – Radio 1
Repeated: 28 January 1969 – 7.45–8.44pm – Radio 1
Rec: 21 January 1969
During a car journey to London, *Daily Express* writer David Wigg interviewed Ringo about the rumours of a Beatles split and the financial state of the group.

SCENE AND HEARD
Br: 8 March 1969 – 1.00–2.00pm – Radio 1
Repeated: 11 March 1969 – 7.45–8.44pm – Radio 1
Rec: 4 March 1969
George was interviewed at the Apple office in Savile Row, London by David Wigg.

SCENE AND HEARD
Br: 12 April 1969 – 1.00–2.00pm – Radio 1
Repeated: 5 April 1969 – 7.45–8.44pm – Radio 1
Rec: 4 March 1969
More from David Wigg's interview with George.

LATE NIGHT EXTRA
Br: 1 April 1969 – 10.00pm–midnight – Radio 1 & Radio 2
Rec: 1 April 1969
An interview with John was broadcast.

THE WORLD AT ONE
Br: 3 April 1969 – 1.00–1.30pm – Radio 4
Rec: 3 April 1969
George talked to Sue MacGregor about his friend and sitar teacher, the virtuoso player Ravi Shankar.

HOW LATE IT IS
Br: 2 May 1969 – 10.55–11.35pm – BBC 1
Rec: 2 May 1969 – 12.30–1.00pm
Studio G BBC Lime Grove Studios, London
John and Yoko interview with Michael Wale about their film *Rape*.

SCENE AND HEARD
Br: 11 May 1969 – 3.00–4.00pm – Radio 1
Repeated: 13 May 1969 – 7.45–8.45pm – Radio 1
Rec: 8 May 1969
John and Yoko talked to David Wigg about their campaign for peace, including their recent Amsterdam Bed-in.

SCENE AND HEARD
Br: 18 May 1969 – 3.00–4.00pm – Radio 1
Repeated: 20 May 1969 – 7.45–8.45pm – Radio 1
Rec: 8 May 1969
More from David Wigg's John and Yoko interview.

LIGHT AND LOCAL
Br: 16 May 1969 – 12.31–1.00pm – BBC Radio Merseyside
Rec: 15 May 1969
Paul gave a very relaxed and candid interview to a former Liverpool Institute school contemporary, Roy Corlett.

EVERETT IS HERE
Br: 20 September 1969 – 10.00am–noon – Radio 1
Rec: 14 August 1969
A Kenny Everett interview with John was delayed until the release of the *Abbey Road* album at the end of September.

SCENE AND HEARD
Br: 21 September 1969 – 3.00–4.00pm – Radio 1
Rec: 19 September 1969
Paul talked to David Wigg about tracks from the forthcoming album *Abbey Road*.

EVERETT IS HERE
Br: 27 September 1969 – 10.00am–noon – Radio 1
Rec: 14 August 1969
More from Kenny's interview with John recorded at Abbey Road Studios.

SCENE AND HEARD
Br: 28 September 1969 – 3.00–4.00pm – Radio 1
Rec: 19 September 1969
More from David Wigg's conversation with Paul.

SCENE AND HEARD
Br: 12 October 1969 – 3.00–4.00pm – Radio 1
Rec: 8 October 1969
George discussed financial matters, songwriting, his spiritual beliefs and his recent production of the Radha Krishna Temple's UK hit 'Hare Krishna Mantra'. David Wigg was in attendance, of course.

SCENE AND HEARD
Br: 19 October 1969 – 3.00–4.00pm – Radio 1
Rec: 8 October 1969
More from the interview with George.

THE WORLD THIS WEEKEND
Br: 26 October 1969 – 1.00–2.00pm – Radio 4
Rec: 24 October 1969
At the time that the 'Paul Is Dead' myth was concocted and disseminated by an American DJ, BBC reporter Chris Drake journeyed to the McCartneys' remote Scottish farmhouse. On the windswept moorland, he talked to the harassed couple who had wanted to retreat from the world for a while.

SCENE AND HEARD
Br: 26 October 1969 – 3.00–4.00pm – Radio 1
Rec: 21 October 1969
Beatle domination of this programme continued with David Wigg's interview with John, in which he discussed the likelihood of The Beatles playing together again.

THE WORLD AT ONE
Br: 27 October 1969 – 1.00–1.30pm – Radio 4
Rec: 24 October 1969
A longer extract was broadcast from Paul's interview recorded in Scotland with Chris Drake.

LATE NIGHT EXTRA
Br: 27 October 1969 – 10.00–midnight – Radio 1 & 2
Rec: 24 October 1969
A repeat of Paul's interview recorded in Scotland with Chris Drake.

TODAY
Br: 26 November 1969 – 7.15–7.45am and 8.15–8.40am – Radio 4
Rec: 25 November 1969

John returned his MBE medal as an act of protest 'against Britain's involvement in the Nigeria-Biafra thing, against our support of America in Vietnam and against "Cold Turkey" slipping down the charts'. Naturally, this generated more publicity for his peace campaign. John's interview with David Bellan was included in two parts of the breakfast news programme.

THE QUESTION WHY
Br: 7 Dec 1969, 6.15–6.50pm – BBC 1 – Live
Studio E, Lime Grove Studios, London
John and Yoko participated in a discussion about evil, in the TV series chaired by Malcolm Muggeridge.

LATE NIGHT LINE-UP
Br: 10 Dec 1969 – 11.07–11.30pm – BBC 2
Rec: 1 Dec 1969
Various London locations
Ringo was interviewed by Tony Bilbow. It was broadcast the evening before the world premiere of the movie *The Magic Christian*, co-starring Peter Sellers and Ringo.

24 HOURS
– The World of John & Yoko
Br: 15 Dec 1969, 10.30–11.05pm, BBC 1
Rec: 2-6 Dec 1969 – Various locations
Much of the footage was used in the 1988 movie *Imagine: John Lennon*.

LATE NIGHT EXTRA
Br: 15 December 1969 – 10.00–midnight
– Radio 1 & 2
Rec: 3 December 1969
An extract from *24 Hours* – the soundtrack of the filmed interview with American writer Gloria Emerson – was broadcast.

WILL THE REAL MR. SELLERS...
Br: 18 Dec 1969 – 9.10–10.pm – BBC 1
Rec: 4 May 1969
Les Ambassadeurs Club
Ringo, Paul and John were filmed at a party marking the end of shooting for *The Magic Christian*.

KENNY EVERETT'S CHRISTMAS SHOW
Br: 25 December 1969 – 10.00am–noon – Radio 1
Rec: 15 December 1969
At 10.15, Ringo was heard making an appeal on behalf of the British Wireless for the Blind Fund.

1970

The Beatles
Today

ON EASTER MONDAY 1970, George was featured in a radio special called *The Beatles Today*. His interview had been recorded nineteen days earlier on 11 March. At this time, things were moving so fast in The Beatles' world that some of what he said was already out of date. George talked about the material Glyn Johns had assembled for the next Beatles album, *Let It Be*. By the time of the Radio 1 broadcast, that version had been ditched and producer Phil Spector was busy creating something very different from the recordings made by Johns in January 1969. On 10 April, a press release from Paul declared his 'break from The Beatles'.

The release of *Let It Be* was linked to the completion of the film documenting the album's creation. This meant the last two Beatles albums did not come out in the chronological order of their recording dates. If they had done so, The Beatles' career would have closed with *Abbey Road* – an LP made with their usual meticulous attention to detail in the studio. Instead, *Let It Be* followed and sounded out of step and a rather scrappy affair. On the other hand, it did contain three American number one singles and one of the most loved of all Beatles songs, 'Across The Universe'. The most successful album of 1970 was *Bridge Over Troubled Water* by Simon & Garfunkel. Having hit their commercial peak, the duo split up. On his first solo album following the dissolution of the partnership, Paul Simon sang 'Everything Put Together Sooner Or Later Falls Apart'.

Everything was falling apart in 1970. Journeys into space had not encountered any major technical problems in recent years. Soon after the first Moon landing made by *Apollo 11*, the next successful American mission placed two more astronauts on the lunar surface in November 1969. But then came the launch of the ill-fated *Apollo 13* on 11 April 1970. Two days into the journey, an oxygen tank exploded. The resulting damage switched the mission objective from landing on the Moon to a challenge to return the astronauts safely to Earth. Through the ingenuity of those at Mission Control and the bravery and skill of the men in space, the Service Module *Odyssey* was brought back home. The dramatic story had gripped millions and the world waited anxiously on 17

April for the spacecraft to splash down in the South Pacific.

Things fell apart for Prime Minister Harold Wilson. The voting age in the UK was lowered from 21 to 18 on 1 January 1970. The first general election to include a younger demographic took place on 19 June. The widely predicted outcome of the contest between Wilson and the leader of the Conservative Party, Edward Heath, was a comfortable victory for the incumbent Prime Minister. But the unexpected happened: the Tories won. Looking for clues, some Labour ministers blamed the upset on the result of a quarter-final match of the World Cup held in Mexico. Just a few days before polling day, West Germany scored a goal in extra time to knock England out of the tournament.

As yet more lives were lost in Vietnam, anti-war demonstrations continued across America. The US had begun military operations in East Cambodia at the end of April 1970. Viewed as heightening the intensity of the war, the incursion provoked more unrest on college campuses. On 4 May, during a demonstration at Kent State University in Ohio, the National Guard opened fire on students. Four were killed and nine injured. The tragedy triggered a strike of four million students across the States. Ten days later, at a student protest against the Cambodian invasion, police killed two and injured twelve at Jackson State College. Over 6,000 Americans died in Vietnam during 1970.

Pop music had taken a central role in the lives of young people and was no longer simply entertainment. Some musicians felt compelled to respond to current events, as Crosby, Stills, Nash & Young did with their rush-released single 'Ohio'. The previous year's Woodstock festival had shown the strength of the bond between performers and their audience. Millions were saddened by the deaths of Jimi Hendrix and Janis Joplin from drug overdoses. If some fans still clung to the hope that The Beatles might reunite – after all, the wording of Paul's 'self-interview' issued on 10 April did not categorically deny it – they would have been disappointed to read the 'Mail Bag' section of *Melody Maker* dated 29 August 1970. A letter from Paul stated: 'My answer to the question "Will The Beatles get together again?" … is "No".'

THE NEW YEAR began with *Abbey Road* on top of the album charts in the UK and America, holding off strong challenges from The Rolling Stones' *Let It Bleed* and the second album by Led Zeppelin. The film documenting the Twickenham sound stage rehearsals and Apple studio sessions of January 1969 was nearing completion. At this point still called *Get Back*, it included footage of an early rehearsal of 'I Me Mine' – a song that had not been properly recorded by the group. Consequently, on 3 January 1970, George's composition was recorded for the film soundtrack album. As John was in Denmark at the time, he was not present for The Beatles' final recording while they were still officially together.

On 27 January – two days after he returned to the UK – John entered Studio Two at Abbey Road with a new song. He wanted it completed and released as quickly as possible. He recorded 'Instant Karma!' with George on guitar, Klaus Voormann on bass and Alan White on drums. Credited to Lennon/Ono with The Plastic Ono Band, the single was rush-released on 6 February 1970. John then enthusiastically accepted numerous promotional duties for 'Instant Karma!' – more than for recent releases by The Beatles. The Plastic Ono Band's third single arrived just a few weeks after the December 1969 release of the album *Live Peace In Toronto*. After a sudden invitation, John had agreed to appear at a 'Rock 'N' Roll Revival Concert' held in September. The LP featured The Plastic Ono Band – John, Klaus Voormann, Alan White and Eric Clapton on guitar – performing onstage three rock 'n' roll favourites and 'Yer Blues' (from 'The White Album'), 'Cold Turkey' and 'Give Peace A Chance'. In his interview with Andy Peebles in 1980, John explained how little preparation there had been for the concert:

'We didn't know what to play, because we'd never played together before, so on the airplane we were running through these oldies – "Are we doing the Elvis version of 'Blue Suede Shoes' or the Carl Perkins with the different break at the beginning?"'

Three months after the Toronto concert, John and Yoko played on stage at the Lyceum Ballroom in London, in aid of UNICEF. Naturally, the Lennons' activities had maintained the media's curiosity about whether The Beatles would continue to work together. BBC reporter David Bellan caught up with John and Yoko just after the session for 'Instant Karma!'

DAVID: How much are you seeing, at the moment, of the other Beatles?

JOHN: Well, George was on the session for 'Instant Karma!' and Ringo's away [in Los Angeles] and Paul's… I don't know what he's doing, you know. At the moment, I haven't got a clue.

DAVID: When did you last see him?

JOHN: Before Toronto. When was it? I'll see him this week actually. If you're listening, I'm coming round!

JOHN AND YOKO had made a return visit to Toronto on 16 December 1969 to discuss plans for a 'Peace Pop Festival' in the city. While they were there, they met the Canadian Prime Minister Pierre Trudeau.

JOHN: We went really to talk about this peace festival these people are going to get together, and we're sort of helping with, and then the next minute we're seeing their Prime Minister Trudeau, which is great, 'cause it's the first time I'd seen one of them, and I was impressed, you know… It wasn't one of those sort of PR photograph bits, and he did talk, and we talked for an hour or more.

DAVID: Of course, he's very young and very switched on and all that, but what did you talk about? How did you get on?

JOHN: We talked about everything on Earth, you know. He wants to know, he's… It's like he's running a business and he can't really know what the doormen and the caretakers are doing, but he cares about them. He was asking us – as like a shop steward of youth maybe – what's going on out there? We were just giving our point of view, not necessarily as representatives of youth, but just as people who have got something to do with youth or had something to do with youth or whatever, and he just wanted to know what's going on, you know, like we did as representatives of youth, what's going on up here, you know. What… where's… it's just a lack of communication, you know.

DAVID: What do you reckon is going on? Big question.

JOHN: Well, there's lack of communication, that's what's going on, you know. He doesn't know what his youth wants, and his youth don't know what he's doing, you know. And I suppose that goes for everywhere.

YOKO: And both sides are creating hatred for each other, you know, which is not helping at all, and actually an establishment like Trudeau is not that bad, you know. I mean he's all right, and if the youth would understand that… because we're playing the same game by hating them. So the more and more communication from now on we hope [for], between those people and the youth.

JOHN: Because I was completely prejudiced. I'm always talking about love and you know, it doesn't matter what length your hair is or what colour you are, but then I'm prejudiced against politicians. I can't help it. I still am.

DAVID: But he won you over, did he?

JOHN: Well, it's not that he won me over. He gave us hope. That's the only one [head of state] I've really met. He was human, obviously, and he did care.

DAVID: How do people regard you generally in Canada? How do you go down over there?

JOHN: Well, it's very nice for us, because they take us seriously there, that's the journalists and the press. I mean they don't agree with everything we say, of course, but they do respect us as human beings with a point of view, which isn't the case back home. But it doesn't worry me unduly, but we have to be able to talk, communicate to people here as well as we do there. It would be great.

DAVID: What about the actual Beatle fans over there? How do they compare? Do they idolize you as much as they do in places where they really do?

JOHN: Oh yeah. Canada's a strong Beatle-hold. I mean because of the Commonwealth association and everything, they hold us a bit special over there.

DAVID: So you've got a bit of power over there in a way, as well as influence?

JOHN: Well I suppose so. Any power I have from the Beatle thing is an abstract power, you know. I mean a lot of Beatle fans have written to me saying, 'What are you doing?' and that. And some of them write back later saying, 'Oh, I understand what you're doing now, so good luck.' So it's not like everything a Beatle says goes with every Beatle fan that ever was, you know. They grow up, they change. Now we've got a new following. I know, just by seeing my son and Yoko's daughter. They're listening to early Beatles stuff

like the kids did in the early days. I couldn't believe it – five-year-olds listening to it. So there's a whole change going on with the Beatle people, whoever they are.

DAVID: Well, you've obviously got a pretty responsible attitude towards the power that you *have* got. But does it worry you, or do you always feel that you know exactly what you want to do?

JOHN: I don't worry about it, because if I'm depressed, I don't have the ability to use or influence anybody if I'm not in a good state of mind. And when I'm in a good state of mind, I use whatever power I have carefully.

DAVID: If we can talk a bit about your musical activities again, do you think you're still a rock and roller at heart?

JOHN: Sure. I mean, listen to 'Instant Karma!', folks. I keep saying that – you see I'm an old plugger. It's rock 'n' roll, you know, plain and simple.

DAVID: Do you still get excited by the prospect of recording or appearing before a live audience?

JOHN: You never lose the excitement or the fear, or the nerves before a performance and we are both hysterical about making this new record. I mean, I know it was only three months ago when we made the last one. But there's this one of ours coming out, then there's a Beatle one coming out a couple of weeks later, and I'm still as excited by the whole scene, you know. When I haven't got a nice song in my head or to record, I'm thinking, 'Oh well, I'm not really interested. I don't care.' But as soon as I've got a song I like, and a record I like, I'm back on.

DAVID: What about live appearances? They're rarer and rarer, aren't they, really? What are your plans?

JOHN: I don't know. I've done more live appearances in the last year than I did in the last five. I've appeared… last year, I appeared live about five times altogether, probably.

DAVID: Yeah, but what about, The Beatles all together as a group?

JOHN: As soon as they're ready. You know we had half The Beatles on again at the Lyceum Ballroom, that was George and me. But we also had Delaney and Bonnie and millions of people. A seventeen-piece band we had on. It was a great experience. It should be like that, you know. If we were doing that and all The Beatles wanted to come, it'd be great. Then there'd be no great thing about: 'Oh, The Beatles are coming back on stage' and all that. Like they expect sort of Buddha and Mohammed to come on and play. I keep saying that, but that's the fear The Beatles have – you know, that's including me as a Beatle – about performing. It's such a great… so much is expected of us, you know. But you see George has been on tour with Bonnie and Delaney playing, and I've been drifting round playing. It's just… playing isn't the hang-up. It's the going on as The Beatles that's the problem for us.

DAVID: Well this, I think, was one of the problems with *Abbey Road*. I think a great deal is always expected of you. Were you disappointed with the critical reaction? I mean it wasn't bad, but it wasn't as ecstatic as…

JOHN: I tell you honestly, I don't remember it, you know, because *Abbey Road* for me, as always with all the albums, I like some of the tracks and I don't like others of the tracks, and it's always been the same. I've never been a knocked-out Beatle fan by any of our albums. You know, I like some of the work we do, and some of it I don't. And *Abbey Road* was a competent album. I don't think it was any more than that or any less.

DAVID: Yeah, it was certainly competent. Yeah. You say you're still a rock and roller at heart, and that you're turning back in this direction a bit now.

JOHN: I've never left it.

DAVID: You never left it?

JOHN: Just trace John Lennon songs, if you'd care to, and you find I never left it, you know.

DAVID: No, I know, that's true actually. But do you ever feel at all nostalgic for the early days of The Beatles?

JOHN: You just get any musician over 26 sitting round with me, and it's all about 'Remember?' Yoko knows more about rock 'n' roll than she does about present-day pop, 'cause I talk about it so much. There's a great [Frank] Zappa album, *Reuben & The Jets*, and he does all this parody of the Fifties rock 'n' roll, but it's beautifully done and he means it as well as making a parody of it. And there's a beautiful sleeve note saying about they're just four old rock 'n' rollers in their rock 'n' roll suits, talking about rock 'n' roll in the studio all the time. In between every Beatle session, and in fact probably on the *Get Back* album, there'll be one or two bits. Whenever there's a break we go into rock 'n' roll, you know, the

old 'Good Golly Miss Molly' or whatever it is, and that's our era. We're already old folks talking about our 'Those were the days', and that's what we're like already.

DAVID: Can we look… [motorbike engine] Gosh, roar, roar from the motorbike. Can we just look at the future for a minute.

JOHN: Yes, I'll just get my crystal [ball].

DAVID: Yes, your crystal, not just *your* future, but, you know, the future of young people and what they're doing. Do you feel, when you look at the 1970s, optimistic or rather sad?

JOHN: No, I feel very optimistic. I don't look upon the Sixties as the decade like that ad for drink. There's one ad for drink that has a horrible drawing of Yoko and I, and a few other people, and Wilson, all saying what a terrible… at least you've got this drink to look forward to. And that's to me, is the right wing, 'Let's keep it like it is' faction of society [that] thinks like that. I think the youth, whatever way they voted, don't think like that, you know and they do have hope, because… it's their future that they're hopeful about, and if they're depressed about their own future, well then we are in a bad state. And we keep hope alive by keeping it alive amongst ourselves, you know. And I have great hope for the future. I think the Sixties was a great decade. I think the great gatherings of youth in America and in the Isle of Wight, they might have just been a pop concert to some people, but they were a lot more than that. They were the youth getting together and forming a new church, as it were, and saying, 'We believe in God. We believe in hope and truth, and here we are 20,000 or 200,000 of us, all together in peace.' And that's what I think about the youth. I think that's where the youth is at, you know.

YOKO ONO: I think the next generation is much wiser than the older generation. I mean when we get together we don't get drunk and, you know, fist-fight or something, but we just sit around quietly in all those pop festivals. And just the fact that we can do that means that we are much more mature than the older generation, in that sense.

DAVID: So you both look into the seventies with confidence, really.

JOHN: Yeah, we named 1970, Year One. For us it's Year One, yes.

DAVID: Well let's hope it will be. Thank you both very much, John and Yoko.

JOHN: It's a pleasure. Bye bye.

ABOVE Yoko and John pictured in the Apple Studio in January 1969 during sessions for an album that was called for most of its evolution *Get Back*. By the time the album and accompanying documentary film were released in May 1970, the title had changed to the fitting *Let It Be*.

JOHN'S VISITS TO Canada in 1969 were partly because he was denied entry into the United States due to his UK conviction for possession of illegal drugs. Following the Amsterdam Bed-in, he and Yoko chose Montreal as the location for their second peace event in a hotel bedroom. The city's proximity to the United States was seen as advantageous when seeking attention from the media.

On 1 June 1969 – the seventh of the couple's eight days in bed – 'Give Peace A Chance' was recorded in Room 1742 of the Queen Elizabeth Hotel, Montreal. By the time of this 1970 interview, the wider significance of pop music was a credible subject to discuss. David Bellan believed that the Lennons had a powerful effect on young people and had a responsibility to use such influence wisely. Canadian Prime Minister Pierre Trudeau met John and Yoko on 23 December 1969. The discussion of *Abbey Road* does reflect its contemporary critical reception. However, over time, the LP has grown in stature. It now rivals *Sgt. Pepper's Lonely Hearts Club Band* as the bestselling Beatles album. John's description of it as merely 'competent' is typical of the dismissive way he often assessed his and The Beatles' musical achievements.

When 'Instant Karma!' was released on 6 February 1970, David Wigg returned to Apple to talk to John and Yoko.

DAVID: Are you in fact going your own way with Yoko these days? Because that is the impression one has.

JOHN: Well, each Beatle's doing his own thing at the moment and it's like… it could be a rebirth or a death, you know. We'll see what it is. It'll probably be a rebirth… for all of us.

DAVID: When do you in fact plan to record with The Beatles again?

JOHN: At the moment, there is no plan whatsoever. And maybe if one of us starts it off, the others will all come round and make an album. It's just like that at the moment. To open The Beatles up, you know. And I've no idea if The Beatles will work together again or not… I never did have, it was always open.

DAVID: It's the first time this situation has ever arisen, isn't it?

JOHN: Well, let's say before *Sgt. Pepper* there was nine months of nothing. So in between our albums now, there's a lot of other stuff going on, that's all. There might be nine months or a year before we decide that we're interested enough to produce that thing called 'The Beatles' album'. But there was nine months before *Sgt. Pepper* and it's only been since September since we worked together.

DAVID: Do you care about making another one?

JOHN: Yeah, I think Beatles is a good communication media and I wouldn't destroy it out of hand or dissolve it out of hand.

JOHN'S COMMITMENT TO communication led to a rare appearance on BBC TV's weekly chart show *Top of the Pops* to sing 'Instant Karma!' His performance with The Plastic Ono Band filmed on 11 February was the first occasion a Beatle had made a visit to the *Top of the Pops* studio since the group performed 'Paperback Writer' and 'Rain' on 16 June 1966. John sang live over a backing track including another lead vocal. He was again accompanied by the regular Plastic Ono Band rhythm section of Klaus Voormann on bass guitar and Alan White on drums. Yoko was blindfolded and held up cards. In a second take, broadcast a week after the first version was shown, she is seen knitting – still enigmatically blindfolded.

On 30 March 1970, the BBC broadcast what had by now become a rare treat – a Beatles 'bank holiday' special. Called *The Beatles Today*, the Easter Monday programme featured George in conversation with the presenter of *Scene and Heard*, Johnny Moran. They talked about the Apple artists George had produced and The Beatles' album and film project, now entitled *Let It Be*.

JOHNNY: George, I'd like to talk to you about The Beatles and the forthcoming LP, but first about yourself. When did you first start writing songs?

GEORGE: Er, first song I ever wrote was in Bournemouth, it must have been about 1963. After our first success, we were doing weekly shows in holiday resorts so we were in Bournemouth [19–24 August 1963] and I was feeling sick. In fact, I was in bed sick and the doctor was giving me some tonic. And I just thought, 'Oh, I'll see if I can write a song.' So I wrote one and it was an awful song. It was called 'Don't Bother Me', [laughing] which I suppose is how I felt at the time. Then I forgot about songs again for a while. Then gradually… there was a period, I think it must have been about '66, when lots of things happened in my life…

BELOW **A still taken during filming for** *Let It Be*. **Director Michael Lindsay-Hogg recalled the day at Twickenham – 10 January 1969 – when 'we went up for lunch, George came up and said, "I'll see you round the clubs," and he left… They thought it was goodbye forever, and John said, "Let's call Eric Clapton and get him."' By the time of his interview with Johnny Moran on 11 March 1970, George was in a positive mood – 'maybe by the end of the year … we'll do [a] Beatle album.'**

JOHNNY: Yeah.

GEORGE: … which we won't talk about on the BBC! And after that, I suddenly realized that I could write songs and I sat down at home and I wrote lots of them, some of which I haven't recorded yet.

JOHNNY: Did you find it very hard at first to get ideas and think up songs?

GEORGE: The main difficulty was really because of Paul and John having written so many good songs that…

JOHNNY: You're automatically compared with them, I suppose.

GEORGE: Well, automatically… it was difficult for me to write some sort of crummy song and expect The Beatles to record it – already having such fine material. That was the most difficult thing. And also to do a song with The Beatles, it was always a matter of trying to do the song that you thought they'd understand quickest or the song you could get onto the tape the quickest – so not necessarily the song you thought was the best. The last two years has really been good experience for me, because I've been doing more producing. And in a way that's nice, because if I'm a part of the band recording, if I'm playing guitar, then you think so much about that one part. Whereas if you're producing, you tend to withdraw from that situation and see it as a whole. You can see the different parts that make up the record and so it's much nicer in a way to produce.

JOHNNY: Which was the first one that you produced?

GEORGE: The first thing I did on my own, I think, was a Jackie Lomax single and album. I did the album in Hollywood. With most of those sort of songs that you think, 'That's a catchy song,' it's because you've heard it so many times before and it's just a matter of different words or slightly different… I mean there's only certain notes in a scale and if you use a basic sort of chord pattern then it's very easy to get a similar sort of melody. And in a way, maybe that's what people like. I think people just tend to like those tunes they can just hear once or twice and go off to work whistling.

JOHNNY: How did you get to work with Billy Preston?

GEORGE: We met Billy years ago when he was over with Little Richard. At that time, he was just an organist in the church – gospel. And Little Richard – if you remember the history of Richard where he gave up rock 'n' roll when his aeroplane was on fire and all those sorts of things.

JOHNNY: He became a monk or something!

GEORGE: But every time he went home and, I think, must have spent all of his money, he decided to come back on tour again. So he brought Billy Preston. He was supposed to be coming to sing gospel songs. And they started the tour in England, sang one gospel song – there was all the rockers shouting 'Lucille', 'Rip It Up' and so Richard did that. It was the only way he could get by, really, because they didn't want to know about the gospel stuff. So Billy at that time was about 15, straight out of church and he never knew what hit him. You know, all these people jumping about, screaming. And we worked with him in Hamburg for a long time and then sort of lost touch with him until about two years ago I saw him in the *Ray Charles Show*. I thought, 'I'm sure I know that fella there.' I didn't catch the name when he was announced. But then I just realized it was Billy, but he was big Billy now, 'cause before he was just very tiny. He was probably only about four foot three! And he came into Apple. I don't know, just the sort of vibration of 'Where's Billy Preston?' went out and suddenly he walked into the office on the day we were doing 'Get Back' and we set up an electric piano for him and he joined in straight away and he's been there ever since. Really lovely fella – very, very good musician.

RECORD BUSINESS VETERAN Tony Hall had commented that George was '*the* record man' in The Beatles and, indeed, he energetically took on the task of producing a roster of artists for the Apple label. George's selection of who to work with reflected his personal interests and friendships. Jackie Lomax was a bass guitarist and vocalist who had played at the Cavern in Wallasey groups Dee & The Dynamites and The Undertakers. The Radha Krishna Temple had a UK hit in September 1969 with 'Hare Krishna Mantra'. At the time of the broadcast of *The Beatles Today*, their second single 'Govinda' entered the chart.

JOHNNY: It's obviously through your interest in Indian music that you became associated with The Radha Krishna Temple.

GEORGE: Yeah, also with the experience of meditation. I suppose all the listeners remember that… and having experienced that, I could understand really what this Krishna movement was about. And also it's a much more appealing path to God. That is to sing and dance and eat, which is really what their thing is all about – just to eat nice food and to dance a lot and to sing a lot. And they sing the name of God, which is 'Hare Krishna, Hare Krishna, Krishna, Krishna, Hare, Hare, Hare Rama, Hare Rama, Rama…' You know, you've all heard that one. Also, their new record now, I think is so much nicer.

JOHNNY: What's the meaning of the new one?

GEORGE: 'Govinda' is also a name of Krishna and Krishna is the name of God, because God is unlimited and so He can have as many names… you know, like Allah, all those names are all God. And it's the same God, all you listeners, it's not like… we haven't got a different one. It's the same one.

WHILE WORKING ON Billy Preston's first Apple album, George met soul singer Doris Troy. She had moved to the UK in 1965 and along with two other Americans, Madeleine Bell and Marsha Hunt, had established a reputation through many sessions as an accomplished backing singer. George signed her to Apple Records and assembled a stellar line-up of musicians for her solo album released in September 1970. He had been impressed by a record she made in 1963, which The Hollies successfully covered: 'The "soul classic" "Just One Look", somebody said in the paper, and I'll buy that. It was a very, very good record. At that time we were becoming really famous in Britain – The Beatles. But we were being influenced by the American things like The Miracles – the Tamla stuff that was going in those days – Marvin Gaye and Miracles and also that Doris Troy record really stuck in my mind.'

When the subject of The Beatles was raised, George was cheerful and positive.

GEORGE: As far as The Beatles go, we've got the *Let It Be* album. It's been held up really because the best way to do it was to put out the film… We're trying to put the film out in about 40 different cities throughout the world all at once, rather than put on a premiere in New York and then let the critics say, 'Oh, well we think it's this and we think it's that.'

JOHNNY: What's The Beatles' film gonna be about?

GEORGE: The Beatle film is just pure documentary of us slogging, working…

JOHNNY: On *Let It Be*?

GEORGE: Yeah, on the album and the hold-up of the album is because we want this film to go out simultaneously. Originally, we were rehearsing. We were rehearsing the songs that we were planning to do in some big TV spectacular. We had a vague idea of doing a TV show, but we didn't really know the formula of how to do it. Because we didn't really want to do… obviously we didn't want to do a *Magical Mystery Tour*, having already been on that… trip [laughs]. And we didn't want to do sort of the Tom Jones spectacular. And we're always trying to do something slightly different. We were down in Apple rehearsing and we decided to film it on 16 millimetre to maybe use as a documentary. The record happened to be the rehearsal of the record and the film happened to be, rather than a TV show, it happened to be a film of us making the record. Though it's very rough in a way, it's nice. You can see 'our warts'. You can hear us talking, you can hear us playing out of tune and you can hear us coughing and all those things. It's the complete opposite to the clinical approach that we've normally had – you know, studio recording: the balance, everything's just right and there's silence in between each track. This is really not like that. In fact, some people may be put off at hearing it, it sounds maybe… my attitude when we decided to use it as an album was that people may think we're not trying, you know, because it's really like a demo record. But, on the other hand, it's worth so much more than those other records, because you can actually get to know us a bit. It's a bit more human than the average studio recording. But there's nice songs; really good songs on it. 'Let It Be', of course, and 'Don't Let Me Down' – I think they're the two that you people will have heard of.

JOHNNY: Are there any more George Harrison 'Something's or…

GEORGE: No, there's no 'Something's. These songs that we did were done before 'Something'. There's one song which is a twelve-bar [blues], 'cause I've never written a twelve-bar before and that's called 'For You Blue' and it's just a very simple foot-tapping twelve-bar. The other one is a very strange song, which I wrote the night before it was in the film. You see, at this time we were at Twickenham and I wrote this song – it took five minutes just from an idea I had. I went in the studio and sang it to Ringo and they happened to film it. That film sequence was quite nice so they wanted to keep that sequence in the film, but I hadn't really recorded it in Apple with the rest of the songs so we had to go in the studio and re-record it. Also we put on 'Across The Universe', which was a song on the charity album that came out for [the World] Wildlife [Fund]. And that really got lost, it's been around for about three years now – 1967, I think we did that [recorded in February 1968].

BY THE TIME of the interview, the original title of *Get Back* for the delayed film and album had been changed to the name of the current single 'Let It Be'. However, George was talking about the LP as it existed on 11 March 1970. Glyn Johns, who had recorded the songs from January 1969, had compiled a second version of the album in January 1970 reflecting the documentary nature of the film. His mix included 'Don't Let Me Down' – the B-side of 'Get Back' – and the version of 'Across The Universe' included on the World Wildlife Fund LP *No One's Gonna Change Our World*, minus the sound effects of birds and children. Apple allowed Radio 1 to broadcast 'Dig It' in *The Beatles Today*, before its commercial release. The track was heard for over three minutes – much longer than was heard on the record released in May. Phil Spector began work on the project on 23 March 1970. On his version of the album, 'Across The Universe' and 'The Long And Winding Road' had orchestral and choral parts arranged by Richard Hewson.

In addition to revealing details about the group's *Let It Be*, George was careful to stress that there would be solo Beatle projects.

GEORGE: Ringo's completed a great album. I think it's called… what's it called, Ringo? [laughter]

JOHNNY: 'Ringo Sings Ringo'?

GEORGE: No. It was gonna be called 'Ringo Starrdust'… *Sentimental Journey*, it's called and it's all the songs that Elsie and 'Arry – that's his mother and father – and his uncles and aunties, they used to all sing and have parties all the time. So he sings all these old songs with the old arrangements. He doesn't do modern arrangements and it's really a nice album. Then John's doing a Plastic Ono album. I think he's gonna do that with Phil Spector. And I think Paul's doing an album, which is, I should imagine like… if you remember Eddie Cochran did a couple of tracks like 'C'Mon Everybody', where he played bass, drums, guitar and sang. So Paul's doing this sort of thing where he's gonna play all the instruments himself, which is nice. Because he couldn't possibly do that in The Beatles. If it was a Beatle album, automatically Paul

gets stuck on bass, Ringo gets on drums. So in a way, it's a great relief for us all to be able to work separately at the same time and so maybe, if I get a chance, I'd like to do an album as well, just to get rid of a lot of songs. So maybe I'll do…

JOHNNY: Just a George album?

GEORGE: A George album. So I'll try and get that together sometime during this summer. And I expect by that time we should be ready to do a new Beatle album. So I think really the next Beatle album should really be a very good one, because we would have had so much freedom that it will be really a pleasure to get back and to do a compromise. Because Beatles are compromising really, because you've got to allow that he's gonna do that and they're gonna do that… and in a way you lose something by being The Beatles, but what we gain, I think, is so much more than what we lose. It's definitely worth it.

JOHNNY: So as long as you all do your own individual things, you have no objection to being a Beatle indefinitely.

GEORGE: No, no, no. I think that's just part of our life, you know, is to be Beatles and I'll play that game as long as the people want us to.

JOHNNY: George, I know you must have spoken many, many times about *this* particular subject, but we still get letters saying, 'Are The Beatles splitting now? Is it the end of The Beatles?'

GEORGE: It's the end of The Beatles like maybe how people imagine The Beatles. The Beatles have never really been what people thought they were, anyway. So, in a way, it's the end of The Beatles like that, but it's not really the end of The Beatles. The Beatles are going to go on until they die, you know. I mean, we can't get away from being The Beatles. I can see this year us all doing a separate album each and by that time people will probably think there's no chance at all of there ever being Beatles again. And then suddenly, there'll be Beatles again. I think it's just a good thing for us all. It's like if you work together for a long time, it's nice to go away from each other for a while, 'cause then you can appreciate what it's like being together. I think during this year… it's really a good year – everything really feels very good, the vibrations are good. Lennon's had his hair cut! And everything's swinging, you know. So it's really gonna be good and maybe by the end of the year, everybody will be feeling so good that we'll do some other album – you know, Beatle album. And also we've just, on Saturday, done a single for Ringo. Well, I don't know whether he'll put it out or not. It's really his decision. We finish that tonight. It's a song Ringo wrote. ['It Don't Come Easy' was released in April 1971.]

JOHNNY: Will it be coming out as a Ringo single or as a Beatle single?

GEORGE: No, it should come out really as a Ringo single, because it's more interesting. You know, he wrote it and he sings it and there's only Ringo and myself playing on it – I mean, there's not just the two of us, there's other musicians but Paul and John aren't appearing on it. I certainly don't want to see the end of The Beatles and I know I'll do anything… whatever Paul, John, Ringo would like to do, I'll do it.

ON 10 APRIL 1970, eleven days after *The Beatles Today* was broadcast, advance copies of Paul's solo album *McCartney* were distributed with a 'self-interview' press release. The only Beatle who had not wanted to quit the group, now seemed to be doing just that.

Q: Are you planning a new album or single with The Beatles?

A: No.

Q: Is your break with The Beatles temporary or permanent, due to personal differences or musical ones?

A: Personal differences, business differences, musical differences, but most of all because I have a better time with my family. Temporary or permanent? I don't know.

AS FAR AS the media knew, after months of speculation, Paul's statement marked the end of The Beatles. The group's split became headline news around the world. On BBC radio, a report by Chris Drake was introduced with the words 'Now it seems The Beatles' story is almost over.' Drake replayed George's recent optimistic statements about the group's future and revisited his interview recorded with Paul in Scotland – prefacing it with the thought that 'the split will obviously suit Paul, because he's done his best to keep away from the public for several months now.'

PAUL: I haven't enjoyed doing interviews and getting a lot of publicity lately. I've preferred to sit more in the background and

ABOVE **A crowd gathered outside Apple's HQ in Savile Row, London on the day Paul announced he had quit The Beatles – 10 April 1970. George gave an interview at Apple on that day for the BBC TV programme *Fact or Fantasy*. He offered the thought that 'what the physical world is about – is change.'**

be more with the family [rather] than go to clubs and be seen everywhere. Like I used to do an interview a week, almost, for a newspaper or something; just to keep my name in the headlines – because, I don't know, you go through a phase of wanting to be up there in the limelight. Well, I'm going through a phase now of where I don't want to be in the limelight.

LISTENING AGAIN TO the group's BBC interviews from 1969 and early 1970, Paul's announcement in April seems not to have been anticipated by the other Beatles. Even during the most tense times – particularly those in January and May 1969 – all four had been gracious and positive about each other in their radio interviews. There had been bitter disagreements concerning Allen Klein's management of Apple's affairs, yet the music continued. Perhaps the divide between Paul and the others became unbridgeable following a decision by George, John and Klein to give Phil Spector the task of 're-producing' *Let It Be*. Paul was not happy about the *auteur* producer's free rein to salvage an album from the 16-month-old tapes. It might well have been the insensitive way that 'The Long And Winding Road' was tampered with that caused him to lose patience. Paul's press release was issued ten days after the song, without his knowledge, was overdubbed with a lush arrangement for orchestra and celestial choir. He was also upset by an appeal to delay the release of his first solo album *McCartney* until after *Let It Be* had been issued, a request that he refused. Whatever the reasons, as John sang in 'God' – included on *John Lennon/Plastic Ono Band* – the dream was over. More prosaically, John told David Wigg in a Radio 1 interview broadcast in November 1971:

'It's just natural. It's not a great disaster. People keep talking about it as if it's the end of the Earth. It's only a rock group that split up. It's nothing important. You have all the old records there if you want to reminisce. It's like a rugby team. Sometimes you have to get married and leave the boys on a Saturday night… and that's how it is.'

1970 RADIO AND TV APPEARANCES

[radio icon] Radio programme titles
[TV icon] TV titles

[TV icon] TOP OF THE POPS
Br: 12 Feb 1970 – 7.15–8.00pm – BBC 1
Rec: 11 Feb 1970
BBC Television Centre, London
'Instant Karma!' was performed by John with The Plastic Ono Band miming. He sang a live vocal to the record's backing track. One take was broadcast on 12 February and repeated on 5 March 1970. The other version was featured in an episode of *Top of the Pops* broadcast on 19 February 1970. Film of the first broadcast has survived.

[radio icon] SCENE AND HEARD
Br: 15 Feb 1970 – 3.00–4.00pm – Radio 1
Rec: 6 Feb 1970
David Wigg talked to John and Yoko on the day 'Instant Karma!' was released.

[radio icon] MIDDAY SPIN
Br: 21 Feb 1970 – 12.00–1.00pm – Radio 1
John talked to DJ Emperor Rosko about 'Instant Karma!' and answered questions sent in by listeners.

[radio icon] SCENE AND HEARD
Br: 15 March 1970 – 3.00–4.00pm – Radio 1
Rec: 11 March 1970
Studio H25, BBC, Aeolian Hall, New Bond Street, London
Short extracts were included from an interview with George conducted by the programme's presenter Johnny Moran. Their conversation was featured in a 44-minute special two weeks later.

[radio icon] SCENE AND HEARD
Br: 29 March 1970 – 3.00–4.00pm – Radio 1
Rec: 25 March 1970
Ringo was interviewed by David Wigg.

[radio icon] SCENE AND HEARD
Br: 5 April 1970 – 3.00–4.00pm – Radio 1
Rec: 25 March 1970
The programme included a second extract from Ringo's interview with David Wigg.

[radio icon] THE BEATLES TODAY
Br: 30 March 1970 (Easter Monday) 4.31–5.15pm – Radio 1
Rec: 11 March 1970
Studio H25, BBC, Aeolian Hall, New Bond Street, London
George talked about his songwriting, his production of Apple Records' artists and the *Let It Be* film and album.

[radio icon] OPEN HOUSE
Br: 31 March 1970 – 9.00-9.55am – Radio 2
Live
Pete Murray talked to Ringo about his album *Sentimental Journey*, which had been released four days earlier.

[radio icon] FACT OR FANTASY
Br: 26 April 1970 – 6.15–6.50pm – BBC 1
(Repeated 27 April – 12.50–1.25pm)
Rec: 10 April 1970
Apple, Savile Row, London
George was interviewed in his office at Apple for an edition of the series entitled 'Prayer And Meditation'. The recording was made on the day the news broke of The Beatles' split.
'People will say I'm the Beatle who changed the most, but really that's what I see life is about. The point is unless you're God-conscious then you have to change, because it's a waste of time. Everybody is so limited and so really useless when you think about the limitations on yourself. And the whole thing is to change; try and make everything better and better. And that's what the physical world is about – is change.'

FROM US TO YOU: THE SONGS

THE BEATLES' MUSIC has continued to transcend the time when it was created. The most popular hits – 'Hey Jude', 'Yesterday', 'Something' – have been absorbed, as if by osmosis, into the collective consciousness of generation after generation. Usually, it is the second half of The Beatles' career that first attracts new listeners, who recognize connections to both the sound and the image of current artists. For example, the faces on the cover of *Let It Be* still resemble the look of contemporary rock bands. The brilliant innovations made by The Beatles in their latter years are, quite rightly, regarded as pioneering achievements that continue to influence musicians. But if you did not experience the group's musical progression as it happened, listening to The Beatles without that chronological context can distort an historical view of their career. The picture on *With The Beatles* may not seem so now, but in 1963 it was extremely radical. So was the album's music: energetic, visceral and cutting edge. Indeed, the initial years of The Beatles' success, 1963 and 1964, may well be their most revolutionary. There was a breathtaking escalation in the quality of the self-composed songs during that time. Their performances – recorded before they became as John Lennon put it 'the clever Beatles' – made the group unassailable.

When The Beatles conquered all before them, the world reeled from the shock of the new. In fact, the group had assimilated 'underground' music and introduced it to the pop mainstream. Of course, it was the remarkable talent and chemistry within The Beatles that led to their unparalleled success when they did that. Twenty-four cover versions on their discs released up to 1965 give clues to the seminal influences shaping the evolution of their music. During the same period, the group chose an additional 36 cover songs to play on radio shows. In all, there were 275 BBC radio performances of 88 different songs between 1962 and 1965. From a musical perspective, this rich legacy of songs is the most important part of the BBC's Beatles archive.

The rapid rise in popularity of rock 'n' roll in America during 1955 and 1956 was wonderfully exciting for America's teenagers. But there had been something in the air before Elvis broke through in 1956. The music he made was an amalgam of black rhythm and blues and white country music. Although Elvis was a white guy from the segregated South, he was enthralled by black gospel and R&B music. The radio dial could not be segregated. However, most teenagers in Britain had no knowledge of the mix of music that led to the birth of rock 'n' roll. They had grown up with pleasant but lightweight songs by well-groomed singers with 'proper' voices. After the first flush of excitement roused by Bill Haley and His Comets, rock 'n' roll really took hold in the UK with the arrival of Elvis's 'Heartbreak Hotel'. In contrast to the songs in the charts and on the BBC, 'Heartbreak Hotel' seemed to have landed from another planet. It was soon joined on the chart by 'Be-Bop-A-Lula' by Gene Vincent and His Blue Caps. Someone even screamed on that record. The B-side, 'Woman Love', was not played on the BBC, because Gene's panting was deemed too lascivious. This kind of thing was not heard on other records in the Top 20 by Perry Como, Ronnie Hilton, David Whitfield and Michael Holiday.

With a handful of honourable exceptions, it was impossible to make an authentic rock 'n' roll record in the UK. From 1956 onwards, British teenagers looked to America to satisfy their demand for more of the excitement they craved. The first wave of rockers stormed the country on discs. Some did make the charts, but these mysterious artists were rarely heard or seen on the BBC. When seeking the forbidden fruit of rock 'n' roll, there were a number of sources for it: Radio Luxembourg, jukeboxes, fairgrounds and record shops.

Radio Luxembourg had beamed programmes to Britain from its transmitters in the small European country since the 1930s. Offering a welcome alternative to the BBC, its provision of popular entertainment found a large audience in the UK. Travelling hundreds of miles, the medium wave (AM) signal was subject to irritating interference. Its 208-metre frequency faded in and out – always, it seemed, during your favourite record. Despite this, in 1955 the night-time English broadcasts of Radio Luxembourg were attracting close to nine million listeners. The station was unashamedly commercial. During the late 1950s, record-company-sponsored shows started to fill its schedule. These provided a lifeline to listeners eager to uncover the latest American records. The shows were short – usually fifteen minutes – so records were not played in full. The Decca programmes presented by Pete Murray, Jack Jackson and Tony Hall were most significant. The Head of Promotions at Decca, Tony Hall, introduced US hits on his Friday night show *America's Hot Ten*. It was essential listening. He selected records from the US chart that were distributed by the Decca group in the UK. Many were issued on its London American label. Others were on Coral, Brunswick, RCA and Warner Brothers. It is no coincidence that of the 56 cover versions

The Beatles performed for BBC radio, an impressive 31 of the songs were first released in the UK on London American. Another nine were on other labels within the Decca stable.

Living in Liverpool, where ships arrived from America, might have helped The Beatles detect the discs they desired. Bob Wooler, the man who played the records at the Cavern Club, always emphasized that this was not the usual means of discovery. 'The R&B records were available on Pye International and London American; they weren't imported here. It's rather fanciful to say we played very rare records that only we had at the Cavern. We didn't really. We played a lot of pop material of the time, interspersed with lesser-known records, but which were actually available in this country.'

Once you knew who was great – The Coasters, Larry Williams, Johnny Burnette's Rock 'n' Roll Trio, The Shirelles, The Miracles – then a search began to find their records. Fortunately, this era was a golden age for record shops. Hundreds of family-run concerns, like Brian Epstein's NEMS in Liverpool, would take pride in stocking at least one copy of everything released. Consequently, many Liverpool musicians spent hours in the listening booths at NEMS while records were played to them. Occasionally, they might even buy one. It was also usual for a group of friends to pool their limited resources by not duplicating their purchases: 'If you buy the new Jerry Lee Lewis, I'll buy The Everly Brothers'. Listening to records was an experience often shared in each other's homes. As Paul confessed in 1990, these were also desperate times: 'That's what going to parties was about, I'm sad to admit. There would be these lovely people who'd bring their whole record collection to a party…

bad move! Too tempting leaving that kind of stuff around with the likes of us!'

Meanwhile, the jukebox in a local coffee bar might have an esoteric selection picked to click with a cool crowd. Then you could really experience that bass sound on 'A Shot Of Rhythm And Blues' by Arthur Alexander. Paul recorded Little Richard's 'Shake A Hand' in 1999. When interviewed by Patrick Humphries, he remembered that 'There was one bar [in Hamburg] we used to go to that had a pool table and a great jukebox. And that was the only place I heard "Shake A Hand". It made such an impression on me that every time we went there, I put it on. I never had the record.'

Like so many of their contemporaries, The Beatles heard records blasted from the rides at fairgrounds. As you were whirled at breakneck speed on the waltzer or bumped about in dodgem cars, loud rock 'n' roll was the perfect soundtrack.

The large number of Beatles cover versions performed for BBC radio divide into two categories. The first of these includes songs by artists they had loved during the late 1950s, when rock was young. With nine of his songs performed by the group at the BBC, Chuck Berry is the most covered of their heroes. With the exception of George singing 'Roll Over Beethoven', Berry's witty rockers were the property of John. In an interview with Dennis Elsas on WNEW New York in 1974, he revealed how much Chuck Berry meant to him: 'I met him a few times over the years, but I still had that feeling of when I was 16. Those were the records I listened to at what we called milk-bars in England, on the jukebox. I could never quite see him as a human, because there was one of my idols actually talking to me!'

In the summer of 1963, six covers of Carl Perkins' songs were heard for the first time during the radio series *Pop Go The Beatles*. Three – 'Everybody's Trying To Be My Baby', 'Honey Don't' and 'Matchbox' – made it onto record the following year, but 'Glad All Over', 'Lend Me Your Comb' and 'Sure To Fall' remained unique to the BBC. Each Beatle loved Carl's rockabilly material and took a lead vocal on at least one of these six tracks. His biggest hit, 'Blue Suede Shoes', was the first to make the American pop, R&B and country charts. It reached the Top Two on all three listings in 1956, but injuries sustained in a car crash soon afterwards prevented Carl capitalizing on the record's success. His career lost momentum and, by 1963, he was a forgotten man in the States.

But The Beatles, like thousands of British rock fans, had longer memories and loyally mentioned that he was an important influence. Carl Perkins gratefully acknowledged this in 1994, 'I [later] said to them, "What have I ever done that caused you to say that I had anything to do with the great music you write?" They said, "We noticed on your first records that you wrote your songs, you played your own music and you sang your songs… and that's what we wanted to do."' Carl was present when The Beatles recorded 'Matchbox' at Abbey Road. 'They struck right into it and I knew then they'd been listening!' At a party in his honour the night before, John asked Carl to play his version of 'Right String Baby, But The Wrong Yo Yo' in order to determine how the opening guitar lick was played. 'I kicked it off and John said, "See George, I told you, you were wrong!"' It was no coincidence that when three of The Beatles adopted temporary stage-names in 1960, George became Carl Harrison.

The group also performed songs by the three most celebrated figures of the rock 'n' roll era: Elvis Presley, Little Richard and Buddy Holly. An Elvis number did not feature on any of their records, but, at the BBC, they covered four songs from Presley's discs: 'I Got A Woman', 'I'm Gonna Sit Right Down And Cry (Over You)', 'That's All Right (Mama)' and 'I Forgot To Remember To Forget'. The impact of Elvis changed the lives of The Beatles in 1956. Yet when the records of Little Richard eventually exploded in Britain, they seemed even wilder. The Beatles covered four songs by Little Richard at the BBC. Paul's throat-tearing imitation of Richard's untamed whoops and hollers may even have been nurtured a little by the man himself. He had become friendly with the group when they were his support act in 1962.

The Beatles loved the music of Buddy Holly and The Crickets. Back in 1958, the Quarry Men – the skiffle prototype of The Beatles – had made a private recording of The Crickets' British number one 'That'll Be The Day'. In a BBC session on 16 July 1963, John and Paul harmonized on 'Words Of Love' and George took the lead on 'Crying, Waiting, Hoping'. Responding to a questionnaire sent to him by writer Jim Dawson in 1974, John emphasized Buddy Holly's historical importance: 'He was a great and innovative musician. He was a "MASTER". His influence continues. I often wonder what his music would be like now, had he lived…'

The Beatles did not rely solely upon the rock 'n' roll era for their repertoire. The other category of covers consists of contemporary songs. At the time of their BBC broadcasts, they were seeking out the latest rhythm and blues records from the States. Although singles by Arthur Alexander, the Marvelettes and The Miracles did not make the British charts, they were a key influence on The Beatles. These records – and those by The Shirelles, who did score some UK hits – had sophisticated vocal, string and horn parts. Rearranging them for a four-piece line-up helped to create the Beatle sound just as much as the earlier singles by Elvis, Buddy and Little Richard. Current R&B records were not easy to hear in Britain. Once again, Radio Luxembourg provided an outlet. From late 1962 to 1963, American records issued on the Tamla and Motown labels were distributed in the UK by Oriole. Its *Big O Show* on Luxembourg featured the latest by Mary Wells, The Contours, The Miracles, Marvin Gaye, Martha & The Vandellas and Little Stevie Wonder. None was a hit at the time. The group's love of the joyous records from Detroit was demonstrated when they included three Motown songs on *With The Beatles*.

The Beatles' devotion to black music proved crucial to its eventual wider acceptance. In 1971, Craig McGregor wrote an article in the *New York Times* called 'The Beatles Betrayal'. His accusation that the group had made money from black American music without any acknowledgement of the originators provoked a passionate reply from John. 'We didn't sing our own songs in the early days – they weren't good enough. The one thing we <u>always did</u> was to <u>make it known</u> that these were <u>black originals</u>, we <u>loved</u> the music and wanted to spread it in <u>any way we could</u> … Many kids were turned on to black music by us. It wasn't a rip-off. It was a love-in.'

★ Denotes that the song was not on any of The Beatles' records released on the Parlophone and Apple labels between October 1962 and April 1970.

♦ indicates a BBC performance released on *The Beatles Live At The BBC* (1994), the *Baby It's You* EP and *Anthology 1* (both 1995).

Key:
SONG TITLE
Lead singer
[Composer]
BBC programme – date of broadcast

ACT NATURALLY
Ringo
[Russell/Morrison]
TV:
The Beatles at Shea Stadium – 1 March 1966
'Act Naturally' was the last track completed for *Help!*, released in August 1965. A fan of country and western music, Ringo chose this appropriate country number one for his featured vocal on the album. 'Act Naturally' was recorded by Buck Owens, whose records were distinguished by the crisp electric guitar work of Don Rich – just the sort of player George admired. The song was the first of 21 country number ones by Buck Owens. His penultimate hit, in 1989, was a duet with Ringo on 'Act Naturally'.

ALL MY LOVING
Paul
[Lennon-McCartney]
RADIO:
Saturday Club – 21 December 1963
From Us To You – 26 December 1963
Saturday Club – 15 February 1964
From Us To You – 30 March 1964 ♦
TV:
It's The Beatles – 7 December 1963
One of the most popular tracks from the second UK album, *With The Beatles*, released in November 1963, 'All My Loving' became the title track of the group's fourth EP in February 1964. It was the opening song in their live debut on American television during *The Ed Sullivan Show*; a performance available on *Anthology 1*. The Beatles' version has a country feel, especially evident in George's concise solo. When given a jazz interpretation or a mellow arrangement for a solo singer, the song was appreciated by listeners older than The Beatles' fans. In the August 1966 BBC radio show *The Lennon and McCartney Songbook*, John commented that English balladeer Matt Monro 'did it how people imagined it should be done'. Paul agreed: 'It changed a few people's minds about us… everyone said, "Oh, that's a nice song, isn't it?" whereas beforehand they thought it was just a gay little ditty… and it still is!'

ALL YOU NEED IS LOVE
John
[Lennon-McCartney]
TV:
Our World – 25 June 1967
Written specifically for the global television programme *Our World*, the chorus was designed to be as simple and effective as possible. After all, the worldwide audience had to understand the message: 'All You Need Is Love'. The sound transmitted to 350 million people from Studio One in Abbey Road was a mix of a rhythm track recorded earlier and the live elements: vocals, bass guitar, lead guitar, drums and a thirteen-piece orchestra. When the broadcast was over, John re-recorded parts of his lead vocal. A single of 'All You Need Is Love' was released in the UK within two weeks of the historic broadcast. It was a British and American number one during the summer of 1967.

AND I LOVE HER
Paul
[Lennon-McCartney]
RADIO:
Top Gear – 16 July 1964
For this BBC performance, George played his solo on electric guitar rather than the nylon acoustic used for the record. Featured in *A Hard Day's Night* and released on the film soundtrack LP in July 1964, 'And I Love Her' was soon the subject of a variety of cover versions that dispensed with a its simple beat-group arrangement. R&B star Esther Phillips had an American hit with 'And I Love Him' in 1965. The same year jazz singer Shirley Horn also recorded the song and Jack Jones was accompanied by the Nelson Riddle Orchestra for an interpretation on his album *There's Love And There's Love And There's Love*. Beatles favourites Smokey Robinson & The Miracles made a sensitive version for their 1970 LP *What Love Has… Joined Together*.

ANNA (GO TO HIM)
John
[Alexander]
RADIO:
Pop Go The Beatles – 25 June 1963
Pop Go The Beatles – 27 August 1963
Written and recorded by country-soul singer Arthur Alexander, 'Anna' was an American Top Ten R&B hit at the end of 1962. The song was autobiographical – Arthur's wife was called Ann. Following the single's UK release in December 1962, The Beatles taped the song a couple of months later for their debut album, *Please Please Me*. In an interview with Mark Lewisohn in 1987, Paul stated: 'If The Beatles ever wanted a sound it was R&B. That's what we used to listen to and what we wanted to be like: black. That was basically it. Arthur Alexander.'

ASK ME WHY
John
[Lennon-McCartney]
RADIO:
Here We Go – 15 June 1962 (with Pete Best)
Here We Go – 25 January 1963
The Talent Spot – 29 January 1963
Pop Go The Beatles – 24 September 1963
First issued as the B-side of 'Please Please Me' in January 1963, 'Ask Me Why' can also be heard on the amateur recording made in the Star-Club, Hamburg in December 1962. This low-quality audio eventually escaped on record in May 1977 and has made further breakouts since then. 'Ask Me Why' became the first ever Lennon-McCartney song to be broadcast when it was featured during *Here We Go* in June 1962.

BABY IT'S YOU
John
[David-Bacharach-Williams]
RADIO:
Side by Side – 22 April 1963
Pop Go The Beatles – 11 June 1963 ♦
Great admirers of the American girl-groups of the early 1960s, The Beatles covered this American Top Ten hit by The Shirelles for their first album, *Please Please Me*. Each BBC performance has an ending rather than the familiar fade-out heard on the LP. In 1969, the song returned to the US chart in a version by a group called Smith. The Beatles' second BBC recording of 'Baby It's You' was the lead track on an EP issued in March 1995. It reached number seven in the UK and number 67 in the States.

BABY'S IN BLACK
John
[Lennon-McCartney]
TV:
The Beatles at Shea Stadium – 1 March 1966 'Baby's In Black' was the first song recorded for *Beatles For Sale*. In the UK, their policy was not to release a single from an album after the LP had been released. Not so in America where the *Beatles For Sale* side two opener 'Eight Days A Week' reached number one in 1965. However, the album's Lennon-McCartney songs chosen for concerts were 'I'm A Loser' and 'Baby's In Black'. The latter stayed in their stage act from 1964 to the final concert in 1966.

BEAUTIFUL DREAMER ★
Paul
[Foster-Goffin-Keller]
RADIO:
Saturday Club – 26 January 1963
The song was written in the mid-19th century by American writer Stephen Foster. Recordings by crooners Bing Crosby and Al Jolson ensured 'Beautiful Dreamer' remained a popular standard in the next century. In the late 1950s, there was a trend for reviving 'oldies' by adding a faster rhythm. Little Richard had stomped through 'Baby Face' and 'By The Light Of The Silvery Moon', 'Blueberry Hill' was given a New Orleans makeover by Fats Domino and 'You Must Have Been A Beautiful Baby' was rocked by Bobby Darin. Tony Orlando's 'Beautiful Dreamer', updated by songwriters Gerry Goffin and Jack Keller, was released in the UK at the end of 1962. A few weeks later The Beatles' cover of his single, including all the changes to the original lyric and its added 'hully-gully' beat, was recorded for *Saturday*

Club. Later in 1963, Liverpool friends Rory Storm and the Hurricanes, the Searchers and Billy J Kramer plus Parlophone label-mates Cliff Bennett & The Rebel Rousers all used the Tony Orlando single as the blueprint for their versions of 'Beautiful Dreamer'.

BESAME MUCHO ★
Paul
[Velazquez-Skylar]
RADIO:
Here We Go – 15 June 1962 (with Pete Best)
The song's popularity during the Second World War came from recordings by Leslie 'Hutch' Hutchinson, Vera Lynn, Carroll Gibbons' Savoy Hotel Orpheans and Joe Loss. The Beatles' decision to cover it was prompted by a quirky version by one of their favourite American R&B groups, The Coasters. Their take on the song was spread over two sides of a single released in 1960. As Paul recalled in 1987, 'I looked at the recording scene and realized that a few people were taking offbeat songs, putting them in their acts and modernizing them a bit.' With Pete Best playing drums, The Beatles performed 'Besame Mucho' at their Decca audition on 1 January 1962 and also at their first EMI session six months later. The Abbey Road recording did not emerge until the release of *Anthology 1* in 1995. The group are seen having fun with it on 29 January 1969 in their movie *Let It Be*.

BOYS
Ringo
[Dixon-Farrell]
RADIO:
Side by Side – 13 May 1963
Saturday Club – 25 May 1963
Side by Side – 24 June 1963
Pop Go The Beatles – 25 June 1963 ♦
Pop Go The Beatles – 17 September 1963
From Us To You – 26 December 1963
From Us To You – 3 August 1964
TV:
It's The Beatles – 7 December 1963
The Shirelles' original was the flip-side of the biggest of their three British hits – 'Will You Love Me Tomorrow', which reached number four in 1961. It topped the American charts – one of 22 pop hits scored by The Shirelles in the States. Included on The Beatles' first album, the large number of BBC performances of 'Boys' reflects its status as one of the few vocal showcases for Ringo.

CAN'T BUY ME LOVE
Paul
[Lennon-McCartney]
RADIO:
From Us To You – 30 March 1964 ♦
Saturday Club – 4 April 1964
From Us To You – 18 May 1964
TV:
Top of the Pops – 25 March 1964 (mimed)
Released as a single in March 1964, 'Can't Buy Me Love' featured in the movie *A Hard Day's Night* and on the accompanying album. There is a live version recorded on 30 August 1965 at the Hollywood Bowl and also an early EMI take on *Anthology 1*. When the acclaimed jazz singer Ella Fitzgerald selected the song, the group gained recognition as something other than a mere teen phenomenon. 'I love it,' said Paul of her swinging seal of approval. 'She was the first [to do a Lennon-McCartney song] of the sort of great, big, all-time "Who do you like? Oh, Ella!" singers.' In the same interview, for *The Lennon and McCartney Songbook*, John reflected: 'That was a little click of time. We thought, "Oh, one of those has done one, have they?"' The Beatles' producer George Martin supervised Ella's recording at EMI Studios, Abbey Road in April 1964. It was released four months later on her album *Hello, Dolly!*

CAROL ★
John
[Berry]
RADIO:
Pop Go The Beatles – 16 July 1963 ♦
Chuck Berry's thirteenth Chess single was a Top 20 US hit following its release in August 1958. His ninth single in the UK, it failed to chart. However, his songs were being performed by many of the fledgling British groups who eventually secured success from 1963 onwards. For example, The Rolling Stones included 'Carol' on their first album, released in June 1964. It is interesting to compare the Stones' rougher take with the lighter touch of The Beatles' BBC performance. 'If you tried to give rock 'n' roll another name, you might call it Chuck Berry,' John suggested.

CHAINS
George
[Goffin-King]
RADIO:
Here We Go – 25 January 1963
Side by Side – 13 May 1963
Pop Go The Beatles – 25 June 1963
Pop Go The Beatles – 17 September 1963

The original by The Cookies – female backing singers on many other Gerry Goffin and Carole King hits on the Dimension label – was climbing the US charts when The Beatles first tried 'Chains' in a studio. The group's performance was released on *Please Please Me* in March 1963 and on the EP *The Beatles (No.1)* six months later.

CHRIMBLE MUDDLEY ★
John
[Lennon-McCartney; Marks; Eddy-Hazlewood]
RADIO:
Saturday Club – 21 December 1963
A half-minute of Christmas fun, in which John (double-tracked) sang the titles or extracts of lyrics from the five Beatles hits so far ('Love Me Do', 'Please Please Me', 'From Me To You', 'She Loves You' and 'I Want To Hold Your Hand') … and 'Rudolph The Red-Nosed Reindeer'. Presenter Brian Matthew described it as a 'muddley… I'm sorry… medley'. The linking riff played on guitar and bass was borrowed from Duane Eddy's 'Shazam!'.

CLARABELLA ★
Paul
[Pingatore]
RADIO:
Pop Go The Beatles – 16 July 1963 ♦
In The Beatles' set list since 1960, this obscure favourite of Paul's was originally recorded by The Jodimars – **Jo**ey Di'Ambrosia, **Di**ck Richards and **Mars**hall Lytle. They were refugees from Bill Haley's Comets, having defected over a dispute concerning the distribution of money. 'Clarabella' was the B-side of The Jodimars' fifth single, 'Midnight', released in the UK on Capitol in November 1956.

CRYING, WAITING, HOPING ★
George
[Holly]
RADIO:
Pop Go The Beatles – 6 August 1963 ♦

The song was recorded by Buddy Holly in his New York apartment less than two months before he died in a plane crash on 3 February 1959. His rudimentary demo was overdubbed in a session supervised by Jack Hansen for release as the B-side of 'Peggy Sue Got Married' in September. 'Crying, Waiting, Hoping' also opened side two of the 1960 album *The Buddy Holly Story Vol. II*. A second version with accompaniment by The Fireballs was created in 1963

by Buddy's former producer Norman Petty. The Beatles played 'Crying, Waiting, Hoping' at their audition for Decca Records on 1 January 1962. When The Beatles recorded the song at the BBC, Buddy Holly was in the UK singles list with 'Bo Diddley' and also on the album chart with *Reminiscing*. In the States, Buddy never had another hit single after 1959.

DEVIL IN HER HEART
George
[Drapkin]
RADIO:
Pop Go The Beatles – 20 August 1963 ♦
Pop Go The Beatles – 24 September 1963
The first BBC performance of this song was released on the *Baby It's You* EP in 1995. It was one of eighteen songs The Beatles recorded during a marathon session on 16 July 1963. Two days later, the group taped it for their second album, *With The Beatles*. 'Devil In His Heart' was the B-side of 'Bad Boy' – the only record made by four Detroit school girls called The Donays. Their American single on Brent was picked up by the British label Oriole for release in September 1962 – the same month the company began distributing Tamla and Motown records in the UK. Perhaps it was that connection which had led George to discover this obscure song.

DIZZY MISS LIZZY
John
[Williams]
RADIO:
The Beatles Invite You to Take a Ticket To Ride – 7 June 1965 ♦
TV:
The Beatles at Shea Stadium – 1 March 1966
A minor US hit on Specialty Records, the label that issued Little Richard's classics, 'Dizzy Miss Lizzy' was one of three Larry Williams rockers found on Beatles records. The other two were 'Slow Down' – featured on their *Long Tall Sally* EP – and 'Bad Boy' released in the UK on *A Collection Of Beatles Oldies* eighteen months after its inclusion on the American album *Beatles VI*. 'Dizzy Miss Lizzy' closed side two of the *Help!* album.

DON'T EVER CHANGE ★
George
[Goffin-King]
RADIO:
Pop Go The Beatles – 27 August 1963 ♦
The Crickets enjoyed a UK Top Five hit in the

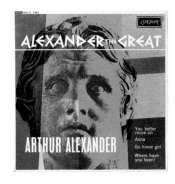

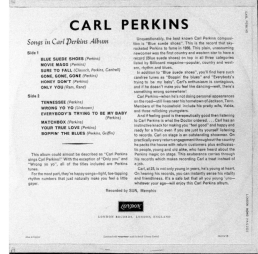

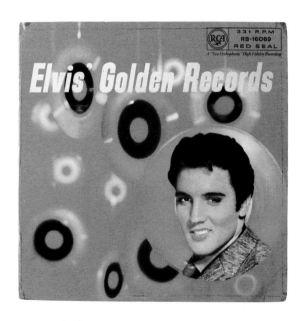
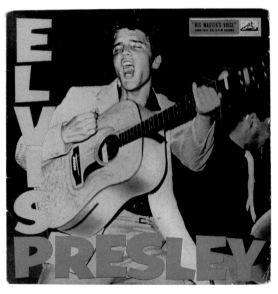

summer of 1962 with this song written by Gerry Goffin and Carole King. Having backed Buddy Holly on most of his hits, The Crickets continued making records after his death in February 1959. They had no chart success in the States during the 1960s, but enjoyed a string of British hits until 1964.

DO YOU WANT TO KNOW A SECRET

George
[Lennon-McCartney]
RADIO:
Here We Go – 12 March 1963
On the Scene – 28 March 1963
Side by Side – 22 April 1963
Saturday Club – 25 May 1963
Pop Go The Beatles – 4 June 1963
Pop Go The Beatles – 30 July 1963
The first BBC performance of 'Do You Want To Know A Secret' was heard ten days before its release on the *Please Please Me* album. Producer George Martin recorded the song again for a Parlophone single by another Brian Epstein act – Billy J Kramer with The Dakotas. Their version of 'Do You Want To Know A Secret' peaked at number two in June 1963 – stuck behind The Beatles' second chart topper, 'From Me To You'.

DREAM BABY (HOW LONG MUST I DREAM) ★

Paul
[Walker]
RADIO:
Teenagers Turn – Here We Go – 8 March 1962 (with Pete Best)
Roy Orbison's record of Cindy Walker's 'Dream Baby' had just entered the UK Top 30 when the group performed it for their radio debut. A little over a year later, The Beatles and 'The Big O' appeared together on a 21-date tour of Britain. In 1988, Roy (as Lefty) played with George (as Nelson) in the Traveling Wilburys.

EVERYBODY'S TRYING TO BE MY BABY

George
[Perkins]
RADIO:
Pop Go The Beatles – 4 June 1963
Saturday Club – 4 April 1964
Top Gear – 26 November 1964
Saturday Club – 26 December 1964 ♦
The Beatles Invite You to Take a Ticket To Ride –

7 June 1965
Featured on the 1959 UK LP on the London label called *Dance Album Of Carl Perkins*, the group had been performing 'Everybody's Trying To Be My Baby' for at least three years before its inclusion on *Beatles For Sale* in December 1964. They recorded the first BBC performance seventeen months before it was captured in one take at Abbey Road. *Anthology 2* features a live recording from their first groundbreaking – and ear-piercing – 1965 concert at Shea Stadium in New York, but it was not seen in the TV film of the event.

FROM ME TO YOU

John & Paul
[Lennon-McCartney]
RADIO:
Easy Beat – 7 April 1963
Swinging Sound '63 – 18 April 1963
Side by Side – 22 April 1963
Side by Side – 13 May 1963
Saturday Club – 25 May 1963
Steppin' Out – 3 June 1963
Pop Go The Beatles – 4 June 1963
Pop Go The Beatles – 18 June 1963
Easy Beat – 23 June 1963
Side by Side – 24 June 1963
Saturday Club – 29 June 1963
The Beat Show – 4 July 1963
Pop Go The Beatles – 3 September 1963
Pop Go The Beatles – 17 September 1963
Easy Beat – 20 October 1963
Royal Variety Performance – 10 November 1963
TV:
The 625 Show – 16 April 1963
Pops and Lenny – 16 May 1963
It's The Beatles – 7 December 1963
Played in sixteen radio shows and three TV programmes, 'From Me To You' is The Beatles' most frequently performed song at the BBC. Its last broadcast was during the television concert called *It's The Beatles* – at the end, the group played an instrumental version of 'From Me To You' while the credits rolled on screen. When they were off the air, they slipped in a snatch of 'The Harry Lime Theme'.
Number one in the UK throughout May and June 1963, the song was the first by Lennon-McCartney to crack the US charts when Del Shannon covered it. *Cashbox* described his single as 'an infectious thump-a-twist version', but it could only dent the lower end of the magazine's Top 100 in July. Del Shannon had topped the bill of the live radio concert *Swinging Sound '63*. He was impressed by the developing Beatles phenomenon when,

with screams echoing in his ears, he followed the group onto the stage of the Royal Albert Hall.

FROM US TO YOU ★

John & Paul
(Two versions: Opening theme and Closing theme with an extended instrumental)
[Lennon-McCartney]
RADIO:
From Us To You – 26 December 1963
From Us To You – 30 March 1964 ♦
From Us To You – 18 May 1964
From Us To You – 3 August 1964
'From Us To You' was used as the theme tune of four programmes broadcast on public holidays. The adaptation of their third single was heard on Boxing Day 1963 and in three shows broadcast on Easter, Whitsun and August bank holiday Mondays in 1964. In this lyrical variation, the title was closer to the phrase that had inspired John and Paul to write 'From Me To You': the name of the *New Musical Express* letters page 'From You To Us'.

GLAD ALL OVER ★

George
[Bennett-Tepper-Schroeder]
RADIO:
Pop Go The Beatles – 20 August 1963 ♦
Saturday Club – 24 August 1963
The third British single by Carl Perkins was released in December 1958. Not a hit on either side of the Atlantic, 'Glad All Over' entered The Beatles' live repertoire in 1960. George played the song in 1985 with a 'dream team' band assembled to pay tribute to Carl in a TV special. The concert was the first occasion since 1966 that Ringo and George had appeared together on a British stage. They happily 'bopped the blues' with Eric Clapton, Dave Edmunds and their rockabilly hero.

HAPPY BIRTHDAY DEAR SATURDAY CLUB ★

John, Paul & George
[Hill-Hill]
RADIO:
Saturday Club – 5 October 1963
To celebrate the fifth birthday of the BBC Light Programme's most successful music show, The Beatles performed 'Happy Birthday'. Their musical arrangement was inspired by a Top Ten hit by Heinz – 'Just Like Eddie' (Cochran, that is). Brian Matthew's response was: 'Isn't that nice? And thank you, Dear Beatles!'

A HARD DAY'S NIGHT

John & Paul
[Lennon-McCartney]
RADIO:
Top Gear – 16 July 1964 ♦
From Us To You – 3 August 1964
TV:
Top of the Pops – 8 July 1964 (mimed)
The Beatles at Shea Stadium – 1 March 1966
The Beatles' first movie was about to open and the title song was on its way to number one when they taped the first BBC performance of 'A Hard Day's Night'. *Top Gear* producer Bernie Andrews remembered that they were expecting George Martin to play the piano part heard on the single, but he failed to arrive. Instead, the instrumental solo of 12-string guitar doubled with piano was dubbed from the record and cut into the session tape. The solo on the *From Us To You* version, made three days later, was picked out on electric 12-string with added echo. A performance recorded in August 1965 appeared on the 1977 LP *Live At The Hollywood Bowl*. Peter Sellers' oration of 'A Hard Day's Night', as if he were Laurence Olivier acting the part of Shakespeare's Richard III, was produced by George Martin for Christmas 1965.

HELP!

John
[Lennon-McCartney]
TV:
The Beatles at Shea Stadium – 1 March 1966
While filming their second movie in April 1965, a name for it was finally agreed upon. The working title of 'Eight Arms to Hold You' was abandoned in favour of *Help!*. John and Paul somehow found time to write the title song, which was recorded in one productive evening at Abbey Road. It was number one, of course.

THE HIPPY HIPPY SHAKE ★

Paul
[Romero]
RADIO:
Saturday Club – 16 March 1963
Pop Go The Beatles – 4 June 1963
Pop Go The Beatles – 30 July 1963 ♦
Pop Go The Beatles – 10 September 1963
Saturday Club – 15 February 1964
Although not a hit, 'The Hippy Hippy Shake' by Chan Romero became popular in Liverpool when DJ Bob Wooler played it at the Cavern Club. He recalled lending his copy of the UK

Columbia single to Paul so The Beatles could learn it. The Swinging Blue Jeans also borrowed the prized disc and scored a British and American hit with 'The Hippy Hippy Shake' in 1964. Cheekily, The Beatles made their last BBC recording of the song when the version by their Merseybeat mates was in the UK Top Three. A live Beatles performance was captured on the 1962 Star-Club tape. Chan Romero had recorded his song in 1959 at Gold Star studio in Los Angeles with the same musicians who played on 'La Bamba' by his hero Ritchie Valens.

HONEY DON'T (★ with John singing)
Ringo
[Perkins]
Pop Go The Beatles – 3 September 1963 (John singing) ♦
From Us To You – 18 May 1964 (John singing)
Top Gear – 26 November 1964
The Beatles Invite You to Take a Ticket To Ride – 7 June 1965
The B-side of Carl Perkins' Top Ten UK hit 'Blue Suede Shoes', 'Honey Don't' was a Beatles stage favourite for several years before appearing on their fourth album in December 1964. The BBC recordings reveal how brilliantly John swaggered through the song until he generously surrendered it to Ringo for a featured vocal on *Beatles For Sale*. The first record with Lennon singing Perkins was The Plastic Ono Band's LP *Live Peace In Toronto*, released in December 1969. The opening track was 'Blue Suede Shoes'.

THE HONEYMOON SONG ★
Paul
[Theodorakis-Sansom]
Pop Go The Beatles – 6 August 1963 ♦
Greek composer Mikis Theodorakis wrote the theme tune for the 1959 film *Honeymoon*. Although it was set in Spain, Italian group Marino Marini and his Quartet performed a vocal version in the movie. They had three British hits during 1958 and 1959, but 'The Honeymoon Song' failed to find chart success. Marino Marini and his Quartet made a big impression when they played in Liverpool. Their concert inspired a local group, including two of Paul's Liverpool Institute classmates, to invent the Italian-sounding name The Remo Quartet – later changed to The Remo Four. Clearly fond of 'The Honeymoon Song', Paul selected it for the *Postcard* album he produced in 1969 for Apple Records artist Mary Hopkin.

I CALL YOUR NAME
John
[Lennon-McCartney]
RADIO:
Saturday Club – 4 April 1964
The song was originally given to Billy J. Kramer with The Dakotas, who placed it on the B-side of another gift from their label-mates, the 1963 number one 'Bad To Me'. The Beatles' own recording of 'I Call Your Name' was released almost a year after Billy J. Kramer's on the *Long Tall Sally* EP. As John pointed out in an interview with Andy Peebles, the instrumental section was influenced by a form of Jamaican music permeating the trendiest London night clubs during the early 1960s: 'The solo on "I Call Your Name" was ska – deliberate and conscious.' A lustrous cover by The Mamas and The Papas was included on their debut album, *If You Can Believe Your Eyes And Ears*.

I FEEL FINE
John
[Lennon-McCartney]
RADIO:
Top Gear – 26 November 1964 ♦
Saturday Club – 26 December 1964
TV:
Top of the Pops – 3 December 1964
The Beatles at Shea Stadium – 1 March 1966
The same BBC performance of 'I Feel Fine' was used in both broadcasts. An unedited *Top Gear* session tape of 'I Feel Fine' reveals that the opening feedback took several attempts to perfect. That riff was tricky too. A Cavern Club favourite – 'Watch Your Step' by Bobby Parker – may have inspired it. The Beatles' eighth single topped the UK and US charts during Christmas 1964, bringing their tally of American number ones in that year to six.

I FORGOT TO REMEMBER TO FORGET ★
George
[Kesler-Feathers]
RADIO:
From Us To You – 18 May 1964 ♦
During their second *From Us To You* with Alan Freeman, the group played this unusual Elvis cover. Presley's final single on Sun Records, 'I Forgot To Remember To Forget' brought him his first national success when it topped the country chart for five weeks during February and March 1956. In the UK, it first appeared in October 1958 on the album *Elvis' Golden Records Vol. 1*. 'I Forgot To Remember To

Forget' was also recorded by its composer, Charlie Feathers, and two other Sun luminaries – Johnny Cash and Jerry Lee Lewis.

I GOT A WOMAN ★
John
[Charles-Richard]
RADIO:
Pop Go The Beatles – 13 August 1963 ♦
Saturday Club – 4 April 1964
An American R&B number one for Ray Charles in 1955, 'I Got A Woman' was not available in the UK until the release of the LP *The Ray Charles Story Volume One* in January 1963. The Beatles heard it on Elvis Presley's first British album, *Rock 'n' Roll*, released in October 1956. Both BBC takes are assured performances. The later version – with a double-tracked vocal by John – is a little more studio polished than the earlier recording.

I GOT TO FIND MY BABY ★
John
[Berry]
RADIO:
Pop Go The Beatles – 11 June 1963 ♦
Saturday Club – 29 June 1963
A Chuck Berry rocker that developed from a 1954 recording by his Chess label-mate and ace harmonica man, Little Walter. An earlier incarnation of the song titled 'Gotta Find My Baby' was recorded in 1941 by Doctor Clayton. Berry's record was released on an American Chess single in August 1960, but failed to chart. It could not have helped that Chuck Berry was facing legal problems following his arrest for the transportation of a minor over state lines in violation of the Mann Act. 'I Gotta Find My Baby' eventually emerged in the UK on the LP *Chuck Berry* in 1962. By that time, the singer was serving a prison sentence.

I JUST DON'T UNDERSTAND ★
John
[Wilkin-Westberry]
RADIO:
Pop Go The Beatles – 20 August 1963 ♦
Swedish-born movie starlet Ann-Margret (Olson) had an American Top 20 hit with 'I Just Don't Understand' in September 1961. Freddie and The Dreamers, who later covered the song, may have discovered it through The Beatles. Paul is convinced their first hit – 'If You Gotta Make A Fool Of Somebody' – went into their set list once The Beatles had played

it at the Manchester group's local club, the Oasis. Both songs are rock 'n' roll waltzes, a musical hybrid the group experimented with for 'Baby's In Black' and an early take of 'I'll Be Back' included on *Anthology 1*.

I SAW HER STANDING THERE
Paul
[Lennon-McCartney]
RADIO:
Saturday Club – 16 March 1963
Side by Side – 22 April 1963
Saturday Club – 25 May 1963
Steppin' Out – 3 June 1963
Pop Go The Beatles – 25 June 1963
Easy Beat – 21 July 1963
Pop Go The Beatles – 24 September 1963
Saturday Club – 5 October 1963
Easy Beat – 20 October 1963 ♦
From Us To You – 26 December 1963
From Us To You – 18 May 1964
TV:
It's The Beatles – 7 December 1963
Written towards the end of 1962, the song was captured on tape at their final Star-Club performance. Six weeks later, they recorded 'I Saw Her Standing There' at Abbey Road during the one-day session that yielded all ten tracks needed to complete the debut album *Please Please Me*. Paul's bass line was inspired by the playing on Chuck Berry's 'I'm Talkin' About You'. The first BBC performance during *Saturday Club* was directly onto the air from a small 'talks' studio. *Easy Beat* was recorded in front of an audience. By the time of The Beatles' second appearance on the show in October 1963, the audience was full of very vocal fans. Presenter Brian Matthew pleaded for the screams to cease and then commented, 'Alfred Hitchcock's Birds have got nothing on you lot!' It was a topical reference, because the director's movie, with a soundtrack of avian screeching, had opened that year.

I SHOULD HAVE KNOWN BETTER
John
[Lennon-McCartney]
RADIO:
From Us To You – 3 August 1964
The Beatles appeared in the first edition of *Top Gear* broadcast 16 July 1964. The extant running order reported that 'I Should Have Known Better' was recorded at the BBC with five others from the current album, *A Hard Day's Night*. A tape of the programme reveals that the song was, in fact, played from a disc.

However, three days later, 'I Should Have Known Better' was taped in a BBC session for the final *From Us To You*.

I WANNA BE YOUR MAN

Ringo
[Lennon-McCartney]
RADIO:
Saturday Club – 15 February 1964
From Us To You – 30 March 1964 ♦
Ringo's vocal spotlight on *Please Please Me* was 'Boys'. On the second album, *With The Beatles*, he was given a Lennon-McCartney composition to sing. The Rolling Stones' manager Andrew Oldham, a former Epstein employee, had received the song from John and Paul after bemoaning his group's lack of chart success during a chance meeting with them. 'I Wanna Be Your Man' entered the chart a week before the release of *With The Beatles* and earned The Rolling Stones their first Top 20 hit single.

I WANT TO HOLD YOUR HAND

John & Paul
[Lennon-McCartney]
RADIO:
Saturday Club – 21 December 1963
From Us To You – 26 December 1963
Saturday Club – 15 February 1964
TV:
It's The Beatles – 7 December 1963
With advance orders of a million, The Beatles' fifth single soon replaced their previous disc – 'She Loves You' – at the top of the UK charts. Just two months later, 'I Want To Hold Your Hand' became only the fourth record by a British act to reach number one in the US charts. The single's success launched The Beatles' musical domination of the world. In January 1964, the group recorded a German translation 'Komm, Gib Mir Deine Hand'. Howard Morrison and the Hu Hus articulated the view of some worried parents when they sang 'I Wanna Cut Your Hair'.

I'LL BE ON MY WAY ★

John & Paul
[Lennon-McCartney]
RADIO:
Side by Side – 24 June 1963 ♦
The BBC recording of this Lennon-McCartney composition is the only one by The Beatles to have survived. 'I'll Be On My Way', written in 1961, was given to another Epstein-managed group – Billy J. Kramer with the Dakotas – and

released on the B-side of their hit version of 'Do You Want To Know A Secret' in April 1963. The writers also provided exclusive hit songs for Tommy Quickly, The Fourmost and Cilla Black in 1963. As John commented in the radio programme *The Lennon and McCartney Songbook*, 'We thought we had some to spare!'

I'LL FOLLOW THE SUN

Paul
[Lennon-McCartney]
RADIO:
Top Gear – 26 November 1964 ♦
This early song of Paul's was at least four years old by the time it was revisited for *Beatles For Sale*. In 1965, Glyn Johns released a version, but it made little impact. His career as a recording engineer and producer was more successful. He worked closely with The Beatles amid the tense conditions of the *Get Back / Let It Be* sessions of January 1969.

I'LL GET YOU

John & Paul
[Lennon-McCartney]
RADIO:
Pop Go The Beatles – 13 August 1963
Saturday Club – 24 August 1963
Pop Go The Beatles – 3 September 1963
Pop Go The Beatles – 10 September 1963
Saturday Club – 5 October 1963
The other side of the 'She Loves You' single, 'I'll Get You' is a Beatles B-side gem. *Anthology 1* presents a live TV performance of the song from *Sunday Night at the London Palladium*, broadcast on 13 October 1963. The British press described the screaming enthusiasm of fans outside the theatre that night as 'Beatlemania'. The hysteria was set to increase from that date.

I'M A LOSER

John
[Lennon-McCartney]
RADIO:
Top Gear – 26 November 1964 ♦
Saturday Club – 26 December 1964
The Beatles Invite You to Take a Ticket To Ride – 7 June 1965
The first broadcast of 'I'm A Loser' was ten days before its release on *Beatles For Sale* in December 1964. Unusually, the *Top Gear* recording was used again in *Saturday Club*. In The Beatles' last BBC music session in 1965, John changed 'Beneath this smile, I am wearing

a frown' to the rather less emotional 'Beneath this wig, I am wearing a tie'.

I'M DOWN

Paul
[Lennon-McCartney]
TV:
The Beatles at Shea Stadium – 1 March 1966
When you turned over the 'Help!' single, Paul's Little Richard-style high-pitched vocal on 'I'm Down' exploded from the 45. After it was recorded during the afternoon of 14 June 1965, Paul calmed things down in the evening session when he sang 'Yesterday'. Released in July 1965, 'I'm Down' was used as the closing number for most Beatles concerts played from then until August 1966.

I'M GONNA SIT RIGHT DOWN AND CRY (OVER YOU) ★

John
[Thomas-Biggs]
RADIO:
Pop Go The Beatles – 6 August 1963 ♦
Three Elvis Presley covers performed for the BBC, including this song, were first released in the UK on his 1956 debut album *Rock 'n' Roll*. The Beatles can also be heard performing 'I'm Gonna Sit Right Down And Cry (Over You)' on the Star-Club tape recorded 31 December 1962.

I'M HAPPY JUST TO DANCE WITH YOU

George
[Lennon-McCartney]
RADIO:
From Us To You – 3 August 1964
As he had on 'Do You Want To Know A Secret', George took the lead vocal on a song written by John and Paul. 'I'm Happy Just To Dance With You' is on *A Hard Day's Night* – the only Beatles album to feature entirely Lennon-McCartney songs. Brian Epstein managed an American folk-rock group The Cyrkle (spelling courtesy of John), who covered this song in 1967.

I'M TALKING ABOUT YOU ★

John
[Berry]
RADIO:
Saturday Club – 16 March 1963
Chess Records released Chuck Berry's song

in February 1961. It arrived on a single in the UK seven months later and was then featured on the LP *Juke Box Hits* in June 1962. The Star-Club tape documents The Beatles' fiery interpretation from New Year's Eve 1962. This BBC version was performed live from the *Saturday Club* on-air studio. Their songs for the show could not be pre-recorded as usual, because a heavy cold had made it impossible for John to sing. There were subsequent covers by leading British groups The Yardbirds (a demonstration tape from 1964), The Hollies (*Stay With The Hollies* LP 1964) and The Rolling Stones (*Out Of Our Heads* LP 1965).

IF I FELL

John & Paul
[Lennon-McCartney]
RADIO:
Top Gear – 16 July 1964
From Us To You – 3 August 1964
'If I Fell' is a sophisticated ballad rooted in the classic American songbook tradition. It features an introductory verse that occurs nowhere else in the song; a frequent ploy of writers in the 1930s. A high point of *A Hard Day's Night*, it was coupled with Paul's ballad 'And I Love Her' on an American single and also featured on the British EP *Extracts From The Film A Hard Day's Night*.

JOHNNY B GOODE ★

John
[Berry]
RADIO:
Saturday Club – 15 February 1964 ♦
The song was a Top Ten American hit for Chuck Berry in 1958. Although it did not register in the British charts, 'Johnny B Goode' (coupled with 'Around And Around') must have been bought by every British beat group of the early 1960s. It was one of the most frequently performed songs on *Saturday Club*. 'Johnny B Goode' was given extra prominence in 1962 when included on the influential British LP compilation *Chuck Berry*.

KANSAS CITY/HEY-HEY-HEY-HEY!

Paul
[Leiber-Stoller]/[Penniman]
RADIO:
Pop Go The Beatles – 6 August 1963 ♦
From Us To You – 18 May 1964
From Us To You – 3 August 1964
Saturday Club – 26 December 1964

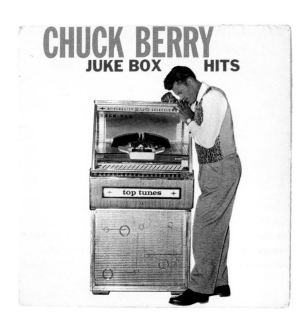

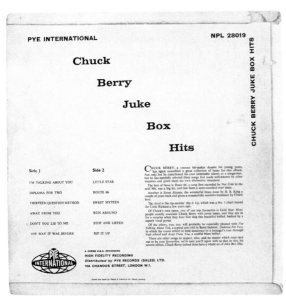

'Kansas City' was an American number one for Wilbert Harrison in May 1959. Originally called 'K. C. Loving', it was composed in 1952 by Jerry Leiber and Mike Stoller – the production and song writing duo who devised The Coasters' records that The Beatles loved so much. Little Richard's 1959 medley of 'Kansas City' with his previously released 'Hey-Hey-Hey-Hey! (Goin' Back To Birmingham)' was a Top 30 UK hit during the summer of 1959. That single was the model for The Beatles' version. The first BBC broadcast of 'Kansas City' was over a year before it was recorded for *Beatles For Sale*.

KEEP YOUR HANDS OFF MY BABY ★
John
[Goffin-King]
RADIO:
Saturday Club 26 January 1963 ♦
Searching for someone to sing on their novelty dance record 'The Loco-Motion', married songwriters Gerry Goffin and Carole King chose their babysitter, Little Eva. The single was an American number one and a British number two. The same team made 'Keep Your Hands Off My Baby'. The Beatles played it during their *Saturday Club* debut in the week Little Eva's record dropped out of the UK Top 40. The song was in the group's set list during the Helen Shapiro tour that opened in Bradford in February 1963.

LEND ME YOUR COMB ★
John & Paul
[Twomey-Wise-Weisman]
RADIO:
Pop Go The Beatles – 16 July 1963 ♦
In the States, 'Lend Me Your Comb' was released in December 1956 on the flip-side of 'Glad All Over'. Its British release came in April 1958 on the fourth Carl Perkins single on London. It was a staple of The Beatles' act for several years before they made their BBC recording. John and Paul replicate the harmony singing of Carl and his brother Jay heard on the original. When the infamous *Live! At The Star-Club* album became available in 1977, it was just possible to discern the song through the muffled recording quality of the tape.

LONESOME TEARS IN MY EYES ★
John
[J and D Burnette-Burlison-Mortimer]
RADIO:

Pop Go The Beatles – 23 July 1963 ♦
The ten-inch LP *Johnny Burnette and the Rock 'n' Roll Trio* was released in the UK in 1957. It did not sell, but became a treasured item for those who enjoyed the excitement generated by the early records of Elvis, Carl Perkins and Gene Vincent. The music on the influential album was certainly devoured by The Beatles. On *Pop Go The Beatles*, John announced: 'This is a Dorsey Burnette number – brother of Johnny – called "Lonesome Tears In My Eyes", recorded on their very first LP in 1822!' The shuffle rhythm and closing guitar riff heard on The Beatles' 1969 single 'The Ballad Of John And Yoko' echo the feel of this BBC performance.

LONG TALL SALLY
Paul
[Johnson-Penniman-Blackwell]
RADIO:
Side by Side – 13 May 1963
Saturday Club – 25 May 1963
Pop Go The Beatles – 13 August 1963 ♦
Saturday Club – 24 August 1963
Saturday Club – 4 April 1964
Top Gear – 16 July 1964
From Us To You – 3 August 1964
TV:
Top of the Pops – 8 July 1964 (mimed)
Five of the seven BBC recordings were broadcast before The Beatles' version was released in June 1964 on the EP *Long Tall Sally*. The group had performed the song ever since it had erupted on a Little Richard record in 1957. The UK single coupled the first two American hits from a year before: 'Long Tall Sally' and the equally thunderous 'Tutti Frutti'. 'Long Tall Sally' endured as a stage number to the very end. It was the last song played at the final official Beatles concert in San Francisco on 29 August 1966. Other versions can be found on the Star-Club tape, the *Hollywood Bowl* album and *Anthology 1*.

LOVE ME DO
John & Paul
[Lennon-McCartney]
RADIO:
Here We Go – 26 October 1962
The Talent Spot – 4 December 1962
Saturday Club – 26 January 1963
Parade of the Pops – 20 February 1963
Pop Go The Beatles – 11 June 1963
Side by Side – 24 June 1963
Pop Go The Beatles – 23 July 1963 ♦
Pop Go The Beatles – 10 September 1963

Easy Beat – 20 October 1963
TV:
The Mersey Sound – 9 October 1963 [disc used to accompany concert footage]
Their first British Top 20 hit in 1962, 'Love Me Do' eventually became a US number one in May 1964. EMI's American outlet Capitol had decided not to issue it, allowing Tollie to license the song. The small independent label rode the wave of Beatlemania, engendered by Capitol's campaign for 'I Want To Hold Your Hand', all the way to the top. There are three EMI recordings of the song, each with a different drummer: the British single take with Ringo, the *Please Please Me* album track with session player Andy White and the earliest recording with Pete Best included on *Anthology 1*.

LUCILLE ★
Paul
[Collins-Penniman]
RADIO:
Pop Go The Beatles – 17 September 1963
Saturday Club – 5 October 1963 ♦
Little Richard's rocker made the UK Top Ten during the summer of 1957. The Beatles' second BBC performance of 'Lucille' was recorded for the fifth-birthday edition of *Saturday Club*. Brian Matthew made a reference to the Everly Brothers over the opening bars, because Don and Phil were also guests in the show and had scored a Top Five UK hit with 'Lucille' in 1960. The *Pop Go The Beatles* version is equally good, with a wild tremolo guitar solo by George. Paul returned to the song at the 1979 Concert For Kampuchea and for his 1988 album, initially available only in the USSR, *CHOBA B CCCP*.

MATCHBOX
Ringo
[Perkins]
RADIO:
Pop Go The Beatles – 30 July 1963 ♦
From Us To You – 18 May 1964
Rooted in a blues recorded in 1927 by Blind Lemon Jefferson, 'Matchbox' by Carl Perkins was the unsuccessful follow-up single to his huge hit 'Blue Suede Shoes'. Pete Best first sang it with The Beatles then, after the drummer's departure, John took it over. As with 'Honey Don't', he passed the song to Ringo for these BBC performances and the version included on the EP *Long Tall Sally*. Carl Perkins witnessed the first Beatles EMI recording of

one of his songs when he attended the Abbey Road session held on 1 June 1964.

MEMPHIS, TENNESSEE ★
John
[Berry]
RADIO:
Teenagers Turn – Here We Go – 8 March 1962 (Pete Best on drums)
Pop Go The Beatles – 18 June 1963
Saturday Club – 29 June 1963
Pop Go The Beatles – 30 July 1963 ♦
Saturday Club – 5 October 1963
First released on the flip-side of Chuck Berry's 'Back In The USA' in the summer of 1959, 'Memphis, Tennessee' reached number six in the British charts four years later. A cover by Sheffield group Dave Berry and The Cruisers was also in the UK Top 20 at the time. In the States, an instrumental version by Lonnie Mack reached number five in 1963 and a cover by Johnny Rivers peaked at number two in 1964. Paul remembers learning 'Memphis, Tennessee' in John's bedroom when the two lads decided it had 'the greatest riff ever, it killed us!'

MISERY
John & Paul
[Lennon-McCartney]
RADIO:
Here We Go – 12 March 1963
Saturday Club – 16 March 1963
On the Scene – 28 March 1963
Easy Beat – 7 April 1963
Side by Side – 22 April 1963
Pop Go The Beatles – 4 June 1963
Pop Go The Beatles – 17 September 1963
While The Beatles were on tour with Helen Shapiro in 1963, John and Paul suggested she record 'Misery'. The 16-year-old had had eight hits by this time, including two number ones, so they hoped a version by her might promote their music. Instead, the song was picked up by Liverpool actor and singer Kenny Lynch, who was also on the tour. The Beatles' BBC performances lack the descending piano runs overdubbed by George Martin onto the tape made at EMI on 11 February 1963.

MONEY (THAT'S WHAT I WANT)
John
[Bradford-Gordy]
RADIO:
Saturday Club – 25 May 1963
Pop Go The Beatles – 18 June 1963

Saturday Club – 29 June 1963
Pop Go The Beatles – 3 September 1963
From Us To You – 26 December 1963
Saturday Club – 15 February 1964
TV:
It's The Beatles – 7 December 1963
Motown founder Berry Gordy gained his first national hit as a label owner with this song. He had co-written it with the company's receptionist Janie Bradford. Recorded by Barrett Strong, 'Money' was an American R&B number two and reached 23 in the pop chart. It was released on a London American single in April 1960, but made little headway in the UK. Motown's first British hit was not to come for another four years. Mirroring the exciting way 'Twist And Shout' had brought the debut album to a close, 'Money' provided a powerful climax to the second LP *With The Beatles*. John's live version with Eric Clapton, Klaus Voormann and Ringo Starr was featured on the 1969 album *Live Peace In Toronto*. The B-side of 'Money' had an influence too. Compare the middle sections of Barrett Strong's 'Oh I Apologize' and 'Isolation' from the 1970 album *John Lennon/Plastic Ono Band*.

THE NIGHT BEFORE
Paul
[Lennon-McCartney]
RADIO:
The Beatles Invite You to Take a Ticket To Ride – 7 June 1965
The last radio show featuring specially re-corded Beatles tracks gave this song its 'first airing', as the host Denny Piercy put it. It was featured in the film *Help!*.

NOTHING SHAKIN' (BUT THE LEAVES ON THE TREES) ★
George
[Fontaine-Colacrai-Lampert-Gluck]
RADIO:
Pop Go The Beatles 23 July 1963 ♦
'Nothin' Shakin'' was first recorded by Eddie Fontaine, who had sung 'Cool It Baby' in The Beatles' favourite rock movie, *The Girl Can't Help It*. A cover version made in 1958 by Craig Douglas was – as with most British attempts at rock 'n' roll – light years away from the sound and spirit infusing the American original. A comparison of Craig's dreary version with the rollicking BBC performance by The Beatles reveals why the quality of most British pop music can be determined by whether it was released before or after 'Love Me Do'.

OOH! MY SOUL ★
Paul
[Penniman]
RADIO:
Pop Go The Beatles – 27 August 1963 ♦
In an 18-month period, from February 1957 to July 1958, Little Richard placed nine songs in the UK chart. 'Ooh! My Soul' was the last of that sequence of hits. His highest British chart position – number two – came with 'Baby Face' in early 1959, by which time he had renounced rock 'n' roll during a tour of Australia. 'Ooh! My Soul' was one of four Little Richard rockers performed by The Beatles at the BBC.

PAPERBACK WRITER
Paul
TV:
Top of the Pops – 16 June 1966 (mimed)
'Paperback Writer' was released after a long wait of six months since The Beatles' last sin-gle. Recorded in April 1966 during the making of the album *Revolver*, both sides of the single revealed a change in the group's sound. The layered harmonies at the start of 'Paperback Writer' are punctured by the loudest bass heard on a Beatles record to that date. As with their previous single, promotional films were supplied to TV stations. However, the group did agree to make a live appearance miming to both sides of their single on *Top of the Pops*. It was The Beatles' final performance on the show.

A PICTURE OF YOU ★
George
[Beveridge-Oakman]
Here We Go – 15 June 1962 (with Pete Best)
'A Picture Of You' was a Top Ten hit for Joe Brown and The Bruvvers when The Beatles played it during *Here We Go*. With his slick finger work on an impressive Grimshaw guitar, Joe's was a more credible face – cheeky grin, spiky hair and all – of pre-Beatles British pop. George also used to sing songs from Brown's early repertoire: 'Darktown Strutters Ball', 'What A Crazy World We're Living In', 'I'm Henry The Eighth, I Am' and 'The Sheik Of Araby' (recorded at the audition for Decca Records). They became close friends. In 2002, Joe Brown's moving performance of 'I'll See You In My Dreams' closed *Concert For George*, staged a year after George's death.

PLEASE MISTER POSTMAN
John
[Dobbins-Garrett-Holland-Bateman-Gorman]
RADIO:
Teenagers Turn – Here We Go – 8 March 1962 (with Pete Best)
Pop Go The Beatles – 30 July 1963
From Us To You – 30 March 1964
In December 1961, The Marvelettes' record on the Tamla label was the first American pop number one for the Motown company. There was no breakthrough in Britain, where it was released on Fontana. Berry Gordy's American hits issued on Tamla and Motown struggled to be heard on the BBC in the early 1960s. When The Beatles became successful, they were tireless champions of the labels' artists, particularly Marvin Gaye, The Miracles and Mary Wells. Even on their humble Light Programme debut, the group gave Gordy's company some rare BBC radio exposure.

PLEASE PLEASE ME
John & Paul
[Lennon-McCartney]
RADIO:
Here We Go – 25 January 1963
Saturday Club – 26 January 1963
The Talent Spot – 29 January 1963
Parade of the Pops – 20 February 1963
Here We Go – 12 March 1963
Saturday Club – 16 March 1963
On the Scene – 28 March 1963
Easy Beat – 7 April 1963
Side by Side – 22 April 1963
Steppin' Out – 3 June 1963
Pop Go The Beatles – 13 August 1963
Easy Beat – 20 October 1963
TV:
The 625 Show – 16 April 1963
Pops and Lenny – 16 May 1963
When 'Please Please Me' was completed at Abbey Road, George Martin was sure the group had made a number one record. The single's release on 11 January was accompa-nied by a flurry of media activity. Following their *Thank Your Lucky Stars* TV appearance on 19 January 1963, three days later the group were heard promoting their new single on *Pop Inn*. Three live radio performances followed in quick succession. The next week 'Please Please Me' entered the Top 20 and rapidly rose to number one on most charts, including that used by the BBC's *Pick of the Pops* programme. For British fans, if DJ Alan Freeman announced

'Please Please Me' was number one, then it was a genuine number one.

POP GO THE BEATLES ★
Instrumental
Opening and closing theme tunes
[Arrangement of the nursery rhyme 'Pop Goes The Weasel']
RADIO:
Pop Go The Beatles – All fifteen programmes
A short 20" version always opened the show and the longer take was fadeable play-out music to close the programme on time. Featuring wailing harmonica and falsetto whooping that was characteristic of the mid-1963 Beatles sound, 'Pop Go The Beatles' was recorded in a session for the first show on 24 May 1963. The programme featured The Lorne Gibson Trio, whose leader remembered lending a hand on this recording.

P.S. I LOVE YOU
Paul
[Lennon-McCartney]
RADIO:
Here We Go – 26 October 1962
The Talent Spot – 4 December 1962
Pop Go The Beatles – 25 June 1963
'P.S. I Love You' was the B-side of 'Love Me Do', released in October 1962. The Cavern Club DJ Bob Wooler remembered that one reason it had not been made the A-side was to avoid confusion with another song bearing the same title. Written in 1934 by Gordon Jenkins and Johnny Mercer, their 'P.S. I Love You' was released by Frank Sinatra in 1957. Five years later, it was revived again when Ketty Lester included it on the album named after her big hit 'Love Letters'.

RAIN
John
[Lennon-McCartney]
TV:
Top of the Pops – 16 June 1966 (mimed)
The B-side of 'Paperback Writer' was a star-tling foretaste of what was to come on their long-awaited next LP. 'Rain' was saturated in sounds that were later described as 'psyche-delic', including a tape of John's voice played backwards during the fade. Ringo's remark-able drumming on 'Rain' is an example of how skilfully he could support the group's different styles of music.

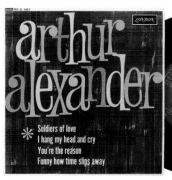

ROCK AND ROLL MUSIC

John
[Berry]
RADIO:

Saturday Club – 26 December 1964 ♦
Chuck Berry's record went to number eight in the Billboard Top 100, but had no chart success in the UK. That did not stop The Beatles unearthing the song. It was released in the UK on a London American single in December 1957 and the *Reelin' And Rockin'* EP in March 1959. It was part of The Beatles' repertoire from 1959 to 1966. With a pressing deadline to complete their fourth album, *Beatles For Sale*, The Beatles selected six favourites from the 1950s. They nailed Chuck Berry's tribute to rock 'n' roll in one take at Abbey Road.

ROLL OVER BEETHOVEN

George
[Berry]
Steppin' Out – 3 June 1963
Saturday Club – 29 June 1963
Pop Go The Beatles – 3 September 1963
Saturday Club – 21 December 1963
From Us To You – 26 December 1963
Saturday Club – 15 February 1964
From Us To You – 30 March 1964 ♦
TV:

It's The Beatles – 7 December 1963
A year after its stay in the American Top 30 during 1956, Chuck Berry's single became available in the UK but had no success. John sang it until 1961; then it was George who invited Beethoven to roll over. Following three BBC broadcasts in summer 1963, the group made it the side two opener of *With The Beatles*, released in November. Three live versions have been issued from concerts in Germany (*Star-Club*), the USA (*Hollywood Bowl*) and Sweden (*Anthology 1*).

SHE LOVES YOU

John & Paul
[Lennon-McCartney]
RADIO:

Pop Go The Beatles – 13 August 1963
Pop Go The Beatles – 20 August 1963
Saturday Club – 24 August 1963
Pop Go The Beatles – 27 August 1963
Pop Go The Beatles – 10 September 1963
Pop Go The Beatles – 24 September 1963
Saturday Club – 5 October 1963
Easy Beat – 20 October 1963
The Ken Dodd Show – 3 November 1963

(repeated 6 November 1963 and 1 February 1964)
Saturday Club – 21 December 1963
From Us To You – 26 December 1963
TV:

The Mersey Sound – 13 November 1963
It's The Beatles – 7 December 1963
The Beatles' fourth single became their biggest seller in Britain, spending twelve weeks in the Top Three including two stints at number one. In the States, Capitol declined to release it so the Philadelphia-based independent Swan Records distributed the record. On 3 January 1964, NBC's *The Jack Paar Show* featured footage of The Beatles taken from BBC TV's *The Mersey Sound*. The clip of 'She Loves You' was America's first glimpse of The Beatles, who were already causing excitement with the rush-released 'I Want To Hold Your Hand'. A month later, that single was number one. After seven weeks at the top, it was replaced by 'She Loves You' (which was then followed by 'Can't Buy Me Love'). Other Beatles versions of 'She Loves You' include the German translation 'Sie Liebt Dich' and live performances in the 1963 Royal Variety Show (included on *Anthology 1*) and at the Hollywood Bowl in August 1964.

SHE'S A WOMAN

Paul
[Lennon-McCartney]
RADIO:

Top Gear – 26 November 1964 ♦
Saturday Club – 26 December 1964
The Beatles Invite You to Take a Ticket To Ride – 7 June 1965
TV:

Top of the Pops – 3 December 1964
'She's A Woman' was released on the flip-side of the Christmas 1964 single 'I Feel Fine'. During *Top Gear*, John and Paul described how they completed writing 'She's A Woman' on the morning of the EMI session. John explained they had 'about one verse and we had to finish it off rather quickly, and that's why they're such rubbishy lyrics!' The Sir Douglas Quintet, an American group assuming an English-sounding name, locked into the record's infectious groove on their 1965 hit 'She's About A Mover'.

A SHOT OF RHYTHM AND BLUES ★

John
[Thompson]
RADIO:

Pop Go The Beatles – 18 June 1963
Easy Beat – 21 July 1963
Pop Go The Beatles – 27 August 1963 ♦
The song was first released in the UK in March 1962 as the B-side of Arthur Alexander's 'You Better Move On'. His single had entered the US chart the previous month and peaked at number 24. In a letter written in Hamburg, dated April 1962, John asked his future wife Cynthia to 'send me the words of "A Shot Of Rhythm + Blues" please? There's not many.' Other Merseyside acts covered it, including Gerry and The Pacemakers, Lee Curtis and Cilla Black. It was a minor British hit in early 1963 for Johnny Kidd and The Pirates. Arthur Alexander never enjoyed British chart success, but his records were very influential. The Rolling Stones' version of 'You Better Move On' was on their first EP in January 1964.

SIDE BY SIDE ★

Karl Denver with John and Paul
WITH THE KARL DENVER TRIO
[Woods]
RADIO:

Side by Side – 22 April 1963
Side by Side – 13 May 1963
Side by Side – 24 June 1963
The format of the *Side by Side* radio series allowed one group to play host to another. During their run in the series, The Karl Denver Trio invited The Beatles to trade numbers on three programmes. Named after the popular song written in 1927, the series required the visiting group to sing 'Side By Side' with a yodelling Karl. The Trio's biggest hit had been 'Wimoweh' in 1962.

SLOW DOWN

John
[Williams]
RADIO:

Pop Go The Beatles – 20 August 1963 ♦
This Larry Williams song was broadcast almost a year before its inclusion on The Beatles' EP *Long Tall Sally*. The B-side of Larry's 'Dizzy Miss Lizzy', 'Slow Down' was a Merseybeat favourite. Gerry and The Pacemakers covered it on their album *How Do You Like It?*. John recorded another Williams classic – 'Bony Moronie' – on his 1975 album *Rock 'N' Roll*. Paul covered Larry's 'She Said Yeah' on *Run Devil Run*, released in 1999.

SO HOW COME (NO ONE LOVES ME) ★

George
[Bryant/Bryant]
RADIO:

Pop Go The Beatles – 23 July 1963 ♦
'So How Come (No One Loves Me)' was included on *A Date With The Everly Brothers*, a UK Top Three album in 1961. It was written by the husband and wife songwriting team of Boudleaux and Felice Bryant, who wrote so many of the hits by Don and Phil. The Beatles are known to have played three other Everly Brothers songs: 'I Wonder If I Care As Much', 'Love Of My Life' and 'Cathy's Clown'.

SOLDIER OF LOVE ★

John
[Cason-Moon]
RADIO:

Pop Go The Beatles – 16 July 1963 ♦
The group covered four songs released by Alabama-born Arthur Alexander. 'Anna' is on their first album, and 'A Shot Of Rhythm And Blues' was recorded three times at the BBC. They also performed both sides of an Arthur Alexander single released in June 1962. 'Where Have You Been' is heard on the tape of the group at the Star-Club on New Year's Eve 1962. Their BBC recording of its B-side 'Soldier Of Love' is a Lennon tour de force – compelling evidence that the song would have enhanced any of The Beatles' early discs. During *Pop Go The Beatles*, George introduced 'John shouting "Soldiers Of Love"'. The plural is used on the label of the UK London-American single.

SOME OTHER GUY ★

John & Paul
[Leiber-Stoller-Barrett]
RADIO:

Saturday Club – 26 January 1963
The Talent Spot – 29 January 1963
Easy Beat – 23 June 1963 ♦
'Some Other Guy' was first recorded by Richie Barrett in direct imitation of the gospel call-and-response style of the Atlantic records of Ray Charles. Its UK release was on a London American single in May 1962. Not a hit anywhere, it was loved in Liverpool where local groups latched onto it. The Big Three's version was a minor hit in 1963. The Searchers not only recorded 'Some Other Guy', but also its B-side 'Tricky Dicky'. On 22 August 1962,

Granada Television filmed The Beatles playing 'Some Other Guy' at the Cavern Club. The footage remained unseen until November 1963, when it gave an historic glimpse of the group before they had scored a hit. Their last concert in what Cavern compere Bob Wooler described as 'the best of cellars' took place on 3 August 1963.

SURE TO FALL (IN LOVE WITH YOU) ★

Paul

[Perkins-Claunch-Cantrell]

RADIO:

Pop Go The Beatles – 18 June 1963 ♦

Pop Go The Beatles – 24 September 1963

Saturday Club – 4 April 1964

From Us To You – 18 May 1964

The song was included on *Dance Album Of Carl Perkins*, recorded in 1956. The sleeve note for the London LP released in November 1959 described its contents: 'For the most part, they're happy songs – light, toe-tapping rhythm numbers that just naturally make you feel a little gayer.' Paul, who took the lead on these BBC performances, produced Ringo singing it on the 1981 album *Stop And Smell The Roses*. On his 1982 album *Tug Of War*, Paul sings a duet with Carl on 'Get It'. In 1999, Paul recorded 'Movie Magg' – another song from *Dance Album Of Carl Perkins* – for the album *Run Devil Run*.

SWEET LITTLE SIXTEEN ★

John

[Berry]

RADIO:

Pop Go The Beatles – 23 July 1963 ♦

Chuck Berry's biggest American hit of the rock 'n' roll era reached the top of the R&B chart and number two in the list of Best Sellers. It became his second British hit single with five weeks in the Top 20 during 1958. The Beatles were recorded romping through it at the Star-Club at the close of play 1962. Eleven years later John revived the song during the unruly, Phil Spector-produced sessions for his album *Rock 'N' Roll*.

A TASTE OF HONEY

Paul

[Marlow-Scott]

RADIO:

Here We Go – 26 October 1962

Side by Side – 13 May 1963

Pop Go The Beatles – 18 June 1963

Easy Beat – 23 June 1963

The Beat Show – 4 July 1963

Pop Go The Beatles – 23 July 1963 ♦

Pop Go The Beatles – 10 September 1963

The Beatles learnt 'A Taste Of Honey' from the first vocal version of the tune released by Lenny Welch in September 1962. The melody was written by Bobby Scott for the 1960 Broadway production of Shelagh Delaney's play *A Taste of Honey*. A version by Herb Alpert & The Tijuana Brass was a Top Ten American hit in 1965 and won Grammy Awards for Record of the Year and Best Pop Instrumental.

THANK YOU GIRL

John & Paul

[Lennon-McCartney]

RADIO:

Side by Side – 13 May 1963

Steppin' Out – 3 June 1963

Easy Beat – 23 June 1963 ♦

TV:

The 625 Show – 16 April 1963

'Thank You Girl' was the B-side of third single 'From Me To You' and also included on the second EP, *The Beatles' Hits*.

THAT'S ALL RIGHT (MAMA) ★

Paul

[Crudup]

RADIO:

Pop Go The Beatles – 16 July 1963 ♦

Written by Arthur 'Big Boy' Crudup, 'That's All Right (Mama)' was on Elvis Presley's first Sun single released in July 1954. It was first made available in the UK in October 1956 when it was included on the Elvis LP *Rock 'n' Roll*. This led to Paul singing 'That's All Right (Mama)' as early as the skiffle days of the Quarry Men. He recorded it in 1987 for *CHOBA B CCCP* – his rock 'n' roll album made exclusively for the Soviet Union.

THERE'S A PLACE

John & Paul

[Lennon-McCartney]

RADIO:

Pop Go The Beatles – 16 July 1963

Easy Beat – 21 July 1963

Pop Go The Beatles – 3 September 1963

John's mature lyric explored a theme revisited in one of his last songs, 'Watching The Wheels'.

The penultimate track on *Please Please Me*, in the USA it was on the B-side of 'Twist And Shout'. In his 1980 interview with David Sheff, John described 'There's A Place' as 'my attempt at a sort of Motown black thing'. Indeed, its stop-start structure and melisma on the opening word of each verse is very similar to 'I Want A Guy' by the Marvelettes – the B-side of 'Twistin' Postman' released in the UK on Fontana in March 1962.

THINGS WE SAID TODAY

Paul

[Lennon-McCartney]

RADIO:

Top Gear – 16 July 1964 ♦

From Us To You – 3 August 1964

TV:

Top of the Pops – 29 July 1964

'Things We Said Today' was issued in July 1964 on side two of the UK LP *A Hard Day's Night* and on the B-side of the title song. In the States, the song was included on the album *Something New*.

THIS BOY

John, Paul & George

[Lennon-McCartney]

RADIO:

Saturday Club – 21 December 1963

From Us To You – 30 March 1964

TV:

It's The Beatles – 7 December 1963

Released in the UK on the flip-side of 'I Want To Hold Your Hand', the tune was orchestrated by George Martin for the movie *A Hard Day's Night*. As 'Ringo's Theme', it accompanies a sequence in which the errant drummer is seen 'parading' through the streets of Twickenham and on a bank of the River Thames. The 1995 'Free As A Bird' single featured two giggly EMI out-takes of 'This Boy'.

TICKET TO RIDE

John

[Lennon-McCartney]

RADIO:

The Beatles Invite You to Take a Ticket To Ride – 7 June 1965 ♦

TV:

Top of the Pops – 15 April 1965

A single included on the soundtrack album of the second movie *Help!*, 'Ticket To Ride' was heard in the last show to feature songs

recorded by The Beatles for BBC radio. *Anthology 2* has a live television performance of the song broadcast from the ABC Theatre in Blackpool on 1 August 1965. The *Live At The Hollywood Bowl* album includes a scream-drenched version from the same month.

TIE ME KANGAROO DOWN, SPORT ★

Rolf Harris

[Harris]

RADIO:

From Us To You – 26 December 1963

The Beatles' first bank holiday special was presented by Rolf Harris, who at the time of the broadcast was appearing in *The Beatles Christmas Show* at the Astoria in Finsbury Park, London. 'Fellas, do you feel like singing a chorus with me?' Rolf enquired. With The Beatles as his backing group, Rolf customized the lyric of 'Tie Me Kangaroo Down, Sport' with a verse about each of them. For example, 'Don't ill-treat me pet dingo, Ringo'. There was also a reference to the distinctive Beatle hairstyle: 'Cut your hair once a year, boys' – and Rolf also extracted some 'She Loves You'-style falsetto woos from the group. 'Tie Me Kangaroo Down, Sport' made the British Top Ten in 1960, but at the time of this unusual collaboration his single (produced by George Martin) had recently hopped to number three in the States.

TILL THERE WAS YOU

Paul

[Willson]

RADIO:

Pop Go The Beatles – 11 June 1963

Saturday Club – 29 June 1963

Pop Go The Beatles – 30 July 1963

Pop Go The Beatles – 10 September 1963

Royal Variety Performance – 10 November 1963

Saturday Club – 21 December 1963

From Us To You – 26 December 1963

From Us To You – 30 March 1964 ♦

TV:

It's The Beatles – 7 December 1963

'Till There Was You' was a highlight of Meredith Willson's Broadway musical *The Music Man*, which also included a BBC Light Programme perennial, 'Seventy-Six Trombones'. Paul was inspired to sing it by Peggy Lee's silky version, which made the UK Top 30 in April 1961. Having been in their stage act for two years, 'Till There Was You' was released on *With The Beatles* in November

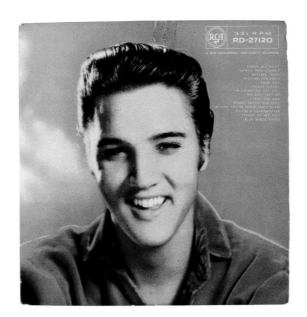

The records photographed for this chapter come from the cherished collections of Roger Armstrong and Tony Rounce at Ace Records, Rob Finnis, Brian Howlett, Kevin Howlett and Bill Millar.

1963. One of The Beatles' choices for the 1963 *Royal Variety Performance*, a recording from the show was eventually released on *Anthology 1*. It was preceded by Paul's introductory quip that the song had also been recorded by 'our favourite American group… Sophie Tucker!'

TO KNOW HER IS TO LOVE HER ★

John, Paul & George

[Spector]

RADIO:

Pop Go The Beatles – 6 August 1963 ♦

The Teddy Bears' American number one was written by Phil Spector, who had been moved to write the song by the inscription on his father's gravestone: 'To know him was to love him'. In the UK, the record climbed to number two during the first months of 1959. John, Paul and George sang three-part harmony on 'To Know Her Is To Love Her'. This distinctive blend of their voices was also heard on their ballads 'This Boy' and 'Yes It Is'.

TOO MUCH MONKEY BUSINESS ★

John

[Berry]

RADIO:

Saturday Club – 16 March 1963

Pop Go The Beatles – 11 June 1963

Side by Side – 24 June 1963

Pop Go The Beatles – 10 September 1963 ♦

On 16 April 1956, Chuck Berry rocked Chess Studios with a session that produced three Top Ten American R & B hits: 'Roll Over Beethoven', 'Brown Eyed Handsome Man' and this song. 'Too Much Monkey Business' was first released in the UK on the Pye International R&B Series LP *More Chuck Berry* at the end of 1963. It then became a British beat group favourite with versions on record by The Kinks, The Hollies, Wayne Fontana and The Mindbenders, The Applejacks and The Yardbirds. The Beatles had performed it on stage since 1960 so must have heard an American copy of 'Too Much Monkey Business' – either a Chess single or Chuck Berry's album *After School Session*, released in the US in May 1957.

TWIST AND SHOUT

John

[Medley-Russell]

RADIO:

The Talent Spot – 4 December 1962

Swinging Sound '63 – 18 April 1963

Pop Go The Beatles – 25 June 1963

The Beat Show – 4 July 1963

Easy Beat – 21 July 1963

Pop Go The Beatles – 6 August 1963

Saturday Club – 24 August 1963

Pop Go The Beatles – 27 August 1963

Pop Go The Beatles – 24 September 1963

Royal Variety Performance – 10 November 1963

TV:

The Mersey Sound – 9 October 1963

It's The Beatles – 7 December 1963

The Beatles at Shea Stadium – 1 March 1966

'Twist And Shout' made its initial impact through a single by The Isley Brothers. The Beatles used their version as the rousing closer of their debut album and many live shows. The song was written under a pseudonym by Bert Berns, who witnessed Phil Spector supervising its first recording by The Top Notes for the Atlantic label. The frantic pace of that performance did not help make it a successful record. In 1962, the Isleys gave the song a slower sensuous swing that took it into the US Top 20 and to number two in the R&B chart. The Beatles' take has more urgency. It is a dramatic illustration of how successfully the group stripped down the sophisticated arrangements of American originals into powerful reinventions for a four-piece beat group. Brian Poole and The Tremeloes – signed by Decca in preference to The Beatles – took the song to number four in the singles chart of July 1963. However, their record was outsold by The Beatles' first EP, featuring 'Twist And Shout' as its title track. The Beatles' characteristic falsetto whoops had been sparked by Little Richard, but the vocal gymnastics on the Isleys' 'Twist And Shout' and their earlier American hit 'Shout' also influenced the group's sound in 1963.

WORDS OF LOVE

John & Paul

[Holly]

RADIO:

Pop Go The Beatles – 20 August 1963

'Words Of Love' was released in the UK on an album simply called *Buddy Holly* in July 1958. The BBC recording was broadcast fifteen months before the song's inclusion on *Beatles For Sale*. John and Paul sang the two-part harmony which, through primitive but effective overdubbing, Buddy had sung with himself. Responding to a questionnaire supplied by writer Jim Dawson, John confirmed the enormous impact made by Buddy Holly and The Crickets in the UK: 'Every group tried to be The Crickets. I

think the greatest effect was on the songwriting (especially mine and Paul's). He made it OK to wear glasses! I WAS Buddy Holly.'

YES IT IS

John, Paul & George

TV:

Top of the Pops – 15 April 1965 (mimed)

'Yes It Is' was released on the B-side of 'Ticket To Ride' in 1965. With its 12/8 time signature and three-part harmony vocal, it is similar to an earlier B-side, 'This Boy'. Another distinguishing feature on the recording of 'Yes It Is' is the unusual guitar sound created by a foot-controlled volume pedal. George also used the effect for 'I Need You' recorded on the same day – 16 February 1965.

YOU CAN'T DO THAT

John

[Lennon-McCartney]

RADIO:

From Us To You – 30 March 1964

Saturday Club – 4 April 1964

From Us To You – 18 May 1964

Top Gear – 16 July 1964

TV:

Top of the Pops – 25 March 1964 (mimed)

Although released as the flip-side of 'Can't Buy Me Love', by March 1964 it was clear that B-side status did not indicate a song was inferior to the A-side. 'You Can't Do That' is a swaggering R&B workout that became a highlight of the non-film-songs side of *A Hard Day's Night*. A vibrant EMI out-take of 'You Can't Do That' was released on *Anthology 1*.

YOUNG BLOOD ★

George

[Leiber-Stoller-Pomus]

RADIO:

Pop Go The Beatles – 11 June 1963 ♦

The Coasters made the US Top Ten in 1957 with both songs on their third Atco single: 'Searchin'' and 'Young Blood'. The record even scraped into the British Top 30 for one week. Paul has recalled cycling across Liverpool on a quest to find someone rumoured to own a copy of the London American single. Both sides were performed by The Beatles. 'Searchin'' – sung by Paul – was one of the fifteen songs recorded at their Decca audition. As George usually took the lead for the quirkier numbers in their early repertoire, he

was upfront for 'Young Blood' (as he was on another of The Coasters' musical cartoons 'Three Cool Cats').

YOU REALLY GOT A HOLD ON ME

John

[Robinson]

RADIO:

Pop Go The Beatles – 4 June 1963

Pop Go The Beatles – 13 August 1963

Saturday Club – 24 August 1963 ♦

Pop Go The Beatles – 17 September 1963

All four BBC performances of 'You Really Got A Hold On Me' were broadcast prior to the release of the EMI version on *With The Beatles* in November 1963. Smokey Robinson had been moved to write his song by the uncredited duet of Sam Cooke and Lou Rawls on 'Bring It On Home To Me'. On The Miracles' recording of 'You Really Got A Hold On Me', Smokey is supported by Bobby Rogers. In The Beatles' performance, it is George who underpins John's lead vocal. The Miracles' single climbed into the Billboard Top Ten at the beginning of 1963. At this time, the humble Oriole label was the British conduit for Berry Gordy's Tamla and Motown releases. Like Fontana before it, Oriole had no chart success with the songs licensed from Gordy. The UK breakthrough eventually came in May 1964 with 'My Guy' written by Smokey Robinson for Mary Wells. Always eager to bang the drum for Motown, The Beatles invited her to close the first half of their 1964 British tour.

RECORDING THE BEATLES' BBC RADIO SESSIONS

The archive of The Beatles' music made in BBC radio studios between March 1962 and May 1965 forms an important part of the group's legacy. As discussed earlier, its value derives from the alternative versions of tracks heard on The Beatles' records and many songs never taped elsewhere for commercial release. The significance of the radio sessions also stems from the way the sound of The Beatles was captured for their broadcasts.

In this period, artists were not indulged with large amounts of studio time. At EMI Studios in Abbey Road, London, on 11 February 1963, The Beatles had to record ten songs for their debut album *Please Please Me*. The fact that this was achieved in under ten hours came to be regarded as a remarkable achievement. It is, of course, but that is mainly because of the high quality of those tracks. It was common practice in 1963 to complete a minimum of two songs in a standard three-hour session. As Paul has pointed out, 'It was just the rate people worked at. You were expected to do at least a couple of songs in that three-hour session. Looking at it now, it seems so fast, but then it seemed very sensible.' At the BBC, the work rate was even higher. Apart from when they were performing in front of an audience for a broadcast, The Beatles had to complete five or six songs in a short session. They were not fazed by this requirement. On 16 July 1963, the group recorded all the music and speech needed for three editions of *Pop Go The Beatles* in less than seven hours. That was a total of *eighteen* songs taped between 3.00 and 10.30pm, including a few short breaks, at the BBC Paris Theatre in Lower Regent Street, London. Fifteen of them were not available on Beatles records at the time.

It was the combination of the time pressure of a radio session and the limitations of the studio equipment that gave The Beatles' BBC musical performances their distinctive quality and historic importance. The group began using a four-track machine at EMI in October 1963, but multi-tracking did not begin at the BBC until the 1970s. Recording on mono tape machines at the BBC meant that if any mistakes were made they could not be isolated from the rest of the music and repaired. The group's performances could only be enhanced by two methods. Occasionally, the best sections of different takes of a song were edited together. Secondly, there was the option to 'overdub' by copying a first recording to another tape, while at the same time adding more instruments or vocals. Any error during this primitive method of overdubbing would necessitate starting again from the beginning, so it could be a time-consuming process. Consequently, mostly what we hear on the BBC tapes is the sound of the group performing live, direct to tape – or, sometimes, straight onto the air. Minus the distraction of the noisy hysteria omnipresent in their public concerts, recordings of their BBC appearances show how accomplished and exciting The Beatles were when they played live.

In many ways the BBC was very similar to EMI. Each had a reputation for striving for excellence but, at the same time, could exude an air of stuffy bureaucracy. Unlike the engineers at EMI, BBC studio managers (SMs) did not have to don white coats in the studio, but all wore jackets and ties. Although performing an equivalent role to a sound balancer in a commercial studio, an SM was never referred to as an engineer. That term was too synonymous with the image of a technical chap wielding a soldering iron and a screwdriver. During the *Pop Go The Beatles* series, the group gained a regular sound balancer, who was around the same age and shared similar interests. As Keith Bateson recalled, he was very different to the first SM at the controls. 'The original chap who did the balance on *Pop Go The Beatles* was a lovely guy called Charles Clark Maxwell, who was an old Etonian. He might just as well have been an old Martian as far as The Beatles were concerned … and there was, I think, a slight communication problem in the language. So I was put in his place, because I could become very Mersey when it suited me!'

Actually born in Bolton in Lancashire, Keith Bateson proved popular with The Beatles and not just because he had moved the provenance of his accent 37 miles to Liverpool. Brian Epstein often made The Beatles' BBC bookings conditional upon him being at the mixing desk. Like several of his pioneering colleagues, Keith wanted to bring the sound of BBC pop recordings up to date:

'The BBC was still recovering from the wartime scenario of "Keep the drums down, don't get the workers jiving in the aisles, keep production up, damp the drums." And we were trying to establish a new sort of pattern to rhythm. We were trying to copy the commercial people and we had a few problems with our microphones [on the drums] at the time, because they were rather old. They were ribbon microphones and as soon as you expended any energy at them above the normal, the ribbon used to break – which was quite handy!'

John Andrews, the assistant SM on *Pop Go The Beatles*, remembered, 'We were the first people to start taking the front skin off the bass drum and putting blankets inside along with the old 4033 – the gin-bottle we used to call it – a very robust microphone designed for television use.'

The studio managers also had to deal with the cavernous echo of a BBC theatre studio – an acoustic that could be attractive when recording an orchestra or big band, but problematic when creating the drier sound required for an amplified beat group. When attempting to screen instruments to avoid their sound spilling into other microphones, the SMs were forced to improvise. John Andrews recalled that in the Paris Theatre in Lower Regent Street 'there were quite heavy curtains on either side of the stage to cover sound effects for audience shows, and Keith decided he would put Ringo behind these curtains. The group had never seen this before and they thought it was hilarious.' When it was Ringo's turn to sing, a Heath Robinson-like array of heavy BBC metalwork was constructed to poke a microphone at him through the curtains. It was an odd sight, as John Andrews explained:

'The only microphone that was good for drum vocals was the old C12 – a great silver cylinder about twelve inches long and two inches in diameter – and the windshield was a great mesh job about four inches in diameter. We didn't have your modern steel booms with the little adjustments… we had a huge great hanging device with elastic strings on it and for it to reach Ringo we had two very large booms with three wheels, a tri-pod and a great big handle.'

A basic but effective method was used to record the sound of a guitar amplifier. Producer Ian Grant remembered that to place a microphone close enough, it was tied to the handle at the top of the amp so that it dangled in front of the speaker cabinet. In the control cubicle, a BBC mixing board did not have linear faders to move up and down. Instead, large black rotary faders were used to adjust sound levels, which made the studio mixing desk look more like the flight deck of a wartime Lancaster bomber than something to blend musical sounds. The control panel usually had only one 'equalization' device to adjust the treble or bass on one input, so microphones were chosen according to their tonal qualities. A ribbon microphone gave a warm bass sound and a condenser mic had a brightness suitable for vocals and guitars. Studio managers employed ingenious tricks to change these characteristics. One famous ploy devised by Freddy Harris to produce a 'bass-cut' involved stuffing a cigarette packet behind the back-clip of a 4038 ribbon microphone. SM Bev Phillips recalled:

'In the early 1960s, once you had enhanced the vocal mic, you were technically stuffed. I used to solder resistors and capacitors between jack plugs housed in my father's tobacco tins in order to create high-pass filters. There was once hell to pay when my boss came round with some engineering top-brass and saw these tobacco tins dangling from the jackfield on the wall.'

Similarly, adding any controlled reverberation to the music was not an easy push-button process. At the BBC's studios in Aeolian Hall, an echo chamber was set up with a loudspeaker and microphone at either end. As the sound of the music coming out of the speaker bounced around the reverberant room, it was picked up by the mic and added to the mix. Ian Grant was fond of experimenting with reverb. 'The only way to change the delay time was to move the speaker towards the microphone or further away. If you pointed the speaker at the wall, you got – not quite slap-back echo – but a different effect. I'd get the keys to the room and mess around!'

Bernie Andrews, producer of *Saturday Club* and *Top Gear*, took very seriously his responsibility to present The Beatles to listeners in the best

ABOVE The control room of a BBC studio in 1959: Bernie Andrews marks a tape on a TR90 machine. Johnny Beerling, sitting at a Type A control desk, and producer Jack Singleton wait for the edit to be completed. Presenter and guitarist Ken Sykora studies his script. This equipment was still prevalent at the BBC when The Beatles did their music sessions from 1962 to 1965.

possible way. His dedication to improving the standard of BBC sessions was certainly appreciated. At the start of John's last BBC interview on 6 December 1980, he talked to presenter Andy Peebles about his memories of working on *Saturday Club* sessions: 'Bernie Andrews… I was just saying I heard some of the tracks. Somebody must have pirated them, Bernie! We did a lot of tracks that were never recorded on record for *Saturday Club*. All the stuff we'd been doing at the Cavern or Hamburg and that. There was some good stuff and they were well recorded too.'

Many of the archive recordings were eventually released on disc in November 1994. On *Live At The BBC*, the world heard The Beatles in the way British listeners had first fallen in love with them – affectionately sending up announcers, laughing at their own crazy success and bringing a rush of musical energy to radio shows creaking with outmoded dance bands and crooners. It was joyous stuff and proved irresistible. Seven million copies were quickly sold. The album's success was a fitting tribute not only to the enduring power of The Beatles, but also to the dedication and ingenuity of BBC producers and studio managers. Thanks to them, subsequent generations have been able to enjoy these remarkable performances from an age of wireless innocence.

MUSICAL DISCOVERY

THE BEATLES AT THE BBC

Live At The BBC (Apple)
First released in November 1994 – remastered and reissued in November 2013 – the album includes 56 songs and various speech tracks featuring The Beatles in conversation with presenters Rodney Burke, Alan Freeman, Brian Matthew and Lee Peters.

Baby It's You (Apple)
Released in March 1995, the EP included 'Baby It's You' from *Live At The BBC* and three previously unavailable BBC recordings: 'Boys', 'I'll Follow The Sun' and 'Devil In Her Heart'.

Anthology 1 (Apple)
First released in November 1995, this collection features 'Lend Me Your Comb' from *Pop Go The Beatles* and two other BBC-related tracks. In addition to a commercial television broadcast, 'Till There Was You' and 'Twist And Shout' from the Royal Variety Performance were broadcast in a BBC radio highlights programme on 10 November 1963.

THE BEATLES' BBC INTERVIEWS

The Beatles Tapes (Polydor)
This collection was originally a double LP released in 1976 and features *Scene and Heard* interviews with David Wigg, plus instrumental versions of songs by The Beatles. The interview recording dates are unreliable. These are the correct dates for the double CD:

DISC ONE:
John And Yoko: Tracks 1 and 3: 8 May 1969; Track 5: 21 October 1969 and 6 February 1970; Track 7: October 1971
Paul: Tracks 8 and 10: 19 September 1969
DISC TWO:
Paul: Track 1: 19 September 1969
George: Tracks 3 and 5: 8 October 1969
Ringo: Track 7: 21 January 1969; Track 8: 25 March 1970; Tracks 9 and 11: 3 January 1973

Paul McCartney – In His Own Words (BBC/AudioGo – 2012)
(includes an interview from *The World At One* broadcast on 26 March 1968)

John Lennon – In His Own Words (BBC/AudioGo – 2013)
(includes three interviews from 1965, one each from 1968, 1969 and 1970, plus an extract from the interview recorded with Andy Peebles on 6 December 1980)

EARLY INFLUENCES

Arthur Alexander *The Greatest* (Ace Records)

Chuck Berry *The Chess Box* (MCA/Universal) [Box Set]

Johnny Burnette *Rock 'N' Roll Trio/Tear It Up* (Beat Goes On Records)

The Coasters *50 Coastin' Classics* (Rhino)

Eddie Cochran *The Eddie Cochran Story* (EMI/Liberty) [4 CD set]

Fats Domino *Greatest Hits – Walking To New Orleans* (EMI)

Duane Eddy *Twang Thang – The Duane Eddy Anthology* (Rhino)

The Everly Brothers *The Original British Hit Singles* (Ace Records) and *It's Everly Time/A Date With the Everly Brothers* (WSM/Warner Bros.)

Marvin Gaye *That Stubborn Kinda Fellow/How Sweet It Is To Be Loved By You* (Motown/Universal) and *The Very Best Of Marvin Gaye* (Universal)

Buddy Holly *From Original Master Tapes* (MCA/Universal) and *Not Fade Away: The Complete Studio Recordings And More* [Box set]

The Isley Brothers *Shout And Twist With Rudolph, Ronald And O'Kelly* (Ace Records)

The Jodimars *Let's All Rock Together* (Rockstar)

Jerry Lee Lewis *The Essential Sun Collection* (Recall)

Little Richard *The Original British Hit Singles* (Ace Records) and *The Very Best of "Little Richard"* (Specialty Records/Universal)

The Marvelettes *Forever – The Complete Motown Albums Volume 1* (HIP-OSelect.com/Motown)

Roy Orbison *For The Lonely: 18 Greatest Hits* (Rhino)

Carl Perkins *Original Sun Greatest Hits* (Rhino) and *Dance Album Of Carl Perkins* (Charly)

Elvis Presley *The King Of Rock 'N' Roll – The Complete 50s Masters* (BMG/RCA) [Box Set]

Smokey Robinson & The Miracles *Anthology* (Tamla Motown) and **The Miracles** *Depend On Me – the early albums* (HIP-OSelect.com/Motown)

The Shirelles *The Best Of* (Ace)

Barrett Strong *The Complete Motown Collection* (Tamla Motown/Spectrum)

Gene Vincent and His Blue Caps *The Best Of* (EMI)

Mary Wells *The Motown Collection* (Motown/Universal) and *The One Who Really Loves You/Two Lovers And Other Great Hits* (Ace Records)

Larry Williams *At His Finest: The Specialty Rock 'n' Roll Years* (Ace Records)

The Golden Age Of American Rock 'n' Roll series on Ace Records features the many styles of music that made the US charts in the late '50s and early '60s. These are the songs The Beatles listened to in their formative years. 'Nothin' Shakin'' by Eddie Fontaine is on Volume 5.

'Devil In His Heart' by The Donays is on *The Time, Brent, Shad Story – Rockin' On Broadway* (Ace Records)

BIBLIOGRAPHY

THE BEATLES IN THEIR OWN WORDS

The Beatles: *Anthology*
(Cassell & Co, 2000)

Davies, Hunter, ed.: *The John Lennon Letters*
(London: Weidenfeld & Nicolson, 2012)

Harrison, George: *I Me Mine*
(London: WH Allen, 1982)

Harrison, Olivia; Mark Holborn, ed.: *George Harrison Living in the Material World*
(New York: Abrams, 2011)

Lennon, John: *In His Own Write*
(London: Jonathan Cape, 1964)

Lennon, John: *A Spaniard in the Works*
(London: Jonathan Cape, 1965)

The Lennon Tapes: John Lennon and Yoko Ono in conversation with Andy Peebles 6 December 1980
(London: BBC, 1981)

McCartney, Paul; Mitchell, Adrian, ed.: *Blackbird Singing - Poems and Lyrics 1965–1999*
(London: faber and faber, 2002)

Miles, Barry: *Paul McCartney Many Years from Now*
(London: Secker & Warburg, 1997)

Starr, Ringo: *Postcards from the Boys*
(London: Cassell Illustrated, 2004)

Wenner, Jann, ed.: *Lennon Remembers*
(New York: Verso, 2000)

BIOGRAPHIES

Braun, Michael: *Love Me Do! The Beatles' Progress*
(London: Penguin, 1964)

Davies, Hunter: *The Beatles*
(London: Heinemann, 1968)

Lewisohn, Mark: *The Beatles – All These Years Volume One: Tune In*
(London: Little, Brown, 2013)

Norman, Philip: *Shout! The True Story of The Beatles*
(London: Elm Tree, 1981)

REFERENCE WORKS

Carr, Roy; Tyler, Tony: *The Beatles: An Illustrated Record*
(London: New English Library, 1975)

Frame, Pete: *The Beatles and Some Other Guys – Rock Family Trees of the Early Sixties*
(London: Omnibus Press, 1997)

Lewisohn, Mark: *The Complete Beatles Recording Sessions: The Official Story of The Abbey Road Years*
(London: Hamlyn, 1988)

Lewisohn, Mark: *The Complete Beatles Chronicle*
(London: Pyramid Books, 1992)

MacDonald, Ian: *Revolution in the Head*
(London: Fourth Estate, 1994)

Pieper, Jörg; Path, Volker: *The Beatles Film & TV Chronicle 1961–1970*
(Stockholm: Premium Publishing)

Schreuders, Piet; Lewisohn, Mark; Smith, Adam: *The Beatles London*
(London: Hamlyn, 1994)

BROADCASTING

Chapman, Rob: *Selling The Sixties – The Pirates and Pop Music Radio*
(London: Routledge, 1992)

Garner, Ken: *In Session Tonight – The Complete Radio 1 Recordings*
(London: BBC Books, 1993)

BEFORE THE BEATLES

Frame, Pete: *The Restless Generation – How Rock Music Changed the Face of 1950s Britain*
(London: Rogan House, 2007)

INDEX

To Prue, Hugh, Oli and Amy

Main body text © Kevin Howlett 2013
Transcripts reproduced with kind permission from Apple Corps Ltd and the BBC
All BBC memos and documents © BBC
Document photography © Woodlands Books Ltd 2013

Kevin Howlett has asserted his right to be identified as the author of this
Work in accordance with the Copyright, Designs and Patents Act 1988

HarperCollins books may be purchased for educational, business, or sales
promotional use. For information please e-mail the Special Markets Department
at SPsales@harpercollins.com.

First published in 2013 by
Harper Design
An Imprint of HarperCollins*Publishers*
10 East 53rd Street
New York, NY 10022
Tel: (212) 207-7000
Fax: (212) 207-7654
www.harpercollinspublishers.com
harperdesign@harpercollins.com

Distributed throughout the world by
HarperCollins *Publishers*
10 East 53rd Street
New York, NY 10022

ISBN: 978-0-06-228853-0
The Library of Congress Control Number: 2013940370

LBI – Nov 8/13

Commissioning editor: Lorna Russell
Project editor: Joe Cottington
Editor: Steve Tribe
Design: Karin Fremer
Packaging design: Two Associates
Document photography: Karl Adamson
Picture research: Claire Gouldstone
Production: Antony Heller
Development and strategic consultation: Les Krantz

First printing, 2013

It is 32 years since I started to uncover the history of The Beatles' BBC broadcasts.
It has proved a rich subject to explore – leading to the production of radio
programmmes, books and albums. My sincere thanks for help along the way to:
Bernie Andrews, John Andrews, Neil Aspinall, Keith Bateson, Johnny Beerling,
Aaron Bremner, Rob Chapman, Derek Chinnery, Jonathan Clyde, Pete Dauncey,
John Fawcett Wilson, Pete Frame, Alan Freeman, Paul Gambaccini, Ian Grant,
Jeff Griffin, Stuart Grundy, Tony Hall, Bob Harris, Guy Hayden, Mike Heatley,
Terry Henebery, Brian Howlett, Jeff Jones, Phil Lawton, Stuart Leaver, Spencer Leigh,
Mark Lewisohn, George Martin, Guy Massey, Brian Matthew, Jeremy Neech,
Staffan Olander, Andy Peebles, Ian Pickavance, Peter Pilbeam, Allan Rouse,
Roger Scott, Richard Skinner, Derek Taylor, Monica Thapar (and her colleagues at
the wonderful BBC Written Archives Centre), Brian Thompson, John Walker,
John Walters, Alex Wharton and Tony Wilson.

– Kevin Howlett

S/13
K